The Politics of Cocaine

How U.S. Foreign Policy
Has Created a Thriving
Drug Industry in Central
and South America

Baker College of Clinton Twp Library

William L. Marcy, Ph.D.
Foreword by Jorrit Kamminga

Lawrence Hill Books

Library of Congress Cataloging-in-Publication Data
Marcy, William L.
  The politics of cocaine : how U.S. policy has created a thriving drug industry
in Central and South America / William L. Marcy.
     p. cm.
  Includes bibliographical references and index.
  ISBN 978-1-55652-949-8 (hardcover)
  1. Cocaine industry–Latin America. 2. Latin America–Economic conditions–
20th century. 3. United States–Foreign relations–Latin America. 4. Latin
America–Foreign relations–United States. 5. Drug control–Latin America.
6. Drug control–United States. 7. Organized crime–Latin America. I. Title.

HV5840.L3.M37 2010
363.45098–dc22

                                                              2009033243

Interior design: Jonathan Hahn
Maps: Chris Erichsen
Charts: Rattray Design

Published by Lawrence Hill Books
An imprint of Chicago Review Press, Incorporated
814 North Franklin Street
Chicago, Illinois 60610
ISBN 978-1-55652-949-8
Printed in the United States of America
5 4 3 2 1

Contents

Foreword

More than ten years ago, world leaders gathered in New York for the United Nations General Assembly Special Session (UNGASS) on the World Drug Problem, committing to a drug-free world by 2008. However, despite multibillion-dollar programs such as Plan Colombia and other bilateral and multilateral efforts implemented around the world in the intervening decade, the problem has not gone away. In many ways, it has become worse: in nearly every nation, abundant availability of all types of illicit drugs, stable levels of purity, stable or decreasing price levels, and increasing numbers of ever-younger drug users is the norm. How is it possible that the illegal drug trade is still one of the most persistent and most damaging forms of international crime, corrupting officials, fueling insecurity and insurgency, and hijacking the economic development of too many countries?

William Marcy goes a long way toward explaining the dynamics at play by focusing on the Northern Andes and Central America, a geopolitical hotspot where for decades intractable problems of violence, leftist insurgency, paramilitary force, governmental instability, and the illegal drug trade have come together in a deadly and explosive mix. In this region and elsewhere the illegal drug trade–the production and trafficking of drugs–has manifested itself as both a cause and a symptom in a broader framework of security and development crises. As a symptom, it is both indicator and outcome of instability, poverty, and unemployment–in other words, of underdevelopment. Latin America's economic crisis of the 1980s, the resulting rise in unemployment in many of its countries; the growing burden of external debt; and profound changes in the structure of the rural economy, guerrilla movements, and counterinsurgency warfare are all indicators of the narcotics economy operating in an underdeveloped region.

But the illegal drug economy is not only a symptom. As a cause, drug cultivation, production, and trafficking create, maintain, and boost violence, corruption, arms trafficking, money laundering, and a host of other crimes. It is a direct cause of an interrelated set of destabilizing factors that hamper security and development in the countries involved.

William Marcy ably illustrates this relationship, showing how the illegal drug trade has exacerbated leftist guerrilla insurgencies, deepened poverty, and disrupted the economic life of the northern Andes and Central America. Yet policymakers have never really paid much attention to the cause-and-symptom aspect of the illegal drug trade in this part of the world. On those occasions where the United States, for example, has tried to integrate the drug problem into a broader framework, the effort has always been tied to a military counterinsurgency campaign cloaked in Cold War rhetoric, aggravating and intensifying regional conflicts rather than resolving them.

To a large extent, the failure of the Andean Strategy, Plan Colombia, and other such ambitious and expensive programs has resulted from fighting the symptoms of the illegal drug trade while forgetting about the broader security and development situation that produces it. As the author rightly points out, this one-sided approach targets the weakest elements within the illegal production chain and within consumer societies: on the one hand, *cocaleros* (and poppy farmers in countries such as Afghanistan, where I have been working now for many years), and on the other hand, the consumers of illegal drugs, who for decades have been stigmatized as criminals instead of victims who need carefully targeted information and prevention programs to limit the harm caused by their addictions.

In *The Politics of Cocaine*, William Marcy gives us a better understanding of how and why drug policy went wrong in the northern Andes and Central America and how we can improve current efforts at curtailing the illegal drug trade and softening its impact around the world. The problem is still there, and spreading. While we waste precious time, West Africa is becoming the next cocaine-trafficking hub en route to Europe. Where legal trade fails, illicit trafficking is going to prevail.

JORRIT KAMMINGA,
Director of Policy Research,
International Council on Security and Development

Acknowledgments

I want to thank certain people who have aided me along the way. These include Albert L. Michaels, PhD; Gregg B. Johnson, PhD; Harold L. Langfur, PhD; John A. Larkin, PhD; Edward O. Smith, Jr., PhD; Jaíme Martínez-Tolentino, PhD; Bruce Jackson, PhD; Jeffrey Shaw; Cynthia Lane; and the people at the National Security Archive. I would also like to thank my agent, Ronald H. Irwin, and my editors Sue Betz and Linda Matthews for keeping me in line and the book on track.

Second, I owe a great deal of thanks to my mother. I would also like to mention my father, William L. Marcy, and my aunts, Joan Luke and Betsy Sinks, all of whom passed away too young.

Finally, I would like to state that this book presents the views of this author only. No support from any institution has influenced this publication. Also, there should be no deconstructionist questions regarding the sources. What has happened in the northern Andes and Central America is real. Honest and innocent people have died. There is much hypocrisy on all sides of the narcotics control issue, but the losers always seem to be the campesinos or the drug addicts whose lives are ruined by their need for narcotics in order to survive.

Map 1. Coca Cultivation and Cocaine-Processing Areas of the Northern Andes

Map 2. Strongholds of the Peruvian Sendero Luminoso

Map 3. Colombia: Poppy-Growing Regions and Guerrilla Safe Havens

Introduction

U.S. Drug Policy in the Northern Andes and Latin America

On November 6, 1985, fifty members of the Colombian M-19 guerrilla organization, disguised as policemen, broke into the Palace of Justice and took the entire Colombian Supreme Court hostage.[1] This began a two-day siege of the building by the Colombian army and police. The M-19 and the military exchanged heavy fire as people sporadically attempted to escape. Twenty-seven hours into the siege, the military decided to assault the building with dynamite to dislodge the M-19 guerrillas holding out on the fourth floor.[2] Gunfire from this assault partially destroyed the palace, and nearly one hundred people died, including eleven Supreme Court judges and all of the guerrillas.[3]

In the aftermath, people asked what the M-19 had expected to achieve by such a suicidal operation. Was it a protest against the Colombian government, or did it have less obvious objectives? Since the government refused to negotiate with the M-19 during the crisis, no one will ever know exactly what the guerrillas had in mind. However, as the dust began to settle, evidence appeared that linked the M-19 attack to the War on Drugs. In particular, all the files related to the extradition of narco-traffickers from Colombia to the United States had been intentionally burned.[4] Moreover, evidence found in the ruins of the Palace of Justice revealed that the M-19 had used weapons allegedly supplied by Nicaragua's Sandinista government, which the Reagan administration had accused of being a narco-communist state.[5] The remnants of the M-19 leadership denied any drug connection in the attack; yet the assault brought the issues of narco-terrorism and the specter of a narco-communist nexus to the forefront of international politics.[6] The most important question about the incident persisted: was the M-19's purported involvement in the War on Drugs an isolated incident, or were guerrilla organizations and narcotics traffickers linked throughout the northern Andes?

U.S. counternarcotics efforts in the northern Andes (Bolivia, Colombia, and Peru) and Central America from 1975 to 2008 seemed to reveal an evolving symbiotic relationship between leftist guerrilla insurgents and narco-traffickers. Immersed in Cold War psychology, the United States came to perceive the narcotics industry as a partnership between procommunist guerrilla insurgents and narco-traffickers to promote drug production and revolution throughout the region.

Narcotics production in the northern Andes grew steadily throughout the 1970s, supported by emerging narcotics networks and a rise in U.S. demand, only to be followed by the collapse of the region's economies in the 1980s. The United States consistently underestimated the long-standing socioeconomic problems plaguing the northern Andes as well as North America's mounting hunger for drugs. U.S. officials ignored the fact that the narcotics trade benefited many players, including *campesino* coca farmers, bankers, corrupt officials, and guerrillas, as well as national economies; and their proscriptive, supply-side drug policy met mass resistance to narcotics control through military operations.

Even under the best-formulated policy, the shifting and highly adaptable nature of the narcotics industry would have made it almost impossible for the United States to suppress narcotics production completely in the northern Andes. However, its misdiagnosis of the issues, its choice virtually to ignore internal demand, and its high-handed approach to implementing its policies made the United States an instrument of increasing political instability, which in turn fostered a sociopolitical and economic climate that has enabled narcotics to flourish in the region for more than four decades.

Throughout the 1970s and 1980s, the United States gradually came to conflate the War on Drugs in the northern Andes with its Cold War struggle against Cuba and Nicaragua. The bitter struggle in Central America and U.S. animosity toward communist Cuba led to allegations that certain Cuban and Sandinista government officials had been involved in narcotics trafficking. The available evidence does appear to connect elements in the Cuban and Nicaraguan governments to narco-trafficking, and the Reagan and the Bush administrations used this information to link those nations with a larger narco-communist nexus in the northern Andes. However, the same evidence points to narcotics smuggling by the CIA-backed Contras, suggesting that narcotics trafficking transcended ideology. Faced by a crack cocaine epidemic in the United States and deeply entrenched in the belief in a narco-communist nexus, the Reagan administration deemed narcotics a national security threat and started to militarize the War on Drugs in the early to mid 1980s. The subsequent Bush administration finalized this militarization, although many within the Pentagon believed that narcotics control was a civilian law enforcement matter and that the administration's approach could corrupt military institutions. In the northern Andes, militarization ultimately promoted political instability in coca-growing areas, which in turn enabled guerrillas to expand their involvement in the narcotics industry and thereby continue financing their revolutions. U.S. policy fostered precisely the outcome that Washington feared.

The invasion of Panama during the presidency of George H.W. Bush, the first real demonstration of U.S. willingness to use military force in the War on Drugs, served dual purposes. By using its armed forces to overthrow Manuel Noriega, the rogue Panamanian dictator who had purportedly facilitated narco-trafficking, the United States showed its determination to shut down the drug industry in the Western Hemisphere. The invasion also strengthened the U.S. bargaining position in Central America to confront the Sandinistas and their Cuban allies.

Despite this victory, the United States' militarized approach to the northern Andean drug trade proved counterproductive in the end. It stirred up greater campesino political opposition to eradication programs, fostered corruption in the Andean militaries, fomented policy disagreements between the United States and its northern Andean counterparts, and intensified narcotics-related violence by both the guerrillas and the narcotics cartels.

Clinton's attempted reformulation of U.S. drug policy did not significantly change what he had inherited from Reagan and Bush. Early in his administration, Clinton de-emphasized narcotics control as a national security issue and focused on diminishing U.S. demand. In the northern Andes, Clinton trimmed military and counternarcotics aid but pursued a supply-side approach that expected the northern Andean governments to continue cutting narcotics production at the same levels they had during the Bush years. Clinton's decision to withhold military aid while maintaining a strict supply-side strategy was as destructive as Bush's decision to militarize the conflict. His policy created a vacuum in the coca-growing regions and at the same time failed to address the socioeconomic and political conditions that drove the narcotics industry and its violence.

Under U.S. pressure, Peru and Bolivia achieved short-term progress in cutting narcotics production, largely due to the repressive supply-side policies directed by their armed forces. However, a number of factors undermined long-term gains: the military presence in counternarcotics operations, human rights abuses, corruption, and confrontations with coca-growing campesinos over coca control and economic liberalization.

U.S. drug policy in the northern Andes consistently shortchanged the campesino population and drove them further and further from their governments. Crop substitution has never had the same priority as coca eradication and interdiction. Economic liberalization did not help coca farmers because few markets for alternative crops existed, limiting their profit potential from the start. Rigidly enforced coca eradication and the inability to develop successful crop substitution programs enhanced the strength of anti-government factions. The United States saw any form of resistance to its narcotics control efforts as part of a narco-guerrilla conspiracy to overthrow the governments of the northern Andes. U.S. counternarcotics and Cold War policies turned the drug war into an intractable battle with no end in sight.

Even when the Cold War ended, these policies ensured that guerrilla insurgencies, rural instability, and narcotics production and trafficking lingered on. Except for a slight decline during the late 1990s, overall drug production in the northern Andes has remained at constant or rising levels since 1970. Campesino resistance to U.S.-Andean antinarcotics programs and the resultant political instability have forged anti-government and guerrilla-campesino alliances that continue to thwart counternarcotics efforts. Moreover, establishing the security conditions necessary to minimize drug cultivation has been fruitless in the absence of an economic option that reduces the campesinos' incentive to grow narcotics. The United States will never win the War on Drugs unless it develops a more comprehensive policy that reduces demand, presents economic incentives to limit narcotics production, and offers political openings to preempt the political and economic forces that have given impetus to radical leftist and guerrilla movements throughout the region. In considering the northern Andes as a whole and in shedding light on how and why the United States mixed Cold War politics into the problem of drug abuse to create a narrow and ineffective narcotics policy, *The Politics of Cocaine* presents a straightforward, comprehensive look at our nation's policy errors and can lay the groundwork for an effective strategy. The War on Drugs is not over; it may yet come to a successful conclusion that reduces the power of the narcotics industry and all the human damage it perpetuates.

1

The Growth of the Narcotics Industry in the Northern Andes, 1971–1980

On July 17, 1980, paramilitary men dressed in army fatigues and wearing black masks and armbands with Nazi swastikas took over Bolivia's capital, La Paz. The paramilitaries were joined by mutinying Bolivian soldiers. Tanks and armored personnel carriers with troops in combat dress patrolled the city's streets. The sound of shooting was heard in various areas of the capital.[1] The paramilitary men—also called Los Novios de la Muerte—and the mutinying soldiers called for the replacement of acting President Lidia Gueiler Tejada and the dissolution of the election that had selected Hernán Siles Zuazo's socialist coalition to lead Bolivia. The military declared that they were launching this coup "for the dignity of Bolivia, to reject the results of the general elections and to declare the Congress and its actions unconstitutional."[2]

On July 18, Gueiler Tejada, who had been cooperating with the DEA on narcotics control, stepped down from power. A right-wing military junta led by General Luis García Meza, acting as president, and Colonel Luis Arce Gómez, acting as minister of the interior, replaced her. The junta disbanded the Bolivian Congress and declared Bolivia a military zone. The revolt appeared to be a right-wing Latin American military coup against a leftist government when the junta announced over the radio that "the armed forces . . . will not allow Communists to assault the country."[3]

However, a more insidious reason for the coup began to circulate alongside the junta's claims. Allegations arose that the military junta was involved in the narcotics trade. The U.S. government withdrew State Department and DEA personnel from Bolivia since they now had no basis "to expect the kind of cooperation" from the military junta that would make it "worthwhile to continue the drug enforcement program."[4] For the U.S. government, it appeared as though millions of dollars and almost a decade of narcotics control efforts with the Bolivian government were lost.

The Origins of the Narcotics Crisis and Nixon's War on Drugs, 1969–1974

In 1969, when Richard Nixon became president, narcotics usage had already reached crisis levels in the United States. According to a State Department study on narcotics control, in the late 1960s and early 1970s "the turmoil in U.S. society, increased addiction, and the war in South East Asia" that "provided easy access to drugs for U.S. servicemen" all became "a part of the same problem."[5] "From an internal security standpoint," the student unrest and political turmoil created by the Vietnam War were a result of "the heavy overlapping between the propagation of the drug culture" in the United States and the "new left radicals who were committed to violent overthrow" of U.S. "institutions."[6] Nixon felt that he had a "national responsibility" to stop the nation from being "destroyed" by drugs.[7] In his administration's view, narcotics threatened the very fabric of U.S. society.

The U.S. military was one of the institutions most threatened by narcotics abuse. Heroin addiction had reached unprecedented levels among U.S. soldiers during the Vietnam War, jeopardizing U.S. national security by undermining military readiness and discipline.[8] In early 1966, military authorities began to investigate the levels of illegal drug use in their ranks. Based on this study, Frank Bartimo, assistant general counsel to the Department of Defense, estimated that between 1967 and 1970, the use of marijuana, heroin, and hard narcotics in the armed forces had doubled each year.[9] In 1971 Egil "Bud" Krogh Jr., Nixon's deputy assistant for domestic affairs, warned him that 15 to 20 percent of U.S. soldiers used heroin.[10] High-ranking generals and members of the administration believed that Chinese communist and Soviet-North Vietnamese operators had flooded South Vietnam with heroin, facilitating the escalation of use by U.S. soldiers.[11]

Along with the high rates of drug abuse among U.S. soldiers returning from Vietnam, drug use among the civilian population also skyrocketed.[12] In a special message to Congress on the "Control of Narcotics and Dangerous Drugs" in 1969, President Nixon stated that narcotics usage was "estimated to be in the hundreds of thousands," and "several million college students had experimented with marihuana [sic], hashish, LSD, amphetamines and barbiturates."[13]

Between 1960 and 1967, juvenile arrests involving drugs had risen almost 800 percent.[14] In 1970 New York City had more than forty thousand heroin addicts, and the city's chief medical examiner estimated that a record 1,050 people had died that year alone from narcotics-related causes.[15] The Nixon administration maintained that the problem was "not limited to any region of the country" or "segment of society."[16] The implications were enormous. Narcotics touched all facets of life within the United States as the scourge of drugs threatened government and family institutions. Drug abuse had become the country's "public enemy number one."[17]

To address the narcotics epidemic, the Nixon administration proposed the Comprehensive Drug Abuse Prevention and Control Act in 1969. Put into force on May 1, 1971, it replaced more than fifty pieces of drug legislation and established a single system of control for both narcotic and psychotropic drugs for the first time in U.S. history.[18] Notably, the act attempted to address the issue of supply and demand within the United States. It created federal and state legislation to strengthen law enforcement procedures and initiated education and rehabilitation programs. Furthermore, it increased law enforcement training and cooperation between the Bureau of Narcotics and Dangerous Drugs (BNDD) and the Customs Bureau and created two new enforcement agencies: the Office of Drug Abuse Law Enforcement (ODALE) and the Office of National Narcotics Intelligence (ONNI).

Nixon hoped that the new legislation would provide "in a single statute" a comprehensive, "revised and modern plan" leading the federal government into a "full scale attack on the problem of drug abuse" in the United States.[19] However, the administration knew that for this domestic narcotics policy to be a success it had to confront the narcotics supply from foreign sources. As a result, the domestic War on Drugs spilled over into the international arena.

The Nixon administration demanded a strong international narcotics control policy and directed its efforts toward decreasing and interdicting the supply of narcotics reaching the United States. To cut supply, signatories to the 1961 United Nations Single Convention on Narcotic Drugs were for the first time required to fulfill their international obligation to limit the illicit cultivation, production, and trafficking of narcotics, including opium, marijuana, and cocaine.[20] Nixon used both military and economic aid to force those nations to reduce the manufacture and trafficking of narcotics within their borders. However, the demand for narcotics in the United States continued. When the War on Drugs stopped the flow of narcotics from nations such as Turkey and Mexico, the industry moved its operations to South and Central America. In the northern Andean nations of Colombia, Bolivia, Peru, and the Central American republic of Panama, the narcotics industry quickly became a nascent force.

The Rise of the Narcotics Industry in the Northern Andes

The Nixon administration's efforts at international narcotics control during the late 1960s were focused on stemming the flow of heroin from Turkey, France, and Mexico into the United States.[21] A lack of resources limited U.S. attention to the budding South American narcotics industry, so that narcotics smugglers tied to the French Connection and South America's *contrabandistas* were able to develop sophisticated production and trafficking networks more or less unobserved. When, in the 1970s, international demand for cocaine supplanted demand for heroin, the South American narcotics industry quickly adapted. In Peru and Bolivia, coca growing had been an important part of indigenous culture since time immemorial. Traffickers now used that coca to make cocaine. They transported the cocaine to their northern Andean neighbors and then shipped it to the United States. Colombia soon became a major transit point for refining and distributing coca as well as heroin and marijuana. Smuggling in Panama, which that government almost tacitly condoned, further contributed to the development of narcotics networks. The Andean narcotics industry had grown deeply entrenched years before the United States recognized its existence.

As early as 1957, several French Corsican families settled in South America and quickly formed a loose alliance with the existing contrabandista system that had smuggled loads of "liquor, tobacco, TV sets, and other high value items" for decades throughout Latin America.[22] From their control centers in South America—Colombia, Panama, and Paraguay—the Corsicans "organized large-scale courier operations" and began to "send large bulk shipments" from Europe "into the United States" via "South America."[23] The border region between Ecuador and Colombia provided some of the heroin, although poppy cultivation in the northern Andes was considered a limited industry.[24] Thus, "unknown to U.S. enforcement officials . . . heroin had been regularly shipped" from Europe "through South America to the United States" as early as 1967.[25]

Before 1972, BNDD headquarters in Mexico City directed all U.S. narcotics operations in South America.[26] The BNDD did not set up a regional headquarters in Buenos Aires to cover South America until 1972. In 1973, when the BNDD was restructured as the Drug Enforcement Administration (DEA), a mere sixteen DEA agents covered all of Latin America and Panama. Of that sixteen, five were in Buenos Aires, which had become a major drug transshipment point, and the other eleven were in Paraguay, Colombia, Bolivia, Brazil, Venezuela, Peru, Panama, Ecuador, and Chile.[27] The problem caused by the lack of BNDD/DEA officers on the ground was further "complicated by the enormous physical magnitude of geography." The "topography of the growing areas, the thousands of miles of un-patrolled coastline, and the thousands of remote clandestine airstrips" provided daunting "obstacles to enforcement efforts."[28]

Corsican smugglers relied on three primary routes for bringing heroin from France into South America. The first consisted of sea shipments from Marseilles to various ports in Chile, with occasional deliveries in Panama along the way.[29] The second involved the movement of heroin by ship or aircraft from Marseilles to Buenos Aires; from there dealers delivered it to intermediate points in Paraguay or Chile. The third route was similar to the second, but in this case, the heroin was smuggled to Montevideo from Paraguay.[30] From bases within South America, the heroin networks smuggled their product into the United States via seamen-couriers, commercial airlines, and freight, or through intermediary countries such as Colombia, Panama, and Mexico.[31]

The DEA's Operation Springboard managed a series of arrests in the early 1970s with the objective of breaking up the French–South American heroin networks. Yet those arrests were only temporarily effective.[32] After Mexican police arrested the Corsican Auguste Ricord and killed another Corsican, Lucien Sarti, in 1972, South Americans who served as low-level operators, couriers, and intermediaries began to rise through the heroin rings and organized their own networks independent of Corsican influence.[33] By 1973 the DEA reported that "criminal elements" were "regrouping and restructuring," and had been "only temporarily affected by enforcement developments."[34] When international law enforcement operations finally caught up with the Corsicans, new organizations were in place and ready to expand their operations.

As early as 1964, the BNDD noted that in both Bolivia and Peru, considerable amounts of coca were being cultivated for the manufacture of cocaine.[35] In mountain laboratories, coca was refined into cocaine hydrochloride (HCL), then trafficked to markets in Europe and the United States. Production and trade in cocaine was more difficult to control than trade in heroin, for coca is native to the northern Andes. It grows easily at altitudes between 2,600 and 3,600 feet on the eastern mountains of the Andes and has done so for millennia. Originally, indigenous campesinos, or peasant farmers, consumed 90 percent of the coca crop in leaf form. They chewed it to enhance physical strength, reduce hunger, and make life in the mountains more endurable.[36] Many farmers and miners in the region received their pay in the form of coca leaves. Efforts to control coca production therefore challenged their livelihood as well as their religious and cultural institutions.

Peru was an original signatory to the 1961 UN Single Convention on Narcotic Drugs, but coca farming was nevertheless legal for cultural and economic purposes, including medical exports. To regulate coca production for legal exportation, the Peruvian government forced coca growers to pay a tax to the Empresa Nacional de la Coca (ENACO) for all coca sales.[37] However, convenient narcotics networks, lack of government authority in remote areas, and the need to make extra money soon invited Peruvian coca growers to divert their excess coca leaf to "clandestine laboratories scattered throughout the Andes Mountains."[38]

Prior to 1975, coca cultivation was also legal in Bolivia. In that country, the two major opportunities for extra income lay in "contraband and in the protection of and/or participation in cocaine refining and smuggling activities."[39] Bolivia's "unstable government, poor economic condition, high degree of corruption among officials, plus the indifferent attitude of the general public toward the coca situation," made it "unlikely that any serious measures" could prevent "the coca leaf" from becoming a part of the "illicit narcotics traffic."[40] Thus the BNDD's assessment for narcotics control in Bolivia had been gloomy even in the 1960s.

The difficulties facing U.S. narcotics enforcement agencies accelerated rapidly after 1970. Between 1970 and 1975, the number of first-time cocaine users in the United States jumped from 301,000 to 652,000 people annually. The number of first-time heroin users spiked between 1971 and 1974; first-time cocaine usage surged past first-time heroin usage after 1975.[41] Increasing demand and the shift away from heroin to cocaine as the drug of choice encouraged Latin American narcotics networks to step up production of coca and cocaine throughout Peru and Bolivia.[42] In Bolivia, "small factories" appeared around Santa Cruz, east of Cochabamba. The cocaine was sent on either to Brazil or to the frontier towns of Argentina.[43] In Peru, coca leaves were often refined in laboratories throughout the highlands to make coca paste, which was shipped to Lima to be "converted into cocaine."[44] The traffickers transformed a traditional crop of the northern Andes into a source of contraband whose cultivation was profit driven. As Bolivia and Peru entered the mid-1970s, they became centers for making cocaine.

However, Colombia was the single most prolific producer and transporter of illegal drugs into the United States throughout the 1960s and 1970s. U.S. officials knew it, but the Colombian government denied the existence of cocaine in their country through the 1960s. The chief of the Colombian National Judicial Police at one point went so far as to claim "that traffickers were afraid to operate in Colombia."[45] U.S. officials in Colombia knew this was an "unrealistic position," but owing to the lack of BNDD agents on the ground, they had "no hard evidence to support" the reports that narcotics were being smuggled through the country until the DEA was created and expanded its activities abroad in 1973.[46]

After 1973 this situation changed rapidly. By 1976 it was clear that approximately 90 percent of the cocaine shipments destined for the United States passed through Colombia.[47] In 1977 between three thousand and five thousand kilos of cocaine were traveling through Colombia to the United States every month.[48] Colombia had also become a major marijuana producer. By 1978, as U.S. crop eradication programs began to curb marijuana growth in Mexico, Colombia surpassed Mexico as the major U.S. marijuana supplier.[49]

The Colombian marijuana and cocaine trafficking networks developed separately. The spike in narcotics trafficking in Colombia during the late 1970s coincided with the fall of the French Connection and the rise of the Cali, Medellín, and North Atlantic Coast cartels.[50] The North Atlantic Coast organization was principally responsible for marijuana production and worked in cooperation with the U.S. Sicilian Mafia, which controlled the distribution as well as the price of marijuana.[51]

When it came to cocaine exports, the Medellín and Cali cartels had an advantage over other transnational criminal organizations. Since coca was indigenous to South America, entrance into the market was difficult for other Mafias, because they could not gain access to the raw materials to make cocaine. The contraband networks that the Colombians had used prior to the coca boom gave the Medellín and Cali organizations easy access to coca grown in Peru and Bolivia. Moreover, immigration of family members to the United States helped the Colombian Mafias develop their own distribution networks there, and thus to operate independently of other organized crime networks. These advantages enabled the Medellín and Cali cartels to develop tightly knit criminal organizations whose power ran parallel to that of the Colombian state.[52]

Several other factors contributed to Colombian domination of cocaine distribution in the United States. The first were Colombia's "proximity to Panama and the United States" and a tolerance for contraband smuggling that had existed for several generations.[53] Second, Colombian efforts to control the flow of narcotics remained limited during the 1970s because of weak laws and enforcement procedures as well as government corruption.[54] Colombia's meager narcotics enforcement units lacked interdepartmental coordination; this "hampered the development of an effective program."[55] Third, weak international assistance (the United States offered only token antinarcotics assistance prior to 1973, cumulatively forty-five thousand dollars) and low salaries allowed institutional corruption to infiltrate all areas of the Colombian government, from low-level police agents to high-level government officials, including elements of the judiciary.[56]

Colombian efforts to support narcotics enforcement programs were also limited because Colombia "had so many other pressing economic and domestic priorities." These came down to the absence of basic security: lawlessness in remote areas where the Colombian government had little or no control, and persistent guerrilla activity from Cuban-inspired revolutionary movements (Fuerzas Armadas Revolucionarias de Colombia [FARC], Ejército de Liberación Nacional [ELN], Movimiento 19 de Abril [M-19], and the Maoist organization Ejército Popular de Liberación [EPL]). When these groups renewed their revolutionary struggles around 1974, they gave the government far greater concern than narcotics production. All these factors made it possible for trafficking networks such as the incipient Medellín and Cali cartels to flood "the entire country with distributors and contacts."[57] Colombia was on its way to becoming a nation where the production, refinement, and trafficking of narcotics was nearly impossible to eliminate.

Panama was another difficult case. U.S. officials had no doubt that Panama had become a major haven for the smuggling of cocaine, heroin, and marijuana. In 1964 the BNDD noted that Panama was one of the "pivotal sources in the illicit cocaine traffic stemming from South America." Smuggling narcotics was facilitated by "political indifference, corruption, and untrained investigators."[58] "Between 1971 and 1973," remarked Senator Birch Bayh, the chairman of the Select Committee on Intelligence, "intelligence on narcotics trafficking in Panama" had become "voluminous."[59] Panama's proximity to Colombia, the presence of the canal, and corruption within the Panamanian government made it a safe haven for narcotics trafficking.

In 1970 this became apparent in a highly publicized case. Lieutenant Nicasio Drake, chief of Panamanian leader Omar Torrijos's security detail, was caught receiving one hundred thousand dollars for protecting narcotics-laden aircraft from customs inspection.[60] In another case, the BNDD uncovered evidence that Juaquin Himinez-Gonzalez, Panama's chief of air traffic control at Toucumen Airport, was using his official position to facilitate shipments of narcotics through Panama. The BNDD seized Gonzalez while he was walking in the Canal Zone, creating a diplomatic row over sovereignty that threatened to produce a crisis between the United States and Panama. Nevertheless, the BNDD won the right to hold on to Gonzalez. They subsequently deported him to the United States and convicted him on charges of conspiracy to smuggle narcotics. These revelations that high-ranking Panamanian officials had assisted the narcotics industry seriously embarrassed Torrijos.[61]

But worse was still to come. In 1971, Torrijos's brother, Moisés, the Panamanian ambassador to Argentina, allegedly provided passports to drug smugglers bringing 171 pounds of heroin into the United States.[62] The case against Moisés Torrijos was politically volatile because it had the potential to derail U.S.–Panamanian talks over the canal treaties. Although the BNDD attempted to capture Torrijos while he was traveling outside Panama, they eventually dropped the charges against him due to their political sensitivity.[63] However, another controversial case soon followed. Columnist Jack Anderson and New York Congressman John Murphy leaked this case to the public in an effort to sabotage the talks concerning the Panama Canal Treaties. The BNDD had informed the two that certain diplomats, including Panama's foreign minister, were involved in drug trafficking. When they made the case against the Panamanian diplomats public, Panama deported three BNDD agents for interfering in its national affairs.[64]

Although no conclusive personal evidence against Torrijos ever turned up, Panama was a perpetual thorn in the side of the Nixon administration.[65] Torrijos had expressed a desire to work with the United States, but the political climate resulting from these cases made it difficult for both sides to agree on the terms of narcotics cooperation. In 1972 the two nations promised to renew their cooperative efforts. The United States agreed not to pursue high-level Panamanian officials in return for Panamanian assistance in negotiations with Cuba over the capture of several Central Intelligence Agency (CIA) agents in Cuban waters.[66] Despite this agreement, narcotics trafficking remained a problem in Panama. U.S. officials "in and out of Panama" did not believe that the government of Panama was fully committed to narcotics control.[67] Rather, the country continued "to serve as a conduit through which vast amounts of illegal drugs" were funneled to the United States.[68]

U.S. Narcotics Enforcement Efforts in the Northern Andes, 1973–1980

As narcotics production and trafficking increased in the northern Andes, the United States heightened its diplomatic efforts to coerce the region's governments into developing training programs for counternarcotics officers and cooperating with the extradition of foreign nationals implicated in narcotics trafficking. The United States also advocated and devised crop substitution programs while pushing foreign governments to create stricter laws for narcotics control.

To implement its narcotics policy, the United States used the power of the Cabinet Committee on International Narcotics Control (CCINC), formed in 1971.[69] The CCINC established interagency committees in all the regional bureaus of the State Department to create a worldwide integrated approach to narcotics control.[70] Under the provisions of the Foreign Assistance Act of 1961, the CCINC already had the authority to certify a foreign country's compliance with U.S. narcotics control programs. If a nation failed to take adequate steps to cooperate with U.S. counternarcotics measures, the secretary of state was obligated to inform the president, who then had the right to withhold economic and military assistance.[71]

The ratification of the 1972 amendment to the 1961 Single Convention on Narcotic Drugs enhanced the power of CCINC. By 1973 twenty-four nations had signed it. All signatory nations now agreed to reduce opium poppy cultivation, ease restrictions on extradition, and establish treatment and education efforts to deal with individual drug abusers.[72] The Department of State believed that this treaty would strengthen "the international drug control machinery" by "assuring expert assistance" to countries that needed help "controlling drugs" and "facilitating the prosecution of narcotics law offenders." The amendment allowed signatory nations to single out fellow signatories that failed to adhere to the convention or had become "important centers of illicit activities regarding narcotic drugs."[73]

The Carter administration replaced CCINC with the Bureau of International Narcotics Matters (INM) in 1977, though the INM retained the same functions.[74] The CCINC and its successor, the INM, became significant tools for U.S. counternarcotics efforts abroad because they could wield economic leverage to influence the narcotics policies of foreign nations.

One of the most important policies devised by the CCINC to halt coca leaf cultivation was crop substitution; this was considered a potential solution to the financial incentive that coca provided for the campesinos. Crop substitution was chosen over eradication because "eradication projects in Bolivia and Peru" conflicted with the centuries-old custom of coca chewing and denied the campesinos their "only source of income."[75]

Neither the Bolivian nor the Peruvian government could afford to upset their campesino populations by eliminating coca farming. Both governments were dictatorships during the mid-1970s, and disturbing the campesino populations with government-directed coca eradication would have threatened their political authority. The success of U.S. counternarcotics policy thus hinged on its ability to create a crop substitution program that would support the campesinos and bring stability to the northern Andean governments and their economies, which were emerging from the bitter revolutionary struggles of the 1960s.

In 1975 an experimental program for coca crop substitution in Bolivia was instituted under the guidance of the United States Agency for International Development (USAID). This program accelerated in 1976 as the result of meetings between Secretary of State Henry Kissinger and President Hugo Banzer of Bolivia.[76] In return for Banzer's commitment to ban coca cultivation and limit trafficking, the United States pledged ninety-five million dollars to be divided "between crop or income replacement and increased enforcement."[77]

A similar crop substitution program was also under consideration for Peru. Members of the Ford administration believed that to secure Bolivian and Peruvian cooperation they had to "assure both nations of U.S. financial assistance in the years to follow" by making a "multi-year commitment."[78] Any crop that could successfully replace coca would have to provide a similar income for the campesinos.[79] Campesinos earned roughly $250 per five hundred kilos of coca leaf in the mid-1970s, twice what they earned growing other crops such as coffee.[80] The search for a suitable replacement crop was formidable. First, it would take several years to identify and develop a crop that would grow in coca areas. Second, transportation, storage, and other marketing concerns had to be addressed, especially those associated with bringing crops from remote Andean regions to a market.[81] Crop replacement and income substitution were daunting goals that would later plague U.S. alternative development programs throughout the 1980s and 1990s.

During the 1970s the very feasibility of crop substitution was brought into question. A 1976 USAID study on coca substitution argued that crop substitution would not work in the absence of effective coca control. Moreover, USAID believed that few crops could compete with the income from coca. The agency observed that farmers replaced "less profitable crops before" they replaced coca, and that coca provided "a more rational use of labor" and involved less risk than "growing and marketing . . . competing crops."[82] A 1977 CIA study, "Bolivia: Obstacles to Coca Crop Substitutions," drew similar conclusions. The CIA reported that none of the alternative crops, "such as sugar, coffee, cotton, and certain fruits," were as easy to grow as coca. Moreover, "proposed substitutes" were "subject to wide price fluctuations and . . . without price guarantees and price stability," crop substitution efforts were "likely to fail."[83]

In response to crop substitution's intrinsic problems, USAID argued that rather than just replacing coca with direct subsidies, the program needed to maintain farm family income by giving "preferential market quotas" for alternative crops such as cotton, creating "off farm opportunities," and providing "more acreage under cultivation per farm."[84] According to State Department and DEA officials, the success of crop substitution depended on basic rural development in coca areas, which in turn required an improvement in the quality of life for the farming population. Only with rural development could a "phased ban on production" occur.[85] The State Department and the DEA therefore pursued a policy that advocated "U.S.-financed rural development projects combined with efforts to limit coca production by the governments of Bolivia and Peru."[86]

Despite these recommendations, U.S. officials in Bolivia and Peru remained pessimistic about the success of crop substitution, with or without alternative development projects. The DEA reported that crop substitution was virtually nonexistent or ineffective in both Peru and Bolivia due to a lack of infrastructure. Moreover, "coca had been grown for centuries" in Bolivia and Peru, and "no alternative crop could match the economic return of coca, especially considering the unlimited amount of funds available to encourage production."[87] According to the 1977 CIA report on Bolivian coca crop substitution, the Bolivian government would have to "endure a certain amount of economic risk, social disruption, and political dissatisfaction" for crop substitution to work. The report added that effective crop substitution would be a "long time coming," and that "in the interim, coca production" was "likely to increase."[88]

All the evidence suggested that coca cultivation in the northern Andes could not be terminated. Eradication threatened to place the governments at odds with a large percentage of their citizens. Factors ranging from culture and climate to inadequate infrastructure and campesino poverty worked against replacing coca with an alternative crop. But the real problem lay in the gigantic illicit profits derived from the production and sale of cocaine. Those profits not only fueled the production of coca beyond its traditional purposes but also stimulated a vast and growing clandestine money-laundering economy.

The enormous amounts of money generated through the sale of narcotics in the United States forced traffickers to find ways to legitimize their profits. Underground money-laundering networks were the result.[89] Every money-laundering scheme sought to get around the Bank Secrecy Act of 1970, which required all transactions of ten thousand dollars or more and all currency leaving the country worth five thousand dollars or more, to be reported to the Internal Revenue Service (IRS).[90] To launder money or move it offshore, narcotics traffickers used a wide variety of techniques, including couriers, wire transfers, fraudulent checking accounts, money orders, money transfers using third-country currencies, illegal imports, and the exchange of precious metals.[91]

In one money-laundering method, individuals deposited cash under ten thousand dollars in the bank accounts of narcotics traffickers. This money was moved through different financial institutions and then either "integrated" into the U.S. economy or transferred back to the traffickers in the northern Andes.[92] Another method used money exchange houses instead of banks. Money was deposited into an exchange house that was identified as the sole owner of the currency. The exchange house then transferred the money to another institution without having to report the transaction, thus skirting the requirements of the Bank Secrecy Act.[93] By the mid-1970s, uncut cocaine smuggled into the United States was producing an estimated thirty-eight thousand to forty thousand dollars per kilo in profit. Some U.S. banks began to facilitate money laundering for traffickers who needed to move large sums into the legitimate economy.[94] In 1977 the government indicted Chemical Bank in a narcotics money-laundering operation for failing to report transactions totaling $8.5 million.[95]

Nowhere was the money-laundering industry more prevalent than in Florida, the primary hub for narcotics flowing into the United States from the Caribbean. In 1974 the DEA noticed abnormal levels of surplus currency, exceeding $921 million, flowing into Florida's banks. A large percentage of that currency came in the form of twenty-dollar bills.[96] Federal bank regulators maintained that they had limited responsibility under the guidelines of the Bank Secrecy Act for preventing drug traffickers from making huge cash deposits in banks. They had "very little authority to prevent bankers from accepting drug money," and they could not guarantee that drug dealers were not using the banks to launder money from narcotics sales.[97] After 1976 the currency surplus in Florida's banks increased at about 50 percent annually. The surplus totaled $3.3 billion in 1978 and was expected to reach $4.9 billion in 1979.[98] By 1979 the DEA estimated that the illegal drug trade in Florida was worth roughly ten billion dollars a year. It was the state's biggest industry.[99]

In 1979 the Department of Justice, the IRS, and the Customs Bureau launched Operation Greenback, also known as the Florida Cash Flow Project, to counter the flow of narco-dollars passing through Miami's airports and banks. Its first major success occurred in 1980, when the operation seized $1.5 million at Miami International Airport.[100] By 1982 Operation Greenback had seized more than $20.6 million in cash and property and had indicted ninety individuals and corporations.[101] Following Greenback's initial success, the government established several task forces to investigate violations of the Bank Secrecy Act.[102]

Money laundering helped drug traffickers to solidify their power base. Both within the United States and abroad, they created the necessary contacts to continue laundering long after the U.S. government began to crack down in the late 1970s. Moreover, they continually found new ways to get around U.S. currency laws. Narco-dollars earned though money laundering became an essential part of northern Andean economies.[103]

In Colombia, laundering was accomplished through *la ventanilla siniestra*.[104] Literally, the phrase means "the left-hand window." The ventanilla siniestra was a well-known method of money laundering that the Colombian government took few steps to regulate. Through the ventanilla, Colombian banks bought U.S. dollars, ostensibly to bolster their financial reserves. Colombians were not required to present any identification to sell their U.S. dollars, but Colombian banks would only buy U.S. dollars if they were physically located in Colombia. By selling their dollars to Colombian banks, Colombian drug traffickers avoided identification. The Colombian economy in turn legitimized and absorbed the illicit profits. Moreover, since the Colombian government wanted to maintain a conservative economic policy and acquire foreign exchange, the banks offered a favorable discount exchange rate to traffickers who sold their dollars for Colombian pesos.[105]

In 1977 the combined export value of marijuana and cocaine constituted roughly 16 percent of the Colombian gross national product.[106] In 1978 the DEA estimated that nearly one billion dollars in drug money entered the Colombian economy annually.[107] Moreover, economists believed that Colombia's record 29 percent inflation rate in 1978 resulted from the influx of drug money.[108] The ventanilla siniestra served its purpose very well.

Like Colombia, Panama had no law that "prevented any banking institution from accepting foreign currency from any source."[109] Through the creation of private company accounts (dummy corporations), interbank accounts with other nonregulated banking nations such as the Cayman Islands, and unidentified personal accounts, Panama attracted "criminal capital."[110] By 1980, Panamanian banking institutions were valued at nearly thirty-eight billion dollars. Panama's banking industry represented 9 percent of its gross national product (GNP) and had an annual growth rate of 22 percent.[111] Narco-dollars pouring into Colombia and Panama created a giant economic cushion for both nations.

On the opposite side of the fence, or rather through the legitimate "right-hand window," steady prices for commodities such as tin and natural gas bolstered the Bolivian economy throughout the 1970s.[112] However, a crash in sugar and cotton prices in 1975 turned many Bolivians to coca production to earn U.S. dollars. Bolivia's coca dependence resulted from government policies that discriminated against farmers and produced unfavorable terms of trade for traditional agriculture (see chart 1.1).[113] Consequently, large sums of narco-dollars flowed into Bolivia and were invested in the Bolivian economy in banking, real estate, consumer goods, transportation, and other legitimate businesses. The 1978 decline in prices for tin and natural gas led to the withdrawal of legal investments from Bolivian banks and their transfer abroad. As Bolivia's credit dried up, a large portion of the country's population was forced to rely on narco-dollars to survive, while at the same time narco-dollars were used to stimulate the legitimate economy.[114] Bolivia was truly developing a coca-driven economy.

Chart 1.1 | **Terms of Trade for Bolivia 1975-1980 (in Millions of Bolivianos)**

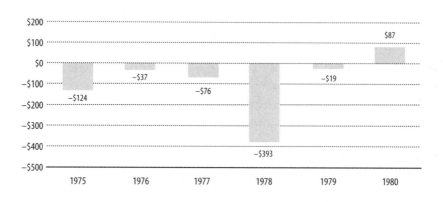

Terms of Trade for Bolivia (in Millions of Bolivianos)

Money laundering sheltered both Colombia and Panama from the Latin American economic meltdown that began in the late 1970s by giving both nations huge reserves of capital. Conversely, Bolivia became dependent on narco-dollars as the crashing commodities market led to the transfer of legitimate capital out of Bolivia. For the region as whole, the tremendous amount of money flooding in threatened national security because it created an inflationary environment that would eventually undermine the legitimate economy.[115]

U.S.–Andean Counternarcotics Cooperation 1968–1980

Through the late 1960s and the 1970s, as crop substitution failed and money laundering thrived in the northern Andes, the U.S. government chafed at the obvious reality that regional governments were negligent on narcotics enforcement. Colombia, Bolivia, and Peru did not have uniform laws setting penalties for the production, possession, or shipment of narcotics. The DEA believed that too many high-level government officials in these countries lacked interest in and knowledge of the local and international drug problem.[116] In the case of Colombia, a 1973 congressional report on Latin America complained that "you get lip service support from the government on narcotics matters—but nothing else."[117] High-level north Andean officials seemed convinced that the local situation was not serious and that the international narcotics trade was a U.S. problem.[118]

In a 1976 report to Congress, investigators determined that northern Andean cooperation in narcotics control efforts was "half-hearted at best" because they "lacked an indigenous addict population to provide a visible reminder" of the problem's severity.[119] The Colombian government felt that the U.S. effort to control marijuana in Colombia was hypocritical because the United States had failed to eradicate its own marijuana fields.[120] Colombian officials also accused the United States of duplicity in placing the blame on Colombia for the U.S. drug epidemic. In their opinion, the United States exported "immorality" by sending "weapons, narcotics such as valium, and pornography" to Colombia, and imported "vice" by "taking out marijuana and cocaine."[121] Northern Andean disinterest in the narcotics problem was aggravated by a shortage of personnel trained in narcotics enforcement and by the absence of a reward system providing incentives for drug interdiction.[122]

In the early 1970s the United States began pushing Andean nations toward a more vigorous counternarcotics policy. In 1972 the CCINC directed the BNDD and the Customs Bureau to begin training competent South American narcotics officers. To gain compliance, the CCINC and its successor, the INM, tied U.S. economic and military assistance to the reorganization of these narcotics suppression units.[123] Between 1972 and 1977, 5,070 new South American officers were trained, including 450 from Bolivia, 714 from Colombia, and 524 from Peru.[124] However, "the drug trade" was "so tempting" and the physical danger of enforcement was so great that the police and military were under constant pressure to yield to bribes or look the other way.[125] To bolster morale and reduce corruption, the United States provided financial support to raise the salaries of the northern Andean counternarcotics forces.[126] In addition, the United States sent advisory teams from agencies such as the Customs Bureau to coordinate narcotics interdiction programs within and between nations.[127]

By pressuring northern Andean governments to use their police forces and militaries to uphold their narcotics laws, the United States forced them into direct confrontation with large sectors of their populations. In Colombia the military's public image declined markedly in rural areas because by eliminating coca, the army deprived the campesinos of "the first real income and dignity" they had known.[128] Nevertheless, by the late 1970s the U.S. effort to increase Andean involvement in counternarcotics activities had expanded their participation in U.S.-sponsored counternarcotics programs.

The United States was also determined to work with foreign governments for the extradition of nationals engaged in drug trafficking. However, most governments refused to surrender their own citizens for trial, partly because doing so would violate their national sovereignty, and partly because narcotics networks had gained significant influence over many northern Andean legal systems.[129] Extradition was also curtailed by the overseas operational limitations set out in the Mansfield Amendment, a law designed to "avoid excessive U.S. interventions in the internal affairs of other nations."[130]

The Mansfield Amendment forbade DEA agents from participating in any direct arrest on the sovereign territory of a foreign nation.[131] The DEA skirted the amendment by arranging for the arrest of foreign offenders when they left their home countries, enabling the agency to seize offenders while claiming that it violated neither national sovereignty nor the Mansfield Amendment. Even so, extradition of foreigners remained a gray area for U.S. and northern Andean governments for many years. It was not until 1979 that the United States signed an extradition treaty with Colombia that allowed U.S. agents to arrest Colombian nationals on their own soil.[132] In Bolivia, Peru, and Panama, extradition of their citizens remained illegal well into the 1980s and 1990s. The issue of extradition ultimately pushed cooperation between the United States and the northern Andean countries to its limits.

Despite these and other complications, the United States, through the CCINC and the INM, gradually pushed northern Andean governments toward greater narcotics control. In 1975 the CCINC coerced Bolivia to sign the UN Single Convention on Narcotics.[133] Bolivia's acceptance of the Single Convention was a major victory for the United States because it forced Bolivia to support U.S.-sponsored crop reduction and experimental crop substitution programs. Nevertheless, corruption within the Bolivian government combined with the DEA's minimal presence in rural areas meant that narcotics production and trafficking continued anyway. Bolivia remained in violation of its international obligations, forcing the United States to apply yet more pressure on the Bolivian government to step up its counternarcotics efforts.[134]

Also in 1975, Colombia, searching for a way to work with the United States, passed a law that made drug trafficking a crime subject to military justice.[135] This measure was a sign that Colombia, like Bolivia, was taking U.S. demands more seriously. By 1976 the CCINC had been able to get ten South American countries to stiffen penalties for traffickers, improve enforcement measures, or change their laws.[136]

In 1977, Bolivia forbade the cultivation of any new plots of coca; however, political, social, and economic difficulties, such as declining commodities prices, corruption in the Banzer government, and campesino resistance to crop control prevented the ban's implementation.[137] In 1978, Peru, an original signatory to the 1961 UN Single Convention on Narcotics, unexpectedly followed Bolivia's suit and tried to create tougher laws and harsher sentences against coca trafficking and production.[138] Although coca cultivation remained legal in areas run by the government-operated ENACO, Peru's adoption of this law signaled its willingness to adhere to its international obligations to control the drug industry.[139]

In 1979 the U.S. Department of State offered financial incentives to encourage the Colombian government to use herbicides to eradicate marijuana.[140] However, a study of Mexico's application of the herbicide paraquat during the 1970s revealed its potential for environmental damage. Colombia consequently refused herbicides because they threatened to destroy the campesinos' legitimate crops as well as the environment.[141] However, in 1984, after continuous pressure from the State Department and the White House, Colombia agreed to use an herbicide, glyphosate, to eradicate marijuana since it was considered less of a danger to the environment.[142]

By the end of 1979, the INM had effectively pressured the northern Andean nations to make significant changes in their narcotics laws. However, this success jeopardized regional stability because the new laws ignored the narcotics industry's political, social, and economic power in the region. In fact, the new narcotics laws began to work against the U.S.

objective of reducing the narcotics supply and its flow into the United States. Jaime Malamud-Goti, the former Argentinean secretary of state and special envoy to Bolivia, called the situation the paradox of the drug war. Goti argued that the political strategies used to control narcotics contradicted the goals of narcotics control.

Instead of stopping production, the proscriptive approach of U.S. policy (tougher laws, stronger enforcement) increased the value of coca.[143] In 1978, sales of coca leaf from the Chapare and Yungas regions in the Bolivian highlands grossed approximately $46.6 million. The new enforcement measures almost doubled the value of coca in these areas to $80.5 million by 1980.[144] The movement of drugs into the United States also increased. In 1973 the United States seized 477 pounds of cocaine and less than one ton of marijuana from South America. In 1978 the United States seized 3,714 pounds of cocaine and 165 tons of marijuana coming from South America.[145]

The ultimate paradox for U.S. policy at the end of the decade was the transformation of the Bolivian government into a narcocracy. Fernando Cepeda Ulloa, the former Colombian minister of government and communications and ambassador to London, defines *narcocracy* as a situation in which drug organizations, or cartels, penetrate the state apparatus as well as key segments of the private sector and begin to exercise de facto authority over the national government.[146] By the late 1970s northern Andean governments recognized the "potential danger" of "shadow governments" directed by narcotics traffickers who had the means to disrupt "the orderly process of government" for their own ends.[147] This threat soon became a reality in Bolivia.[148]

In 1978 economic chaos, strikes by tin miners, allegations of narcotics corruption, and demands for political freedom forced the Bolivian dictator Hugo Banzer to resign from power and promise free elections.[149] Banzer's departure created a power vacuum in Bolivia that resulted in various coups and the election of three different presidents, each of whom failed to gain the support of the Bolivian people and military.

In 1979 Lidia Gueiler Tejada was appointed interim head of the Bolivian government until elections could be held in 1980. Tejada's transitional government worked with the DEA to implement a tough counternarcotics policy that challenged the power of the Bolivian drug baron Roberto Suárez Gómez. In 1980 Tejada oversaw the election of Hernán Siles Zuazo and his party, Unidad Democrática y Popular (UDP), a socialist coalition that promised to intensify narcotics enforcement measures.[150] This triggered what was known as the "cocaine coup" described at the beginning of this chapter. Led by General Luis García Meza, the coup (*golpe*) violently overthrew the government of Gueiler Tejada before Siles Zuazo could take power.[151]

An alliance of anti-leftist forces and narcotics traffickers directed the coup, which initially appeared to be a reaction by right-wing factions to their failure to win the 1980 national elections. Many leftists, union leaders, and progressive clergy, who were perceived to be threats to Bolivian security, were rounded up and executed by right-wing death squads under the direction of the former Nazi, Klaus Barbie.[152] However, in reality, the coup was staged so that García Meza could protect the interests of Suárez and prominent Bolivian military officials, such as Colonel Luis Arce Gómez, who were earning nearly five hundred million dollars annually from cocaine.[153] One of the most obvious indicators that the coup had been driven by coca-dollars was García Meza's release of several prominent narcotics traffickers from jail when he assumed power.

When the reality of what had occurred in Bolivia dawned upon the U.S. government, it withdrew its ambassador and suspended all economic and military aid, estimated at roughly $127 million.[154] These actions did little to change the immediate situation because the loss of U.S. aid was offset by the enormous profits that coca was bringing to Bolivia. In Bolivia, coca had become king.

Meza was forced out of power in 1982, but the events that had transpired in Bolivia proved that the attempts to eliminate narcotics at their source had been counterproductive. U.S. policies had given the drug industry an unprecedented economic presence in the northern Andes, which was translated into political power. In Bolivia, rather than let a proscriptive narcotics regime directed by the United States take over their country, powerful narcotics traffickers like Suárez conspired with elements of the military to overthrow the government and protect the flow of narco-dollars.

This was the essential paradox of the War on Drugs. Socioeconomic and political factors in the northern Andes sabotaged U.S. methods for drug control. The United States could do little to prevent the cocaine coup of 1980 because its strategy did not address the reality that the narcotics industry penetrated nearly every aspect of north Andean economic and political systems. As the 1980s began, northern Andean nations and

Panama were ill-prepared to challenge the growing power of the drug trade, which U.S. policies had paradoxically strengthened. The deeper the United States was drawn into the vortex of narcotics control in the northern Andes and Central America, the further it stood from achieving its goals.

2

The Economic Role of Narcotics in Latin America, 1980–1987

The coca boom of the late 1970s and early 1980s and a Latin American debt crisis precipitated by worldwide increases in the price of oil after 1979 plunged Colombia, Peru, and Bolivia into an ever more destructive dependency on the economic power of narcotics in the last decades of the twentieth century. As prices plummeted for legitimate agricultural exports, money from coca and cocaine production became nearly the sole means of subsistence for northern Andean campesinos. Collapsing prices for tin and other industrial exports destroyed foreign exchange and heightened the need to service foreign debt, creating an increased dependence on narco-dollars and vulnerability to the cartels that brought those dollars into their national economies.[1]

Narco-dollars and the ventanilla siniestra compromised Colombia's ability to maintain a fiscally conservative macroeconomic policy over the long term. In Peru, Alan García's heterodox macroeconomic policies created rampant inflation and a dependence on narco-dollars to keep the economy functioning. In Bolivia, President Paz Estenssoro's questionable economic reforms were facilitated by the infusion of narco-dollars. The cascade of negative consequences precipitated fiscal and political crises in the northern Andes.

The 1979 Debt Crisis and the Demand for Narcotics

The Latin American debt crisis had been long in the making. In the 1930s the Great Depression and the desire to make Latin America less dependent on industrialized countries led to the development of import substitution industrialization (ISI) programs throughout the region.[2] ISI was designed to help Latin America achieve greater economic independence by promoting the expansion of industries that could eliminate the need to import basic goods. Economic planners believed that ISI would end Latin American countries' economic dependence on world markets and help each break its reliance on the export of one or two primary products to earn the foreign currency to import essentials not produced in the region.

However, ISI encountered difficulties right from the start.[3] For one thing, employment in Latin America was inadequate to stimulate demand for substituted products. For another, offering government contracts to purchase ISI products created an artificial demand that allowed these industries to grow when they might not have done so otherwise. Finally, high energy prices and protectionist policies against competitive foreign imports led to slow export growth and a decline in foreign exchange, which in turn generated an overvaluation of national currencies.[4] When national currencies became overvalued and the export sector weakened, internal markets for ISI goods declined, continuing the downward spiral. Lack of demand for ISI products led Latin American nations to borrow more money from abroad to keep their national industries afloat. Increased borrowing led to larger deficits and higher inflation.[5]

When the price of oil exploded in 1979, industrialized nations countered inflationary pressures by raising their interest rates. This produced a severe credit crunch in Latin America. However, Latin American states continued to borrow heavily from U.S. commercial banks to finance their national industries. With the onset of a global recession and a concurrent rise in interest rates, the demand for Latin America's primary exports decreased, and the region's last source of foreign exchange slowly dried up.

In 1982 the announcement that Mexico and Argentina had to suspend payments on their foreign debt sparked a regional economic crisis. International creditors called in their loans to Latin America. The tightening of international interest rates left many Latin American nations unable to finance their foreign debt. In particular, Bolivia and Peru suffered under the credit crunch because of their excessive borrowing and heterodox economic policies. Colombia, on the other hand, initially weathered the storm thanks to its conservative fiscal policy, but it too felt the impact of the debt crisis by the end of the 1980s.

As the regional debt crisis intensified in Latin America, demand for narcotics spiked in the United States. In the early 1980s, narcotics use among the general U.S. population remained at steady or increasing levels. In 1982 the United States had an estimated 4.33 million cocaine users and 22.5 million marijuana users. The National Household Survey on Drug Abuse (NHSDA) estimated that, between 1977 and 1982, the number of monthly cocaine users between the ages of eighteen and twenty-five rose from 10.2 percent to 18.8 percent. The same survey estimated that the number of cocaine users aged twenty-six and above rose steadily, from 0.9 percent in 1977 to 3.8 percent in 1982 (see chart 2.1).[6]

Chart 2.1 | **National Household Survey on Drug Abuse (NHSDA) Survey on Yearly Cocaine Use for Users 18 Years of Age and Older, 1976–1982**

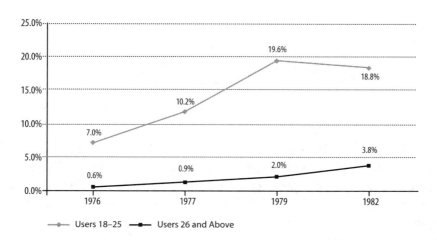

The NHSDA survey noted that, between 1979 and 1985, the number of monthly cocaine users more than doubled, from 3.0 percent to 6.3 percent for people between the ages of twenty-six and thirty-four. The num-

ber of monthly cocaine users 35 and older rose slightly from 0.2 percent
to 0.5 percent, while the number of users between the ages of eighteen
and twenty-five decreased slightly, from 9.9 percent to 8.1 percent (see
chart 2.2).[7] One can surmise from the data in these surveys that the rate
of cocaine consumption among a large sector of the U.S. population rose
continuously. Moreover, rising cocaine consumption was accompanied by
decreasing marijuana use.[8] These trends helped stimulate a coca boom in
the northern Andes during the early 1980s.

The northern Andean economies became "hooked" on drugs. Narcotics
cultivation dramatically increased, while drug processing and distribution
began to provide massive profits for the region.

Chart 2.2 | **NHSDA Survey on Monthly Cocaine Abuse, 1979–1985**

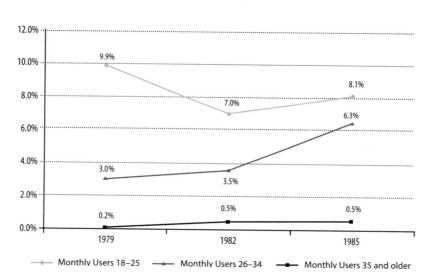

In Peru the USAID estimated that coca cultivation jumped from twelve
thousand hectares in 1981 to sixty thousand hectares in 1986.[9] The INM
embassy report on coca production in Peru projected a jump from 46,000
hectares under cultivation in 1982 to 56,820 hectares in 1985.[10] Bolivia's
cultivation rate remained steady between 1981 and 1983, at roughly
thirty-five thousand hectares, then climbed to forty-five thousand hectares
between 1984 and 1986.[11] Colombia retained its position as the "process-
ing/distribution center for cocaine and coca derivatives . . . coming up
from Peru and Bolivia" because of its proximity to the Caribbean basin.[12]

Colombia's coca leaf production expanded from 2,900 hectares in 1981 to 20,000 by 1985.[13] Colombia also produced nearly 70 percent of the marijuana that flowed into the United States, though the number of hectares devoted to marijuana cultivation increased only slightly, from 8,000 in 1981 to 9,400 in 1984.[14] In 1985, conservative assessments projected that narcotics earnings brought roughly $2 billion to Colombia, $1.5 billion to Peru, and $1 billion to Bolivia annually.[15]

The Narcotics Economy in Colombia

Unlike its neighbors, Colombia did not suffer immediately from the 1980s economic crisis. It benefited from good fiscal management during the 1970s, when most Latin American nations were heading deep into debt to finance their ISI programs. Colombia's fiscal conservatism entailed tight monetary policies to control inflation, as well as economic austerity and avoidance of hyperinflation.[16] Although Colombia was successful in managing its foreign debt payments throughout the 1980s, its foreign debt grew from $6.9 billion in 1980 to almost $14 billion in 1985 (see chart 2.3).[17]

Chart 2.3 | **Colombian External Debt, 1980–1985 (in Billions of U.S. Dollars)**

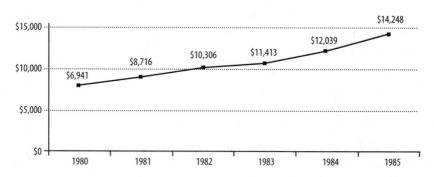

However, the debt crisis among Colombia's neighbors made it difficult for Colombia to obtain loans on favorable terms, and the Colombian peso became highly overvalued due to a lack of foreign exchange.[18] Overvaluation hurt Colombia's ability to export its products and compete in international markets, so the government rapidly devalued its peso in 1984.[19] The exchange rate adjustment was painful for many Colombians, but it helped the country grow, through the export of coffee, gold, and oil. Nevertheless, Colombia's foreign debt slowly continued its movement upward, from $15.5 billion in 1986 to $16.8 billion by 1989 (see chart 2.4), driven in part by the need to fight guerrilla insurgencies and narcotics traffickers.[20]

Chart 2.4 | **Colombian External Debt, 1986–1989 (in Billions of U.S. Dollars)**

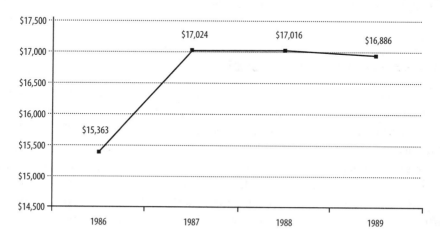

In 1989 the United States allowed the International Coffee Agreement (ICA) to collapse.[21] The ICA had provided price supports for Colombian coffee. As a consequence, Colombia's primary source of foreign exchange declined, and the country was forced to look to its other products for income. By 1990, Colombia faced poor economic growth and higher inflation caused by swelling deficits.[22]

Even so, Colombia's economy was a relative success story during the 1980s, partly because its orthodox fiscal policy kept inflation down. However, the legal economy was not the sole source of its success; narcodollars played an important role, particularly their impact on fiscal policy management and inflation control. As legitimate exports declined, "illicit drugs had become a significant source of foreign exchange."[23]

The mechanism for laundering illicit profits was primarily the ventanilla siniestra. The ventanilla first opened in 1975 as a way to garner foreign exchange, which was in short supply, and much (though not all) of its money came from narcotics.[24] The ventanilla operated with the tacit approval of the Colombian government; banks such as the Banco de la República accepted U.S. dollars from any source with no questions asked.[25] In 1979 the ventanilla earned $1.452 billion; it earned another

$1.281 billion in 1980 and close to $1.008 billion in 1981 (see chart 2.5).[26] In some ways, the ventanilla worked too well: it brought in too many U.S. dollars at a time when the government was trying to control inflation by reducing excess money supply. Thus, in 1982 the Colombian government attempted to regulate it.[27]

Chart 2.5 | **La Ventanilla Siniestra, 1979–1989 (in Millions of U.S. Dollars)**

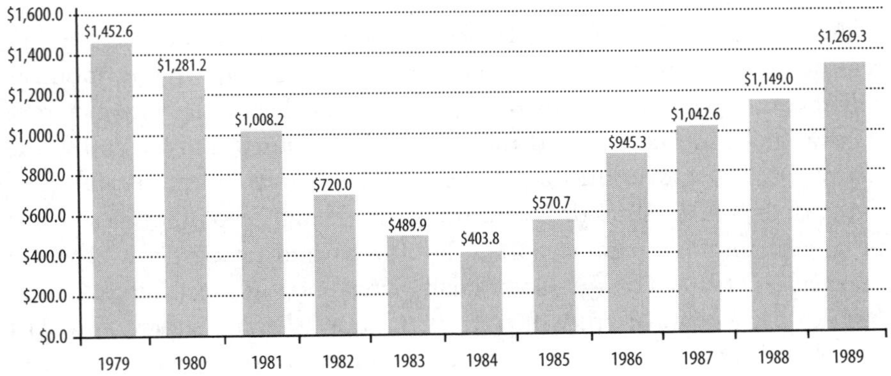

The flow of money through the ventanilla declined from $720 million in 1982 to $403 million in 1984.[28] Colombia's foreign exchange then declined, due both to restrictions on the ventanilla and the country's inability to obtain foreign loans. This led to an overvaluation of the Colombian peso, forcing the government to maintain high interest rates to prevent inflation. In 1984, the same year that ventanilla receipts were at their lowest point, the Colombian government devalued its peso to stop overvaluation and increase its ability to export abroad.

To compensate for the peso's devaluation and to encourage a renewed influx of foreign exchange, the government relaxed its controls on the ventanilla siniestra in 1985, at the same time maintaining high interest rates of roughly 7 percent. U.S. dollars began to move back into the country, temporarily reducing inflationary pressure. Deposits through the ventanilla jumped from $570 million in 1985 to $1.42 billion by 1987, coinciding with the coca boom.[29] The surge of narco-dollars, along with rising incomes from coffee exports, once again pushed up interest rates on the Colombian peso. This hurt Colombia's ability to boost the sale of its nontraditional exports.[30] When the ICA collapsed in 1989, Colombia was faced with slow economic growth due to the decline in coffee revenues and rising inflation related to increasing budget deficits. All wreaked havoc with the national economy.

By 1989, cocaine and marijuana contributed close to 15 percent of Colombia's export earnings.[31] Thus, when Colombia liberalized its economy in 1990, the reduction of tariffs and the freeing of restrictions on the movement of capital did not initially bring in the expected imports. Instead, U.S. dollars inundated the country, more than half of which came from cocaine earnings laundered and repatriated to Colombia by narcotics traffickers.[32]

According to Dr. Miguel Urrutia, Colombia's former planning minister, the massive quantity of drug dollars gave Colombia what economists call the "Dutch Disease." In the late 1970s mushrooming income from natural gas exports distorted the value of the Dutch guilder and made many Dutch exports uncompetitive. Similarly, the enormous influx of narco-dollars after 1985 drove up the value of the Colombian peso, thus pricing Colombia's legal exports (like flowers and textiles) out of world markets.[33] This forced the Colombian government to keep interest rates high to prevent inflation, which in turn attracted more capital and hurt Colombia's ability to open up new, nontraditional export markets.

As narco-dollars continued to deluge the economy, in 1990 the government reduced tariff rates to attract imports and rid itself of excess foreign exchange. However, this decision made it increasingly difficult for legitimate businesses to survive as cheap imports poured into Colombia and replaced local products in the marketplace. In addition, the reduction of tariff rates and the loosening of restrictions on the movement of capital stimulated an influx of illegal contraband, putting hundreds of legitimate importers out of business and cutting government revenue.[34]

As Colombia moved into the new decade, it confronted the results of the 1980s. The manipulation of narco-dollars in the economy had retarded the country's economic growth. The sale and distribution of drugs had generated a great deal of income, but much of it had become concentrated in a few hands, particularly among the Medellín and Cali cartels. The cartels' narco-dollar investments created local inflationary conditions. As early as 1981, the influx of drug money led to "real estate speculation, which caused the price of land to skyrocket."[35] This affected not only the consumer price index but also the ability of middle- and lower-income families to obtain housing.

The role of the Medellín cartel in distorting local economies is a case in point. Colombia's second largest city, Medellín, had an extremely high unemployment rate when the demand for textiles collapsed following the

1980 global economic crisis. Textiles were Medellín's largest industry. In 1983, the city's unemployment rate was 16.7 percent.[36] However, when the ventanilla brought massive amounts of money into Colombia, Medellín witnessed an economic boom based on narco-dollars. Colombian economist Mario Arango estimated that by 1987 roughly $313 million had flowed into Medellín, creating twenty-eight thousand low-skill jobs. As more and more narco-dollars arrived, they triggered local inflation and stimulated a short-term boom in construction.[37] The construction boom inflated property values but failed to create a mass market to support the growth of local industries.

In 1989, according to Medellín's mayor, Juan Gómez Martínez, drug money did not generate enough employment because it wasn't "invested in productive infrastructure." Gómez Martínez explained that "spending on imported bathroom fixtures and expensive art" did not "translate into jobs for skilled tradesmen in Medellín's factories."[38] The short-term construction boom yielded temporary employment for unskilled laborers, but narco-dollars were not invested in high-skill industries. They thus failed to stimulate employment for the skilled industrial workers who suffered from inflation.[39]

Cali and Barranquilla had similar experiences. For example, the Cali cartel kingpin Gilberto Rodríguez Orejuela invested heavily in Cali real estate, drugstores, and radio stations. As observed by a Cali resident, the cartel was "involved in everything, providing jobs for the people." However, the net effect was that the cartel's narco-dollars "pushed up the prices on everything."[40] In Barranquilla, on the north coast, which grew much of Colombia's marijuana, luxury shops appeared, selling "imported apparel," "electrical appliances," and "expensive furniture." Commerce in the Barranquilla region switched from serving an "agro-oriented society" to accommodating an "affluent, drug-related strata."[41] According to an INM Bogotá cable, drug money highly inflated prices and wages on the north coast.[42] The Colombian deputy director of the Department of National Planning stated that, starting in 1986, the "coca-dollar . . . caused the price of real estate and houses to double."[43]

Narco-dollars also distorted life in Colombia's countryside. The coca industry not only employed roughly two hundred thousand to five hundred thousand people in the late 1970s and early 1980s, but it also stimulated the conversion of agricultural land for marijuana and coca cultivation. This resulted in shortages of legitimate agricultural crops in rural drug zones.[44] More important, the increase in illicit wealth allowed traffickers to buy up nearly one-third of the country's best agricultural land as well as many privatized businesses, which they used to launder their money. Much of the illicit earnings in the north coast/Baranquilla area went into real estate, especially ranches and farms. The head of the national real estate organization, Oscar Borrero Ochoa, said traffickers bought $5.5 billion worth of urban and rural property between 1979 and 1988.[45]

Around 1984 the Medellín cartel began investing in cattle land, partly to gain legitimacy among Colombia's traditional landholding oligarchy.[46] This phenomenon became so widespread that the Colombian army's "main drug fighter, General Jaime Ruiz Barrera," coined the term "narco-cattlemen."[47] These land purchases displaced agricultural activity. The new owners turned the land into pasture or utilized improvements in agricultural technology with which small-scale farmers could not compete.[48]

Significantly, the cartels' land acquisitions injured land reform programs, creating a long-term problem. In 1984 an estimated 3.2 percent of rural proprietors owned over half of the country's land. Despite earlier attempts at land reform, land had always been concentrated in a few hands. Often land reform laws were ineffective because landowners managed to find legal loopholes that enabled them to preserve the highly skewed pattern of land distribution.[49] Thus, narco-traffickers' effort to join Colombia's traditional land-owning elite through land purchases exacerbated conflicts over land reform.

Although the government passed a new agrarian reform law in 1987, the cartels' massive drug profits allowed them to purchase some of the best rural land, making the law difficult to implement. Thus, commented Carlos Ossa, manager of the Colombian Institute of Agrarian Reform (INCORA), "an agrarian counter-reform was happening where land was being concentrated in the hands of the drug traffickers."[50] By 1989, INCORA concluded that in an area of twenty-seven thousand square miles, 5 percent of the farms held 54 percent of the land.[51] This eventually led to clashes between Colombia's leftist guerrillas and Colombia's narco-traffickers over land reform and peasants' rights and called into question the concept of a working relationship between guerrillas and traffickers.

The Narcotics Economy in Peru

Peru's deteriorating economic situation after 1979 had a direct and immediate impact on the rise of the coca industry. Fernando Belaúnde Terry's democratically elected government had succeeded the military government in 1979, but it suffered from a deepening external debt burden as well as growing deficits and inflation. In 1978, Peru's debt totaled $9.7 billion. By 1982, Peru's external debt had reached $10.7 billion, and it continued rising—to roughly $14.8 billion by 1986.[52] During Belaúnde Terry's presidency, inflation rose in a linear fashion from 66 percent in 1980 to 104 percent in 1982 to 166 percent in 1984 (see chart 2.6).[53]

Chart 2.6 | **Peruvian External Debt and Inflation, 1979–1986**

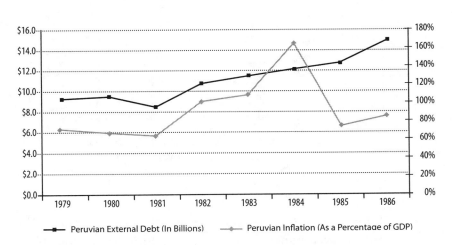

—■— Peruvian External Debt (In Billions)   —◇— Peruvian Inflation (As a Percentage of GDP)

Popular dissatisfaction with Belaúnde Terry emerged as unemployment, debt, and inflation mounted. In 1983, Peru had earned only $3.5 billion in export earnings to finance its $11.5 billion debt (see chart 2.6). Moreover, in 1983, real wages were only three-fifths of Peru's 1973 highs.[54] Per capita income in 1985 remained roughly where it had been twenty years before, while the foreign debt was equal to 80 percent of Peru's GDP.[55]

Under these circumstances, Peruvians pushed for a shift in economic strategy, and Alan García's election in 1985 provided that change. García initiated a series of heterodox economic policies to reactivate the economy. He cut inflation with strict controls on prices and nonessential government spending, while at the same time promoting consumption and increased production through higher salaries.[56] More important, García reduced debt service payments to 10 percent of all export earnings, which allowed him to finance easy credit and offer salary increases to Peruvian workers.[57] García's policies stimulated the Peruvian GDP to a twenty-six-year high of 8.5 percent in 1986, followed by a 7 percent GDP in 1987.[58]

Despite García's initial successes, these advances were not sustainable. The wage hikes created soaring demand, but domestic production could not match the demand. Peru became a net importer, which further diminished the flow of foreign exchange into the economy (see chart 2.7).

Chart 2.7 | **Peruvian Imports vs. Exports, 1986–1990**

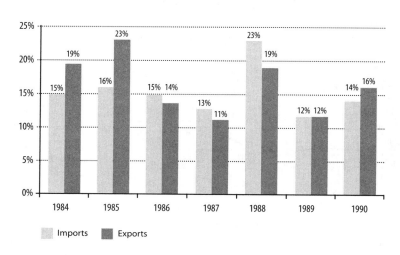

Imports Exports

By 1988 the level of foreign exchange that Peru earned from exports had declined to seven hundred million dollars from its previous high of $1.3 billion in 1985.[59] Much of the decrease was a result of the worldwide collapse in metal prices. When foreign banks tightened credit in reaction to García's 10 percent moratorium on the deficit, the decline worsened. The foreign exchange shortage, national debt, increased currency printing, and increased demand for essential products caused inflation to explode—from 85 percent in 1987 to 6,837 percent by 1990 (see chart 2.8). At the same time, Peru's GDP sank from 8 percent annual growth to –5 percent in 1990, while the external debt steadily rose from seventeen billion dollars in 1987 to twenty billion dollars in 1990 (see charts 2.9 and 2.10).[60] Peru had suffered a severe cash crunch, exacerbated by García's heterodox economic policies. But the question remains: how did coca production influence Peru's economy?

In the midst of Peru's fiscal crisis, the economy surrounding coca production (which stood at between $1.2 billion and $1.5 billion) forced legitimate businesses such as Peruvian banks and Peruvian importers to depend on narco-dollars to operate.[61] For instance, moneychangers on

Ocoña Street in downtown Lima, who traded foreign currency for the Peruvian sol, traveled to Peru's interior to buy narco-dollars at a discount. The moneychangers then sold those narco-dollars on the legal currency market. Nearly three million dollars a day was exchanged on this market, and most of the exchange came from narco-dollars. Without narco-dollars, Peru's importers did not have the dollars they needed to buy goods from abroad. Not only did importers depend on narco-dollars, but so did Peruvian banks. Peru's Banco de Crédito aggressively purchased narco-dollars at its branches in coca-growing regions such as the Upper

Chart 2.8 | **Peruvian Inflation, 1987–1990**

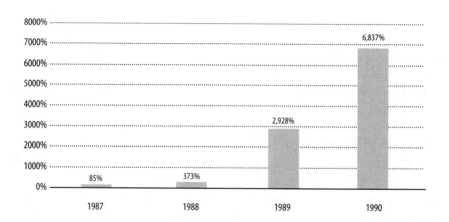

Chart 2.9 | **Peruvian Annual GDP Growth, 1987–1990**

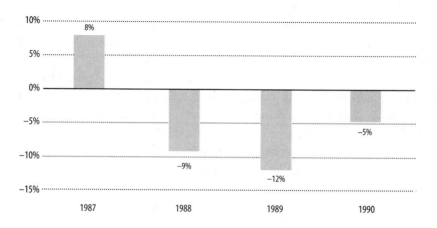

Chart 2.10 | **Peruvian External Debt, 1987–1990 (in Billions of U.S. Dollars)**

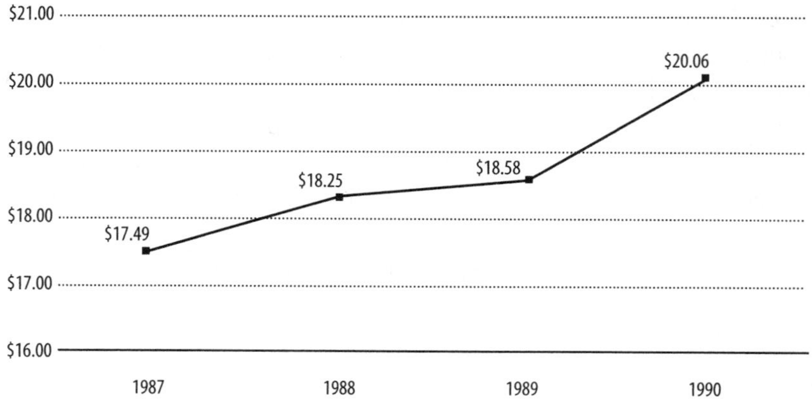

Huallaga Valley. It was able to do so because the Peruvian government had abolished exchange controls in the late 1970s.

The wide-open Central Bank rules governing foreign exchange made Peru an easy place to hide, change, launder, and transfer large amounts of cash through the banking system.[62] In 1988, while Peru was suffering from massive hyperinflation and a burgeoning deficit, President García opened foreign exchange houses, encouraged importers to purchase dollars to buy imports, and declared a tax amnesty on all repatriated dollars regardless of their source. During this same period, coca production and refining increased dramatically.[63]

Unlike Colombia, where the peso had been devalued and exports abroad continued, García's foreign exchange amnesty in Peru flooded the country with narco-dollars, making it possible for citizens to buy needed imports. Though García's heterodox macroeconomic policies created massive hyperinflation, narco-dollars became the source of revenue that "helped reduce the rate of inflation."[64] Peruvian economist Humberto Campodónico argued that without narco-dollars, "exchange rates" would have almost doubled, "making vital imports needed to generate Peruvian growth extremely expensive."[65] Narco-dollars thus acted as a stabilizer for the economy. Yet, as soon as the narco-dollars flowed in, they flowed out to meet the demand for foreign essentials. This situation left Peru with minimal foreign exchange reserves to pay off its national debt. Peru's need for narco-dollars locked it into a vicious cycle of coca dependency.

Legal coca production for domestic consumption in Peru began to rise during the 1970s, mainly in Cuzco, La Libertad, Ayacucho, and the Upper Huallaga Valley (UHV), where three-quarters of illegal coca production later became concentrated (see map 1).[66] It developed into the dominant economic activity in the UHV while the military government concentrated its economic efforts on the Peruvian coast and sierra.[67] Many campesinos in the region turned toward coca as an alternate source of subsistence in the late 1970s, when prices for cacao and coffee fell.[68] By 1980 the UHV was the center for excess illegal production; one hundred thousand campesino families there worked for the coca industry.[69] In the department of San Martín, where the UHV was located, an independent survey concluded that 62.9 percent of the *cocaleros* (coca farmers) planted coca either because it provided the greatest profit that they could earn from farming or because it afforded them the basic necessities for their homes. As one campesino succinctly put it, coca "bettered the level of living" for his family. [70]

A USAID study on the Upper Huallaga Valley estimated that during the mid-1980s, dried coca leaf brought a minimum return of roughly $270 million a year to the area, a great deal of money for a region that had maintained a subsistence economy prior to the coca boom. Coca returned close to $4,500 per hectare for the campesino, whereas other crops averaged a return of only $604.37 per hectare. By 1985, coca grown in the Upper Huallaga Valley represented about 27 percent of Peru's gross national agricultural product.[71]

As campesinos received high prices for coca leaf and coca paste and high wages for work in the coca fields, distortions in the rural economy followed. In 1985, daily wages for coca workers "ranged from 100 to 150 initis, plus food, while the daily wage paid by cultivators of licit products ranged from 30 to 50 initis, with only one or two meals a day."[72] The imbalance created a scarcity of labor for legal crops. A campesino interviewed by a research team investigating the effects of coca explained that "many campesinos" stopped "cultivating corn" because it was "not profitable"; instead, they "dedicated themselves to coca" because "it was profitable."[73]

Consequently, beginning in 1986, "agricultural productivity" for Peru remained "very low" and "did not keep pace with population growth."[74] Between 1987 and 1990, it declined from 4 percent to −8 percent.[75] The decrease in agricultural activity corresponded with an upsurge in imports, suggesting that the coca industry actually weakened Peru's ability to reform its economy and counter inflation: the rising coca industry associated with the declining agricultural sector had made Peru a net importer of essentials.

Campesinos rarely put their profits into anything that would improve their long-term financial position. Since their earnings came from illicit activities, they could not easily launder them via legitimate investments in rural areas. They were afraid to make large bank deposits because they thought doing so would attract the attention of Peruvian authorities. Moreover, they were reluctant to legitimize their profits because exchanging foreign currency through regular bank transactions took a long time. It was easier for campesinos to sell their narco-dollars to the moneychangers, who often gave them better returns than a national bank.[76]

Campesinos also wanted to display their new wealth. They "rarely invested in land, livestock, and tangibles."[77] Instead, they bought luxury goods, which were contraband in the coca-growing regions.[78] Tingo Maria, a town located in the UHV that was noted for the purity of its cocaine, had the largest number of auto dealerships in Peru, although the town had no paved streets.[79] For Peru's campesinos, the life that coca cultivation made possible could not be matched by any other means.

However, within the coca boom, those who created "the commodity" received fewer rewards than those who controlled "the capital." While the campesinos gained financial security and steady employment, they did not earn massive returns on their investments. On the other hand, the traffickers, who controlled the modes of production, made enormous profits, which they laundered through various methods unavailable to the campesinos.[80] Their enormous wealth increased their economic and political position in Peru's coca-growing regions, which allowed them to dictate the terms of the coca trade.[81] In many respects, coca was a destructive force that undermined the campesinos' own long-term economic security: they had relatively few ways to legitimize their profits, and the boom provided only short-term gains in material wealth.

Narco-dollars served as the Peruvian government's greatest source of hard currency throughout the 1980s. "The invisible injection of coca-dollars" lent a "boost to the economy that the Peruvian authorities pretended not to take into consideration in their statistics, but [that] in reality represented a significant contribution."[82] In one study, cocaine represented roughly 6 to 16 percent of Peru's exports in 1984. By 1987 the study concluded that coca provided close to 14.5 percent of Peru's exports.[83] Peru also developed a black market around the narco-dollar economy so that a "substantial percentage of the economically active population in general and the agricultural population in particular" participated in the coca industry. By the end of the decade, an estimated 160,000 families (between eight hundred thousand and one million people) profited from coca.[84] Like Colombia, Peru was addicted to narco-dollars.

The Narcotics Economy in Bolivia

The deterioration of Bolivia's economy in the mid-1980s was closely tied to the rise of the coca industry in that country. In 1980, Bolivia's inflation rate was 25 percent. By 1982 it had reached 158 percent. In 1984 the inflation rate leaped to 1,443 percent and then soared to 12,339 percent in 1985 (see chart 2.11).[85] In addition, between 1980 and 1985, Bolivia's economy suffered from a –4.5 percent GDP growth rate, while its external debt rose from $2.7 billion in 1980 to $4.0 billion in 1985.[86]

Chart 2.11 | Bolivian External Debt and Inflation, 1980–1985 (in U.S. Dollars)

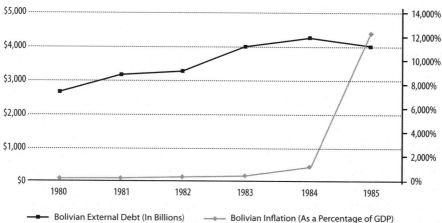

According to a USAID study, "high domestic inflation" caused "interest rates on loans to rise, which in turn" choked "credit" and reduced "the opportunity for small farmers to diversify their farming systems." The report went on to say that "weak local currencies" attracted holders of "financial capital to investments in the dollar-based narcotics trade" because "investing in the production of coca" locked in "the investment to the U.S. dollar."[87]

Between 1980 and 1982, estimates of the total value of coca leaf produced in Bolivia shot upward from $80.5 million to $130.1 million, where it remained steady throughout 1983. In 1984 the total value of coca produced in Bolivia dropped to $92.2 million, but this did not slow production. The total value of coca leaf remained steady or near that price level throughout 1987, although a slight price anomaly occurred during 1986 when the total value of coca leaf declined to $63.1 million because of overproduction (see chart 2.12).[88] Thus, as the Bolivian currency weakened, selling coca became an increasingly attractive proposition because it brought financial returns in the form of nontaxable U.S. dollars.[89]

Chart 2.12 | **Estimate of the Total of Coca Leaves Produced in Bolivia, 1980–1987 (in Millions of U.S. Dollars)**

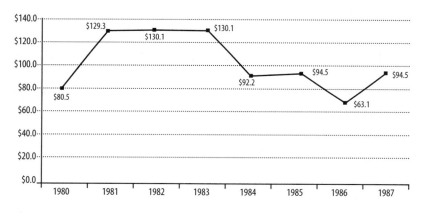

Moreover, as the United States raised interest rates in the 1980s, the value of the U.S. dollar increased, driving up the returns that Bolivian farmers could earn from coca.

Inevitably, the switch to a coca economy created distortions in Bolivia's legitimate economy. According to Interior Minister Fernando Barthelemy, "more than 50 percent of the dollars entering" Bolivia "came from drug trafficking."[90] Planning Minister Gonzalo de Lozada noted in 1986 that "two thirds" of "Bolivia's export economy was from contraband and narcotics," while finance minister Juan Cariaga calculated that narcotics provided "two thirds of the daily foreign exchange demand of approximately $3 million."[91] Another government minister, Samuel Doria Medina, stated in 1987 that the cocaine trade was worth $1.5 billion to Bolivia. He added that roughly $600 million of that $1.5 billion remained in the national economy after producers and traffickers in other countries took their cut. A study on the financial markets of the Chapare (the predominant illicit coca-growing region in Bolivia during the 1980s) showed that savings at one of the region's banks (in Cochabamba) peaked between 1982 and 1983. The report explained that the "large amount of savings in the region" was "due to the huge supplies in liquidity caused by the increasingly favorable prices for coca" and added that the coca growers' income rose rapidly as prices climbed in response to the demand for Bolivian cocaine. Thus, "those farmers placed their savings from this increase" in revenue "in savings accounts," whereby they earned "a nominal interest rate of 30 percent." As a result, estimates showed that credit earned through savings accounts increased from 14 percent in 1978 to 61.7 percent in 1982 at commercial banks located in Chapare.[92]

As in Peru, narco-dollars flooding into the Bolivian economy indirectly stabilized government finances. In 1985 President Victor Paz Estenssoro (1985–1989) relaxed the rules governing the repatriation of dollars and the identification of deposits made at private banks.[93] This allowed the Bolivian government to soak up cocaine dollars in the banking system. As a result, "short-term (30-day) deposits in dollars and dollar-indexed accounts increased from less than $28 million in 1985, to an estimated $270 million in March 1987."[94]

Remarkably, the increase in dollars in the Bolivian Central Bank occurred at the same time that President Paz implemented his New Economic Policy (NEP). The NEP cut government spending, emphasized import liberalization, deregulated the economy, and eliminated subsidies. The NEP's main feature was the creation of a floating exchange rate with the U.S. dollar, which brought Bolivia's hyperinflation under control.[95] Yet the NEP's emphasis on import liberalization caused imports to surpass exports between 1985 and 1988. This raised questions about the source of the increase in U.S. dollar deposits in the Bolivian Central Bank, which were hard to explain—unless they came from the coca economy (see chart 2.13).[96] Economist Roberto Laserna observed that the illegal coca economy increased import capacity by causing Bolivia's parity of exchange to remain relatively low.[97] It was widely believed that relaxation of the rules governing repatriation of dollars allowed narco-dollars to "oil" the implementation of the NEP.[98]

The collapse of Bolivia's traditional export sector in the 1980s created excessive unemployment and pushed more people into the narcotics industry. Even prior to the NEP, many Bolivians had turned to coca production to earn a living. Starting around 1983, a large number of migratory workers, unemployed because of drought and weak prices for agricultural commodities, moved into Bolivia's Chapare region to grow coca.[99]

Chart 2.13 | **Bolivian Imports vs. Exports, 1980–1989**

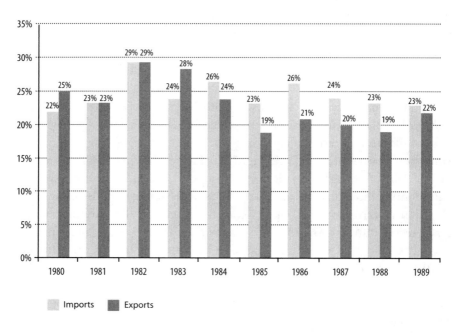

In 1985, when tin prices collapsed and the government implemented the NEP, even more workers adopted coca farming as a livelihood.

Bolivia's soaring unemployment rate climbed from 5.5 percent in 1978 to 20 percent by 1986.[100] By 1987, unemployment in Bolivia had reached 21.5 percent, although economic restructuring was a partial cause of the increase. During this period of unemployment, the coca boom drove the population of the Chapare from an estimated seventy thousand permanent residents to nearly four hundred thousand residents, most of whom worked for the coca trade.[101]

Estimates suggest that, by the mid-1980s, nearly 50 percent of all Bolivians depended on the coca industry for their existence.[102] Coca brought farmers much better prices than alternative crops in legal markets.[103] In the early 1980s a Bolivian farmer could earn from five thousand dollars to nine thousand dollars per hectare of coca, whereas citrus, the next most profitable crop, brought in roughly five hundred dollars per hectare.[104] After 1986 a glut in coca leaf production cut typical campesino earnings to approximately $2,500 per hectare of coca—still four times the return from oranges or avocados.[105] As high coca prices motivated farmers to shift away from legitimate crops, Bolivia was forced to import more food to overcome growing shortages in urban centers.[106]

As in Peru, the influx of narco-dollars in rural coca-growing areas created an inflationary cycle that made those areas permanently dependent on the coca industry. In the cities of La Paz, Santa Cruz, and Cochabamba, prices skyrocketed. Cochabamba, which traditionally had the lowest cost of living in Bolivia, became the country's most expensive city in 1984. The daily cost of living in Cochabamba rose from twenty dollars to two hundred dollars.[107] The market for luxury items also vastly expanded, although some studies argued that this demand came only from high-ranking participants in the drug economy.[108]

In general, campesinos used their profits to improve their families' economic situations. Their consumption fulfilled both basic needs and those created by the market. Some campesinos bought refrigerators even when they did not have electricity, because they were afraid that a change in the coca economy would make refrigerators unaffordable when electricity finally arrived.[109]

More than 40 percent of the Chapare's imports were illegal. A significant black market emerged that undermined legitimate businesses because imports could be offered at discount rates.[110] All transactions on the black market were handled in U.S. dollars earned through coca.[111] Consequently, the black market in coca dollars hurt local economies and made Bolivian towns even more dependent on narcotics production. "Legitimate business saw their sales revenues dwindle," and Bolivian "tax revenues" from the value added tax (VAT) "dried up."[112] Farmers and businessmen could not hire workers—even by tripling their wages—because the workers could still earn more money by working for the coca industry.[113] Bolivia's economic infrastructure deteriorated as local economies became wholly dependent on the fluctuating prices of the coca trade. Anibal Aguilar, Bolivia's subsecretary for Alternative Rural Development and Control of Coca for the Ministry of Campesino and Agricultural Affairs, explained that the drug industry subordinated the national economy because it broke the campesinos' system of diversified agricultural production.[114]

The narco-economy maintained a tight grip over the northern Andes during its darkest financial period. Pressure from the international finance community for debt payment exacerbated reliance on coca to generate money to supplant the shortage of foreign reserves. A contradiction in U.S. policy might have created this dependency: both the U.S. government and banks accepted debt payments and applauded liberalization policies facilitated by narco-dollars.[115]

Narco-dollars were the only means of survival for many suffering through the regional economic crisis. Reliance on narco-dollars transformed coca into a parasite that helped destroy and then replace the legal economy. In Colombia, Bolivia, and Peru, narco-dollars created localized inflation and led to a decline in agricultural activity in coca regions. The coca industry stimulated a rise in black markets that sold contraband to campesino coca growers. This reduced government revenue and made it impossible for legitimate businesses and importers to operate. Narco-dollars hampered each government's ability to manage inflation and ultimately destroyed the region's export sector as each nation tampered with its monetary policy in order to control inflation. Vanishing exports weakened each nation's ability to earn foreign revenue, creating a vicious circle of dependency based on narco-dollars. Like cocaine, narco-dollars were addictive. Breaking the addiction threatened to precipitate economic collapse in nations that had come to rely on it.

3

U.S. Narcotics Control Policies in the Northern Andes, 1980–1987

In February 1982, motivated by rapidly spreading drug use in the United States, President Reagan declared a war on drugs. His administration immediately stepped up efforts toward eradication, interdiction, crop substitution, and law enforcement, including extradition, in the northern Andes. Rather than address the issue of demand at home, Reagan's War on Drugs focused on enhanced military and law enforcement activities to shut off the narcotics supply, particularly from the source countries of Colombia, Peru, and Bolivia.

The War on Drugs began with the passage of the Defense Authorization Act of 1982, which, for the first time, permitted the U.S. Coast Guard and Navy to initiate counternarcotics operations. At the same time, the Reagan administration established the South Florida Task Force, under the direction of Vice President Bush, to intercept drug shipments from

South America.[1] This operation used CIA and DEA agents to gain intelligence about U.S.-bound drug shipments and then used the U.S. Coast Guard, Navy, and Customs Service to seize them.[2] In a speech to the International Association of Chiefs of Police, Reagan announced a foreign policy that would vigorously attack "organized criminal trafficking in drugs, international production, [and the export of] illicit narcotics" wherever those abuses occurred.[3]

However, Reagan's War on Drugs did not result in the victory over narcotics trafficking that the United States hoped to achieve. In Colombia, joint counternarcotics operations by which the U.S. and Colombian governments attempted to rein in the Medellín cartel were met with increasing violence and terror. Instead of being disrupted, the Medellín cartel gradually corrupted Colombia's socioeconomic and political life and manipulated the Movimiento 19 de Abril (M-19) to serve its own purposes. In Bolivia and Peru, campesino resistance to narcotics control burgeoned, while eradication and interdiction programs generated increased anti-government sentiment. Emerging political instability created a lack of security, which in turn allowed traffickers and guerrillas to flourish in coca-growing regions.

U.S.-Colombian Counternarcotics Efforts

By 1980, Colombia had become responsible for approximately 70 percent of the marijuana and more than 50 percent of the cocaine entering the United States. The U.S. State Department felt that the Colombian government's approach to narcotics was negligent. Certain sectors of society strongly opposed implementing any drug control policy at all: some of the Colombian intelligentsia and a few political figures saw no harm in producing or smuggling marijuana. Some opposed narcotics control because they profited personally from the drug trade. Others believed that legalizing marijuana would bring in tax revenue for the government.[4] In 1981 the former president of Colombia, Alfonso Lopez Michelsen (1974–1978), directly blamed the United States for the billion-dollar drug trade, accusing the United States of attempting to "corrupt" Colombia. In particular, Michelsen blamed American youth for the rise in U.S. marijuana consumption.[5] Colombian officials and ordinary citizens believed that the U.S. drug problem should be dealt with first at home, not abroad.[6]

From the U.S. point of view, corruption as well as disinterest made nar-cotics control in Colombia a daunting task. Low police pay—around $150 a month—encouraged the pursuit of personal financial benefit when mil-lions of pesos worth of drugs were involved. According to one U.S. State Department report, the drug Mafia had bought off some highly placed government politicians, while other traffickers were able to "escape prose-cution by bribing judicial officials."[7] Although quite a few Colombians felt that narcotics abuse was a U.S. domestic problem, many realized that nar-cotics-related corruption had "penetrated all levels of society."[8] Colombian officials recognized the narcotics industry's deleterious impact on govern-ment institutions but lacked money and personnel to combat the problem, especially since certain regions fell outside government control.

The 1978 election of Julio Cesar Turbay as president (1978–1982) set a new tone in the drug war. In his inaugural speech, Turbay pledged that he was prepared to "wage an implacable crusade" against the drug industry.[9] He immediately signed Decree 2144, which regulated air traffic into Colombia, and authorized a military operation to gain control over Colombia's Guajira Peninsula on the north coast, where the majority of Colombia's marijuana was grown. Both actions demonstrated Turbay's determination to fight narcotics.

In response, the United States dramatically increased narcotics control assistance to Colombia. In particular, the U.S. government offered to pay sixteen million dollars to supply and maintain helicopters, patrol vessels, fixed radar equipment, transportation vehicles, and fuel used exclusively to interdict drug traffic.[10] Complementing aid to the Colombian government, the United States employed air and naval forces to enhance the interdic-tion campaign. Hawkeye radar planes, similar to Airborne Warning and Control System (AWACS) planes, flew over the Caribbean to detect low-flying aircraft carrying narcotics.[11] With the support of the Colombian government, the United States also stationed navy and coast guard ships along two major shipping lanes off Colombia's coast to stop and board ships suspected of carrying narcotics.[12] Along with the governments of the Bahamas and the United Kingdom, the United States implemented Operation Bahamas Turks and Caicos (OPBAT) in 1982. This operation was designed to "interdict and disrupt" Colombian air and sea smuggling routes that passed through the Caribbean into the southeastern United States.[13]

The United States also dedicated funds to training personnel, especially the U.S.-financed Special Anti-Narcotics Units (SANUs) of the Colombian

Chart 3.1 | **Seizures and Production of Colombian Cocaine, 1981–1983 (in Metric Tons)**

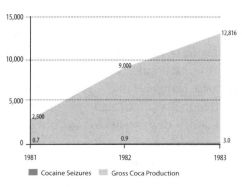

National Police (CNP).[14] These units were expected to set up checkpoints, sweep through the jungle with jeeps, and use American UH-1 helicopters ("Hueys") to knock out HCL production centers that were "processing 14–19 metric tons" of cocaine HCL annually in 1981.[15] The company-sized SANUs assumed primary responsibility for narcotics control by replacing the military in the Guajira region. Colombian armed forces were expected to provide tactical support only.[16] SANU deployments in Guajira were a response to corruption within the Colombian army.[17] The Turbay government wanted the military out of Guajira. Their continued involvement in the War on Drugs threatened to corrupt the armed forces permanently, and the government needed an effective military to fight the guerrillas elsewhere.[18]

With the creation of the SANUs, drug seizures increased each year. In 1981 the government had seized 0.7 metric tons of cocaine; by 1983 it had captured three metric tons (see chart 3.1). Marijuana seizures rose slightly from 3,310 to 3,934 metric tons between 1981 and 1983 (see chart 3.2).[19]

Chart 3.2 | **Seizures vs. Production of Colombian Marijuana, 1981–1983 (in Metric Tons)**

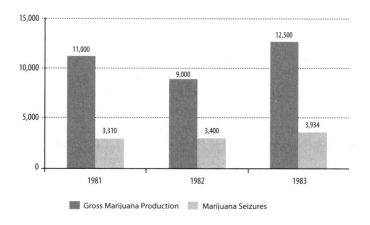

However, even with this improvement in interdiction statistics, coca and marijuana production continued to grow. Coca cultivation rose from 2,500 metric tons in 1981 to 12,816 metric tons in 1983. Marijuana cultivation remained fairly steady, growing from roughly 11,000 to 12,500 metric tons between 1980 and 1983. Although the SANU's efforts were impressive by Colombian standards, the statistics clearly show that drug cultivation outpaced the Colombian government's ability to confiscate drug output.

Since Colombia's borders were porous and the government could not control large portions of the countryside, U.S. officials soon realized that interdiction alone was not sufficient to control coca and cocaine production. The INM became convinced, based on their Mexican experience, that "pressure should also be put on the drug at its source, through eradication."[20]

The United States had been blocked from funding foreign herbicidal eradication programs since the passage of the Percy Amendment in 1978. In 1981, Congress repealed the amendment. Colombia, however, remained reluctant to use herbicides because they threatened to damage the environment and destroy legitimate campesino crops.[21] But under several years of continuous pressure from the State Department and the White House, Colombia agreed to use glyphosate, an herbicide, to destroy marijuana crops in 1984.[22] In that year, over 85 percent of a projected ten million dollars for Colombia from the INM went to herbicidal crop destruction, while 6 percent of the budget was devoted to narcotics interdiction.[23] In 1985, after extensive testing, the Colombian government also allowed the use of Garlon 4.[24] U.S. State Department officials touted the herbicide program and claimed that they could "knock out" coca and marijuana cultivation within "three years."[25] They declared that if they had more U.S. helicopters, they could eliminate the entire marijuana crop by mid-1985. Colombian expectations were more modest. Officials there believed that additional helicopters might bring marijuana cultivation *under control* in three years.[26]

To obtain better results, the CNP unified all eradication and interdiction activity under the Directorate of Anti-Narcotics (DAN).[27] Marijuana production declined rapidly: The eradication program destroyed 1,561 metric tons in 1984 and 8,800 metric tons in 1987. At the same time, the interdiction program netted from one thousand to three thousand metric tons of marijuana.[28] Between 1984 and 1987, while the combined eradication and interdiction program was in progress, the INM estimated that gross marijuana production remained at constant levels, ranging from thirteen thousand to fourteen thousand metric tons.[29] As the graph shows, results from the combined eradication and interdiction operations nearly equaled the levels of marijuana production in Colombia (see chart 3.3).[30] The INM calculated that these efforts had reduced the amount of marijuana available to U.S. consumers from 11,000 metric tons in 1981 to between 1,100 and 2,200 metric tons in 1986.[31] The program's success cut marijuana production in Colombia so extensively that Mexico began to replace Colombia as the major exporter of marijuana to the United States in 1987.[32]

Chart 3.3 | **Combined Eradication and Interdiction Program vs. Gross Potential Production of Colombian Marijuana, 1984–1987 (in Metric Tons)**

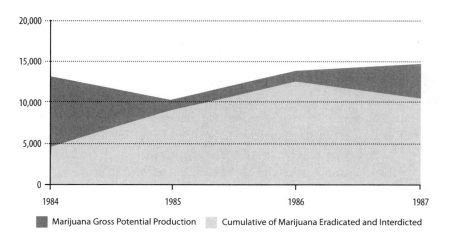

Initially, the coca reduction program was successful as well, but its success was fleeting. The seizure of 21.3 metric tons of cocaine in 1984 was due in large part to the raid on the Tranquilandia site in the Cauqetá department of southeastern Colombia, where authorities captured 8,500 kilograms of HCL and 1,500 kilograms of cocaine base.[33] The achievements of 1984 were not matched in following years. Interdiction declined from 9.46 metric tons in 1985 to 4.32 metric tons in 1986, with only a slight increase in 1987 to 5.94 metric tons of cocaine.[34] Since the Colombian government forbade spraying herbicides on coca, the SANUs attempted to eradicate coca manually. However, local resistance and the lack of resources for destroying coca in remote, guerrilla-occupied areas weakened the Colombian government's commitment to manual eradication.[35] Coca eradication slowly declined from 1,942 metric tons in 1984 to 370 metric tons in 1987 (see chart 3.4).[36] As the demand for coca increased, gross coca production expanded from 12,400 metric tons in 1985 to 20,000 metric tons in 1987.[37] Meanwhile, eradication and interdiction programs in Peru and Bolivia led the Medellín cartel to increase its reliance on Colombian coca growers, augmenting the spike in production.[38]

Chart 3.4 | **Colombian Coca Leaf Production vs. Cumulative of Cocaine Seizures and Coca Leaf Eradication, 1984–1987 (in Metric Tons)**

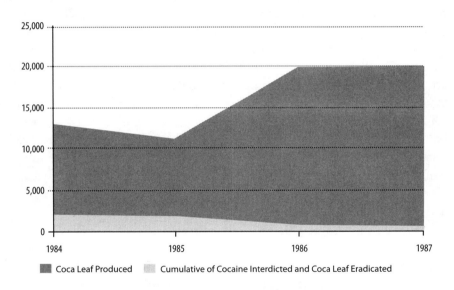

Coca Leaf Produced   Cumulative of Cocaine Interdicted and Coca Leaf Eradicated

Although the effects of the eradication and interdiction programs appeared to be minimal, the combined programs upset Colombia's campesino population. As in Bolivia and Peru, the contradiction in U.S. policy placed the Colombian government in a bind with the populace. The United States did nothing to cut down on domestic consumption but required Colombia to destroy crops where the "Indians made money for the first time in a number of years."[39] Yet, because of previous failures, neither the Colombian nor the U.S. government was prepared to develop an adequate crop substitution program.[40] Further complicating the situation, the SANUs' manual crop elimination efforts became increasingly dangerous. The program to seek and destroy cocaine laboratories like Tranquilandia pitted the SANUs against well-armed traffickers.[41] The presence of guerrillas near the Tranquilandia site gave rise to allegations that they had developed some type of coexistence policy with the traffickers. This revelation made narcotics interdiction and eradication even harder for the SANUs since they were not trained in guerrilla warfare.[42] By 1987, because of coca and cocaine production and control, Colombia had begun a descent toward anarchy.

The Medellín Cartel and Extradition

Extradition was the single most inflammatory issue in U.S.-Colombian counternarcotics policy through the 1980s. In 1979 the U.S. and Colombian governments agreed to "modernize" their existing extradition treaty. The new agreement permitted extradition for "offenses committed outside the territory of the requesting state."[43] However, since Colombian law did not allow extradition of Colombian nationals, the new treaty stated that extradition would not be based solely on nationality. The government could extradite an individual if the requesting state had already convicted him or her, or if the offense for which extradition was sought involved acts taking place in other states and was intended to consummate in the requesting state. Behind all the legalese was the understanding that the United States could request the extradition of a Colombian national if it had credible evidence that the suspect had violated U.S. law by smuggling narcotics into the United States.

The extradition treaty took effect in 1982. U.S. pressure to put the treaty into practice sparked massive resistance by narcotics traffickers. The traffickers initially attempted to provoke an abrogation of the treaty by charging that the extradition of Colombian nationals violated the country's judicial sovereignty.[44] In order to lobby against extradition, Pablo Escobar, one of the Medellín cartel's leaders, went so far as to put himself up for election to the Colombian Congress, where he won an alternate seat as a Liberal Party member in 1982.[45] Carlos Lehder, another Medellín kingpin, who had initially helped form the cartel by putting together shipments of cocaine at his private airstrip on Norman's Cay in the Bahamas between 1978 and 1981, was number one on the United States' list of extraditable subjects. When U.S. and Bahamian authorities forced Lehder to return to Colombia in 1981, he formed his own political party, the Movimiento Cívico Latino Nacional (MCLN), to fight against narcotics control and extradition. To further intimidate the Colombian government, the cartel launched a wave of assassinations against Colombian judges, usually using *sicarios* (assassins), also nicknamed *asesinos de moto* because they murdered their victims from motorcycles, which allowed for quick getaways in heavy traffic.[46] Nevertheless, to increase pressure on the Colombian government to honor the treaty, the Reagan administration appointed Lewis Tambs ambassador to Colombia in 1983. Selecting Tambs, known for his hard-line Republican views, sent a message to the Colombian government to get tough on drugs and terrorism.[47]

President Belisario Betancur (1982–1986), who replaced Julio Cesar Turbay in 1982, was reluctant to move against the cartel by signing the U.S. extradition requests already approved by the Colombian Supreme Court.[48] Still, the court forged on and granted the extradition request for Carlos Lehder, forcing him to go underground in September 1983. To pressure the government to halt further extradition proceedings, the Medellín organization gunned down judges, police inspectors, and other officials at the rate of about one per week.[49] However, immediately following the Tranquilandia bust, the April 1984 assassination of Minister of Justice Rodrigo Lara Bonilla, one of the strongest supporters of extradition and antidrug policies, forced Betancur to declare a state of siege.[50] While he did not directly accuse the traffickers of the killing, he implied that he held them responsible and declared that he was going to launch a war without quarter against drug traffickers.[51]

In response, the Medellín cartel took even more radical measures to avoid extradition. Initially, the cartel denied its involvement in Bonilla's assassination. They attempted to negotiate a secret pact with the Colombian government in Panama City, approaching former president Alfonso Michelsen and offering to dismantle their operations and pay off Colombia's foreign debt if the government dropped extradition.[52] Michelsen reported this offer to Betancur, who sent his attorney, Carlos Jiminez Gomez, to negotiate. However, when the Colombian public found out about the potential deal, an outcry arose over the idea that the government would negotiate with a crime syndicate. Mounting political pressure inside Colombia, as well as from the United States, forced Betancur to declare that "under no circumstances" would he accept the offer.

When Betancur moved to extradite five low-level Colombian narcotics traffickers, the Medellín organization intensified its violence. Sicarios killed many important judges and politicians, including Ivan Dario Morales, a Liberal Party leader, and José Gonzalez Narvaez, a Conservative Party leader, in August 1984; Justice Alvaro Medina Ochoa of the criminal court in April 1985, and Judge Tulio Manuel Castro-Gil, the judge who had indicted Escobar for the murder of Lara Bonilla, in July 1985.[53]

However, the cartel did not restrict itself to Colombian targets. On November 27, 1984, a car bomb exploded outside the U.S. embassy in Bogotá. Unidentified narcotics traffickers threatened to kill five Americans for every Colombian extradited to the United States.[54] As more threats were made against the U.S. presence in Colombia, traffickers succeeded in turning drug industry issues into anti-U.S. nationalism.

Carlos Lehder, known for his pro-Nazi, anti-American sentiments, went on Colombian national television in 1985 to declare that "cocaine and marijuana" had become "an arm of the struggle against American imperialism." He further proclaimed, "[W]e have the same responsibility in this—he who takes up the rifle, he who plants coca, he who goes to the public plaza and denounces imperialism." Lehder claimed that "Lara Bonilla, Tambs and Betancur united to conspire against the interests of this country," and that was why "a political, economic and social battle against extradition" was necessary.[55]

Although their threats remained real, both Lehder and Escobar stayed in hiding. For many Colombians, they had become modern Robin Hoods. Through his social program, Medellín without Slums, Escobar provided a thousand free houses to low-income families in an area he appropriately named Barrio Pablo Escobar. Nationalist feelings ran deep, and the extradition treaty generated resentment among many Colombians who had nothing to do with the drug trade.[56] All these factors made the capture of Lehder and Escobar, as well as other members of the Medellín cartel, a major challenge.

The State Department in Bogotá declared that it would "not be scared off," but Ambassador Tambs took what the State Department described as a "vacation" from his position in Colombia following threats against his life after the first extradition of four Colombian nationals to the United States in 1984. At the time, the United States was seeking the extradition of at least eighty more drug suspects.[57]

Convicting drug traffickers was even more dangerous for Colombian judges. Many were given the choice of *plata o plomo* (silver or lead): a judge could either take a bribe (plata) from the cartel or receive a bullet (plomo) from one of the cartel's sicarios or asesinos de moto.[58]

The case of Jorge Ochoa, a high-ranking member of the Medellín organization along with Lehder and Escobar, illustrates the rule of plata o plomo. In November 1984, Ochoa was arrested in Spain while trying to buy property. Both Colombia and the United States had filed extradition charges with the Spanish authorities, but Spain vacillated when the cartel issued threats against their ambassador to Colombia.[59] Eventually, Spain decided to release Ochoa to Colombian officials. Colombia's extradition charges against Ochoa were not for drug smuggling but for illegally importing fighting bulls.

Over U.S. protests, Colombia released Ochoa on bail, and he then went into hiding. The chief of staff for the House Committee on Narcotics Abuse and Control summed up the reason for Ochoa's release: Colombian judges withheld sentencing because sentencing was their "death warrant."[60] The Medellín cartel's enormous wealth bought cooperation and political influence and paid for the deaths of officers, judges, and newspeople.[61] However, the Betancur government remained determined to fight. Underlying Betancur's commitment was the realization that high-ranking members of the Medellín cartel, and drug traffickers in general, appeared to be more powerful than the Colombian government. Yielding to the cartel over extradition threatened nothing less than Colombia's ability to remain a legitimate democracy.

While the Colombian government and the Medellín cartel struggled over the extradition issue, the Betancur administration initiated a peace process with Colombia's guerrillas. U.S. Ambassador Tambs pushed the idea that the drug traffickers and the guerrillas were working together to turn Colombia into a failed narco-state, but Betancur did not accept this assertion. In fact, he had been elected on the promise of creating a permanent peace with Colombia's major guerrilla organization, the FARC, and he did not believe the FARC was involved in narcotics trafficking.[62] Therefore, coinciding with the assassination of Lara Bonilla in April 1984, President Betancur announced a cease-fire with the FARC, known as the cease-fire of La Uribe.[63] In a televised address, Betancur announced that a "moral peace" between the government and the FARC would allow the government to "dedicate all its energy and many resources [to] recuperate the national dignity taken away by the drug traffic."[64] Betancur went on to assert that drug traffic posed a "more lethal menace" than the guerrillas.

The government invited other guerrilla organizations into the peace process, including the EPL and the M-19, who signed a peace accord in May 1984. The ELN declined to participate.[65] Critics of the peace process complained that the burden of its maintenance rested on the government, whereas the FARC and the other organizations only had to pay lip service by condemning "kidnapping, extortion, and terrorism."[66] Military and civilian critics were concerned that the political resolution might "grant the guerrillas illicit gains."[67] Notably, they feared that the cease-fire would allow guerrillas to consolidate control over coca-growing areas where "the terms of the cease-fire" limited military options.[68]

The cease-fire, however, was soon shattered. On November 6, 1985, the M-19 broke into the Colombian Supreme Court in the Palace of Justice building and killed eleven sitting judges who had the authority to implement Colombia's extradition treaty.[69] The assault by the Colombian military to dislodge the M-19 guerrillas led to nearly one hundred deaths and the partial destruction of the building.[70]

The burning of all files related to pending extradition cases appeared to link the incident to the War on Drugs. The M-19's weapons, supposedly obtained from the Sandinista government, also pointed to a drug industry connection; the Reagan administration had accused the Sandinista government of being a narco-communist state and having ties to the Medellín cartel.[71] The M-19 denied any drug connection.[72] However, this denial seemed insincere, particularly after Carlos Lehder announced on public television that he was in contact with the M-19.[73]

This apparently cordial relationship between the M-19 and the Medellín was quite new. The Movimiento 19 de Abril (M-19) was formed in 1972 in response to the 1970 elections, when Alianza Nacional Popular (ANAPO) candidate Gustavo Rojas Pinilla was defeated by National Front candidate Misael Pastrana (1970–1974) in an election clouded by accusations of vote rigging.[74] In 1980 the M-19 dramatically appeared on the scene when they stormed the Dominican Republic's embassy in Bogotá and took U.S. Ambassador Diego Asencio and thirty more diplomats hostage, including the papal delegate and sixteen other ambassadors.[75] The guerrillas held the hostages for two days and then released them after the M-19 was promised safe passage to Cuba.

Following this event, the M-19 boldly kidnapped a series of wealthy individuals.[76] Most notably, in 1981 they kidnapped the daughter of Medellín cartel kingpin Fabio Ochoa, Jorge Ochoa's brother.[77] In response, Ochoa and the other members of the Medellín cartel pooled seven million dollars and formed Muerte a Secuestradores (MAS), or "Death to Kidnappers."[78] In December 1981, a small plane circled around Cali's soccer stadium dropping leaflets announcing formation of the MAS.[79] The MAS began a brutal war against the M-19 in which it publicly displayed its victims hanging from trees or disemboweled with signs around their necks to discourage the public from supporting the M-19.[80] The M-19's power was no match for the Medellín cartel, and consequently, it was forced to surrender.[81] During peace negotiations between the MAS and the M-19 in Panama, they formed an alliance that made the M-19 an enforcement mechanism for the cartel.

Although the alliance between the Medellín and the M-19 was not public, M-19 activities indicated a deep interest in the drug war raging in Colombia. Signs reading "Down with the Yankees" and "Out with imperialism," emblazoned with the M-19 slogan, were seen on the walls of Bogotá's slums.[82]

By 1984, the M-19 was threatening to fire on helicopters that sprayed marijuana fields in Colombia's Sierra Nevada. They used the belief that herbicides were potentially harmful to the ecology and local inhabitants to rationalize their threats. Colombia's DAN thought that the warnings came from the narco-traffickers, not the M-19, and the U.S. embassy in Bogotá could not "discount the possibility that the narco-traffickers" were the "motivating force behind the threat." [83]

In late 1984, following Betancur's declaration of war on narco-traffickers, the M-19 called on the drug smugglers to carry out their threats against U.S. government employees in Colombia.[84] Significantly, the M-19 enunciated a platform that tied narcotics to nationalism when their leader, Iván Marino Ospina, stated, "[L]et those threats be carried out against the representatives of rapacious imperialism, which live alongside the misery of the exploited people." Ospina maintained that "traffic in drugs . . . acquired special characteristics" because many "Colombians lived off and benefited from that activity," and he encouraged Colombians to use the drug money to "build up their native land."

Following Ospina's comments, criticism of Betancur mounted because of his attempt to maintain peace with the guerrillas. When Marino Ospina was assassinated in September 1985, it was only a matter of time before the M-19 took revenge against the government by breaking the peace accord and attacking the Palace of Justice.[85]

When Virgilio Barco (1986–1990) became president, the power of the Medellín cartel seemed to be reaching its height in the fight against extradition. The cartel murdered Jaíme Ramiréz, head of Colombia's SANUs, in November 1986. In December, the Colombian Supreme Court caved in and nullified its extradition treaty with the United States based on a technicality: President Turbay had not personally signed the treaty.[86] This was viewed as a great victory for the Medellín cartel.[87] U.S. officials were stunned that Colombia's Supreme Court, which had witnessed the deaths of twelve of its twenty-four members in 1986, had capitulated to the cartel.[88]

President Barco, acting as if the issue were an administrative error, re-signed the law himself. The Colombian police captured Carlos Lehder in his Medellín ranch house, and he was whisked off to the United States to stand trial in February 1987.[89] Meanwhile, the Supreme Court continued to debate Barco's decision to affirm the treaty.

In 1987 the Supreme Court split evenly on extradition, their indeci-sion apparently due to cartel intimidation. On December 17, 1986, two days after the court ruled extradition unconstitutional, the cartel assas-sinated Guillermo Cano, a prominent newsman and editor of the news-paper *El Espectador*, which had printed exposés about the cartel. Cano's death stunned the country and caused Barco to declare a national state of siege. The Supreme Court continued to refuse to rule on pending extradi-tion cases. The court also ruled Barco's state of siege unconstitutional in March 1987.[90]

The Barco administration then forced the issue with the Supreme Court. Consequently, in May 1987, the court declared that it needed to hire a temporary justice to break the deadlock. When the outside jurist cast his deciding vote, the treaty was ruled unconstitutional again, thus freezing further extraditions.[91] This decision was a setback for the U.S.-Colombian counternarcotics program, and the State Department complained that the law was in limbo. Barco declared that the government could not enforce extradition until the Colombian Congress approved the treaty; however, it was unclear whether the Congress would pass the law, since the Medellín cartel wielded great political influence through its political contributions and threats.[92]

When Jorge Ochoa was stopped in a routine police check and arrested for jumping bail on the previous charge—illegally importing bulls into Colombia—the Ministry of Justice blocked U.S. efforts to extradite him, because the Supreme Court had ruled the 1979 treaty unconstitutional.[93] The worst that Ochoa faced was a twenty-two-month prison sentence in Colombia; in the end, they only held him for a month.

The suspension of extradition and the failure to extradite Ochoa were major blows to U.S. strategy. U.S. efforts to renew extradition eventually collapsed in 1991, when the Colombian Congress made extradition of its nationals illegal.[94] However, the United States did not give up. It contin-ued to pressure the Colombian government, and as a result, extradition again became a major source of instability in the mid-1990s.

While the battle over extradition was running its course, the cease-fire between the government and the FARC broke down when the Medellín cartel and the military informally united to launch a dirty war against the FARC's entry into the political system with the Union Patriotica (UP). President Betancur believed that the civil war in Colombia was the result of real social problems that needed to be addressed, but the legislature opposed his reforms. Although the UP won political representation in the 1986 election, including thirteen congressional seats, a seat in the Senate, and more than 250 departmental and municipal positions, the newly elected President Barco opposed recognition of the UP.[95] Barco wanted to diminish the guerrillas' social base by promoting government-backed social programs. He therefore did not want the guerrillas to enlarge their source of support at the expense of the government through the UP.[96]

Adding to the collapse of the cease-fire was the fact that some members of the Medellín cartel had become rural property owners linked to the conservative, landholding elite. During the 1970s and early 1980s, Colombia's rural landowners extended their holdings at the expense of campesinos who were forced to sell their land due to debts incurred, ironically, from loans associated with government rural development programs.[97] The displaced campesinos migrated to regions such as Putumayo where there was little governmental authority. In these marginal regions, the FARC provided law and order and defended the campesinos' interests, including participation in the narco-economy. Moreover, the FARC charged the Medellín cartel "revolutionary taxes" in exchange for military protection.[98] As the cartel's landholdings expanded, the FARC's presence and control over Medellín activities in rural areas seriously heightened tensions between the two factions and strengthened the cartel's ties with the landholding elite in their stance against Colombia's guerrilla organizations.

The peace treaty between the FARC and the government rapidly disintegrated as the Medellín cartel and conservative landholders launched their own war against the FARC and the UP. While the Medellín cartel was on the run from the Colombian government, the FARC took over its land. Moreover, the FARC used the taxes it charged the cartel to finance UP activities, including its land reform program in the Colombian Congress, which placed the Medellín cartel's real estate at risk.[99]

Consequently, the Medellín cartel used the MAS and other paramilitary groups to attack the FARC.[100] Many paramilitary organizations such as the MAS were composed of Colombian military officers who defended the interests of large landowners against the interests of landless rural campesinos.[101] At the same time, some paramilitary organizations were formed from campesino *minifundista* (small landowner) self-defense groups that opposed the FARC's decision in the early 1980s to place revolutionary taxes on their land.[102] The FARC warned that paramilitary attacks could disrupt the peace and that, if they were not restrained, greater violence could spread throughout Colombia.[103]

When President Barco unofficially ended the cease-fire by shutting down the peace commission and moving the Colombian military into guerrilla-controlled areas, the MAS and other paramilitary organizations, such as the Magdalena Medio group, teamed up with the military to launch a "dirty war" against the FARC and the UP.[104] By 1987, assassins had murdered at least 450 UP members, including the party's leader, Jaime Pardo Leal, whose assassination in October 1987 was allegedly ordered by the Medellín cartel.[105] The FARC maintained the cease-fire and called for new talks to find a "political solution" to Colombia's internal conflicts, but the Barco administration rejected the offer and stated that it would "only negotiate terms for the guerrillas' demobilization."[106] By the end of 1987, Colombia appeared to be heading toward an all-out civil war.

U.S.-Peruvian Counternarcotics Efforts

Peru's change from a military to a civilian government in 1979 offered the United States an opportunity to reformulate its interdiction, eradication, and crop substitution agenda with the country.[107] In 1981 the United States initiated a program that delivered seventy million dollars in loans and grants from USAID and the INM. It was a five-year rural development plan for the Upper Huallaga Valley, where illegal coca production began to flourish in the early 1980s.[108] According to Larry Thompson, head of the U.S. Narcotics Assistance Unit in Peru, the idea was to substitute economically viable alternative crops for coca. The plan also proposed to reestablish the U.S. government's agricultural services in the UHV, which had been dismantled during military rule in the 1970s.[109] In general, the program was designed to demonstrate concern over legitimate agricultural employment for farmers, while aggressively running eradication and enforcement efforts against coca production.

Peru was expected to provide the forces to fulfill the counternarcotics agenda. The eradication component, directed by both the INM and the Peruvian government, was the Project for Coca Leaf Control and

Reduction in the Alto Huallaga (CORAH), composed of roughly four hundred men. The Peruvian rural police force, known as Unidad Móvil de Patrullaje Rural (UMOPAR), was in charge of the interdiction program as well as the enforcement of narcotics control laws. The Special Project for the Upper Huallaga, also known as Proyecto Especial Alto Huallaga (PEAH), ran the USAID crop substitution program. The PEAH's assignment was to generate alternate support systems for UHV farmers who stopped growing coca.[110] While the CORAH and UMOPAR programs were aimed at shutting down traffickers and eliminating coca leaf cultivation, the USAID-PEAH mission was to help the Peruvian government expand the UHV's legitimate agricultural base.[111]

Defining these goals was one thing, however, and implementing them was quite another. Although the programs went into effect in 1981, they did not make any gains until 1983, when the Peruvian government began to eradicate coca manually.[112] CORAH used various manual eradication techniques, such as cutting, burning, or digging out the roots of coca bushes. CORAH's efforts were coercive, and the workers who carried them out had to be protected by the UMOPAR police. The program generated "resistance and counteraction by the affected population."[113]

CORAH sent the campesinos to PEAH to receive technical assistance, credit, and services. However, the PEAH program could not help the campesinos who grew coca, because their cultivation areas were located on slopes where no crop substitution program could work. Since the slopes in the UHV were only suitable for coca cultivation, PEAH concentrated on supporting large farmers on the valley floor where rice and cacao could grow.[114] Meanwhile, campesinos in the UHV utilized their crop substitution loans to plant more coca. Even after they signed affidavits promising not to use their financial assistance to plant coca, the campesinos continued to do so because they could not meet their financial obligations to the lending institutions with the profits from legitimate crops.[115]

The project made coca growers who did not own land ever more dependent on coca. The banks denied them credit to purchase land or begin alternative crop programs because Peruvian law prevented the distribution of "land titles . . . to farmers who grew coca" illegally.[116] Adding salt to the wound, the deteriorating economic situation in Peru forced the government to implement austerity measures for development ventures, including the UHV project.[117] The campesinos and others indirectly involved in the coca trade in the UHV found no difference between the CORAH, PEAH, and UMOPAR teams.

As early as 1983, the Upper Huallaga District police began to encounter widespread violence and terrorism from coca farmers and drug traffickers.[118] Many coca farmers acted on their own initiative, attacking CORAH and PEAH workers without direct cause and participating in public disturbances, often blocking highways with rocks. Drug traffickers on the other hand perpetrated the majority of violence against members of police forces such as the UMOPAR. Occasionally, they precipitated confrontations with CORAH by inciting local campesinos.[119]

Two types of trafficking organizations now emerged in the UHV: Peruvian groups and those run by representatives of the major Colombian cartels. Both were well armed and possessed their own private armies.[120] They often clashed, fighting to "settle scores" and gain control over coca and basic cocaine paste trading.[121] By the mid-1980s, the Medellín cartel extended overt control over UHV cocaine processing and refinement to guarantee both the quality of coca products from Peru and a constant reliable source of coca to meet international demand.[122] The UHV counternarcotics program was in severe jeopardy.

The Sendero Luminoso (Shining Path) soon became a third component in UHV power struggles, and security plummeted further.[123] The Sendero took its name from José Carlos Mariátegui's revolutionary pronouncement that "Marxism-Leninism will open the shining path to revolution."[124] It picked up strength in the mid-1970s as a result of the military government's land reform program, which left the campesinos indebted to the government's land reform agency. Campesinos were forced into debt so that the government could generate enough revenue to pay off landowners whose land had been expropriated and redistributed to the campesinos. This debt became the justification for state intervention in pricing and marketing agricultural products. Thus, land reform did not release the campesinos from debt-based peonage; it simply transferred their debt to the government.[125]

The lack of true reform led the Sendero to believe that the only way to achieve change was to mobilize the campesinos.[126] Under the leadership of Abimael Guzmán, a professor of agronomics at the University of Ayacucho, the Sendero adopted a radical ideology to alleviate the burdens of the campesinos, many of whom were Quechua Indians. Significantly, the Sendero adopted what was known as the Pensamiento Gonzalo, which incorporated Maoist ideology into a philosophy that professed a desire to return Peru to a traditional, pre-Spanish, Incan way of life.[127] The Sendero presented itself as the champion of the campesinos, arriving in the UHV from the state of Ayacucho to end generations of suffering and exploitation for the Quechua Indians. The mix of anti-eradication programs and the Sendero's radical ideology became a dangerous cocktail that guaranteed violence in the UHV.

The Sendero moved into the UHV in 1983 and forged a natural alliance with the majority of coca-growing campesinos living in the department of San Martín, where the UHV was located (see map 2).[128] The Peruvian army had launched what could be described as a "dirty war" against the Sendero, causing it to lose territory in the mountainous regions around the department of Ayacucho. Under extreme pressure from the Peruvian army, the Sendero moved north into the Upper Huallaga Valley.[129] Lack of order in rural sectors in and around the UHV forced the campesinos to submit to the Sendero, which established its tight rule over the region.[130]

When the Sendero moved into the UHV, some speculated that it had "pre-targeted the UHV in anticipation of the popular support and potential revenue to be gained from the coca industry." [131] DEA and CIA analysts believed that the Sendero recognized a ready source of campesino support, which it exploited by positioning itself as a group of "advocates for the rights of campesino coca growers." This included providing armed protection against government eradication efforts. Moreover, many of the coca growers in the UHV were recent immigrants of Quechua origin with whom the Sendero had connected due to its political philosophy.[132] According to David L. Westrate, the DEA's deputy assistant administrator, the Sendero now "presented the anti-coca issue as an example" of the central government's attempt to "take away the livelihood of the Indian population." Coca eradication programs and the PEAH's failure to provide sufficient credit to the campesinos created a natural partnership between the Sendero and many of the coca growers within the UHV and other parts of the department of San Martín. The inability to break this coalition proved to be the Peruvian government's Achilles' heel for the remainder of the decade.

The Sendero did not seek an alliance with traffickers—at least not to start with. Though the Sendero openly induced the coca growers to defend their crops, it was more interested in carving out a "liberated zone" in the UHV through attacks on police outposts and targeted political assassinations of mayors and local governors. Traffickers tried to keep a low profile to avoid notice by law enforcement, and the Sendero's anti-government activities drew too much attention for their liking.[133] Also, the Sendero had developed a strict code of conduct and was unwilling to make tactical arrangements with traffickers. However, as the Sendero solidified its control in the UHV, evidence began to appear that it had become a primary trafficking organization in the region and was using the narcotics industry to fuel its insurgency.[134]

The combination of peasant opposition, drug-related violence, and Sendero Luminoso terrorism brought all narcotics control programs in the UHV to a near standstill in 1984, and the Upper Huallaga Valley became a no-man's-land. That year, two UHV project encampments were attacked, and fifty campesinos with close links to PEAH were murdered.[135] Ten out of thirteen area police stations were dynamited.[136] Nineteen defenseless CORAH workers were ambushed and killed.[137] The Peruvian government declared a temporary state of emergency beginning in July. Both the U.S. and Peruvian governments suspended all coca control programs in the region, and the Peruvian government sent in the military to defeat the Sendero.[138]

Although military officials were aware that this new effort could be used to "vilify the armed forces," they were determined to regain control of the UHV; to do otherwise meant running up the white flag of surrender to the Sendero.[139] Peru's military argued that "the forces of order" could not "engage both the terrorists and the drug traffickers simultaneously." Only when the "terrorist problem was brought under control, could the trafficking problem be brought under control."[140] Following this strategy, the army, under the command of General Julio Carbajal D'Angelo, received important intelligence from campesinos in the UHV that helped the army to score many successes against the Sendero during the first six months of emergency.

The military's focus on the Sendero inevitably resulted in increased coca production and eradication levels below U.S. expectations.[141] The narco-traffickers took advantage of the situation by launching a terror campaign to bring local cocaleros under their control.[142] The Peruvian army confined UMOPAR narcotics police to their barracks during the emergency, but CORAH teams continued to go out on eradication missions.[143] Since UMOPAR no longer accompanied and protected them, their activities became extremely dangerous.[144] To complicate matters, the PEAH stayed in their headquarters in Tingo Maria. This made the CORAH teams extremely unpopular in the UHV, because they could not provide relief to campesinos who had just had their crops destroyed.

Following his election in 1985, Alan García (1985–1990) lifted the state of emergency, withdrew the army from the UHV, and called for a reinvigoration of narcotics control activities in the region.[145] García reversed the military's strategy in order to continue receiving foreign aid from the United States and to eliminate the perception that Peru was becoming a failed narco-state.[146] Even though the period between 1984 and 1985 was disastrous for coca control, García's policy change made 1985 an extremely successful year in the eyes of the U.S. government. The United States applauded CORAH's ability to "eradicate 5,000 hectares of coca." Although CORAH's achievement and García's change in policy were signs of success, the State Department also noted that "this was less than half of the 12,000 new hectares brought under cultivation" in 1986, "and a mere 2% of the total area under cultivation" (see chart 3.5).[147]

Chart 3.5 | **Peruvian Coca Eradication vs. Gross Coca Cultivation, 1982–1987 (in Hectares)**

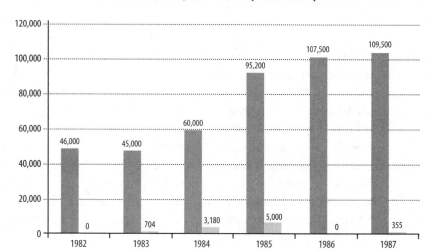

Approximately ten thousand hectares of Peruvian coca had been destroyed manually between 1983 and 1986. However, new fields were planted much faster than crops were eradicated. A USAID report stated that eradication had not been able to "raise the cost of illegal coca production or stop illegal cultivation from expanding into additional fields." The report went on to say that coca producers could earn profits from "3 to 10 times that achieved by legitimate farmers."[148] CORAH paid the campesinos three hundred dollars to eradicate one hectare of coca, whereas the traffickers paid seven thousand dollars for the leaves from that same hectare.[149]

Thus, in mid-1985, the United States and Peru launched multiple operations known collectively as Condor. Condor operations aimed to make the price of coca leaf fall by destroying processing and trafficking facilities, including laboratories and airstrips. They expected the reduction in the number of processing and trafficking facilities to precipitate lower coca prices as the supply of coca began to exceed the capacity to produce coca paste for cocaine.[150] By the end of 1985, Condor had destroyed forty-four cocaine laboratories, forty airstrips, and 725 tons of coca leaf.[151] The price of coca paste fell by 50 percent. It seemed as if the U.S.-Peruvian strategy was working.

However, Condor campaigns in 1986 and 1987 were less effective.[152] The State Department increased the number of helicopters available to Peru's eradication forces, yet coca growers and traffickers quickly adapted. In mid-1987 about a thousand antidrug personnel moved into Tocache. They held the town for two months and then withdrew. Local growers and traffickers returned to business as usual. Colombian traffickers installed more cocaine laboratories to make up for their losses from Condor, while coca growers moved deeper into the UHV. Security continued to deteriorate. On April 23, 1986, five policemen were murdered by traffickers.[153] Six CORAH eradicators were killed in July.

A new guerrilla organization, the Movimiento Revolucionario Túpac Amaru (MRTA), infiltrated the UHV in 1987.[154] Formed from the remnants of the 1960s guerrilla group called Movimiento de la Izquierda Revolucionaria (MIR), it was Marxist-Leninist in character. It took its name from the eighteenth-century rebel leader Túpac Amaru, who had fought against Spanish colonial authority.[155] MRTA's objective was to rid Peru of all imperialist elements that had significant investments in Peru, particularly the United States and Japan.[156] In contrast to the Sendero, which it considered too Stalinist, the MRTA hoped for a more conventional socialist government like that of Cuba or Nicaragua.

The MRTA gained notoriety by using sophisticated armed propaganda techniques, such as hijacking trucks carrying food and then redistributing the food to the poor to win their support. As time progressed, the MRTA also committed acts of terrorism, including bombings of the U.S. embassy, attacks on U.S. corporations and Peruvian banks, and kidnappings.[157] In 1987 the MRTA made its splash in the UHV by launching a massive attack against the town of Juanjuí. The MRTA captured a large cache of arms and held the town for six hours.

In the aftermath of the attack, President García called for a state of emergency for ten provinces in northeastern Peru. García had previously promised "that nothing would deter Peru from its war against narcotics."[158] Yet mounting instability made it nearly impossible to challenge narcotics traffickers in the UHV. In 1987 the government's narcotics control forces destroyed only 355 of roughly one hundred thousand hectares of coca, and seizures of coca leaf remained minimal, at roughly four hundred metric tons.[159] The resources and the security necessary to implement an integrated rural development program in the UHV simply could not be mustered.[160]

As early as 1986, analysts at the U.S. embassy in Lima saw that only a massive commitment could solve the problems in the UHV, reporting to the U.S. Secretary of State that "given the narcotics problem in Peru and throughout the region, we can no longer afford to think in terms of piecemeal solutions."[161] A USAID report agreed that a successful strategy would include "simultaneous actions in the fight against paramilitary groups linked to the Sendero and those linked to the drug trade."[162]

However, Peru had long understood that it could not pursue traffickers and guerrillas at the same time. Antidrug efforts drove peasants into the protective arms of guerrillas, while attacks against guerrillas gave the drug producers a free hand to pursue their business. The militarization of the War on Drugs forced a simultaneous attack on guerrillas and traffickers, placing the Peruvian government and military in an impossible bind.

U.S.-Bolivian Counternarcotics Efforts

In Bolivia, too, alternate crop development programs sponsored by the United States were incapable of creating markets that would reduce campesino dependence on coca. Although Bolivia did not confront guerrilla insurgencies, U.S. pressure on the Bolivian government to step up its counternarcotics operations weakened its ability to maintain control over the country, provoking coup attempts as well as massive campesino demonstrations.

In August 1981 a military junta replaced the García Meza dictatorship. Pressure from political parties and disputes among rival military factions caused the Bolivian Congress to appoint Siles Zuazo (1982–1985) president in 1982. During the García Meza administration, the United States reduced its diplomatic mission and cut off economic aid.[163] However, with the election of Zuazo, the United States offered Bolivia a $140 million aid package. In exchange, the United States expected the government to control narcotics production.[164] The package included fifty-one million dollars for coca substitution programs and thirty-two million dollars in development assistance for the Chapare region between 1983 and 1985.[165] This assistance was critical to Bolivia's efforts to develop a counternarcotics program. The government needed the money to establish a security presence in the Chapare, create a narcotics investigation unit, develop an eradication program, and establish a system of control for licit coca production.

The initial target for coca eradication was set at two thousand hectares in 1983 and four thousand hectares each year thereafter until 1985. The United States would offer additional aid annually, based on results. Bolivia's DIRECO, supported by U.S.-trained narcotics police—the Leopards—carried out the coca eradication program in the Chapare.[166]

The crop substitution program was called the Chapare Regional Development Project (CRDP). The CRDP's intention was to enlarge market demand for Chapare agricultural products. This would stimulate production, thereby improving the farmers' quality of life, while making them less dependent on coca cultivation. Analysts believed that if the government launched a coca reduction program in the Chapare, the farmers' risk from the loss of their coca crop would be too great for them to withstand. Coca interdiction was therefore expected to create "economic uncertainty," which would then stimulate economic development away from coca.[167]

This plan had serious shortcomings. From the outset, funding for the CRDP was insufficient to compete with the thriving coca industry.[168] The project designers "recognized that no one crop and probably no combination of crops would match the income generated from the sale of illegal coca."[169] Limited infrastructure, limited credit acceptance, and a lack of coordination complicated matters further. On the campesinos' side, alternate crops were less hardy than coca; marketing them was costly; and food-pricing policies favored consumers over producers.[170]

Although Zuazo initiated the program in the Chapare, U.S. officials in Bolivia complained that "no progress" was made in coca eradication (see chart 3.6).[171] Moreover, U.S. officials in Bolivia publicly asserted that President Zuazo did little to combat corruption, and many of the military officers related to the Meza regime remained in power. Zuazo acknowledged a lack of progress but maintained that the United States was asking Bolivia "for too much, while offering too little." Zuazo added that if the

United States really wanted to combat cocaine traffic, it would have to commit at least one billion dollars to the purpose.[172]

The lack of progress in the coca control program prompted Bolivia's narcotics police, the Leopards, to take matters into their own hands. On June 30, 1984, military commanders from the Leopards attempted to launch a coup against Zuazo.[173] The coup plotters kidnapped him, claiming that they had received backing directly from the Reagan administration. U.S. Ambassador to Bolivia Edwin Corr denied that the United States was behind the coup and affirmed that the United States opposed any attempt to overthrow Zuazo.[174]

Chart 3.6 | **Bolivian Coca Leaf Eradication vs. Gross Coca Cultivation, 1982–1987 (in Hectares)**

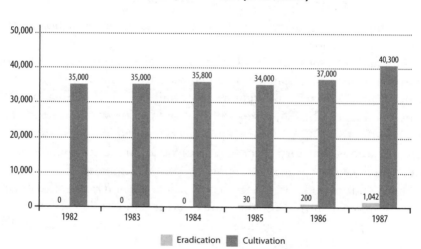

Without support within Bolivia or from the United States, the coup attempt failed to gain momentum and fell apart. However, DEA agents in Bolivia were quoted as saying that the Leopards had "such a bad reputation" that they were not sure if they were "of any use" in drug control.[175] The Leopards' participation in this coup attempt demonstrated the potential for U.S. counternarcotics policies to undermine Bolivia's budding democracy.

Zuazo remained under constant pressure to confront the narcotics problem for the rest of his presidency. Demands from both pro- and anti-coca-control forces undermined his political legitimacy. In July 1984, immediately following the attempted coup, members of the U.S. Senate visiting Bolivia threatened to cut off aid if the country did not begin its crackdown on coca cultivation. The threat of losing economic support during its darkest hour of economic crisis deeply upset the Bolivian Congress.

In October 1984 the Congress censured Zuazo after reports surfaced that his government was negotiating with Roberto Suárez, the main narco-trafficker associated with the García Meza coup, after Suárez offered to pay off Bolivia's foreign debt of $4.3 billion in exchange for immunity against prosecution. Zuazo responded that the censure was a political ploy to "sabotage" his presidency. [176] Nevertheless, his political clout was seriously diminished. Zuazo was forced to remove General Ovis (a military commander whose junior officers were allegedly involved in the cocaine trade) from power in December 1984 after rumors of another coup against Zuazo abounded. [177] The issue of narcotics control became a political football, complicating government attempts to take effective action against narcotics production.

General lawlessness in the Chapare and campesino opposition to coca control further complicated matters for Zuazo. The Bolivian peasant confederation rejected all attempts to curtail coca leaf cultivation. [178] In March and April of 1984, campesinos in conjunction with Confederación de Coca (CONCOCA), the coca producers' confederation, held massive demonstrations that forced the government to announce that "it would not . . . reduce coca growing . . . only prevent its expansion."

During this period, the U.S. embassy believed that narco-traffickers had increased their control over the campesino federation, known as FEAT, in the Chapare. The U.S. embassy declared that the narcotics traffickers alone controlled the region and neither the "police nor any type of government authority could interfere with their operations." [179] In order to prevent the Leopards from entering the Chapare, traffickers encouraged campesino coca growers to seize equipment and occupy the Leopards' headquarters.

To reestablish its authority, the government sent the military into the Chapare; however, the military claimed that the Leopards could not act until they received military permission. The Bolivian military's obstructionist attitude was due in part to interagency jealousy over funding. When the military did permit the Leopards to renew narcotics enforcement operations, they became one of the most vilified forces in the country. Accusations of rape, robbery, and other atrocities committed by the "well-armed" Leopards burgeoned. [180]

Hostility between the campesinos and the government became even more apparent when the national campesino federation, Confederación Sindical Unica de Trabajadores Campesinos de Bolivia (CSUTCB), criticized the government for militarizing the Chapare. The CSUTCB felt that the government did "not touch the big narco-traffickers" but instead repressed "the campesinos who were not responsible for the abuse of the coca leaf."[181] Because the U.S. government was paying eight dollars a day for each Leopard soldier to eliminate coca production, the Leopards' actions indirectly fostered resentment toward the United States.[182] In December 1984, a plot to murder Ambassador Edwin Corr was uncovered.[183] By December 1985 the situation had deteriorated so badly that Bolivian campesinos marching near the U.S. embassy in La Paz shouted "long live coca" and "death to the Yankees."[184]

In August 1985 the election of President Paz Estenssoro (1985–1989) led Bolivia to renew its commitment to control illegal coca processing and cultivation. Estenssoro perceived the traffickers' threat to the government through their sheer economic power. The coca economy in Bolivia was generating roughly $800,000 million to one billion dollars annually, although this money did not always remain in the country. Estenssoro declared, "[If] we do not address the narcotics problem decisively . . . the day could come when the economic power" wielded by the narcotics traffickers "could result in their governing the country."[185] Yet, in attacking coca production, Estenssoro was threatening Bolivia's most profitable cash crop.[186]

Political tensions ran high. Just prior to Estenssoro's election, thousands of coca farmers, urged on by narcotics traffickers, marched against the Bolivian government in Cochabamba City and tried to establish a national road blockade. The campesinos' fury was fueled by the attack upon their livelihood and by continuous allegations (some true, some false) of abuses and murders committed by the Leopards.[187] This demonstration left President Estenssoro with no choice but to negotiate with FEAT after he was elected. Estenssoro offered to give campesinos who abandoned coca cultivation $350 per hectare. Compared to the huge returns the campesinos were earning for each hectare of coca they raised, the offer was laughable.[188]

Nevertheless, Estenssoro was determined to face down narcotics traffickers. He developed a joint counternarcotics operation with the United States known as Operation Blast Furnace.[189] Blast Furnace, which began in July 1986, was a sixty-day operation in the Chapare and Beni regions.

Like Peru's Operation Condor, it sought to destroy cocaine production labs with the hope that lab reduction would drive down demand and, ultimately, the price and production of coca.[190] However, unlike Operation Condor, this operation used U.S. military personnel to support a joint DEA/Leopards strike force against narcotics processing and transportation facilities.[191] This was the first time a U.S. military contingent was sent to another country to fight drug trafficking. The United States contributed six Black Hawk helicopters, several transport planes, and about 160 men to help transport the Bolivian Leopards and maintain the helicopters.[192] Although the U.S. military's participation in Blast Furnace was limited to an initial sixty days, U.S. forces received permission to remain in Bolivia until it was "determined" that the Bolivian government could "continue on its own."[193]

Within Bolivia, Blast Furnace met with instantaneous opposition. The widely publicized operation and the arrival of U.S. troops created a nationalistic fervor against the Estenssoro government. Bolivia's finance minister, Juan Cariaga, went so far as to say that if the cushion of narco-dollars dried up as a result of Blast Furnace, the New Economic Policy could falter, since the lack of foreign exchange in the Bolivian economy would drive up inflation.[194] Politicians from both left and right accused Estenssoro of violating the constitution and compromising national sovereignty by inviting U.S. troops into the country.

Campesinos in the Chapare protested the operation, and Bolivian newspapers carried headlines such as "U.S. Invades Bolivia." A campesino leader stated that the campesinos were "not in accord with the narcotics traffickers," but the government was not able to meet their need for "electricity and better roads in the Chapare," which would "make other types of crops work." The Confederación de Obreros Bolivianos (COB) called for a general strike and threatened to invoke a state of siege in protest of the "Yankee invasion."[195]

Threats of striking at the "gringos" and dynamiting U.S. helicopters became more serious when a large cache of weapons was intercepted in early August 1986.[196] In one demonstration against Blast Furnace, thousands of students, teachers, and campesinos attacked the police in the town of Oruro. In another protest, seventeen thousand coca leaf farmers staged a five-day siege against 245 narcotics officers at the U.S./Bolivian forward operating base in Ivargazama, after the Leopards conducted a number of raids against coca processing laboratories. The Bolivian military threatened to break up the siege, while the campesinos declared that "if the Leopards remained in the area . . . violence and confrontations" would continue.[197]

U.S. troops were slowly phased out by October 1986, but coca control continued to generate massive unrest. In 1987, Bolivia proposed its own three-year plan to reduce coca cultivation. The government designed this plan, known as Plan Trienal, to keep the demand for coca leaf depressed by maintaining pressure on the traffickers and their processing labs after the Blast Furnace operation ended. Its overall goal was to decrease coca leaf production to roughly twenty-four thousand hectares, a number considered "sufficient to satisfy Bolivia's traditional use" of coca.[198] Total funding for the program equaled three hundred million dollars over a three-year period.[199]

The specific terms of the agreement stipulated that the United States would provide funds as well as material and logistical support for the operation based on Bolivia's success in cutting coca cultivation.[200] Bolivia would pay for 20 percent of the budget, or roughly sixty million dollars, while Washington would give seventy-five million dollars.[201] The United States dangled another $14.6 million in economic support funds (ESF) for 1987, and about thirty million dollars in ESF for 1988, if Bolivia reached the coca eradication targets set by the United States.[202] The rest of the money would come from other donors, including Western European governments and international banks such as the IMF.[203]

Paz Estenssoro's Plan Trienal promised to recompense coca growers for the economic fallout from coca destruction. As part of the three-year plan, the United States agreed to give the Bolivian government $350 per hectare of destroyed coca to help cover their administrative and operational costs.[204] However, the Bolivian government determined that it needed to pay two thousand dollars in cash for each hectare of coca that was voluntarily destroyed.[205] In response, the United States stated that the Bolivian government would be responsible for the direct cost of assistance to former coca growers and that financial assistance from the United States could only come in the form of credit, tools, and technical service.

The Bolivian government attempted to distribute cash payments on its own, but U.S. specifications for the release of credit drew criticism from Estenssoro. He wrote to President Reagan that the United States' "financial commitment" was "not sufficient to carry out any responsible and sustained work, particularly with regard to the operative components of coca eradication and family rehabilitation outlined in the three-year plan." Estenssoro went on to write that "payments in kind" were not "sufficiently attractive to the campesinos affected by the eradication program set forth."[206] The campesinos agreed. According to José Antonio Quiroga, an investigator for the Bolivian Center of Information and Development (CID), two thousand dollars was enough to destroy a hectare of coca and pay for a family to return to its community of origin, but the money meant nothing in terms of development and crop substitution for the campesinos.[207]

In the long run, the Blast Furnace operation and the three-year plan did not produce the desired results. Initially, Blast Furnace forced Bolivian, Peruvian, and Colombian narco-traffickers out of the Chapare, although many of them were tipped off about the raids before they occurred.[208] Some analysts argued that Blast Furnace caused the price of coca leaf to drop from an estimated $0.70 to $0.25 per pound.[209] However, the drop in the price of coca could also have been due to overproduction and bad weather, according to Robert Gelbard, the deputy assistant secretary of state for South America (1985–1988).[210] After the withdrawal of U.S. troops from Bolivia at the close of Blast Furnace, the price of coca leaf shot up from an estimated $0.20 to $0.60 per pound.[211]

This rapid recovery caused U.S. officials to maintain that a long-term interdiction and eradication program was necessary.[212] Yet even with the implementation of the three-year plan, in 1987 the government eradicated only 1,042 of an estimated 40,300 hectares and seized merely fifteen metric tons of coca leaf.[213] Mario Mercado, a centrist Bolivian congressman, argued that interdiction and eradication were a "Band-Aid" cure. As Mercado saw it, the country needed a "substitution for the millions of dollars that the drug trade brought into the country."[214] In a message to the congress of the Asociación Nacional de Productores de Coca (ANAPCOCA), Socialist leader Roger Cortéz Hurtado pronounced that the coca farmers would reject and combat the presence of foreign troops supported by a government whose economic restructuring policy made the expansion of coca production the only viable alternative for the campesinos.[215] By the end of 1987, the Chapare-region campesinos declared their own state of emergency. They suspended all coca eradication and called for the removal of all U.S. advisors to the Bolivian government.[216]

Nevertheless, the United States continued to push for aggressive eradication and interdiction policies. Bolivia's political problems with narcotics control frustrated Washington, while the Reagan and Bush administrations' policy of increasing military funding to fight the drug industry created more chaos for Bolivia.

As the end of the 1980s approached, it was clear to all involved that U.S. narcotics control policy in Colombia, Peru, and Bolivia had not been effective. The narcotics industry's vast economic power—it provided an estimated $2 billion to Colombia, $1.5 billion to Peru, and $1 billion to Bolivia each year—was too enormous to counteract with aid provided by the United States.[217] Continuous U.S. pressure on the Andean governments generated massive political instability in the northern Andes, yet the United States did not see its drug control strategy as a major source of this instability. It felt that the northern Andean narcotics dilemma was not a consequence of long-term socioeconomic and political challenges exacerbated by U.S. demand for narcotics; rather, it blamed the northern Andean narcotics problem and the failure to solve it on the influence of communists and narco-terrorists, which the United States considered one and the same.

4

Reagan, the Drug War, and the Narco-Terrorist Nexus

Four years after initiating the War on Drugs, the Reagan administration could show neither a decrease in availability nor a decrease in demand for illicit narcotics in the United States. On the contrary, by 1986 the widely publicized crack cocaine epidemic had put drug abuse and the War on Drugs into the consciousness of every American citizen. Reagan's response was to initiate congressional legislation authorizing even more aggressive narcotics control measures. The Anti-Drug Abuse Act of 1986 sought to combat the rapidly expanding drug trade on both the domestic and international fronts by increasing the military role in counternarcotics activities, particularly in the area of drug interdiction. The act also allowed the Reagan administration to apply more coercion on the governments of Peru, Bolivia, and Colombia through a new certification policy that permitted the president to withhold foreign aid in order to secure cooperation from drug-producing nations.

Although the public considered the Anti-Drug Abuse Act a step in the right direction, many members of Congress felt that it lacked teeth. Due to a budgetary policy that restricted discretionary domestic spending, the Reagan administration was talking about cutting the act's budget the first year after its passage. Moreover, many Pentagon officials opposed the enlarged military role because they saw narcotics control as a civilian matter. Military leaders thought that their involvement in narcotics control would reduce readiness and lead to corruption. Still, narcotics were perceived as a national security threat, and the Reagan administration was convinced that Cuba and its ally Nicaragua were using narcotics to finance insurgencies throughout the hemisphere. In Reagan's mind, the only way to defeat the scourges of narcotics and Marxist revolution was to confront both problems at the source, head on and simultaneously.

Reagan saw political instability in the Western Hemisphere and the thriving narcotics trade as direct threats to his antidrug and Cold War policies. This perception was solidified when evidence surfaced that the Soviet-sympathizing Cuban and Sandinista governments were involved in narcotics trafficking.[1] Little proof existed for a Cuban or Nicaraguan partnership with guerrilla organizations—with the exception of the M-19—to traffic in narcotics. Nevertheless, Reagan and his advisors grouped narcotics production and guerrilla insurgencies into the same category. At the same time, the Reagan administration denied allegations that CIA-backed Contra forces fighting the Sandinista government used narcotics to fund their insurgency after Congress cut off aid to their counterrevolution. Mounting evidence showed that the vast profits generated by narcotics had no ideological boundaries. This situation called into question U.S. objectives as the nation attempted to fight both the War on Drugs and the Cold War in Latin America. Eventually the War on Drugs metamorphosed into the Cold War: the two became one.

The Domestic Crisis

In 1985 crack cocaine began to appear in New York City and elsewhere in the United States owing to its relatively low price—five to ten dollars a hit. Unlike freebase, which required obscure chemicals such as ether for manufacture, crack was easy to make; production required only water or alcohol and baking soda. Crack was also highly addictive. It was described as the "ultimate ego-enhancing" trip; with constant use, a crack high would make addicts out of users in a matter of days.[2] The public began to see crack as an emerging menace as they watched addicts become unproductive members of society who hung out in rundown buildings known as "crack houses." The deaths of two famous athletes in June 1986 brought the lethal nature of the crack cocaine epidemic to the forefront of national conscious-ness. The drug-related deaths of Len Bias, a first-round draft choice for the Boston Celtics from the University of Maryland, and Don Rogers, a player for the Cleveland Browns, turned crack cocaine use into a national crisis. The drug epidemic was declared more dangerous than terrorism.[3]

Hysteria surrounding the drug crisis grew as street purity rose, prices declined, and hospital-related emergencies increased. Constant media attention fed the national panic.[4] Polls across the United States listed drugs as the number one voter concern. In congressional hearings, the drug crisis was called "a pervasive evil" that was "eroding the roots" of U.S. "society."[5]

Chart 4.1 | **Emergency Room Admissions for Cocaine, 1985–1988**

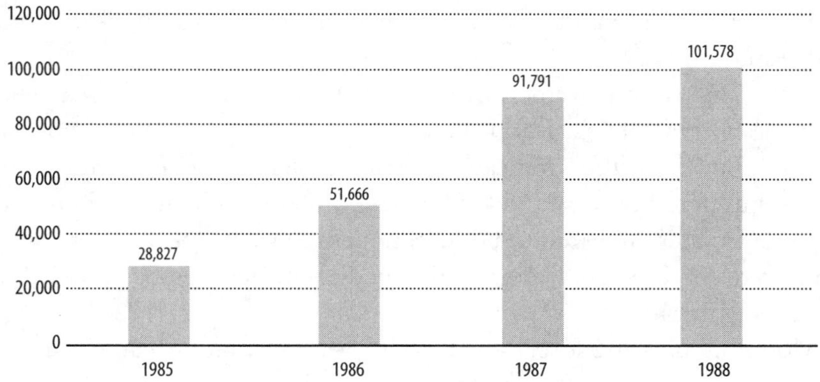

Between 1985 and 1987, emergency room admissions for cocaine over-doses nearly doubled each year (see chart 4.1). By 1988 such admissions surpassed one hundred thousand.[6] Furthermore, as the number of emer-gency room admissions increased, the street price for cocaine went down, and cocaine purity went up. For example, in 1985 the DEA estimated that the price for a pure gram of cocaine was $212 and that cocaine's overall purity was at 58.58 percent. By 1988 the price had dropped to $105 per gram, while purity rose to 79.15 percent (see chart 4.2).[7]

Chart 4.2 | **Street Price and Purity of Cocaine, 1985–1988**

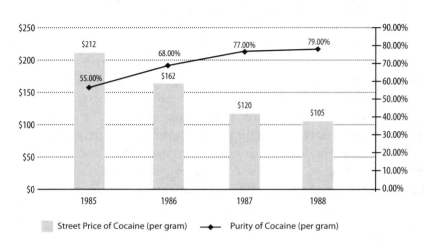

Street Price of Cocaine (per gram)   ◆ Purity of Cocaine (per gram)

The disturbing trend of babies born addicted to cocaine made its appearance in 1986, amplifying national concern. An estimated 10 percent of all pregnant women in the United States were trying cocaine at least once during their pregnancies. Cocaine use during pregnancy produced babies who were born prematurely or who experienced heart attacks, strokes, and respiratory distress.[8]

Physicians were extremely worried that so-called crack babies would suffer long-term physical and mental damage. When estimates became available in 1989, they indicated that crack babies born in the United States numbered between 100,000 and 375,000 each year.[9] Although the higher estimates appeared to be sensationalized by the newspapers, it was obvious to the U.S. public and to the medical profession that cocaine was a national menace.

Mounting pressure forced the Reagan administration to take action. In a speech to the American public, President Reagan declared that "drug use continues and its consequences escalate . . . bringing sorrow and heartbreak into homes across the country."[10] For Reagan, the archconservative reelected to make the United States the "shining city on the hill," drug abuse was "a repudiation of everything" the country stood for.[11] Reagan attributed the drug dilemma to the pervasive "attitude of permissiveness" that had erupted during the 1960s. In his view, illegal drugs were every bit as much of a threat to the United States as "enemy planes and missiles."[12]

After the deaths of Bias and Rogers, many members of Congress feared that the public would hold them responsible for the cocaine epidemic in the 1986 mid-term elections.[13] Congress therefore called on Reagan to develop a new antidrug strategy. On April 16, 1986, Reagan issued National Security Decision Directive 221 (NSDD 221), which designated narcotics a national security threat and called on the Department of Defense to expand its role in counternarcotics operations.[14] He also proposed legislation that became the Anti-Drug Abuse Act of 1986.

The 1986 Anti-Drug Abuse Act was multifaceted, geared to attack the narcotics industry inside and outside the United States for the remainder of Reagan's term in office. The Act escalated the War on Drugs into a "crusade" with the goal of securing a drug-free America. It included law enforcement, protection, and treatment for U.S. citizens. Internationally, Reagan sought to "expand international cooperation while treating drug trafficking as a threat [to] national security."[15] The total budget for the act reached nearly $1.7 billion.[16]

Reagan noted that "all the confiscation and law enforcement in the world" would not stop drug abuse and paid at least lip service to the idea that the United States would have to "go beyond efforts at affecting the supply of drugs" to focus on "not only supply, but demand."[17] In reality, however, roughly 75 percent of the money went to supply-side enforcement, rather than use-reduction and prevention programs.[18] The program budget authorized $200 million dollars for education and $241 million for rehabilitation in 1987. On the other hand, it gave $230 million to local law enforcement, $133 million to the Coast Guard, and $199.5 million to the Customs Service, and allocated $96.5 million to build more federal prisons. The act also ordered the army to provide $277 million in military equipment (primarily aircraft) to support interdiction by the Customs Service and Coast Guard.[19] An additional $45 million was dedicated to provide aircraft and helicopters for Latin American countries to conduct their own interdiction and eradication activities. Notably, only $75.4 million, the smallest portion of the budget, went to the Department of State for international narcotics control.[20] This seemed like a pittance, considering the drug industry's enormous economic power in Latin America; yet a legislative aide who wrote a good deal of the bill believed, ironically, that for the "first time," the United States was going to "give the traffickers a fight on near even terms."[21]

In addition to massive spending, the act initiated two policies that became cornerstones of U.S. international narcotics control policies in Latin America: presidential certification for nations that cooperated in the War on Drugs and tacit congressional approval for military support in narcotics interdiction efforts. The certification law was a modification of previous amendments associated with the 1961 Foreign Assistance Act, which required each signatory to the 1961 Convention on Narcotic Drugs to fulfill its obligation to eliminate illicit drug production.[22] The Hawkins-Rangel-Gilman amendment was the initial step leading to the certification clause in the Anti-Drug Abuse Act of 1986. Signed by President Reagan in 1983, this law differed from previous legislation by authorizing the president to suspend economic and military aid to a nation that failed to take adequate steps "to prevent illicit drugs from *entering* the United States."[23] Although U.S. officials had held some serious discussions on whether Bolivia should receive assistance, the U.S. government had never taken action against a foreign government prior to the 1986 legislation.[24]

Under the new statute, Congress supervised the certification process. The president was required to identify countries that were major producers of illicit drugs, following the recommendations of the International Narcotics Control Strategy Report (INCSR) released each year on March 1. Once the report identified a major trafficking country, the president had to withhold 50 percent of U.S. foreign assistance at the start of the fiscal year in October. However, aid sanctions could be removed if the president determined that a nation had fully cooperated with U.S. counternarcotics policies or had taken adequate steps of its own accord. In addition, the president could remove sanctions if he deemed that vital national interests were at stake.

The act allowed Congress to hold hearings and consult with the State Department on certification decisions. It also gave Congress the power to disapprove the president's determination of certification, but this decision had to pass in both houses. If a nation's decertification continued in subsequent fiscal years, it lost 100 percent of U.S. assistance and could face optional sanctions, such as higher export duties, a reduction of air transportation traffic, and a withdrawal of any pre-customs clearance agreements.[25] Certification became a significant tool because it enhanced U.S. economic leverage over the nations in which the drug industry was thriving; however, in 1987, the first year that the act was implemented, the United States certified all the drug-producing nations in the northern Andes.[26]

The second policy cornerstone was nothing new. As early as 1981, public law 97–86 had mandated military cooperation with civilian law enforcement. At the discretion of the secretary of defense, the Anti-Drug Abuse Act now gave the military the authority to provide intelligence, equipment, and training to federal, state, and local law enforcement officials, as well as support for activities outside the United States. The law also instructed the secretary of defense to issue regulations to prevent military participation in seizures and arrests and to insure that the provision of assistance did not adversely affect military preparedness. [27]

U.S. military participation in the War on Drugs had remained limited under the Defense Authorization Act of 1982, which theoretically had allowed the Coast Guard and navy to participate in counternarcotics operations. U.S. military leaders had been wary of allowing their forces to serve as police officers, and Secretary of Defense Caspar Weinberger (1981–1988) at one point had gone so far as to call the idea "dangerous and undesirable."[28] In what became known as the Weinberger Doctrine, Weinberger had expressed his conviction that U.S. troops should be committed to action only if defined political and military objectives existed. Moreover, Weinberger wrote in 1985 that "reliance on military forces to accomplish civilian tasks" was "detrimental to military readiness and democratic processes."[29]

By mid-1985, Congress demanded that the Reagan administration start taking tougher steps to curb international narcotics traffic, including increased U.S. military involvement. Congressmen Charles Rangel and Henry Hyde, in particular, called for the military to be "pressed into further drug control efforts." Rangel accused the Joint Chiefs of Staff (JCS) of resisting participation in the War on Drugs because they did not consider it "a part of the mandate relating to national security."[30] The calls from Congress motivated the JCS to study the military role in the War on Drugs. National pressure, along with the escalating Central American conflict—Nicaragua, El Salvador, Guatemala, and the borders of Costa Rica and Honduras were all involved—resulted in the JCS recommending that the U.S. armed forces engage, to an unprecedented extent, in fighting Central American drug trafficking.[31]

The JCS proposal also intended to help countries such as Colombia and Peru by training highly mobile teams to stamp out marijuana and heroin, which was then being trafficked through Central America. The military's Special Forces had already conducted military exercises with Colombia and Peru in counterinsurgency, survival, and small unit tactics. In addition, U.S. aircraft and ships were expected to stop the export of drugs through the Caribbean and Central America.[32] The Department of Defense also furnished significant intelligence, using the Defense Intelligence Agency (DIA) and the National Security Agency (NSA), as well as navy aerial surveillance.[33]

With the adoption of the Joint Chiefs' recommendation, the government anticipated curtailing the drug sales that financed insurgents attempting to "topple anti-Marxist governments in the hemisphere."[34] Using the pretext of narcotics control to counter a narco-guerrilla nexus, the United States deepened its commitment to helping the militaries in both Central America and the northern Andes to fight their civil wars.[35] Reagan signed NSDD 221 almost immediately after he addressed the nation on March 16, 1986, announcing that "Nicaragua, a Soviet ally," under the leadership of the Sandinistas, had "involved themselves in the international drug trade."[36] In addition to permitting the use of U.S. forces to help other nations fight narcotics, Reagan's directive authorized an expanded use of intelligence, including electronic eavesdropping, to combat the drug trade in other countries.[37]

Some military officials were not happy about the military's enlistment in the War on Drugs. They felt they were being dragged into an open-ended conflict in which U.S. troops could become casualties in a new kind of unconventional warfare that conflated narcotics traffickers and Marxist guerrillas. Moreover, they felt that America's NATO commitment and other international security interests had already stretched the military's resources thin. [38] Numerous people in Washington speculated that Secretary of Defense Weinberger gave his approval to the national security decision only after Vice President Bush made a personal appeal to President Reagan.[39] In September 1986, passage of the Anti-Drug Abuse Act made military involvement in the War on Drugs official. The act required the president to deploy enough military force "to halt the unlawful penetration of United States borders by aircraft and vessels carrying narcotics," and gave the military permission to track and intercept Colombian planes and speedboats smuggling narcotics into the United States.[40] The militarization of U.S. counternarcotics efforts in the northern Andes had begun.

The Birth of the Narco-Guerrilla

The Reagan administration's claim of a "real link between drugs and terrorism" lay behind the creation of both the National Security Decision Directive and the Anti-Drug Abuse Act.[41] Reagan believed that a nexus existed between Cuba, Nicaragua, and the guerrillas in the northern Andes to facilitate drug traffic in order to finance Marxist revolutions throughout the hemisphere. The Reagan administration alleged that "Cuba and Nicaragua" used their ill-gotten gains from narcotics trafficking as "a source of funds to support insurgencies and subversion."[42] Secretary of State George Shultz called "the complicity of Communist governments in the drug trade" a "cause for grave concern" and "a larger part of international lawlessness by Communist nations that, as we have seen, also includes support for international terrorism and other forms of organized violence against legitimate governments."[43] As if to confirm this, Medellín cartel boss Carlos Lehder pronounced that drugs were the "Third World's atomic bomb," and that they were "a revolutionary weapon against American imperialism."[44]

Narco-Guerrillas in Cuba

In 1989 the trial and execution of General Arnaldo Ochoa Sánchez—officially proclaimed a "hero of the republic"—and Colonel Antonio de la Guardia for involvement in international drug trafficking shocked Cuba and the world.[45] This was the first time that Cuba officially admitted that members of its government were involved in the narcotics trade. However, the trial gave rise to several questions. Was Castro really joining the world community in the fight against illegal drugs, or was this merely a highly publicized show trial to spread disinformation about Cuba's role in the narcotics trade and rid Castro of political opponents? More important, what was the Cuban government's role in facilitating narcotics traffic to the United States?

Allegations about Cuban involvement in the drug trade had persisted since the 1960s.[46] Prior to the Cuban revolution, the Sicilian mob, directed by Lucky Luciano, had used Cuba as a waypoint to traffic heroin from France into the United States.[47] Following the revolution, an intelligence report contended that top Cuban officials, including Che Guevara, discussed creating a drug smuggling network as early as 1961.[48] Other evidence of Cuba's association with the drug trade during the 1960s includes several BNDD memoranda. The BNDD investigated a purported Cuban government operation to sponsor marijuana and heroin crops in Cuba's Oriente province, using a secret department within the country's National Institute of Agrarian Reform.[49] A 1965 letter, written by Commissioner of Narcotics Henry Giordano, described an "increase" in "narcotics trafficking by Cubans . . . to finance subversion following the emergence of the Castro regime." The letter went on to say that the BNDD had uncovered a "pattern of Cuban nationals," who were "suspected Castro sympathizers . . . dominating the traffic" and "operating in Cuba, Mexico, Peru, Bolivia, and Chile to distribute large quantities of cocaine throughout the United States."[50]

In 1966, Giordano changed his position regarding Cuba and narcotics trafficking. In an internal BNDD memo, Giordano wrote that "Cuba, because of its isolation . . . presented less of a problem to the United States," and that "Cuba itself did not appear to be involved" in narcotics trafficking. Although Giordano noted that some drug smuggling from Cuba had occurred in 1962, he placed the blame for the trafficking increase during 1966 on "certain Cuban nationals." These individuals were "motivated by greed alone," or were attempting to finance "either pro- or anti-Castro movements in the United States through their narcotics profits."[51]

David Acheson, the special assistant to the secretary for enforcement, repeated Giordano's opinion. He stated in a letter that there was "no indication that narcotics from Cuba" were "entering the United States," though a "certain number of Cuban nationals" had been "involved in this country and elsewhere in Latin America in smuggling narcotics of various kinds." Still, Acheson added, "it may be that certain . . . Cuban nationals involved in this traffic are in it, to earn dollar exchange for Cuba." Nevertheless, "the scale of that operation" appeared "too small to have much of an effect on the supply of dollars to that country."[52]

Differing evidence collected by Giordano indicated that Cuba was initially involved in the narcotics trade following the revolution. However, as the country became isolated in the hemisphere, its connection to the narcotics trade decreased. It can also be deduced that many Cuban nationals continuously involved in the narcotics trade were exiles working for the U.S. Sicilian Mafia, with whom they had formed relationships during the Battista years.

However, Cuba's role in the narcotics trade appears to have taken a sinister turn in the late 1960s. In the book *Red Cocaine*, Professor Joseph Douglass argues that Raúl Castro went to Czechoslovakia in 1967 to discuss narcotics operations. The ultimate goal of these operations, according to Douglass, was to undermine American society from within by facilitating the proliferation of narcotics. Utilizing Gramscian–Marxist strategy, which sought to radicalize the cultural institutions of the West, Cuba's drug operations targeted the youth of the United States. They expected the proliferation of drugs among America's youth (and Western youth in general) to corrode and weaken societal values. Thus, when members of the affected generation matured and assumed positions of power, their weakened values and loyalties would make them more susceptible to supporting socialist revolution.[53]

There is some evidence for Douglass's claim, and it appears that Raúl Castro may have wasted no time in getting this operation up and running. In September 1967 a letter addressed to J. Edgar Hoover, director of the Federal Bureau of Investigation (FBI), alleged that three communist Cuban agents were attempting to bring "arms and marijuana" through Tampa and New York in coffee sacks.[54] Another letter, written by Hoover, reported that several Colombian airplanes taken to Cuba in 1967 were hijacked on behalf of the Cuban government for the purpose of obtaining the cargo—smuggled heroin. The Federal Bureau of Narcotics (FBN) and the FBI estimated that the hijacked heroin was worth about twenty million dollars. According to Hoover's source, Cuba wanted to send the heroin to North Vietnam via China, where it would be used to demoralize U.S. troops and the war effort in South Vietnam.[55] The spread of heroin would not only undermine the war effort in Vietnam and military readiness, but it would also enhance the societal burden for the United States when many Vietnam veterans returned home as addicts.[56] A massive heroin bust in Yonkers, near New York City, provided the last bit of evidence to support the claim that Cuba was actively engaged in spreading narcotics in the United States. The DEA estimated that the street value of the recovered heroin was nearly $480,000. Most important, the heroin came not only from Mexico but also from Cuba.[57]

Substantial evidence against Cuba began to appear in the mid-1970s. In congressional hearings during the 1980s, the Reagan administration used this evidence as proof that Cuba was a narco-communist state. Around 1975, the Departamento de América (Department of America) allegedly broke away from the Dirección General de Información (DGI), which was Cuba's intelligence service within the Ministerio del Interior (MININT).[58] The Departamento de América was in charge of subversion and sabotage operations in the Western Hemisphere, including disinformation, terrorism, and drugs.[59] The Departamento de América broke away from the KGB-directed DGI as a result of a dispute between the USSR and Cuba over Cuba's support for guerrilla insurgencies during the era of détente. The Departamento de América then turned to narcotics smuggling to finance guerrilla insurgencies throughout the hemisphere.[60]

During this same period, Cuban authorities initiated a cooperative program with the United States to interdict drugs moving through Cuba's territorial airspace and water.[61] Consequently, Cuba started to seize drug shipments, boats, and crews traveling out of Colombia. In response, members of the newly formed Medellín cartel approached Fernando Ravelo Renedo, Cuba's ambassador to Colombia, who supposedly worked for the DGI, to negotiate the release of their crews and ships.[62] In return for payments estimated at eight hundred thousand dollars per vessel, Cuba agreed to provide safe passage for the cartel's ships.[63] Captured Cuban DGI agent and smuggler Mario Estevez Gonzalez testified that the Departamento de América and the DGI also infiltrated agents into the United States during the Mariel boatlift in 1980 to facilitate narcotics trafficking, spy on anti-Castro elements, or act as sleeper agents until a conflict between the United States and Cuba broke out.[64] Thus, during the mid-1970s, while Cuba made overtures to the United States to cooperate on narcotics control, elements within Cuba's intelligence community simultaneously cultivated a relationship with the Medellín cartel, which was busy setting up narcotics trafficking networks in the United States, particularly in Florida.

In 1982 the Reagan administration presented damning evidence against Cuba during the Guillot Lara case. This case showed that Cuba was not only smuggling narcotics into the United States but was also using the proceeds from the operation to finance the Colombian M-19. The evidence assembled against Cuba came from Juan Lozano Perez, also known as Johnny Crump, a convicted Colombian drug dealer who was an associate of Jaime Guillot Lara.[65] According to Crump's testimony, Crump and Guillot Lara, a Colombian marijuana smuggler, met with Cuban Ambassador Ravelo Renedo in late 1979. During this meeting, Lara proposed using Cuba as a stopover point for his cargo. Rene Rodríguez Cruz, a member of the Central Committee of the Communist Party of Cuba, warmed to this idea and ordered Gonzalo Bassols Suárez, the Cuban minister-counselor to Colombia, to serve as a liaison between Lara and Cuba. Crump, Lara, and the Cuban government agreed that in exchange for five hundred thousand dollars per boatload, Cuba would offer safe passage for vessels loaded with drugs.[66]

Crump and Guillot Lara's venture with the Cubans started out poorly. They had to transfer the first major shipment of marijuana from the mother ship, the *Viviana*, to an intermediary ship, the *Lazy Lady*, which was run by Cuban agents, including Mario Estevez Gonzalez. Further complicating the operation, Estevez Gonzalez intentionally sabotaged the *Lazy Lady* in order to pick up a separate shipment of quaaludes waiting at the Cuban port of Cayo Paredón Grande on Cuba's north shore. At Paredón Grande, the vice admiral of the Cuban navy, Aldo Santamaría Cuadrado, oversaw the loading of the quaaludes and the repair of the *Lazy Lady*. The *Lazy Lady* eventually set out to sea again. As it neared U.S. territorial waters to rendezvous with speedboats waiting to run the narcotics into Florida, a U.S. Coast Guard helicopter appeared and the crew dumped the narcotics overboard.

In the aftermath of this failure, Guillot Lara attempted to send another shipment of marijuana, but the Cuban navy seized it. Ambassador Renedo intervened on his behalf, and the ship was released. The load of marijuana was of such poor quality, however, that Crump and Lara just broke even. Nevertheless, the Cubans expected payment for their assistance. Lara went to Crump and an associate in Florida named David Lorenzo Perez and explained that they could work off the money they owed the Cubans "by carrying guns to South America's rebels" and by shipping "500 kilos of cocaine" a month from Bolivia to Florida. In exchange for allowing the transportation of narcotics through Cuba, the Cubans would receive money and weapons purchased in Florida with the illegal proceeds.[67]

Though historian Rachel Ehrenfeld argues that the operation went "too well" and that Lara and Crump smuggled weapons for the Cuban DGI, it seems more likely that the DGI put Lara and Crump in such a position that they had no alternative but to help the Cubans.[68] It also appears that the DGI targeted Lara for this operation because he was a schoolmate of Jaime Bateman, who headed the M-19 before Mario Ospina. Their predicament forced Crump and Lara to help Cuba smuggle weapons to the M-19 in Colombia and to anti-Pinochet groups in Chile.[69]

The arms smuggling operation with the Colombian M-19 also went poorly. On November 15, 1981, one of Guillot Lara's ships, the *Karina*, was destroyed off Colombia's west coast.[70] It carried an estimated one hundred tons of weapons when it sank. Following this incident, another Lara ship, the *Monarca*, was seized after it offloaded a large quantity of weapons for the M-19. The seizures forced Lara to flee from Colombia. He went to Managua, where he met with Bateman and First Secretary Gonzalo Bassols Suárez of Cuba. They told Lara to go to Mexico City and meet with a Bolivian Air Force officer to arrange the purchase of five hundred kilograms of cocaine to sell in the United States; but this deal fell through when the Mexican police arrested him for carrying false identification. Although the United States tried to have Lara extradited from Mexico, the Mexican police released him, and he went into hiding. Soon after, U.S.

authorities arrested Crump for narcotics trafficking. In exchange for his testimony, he received a twenty-five-year suspended sentence with six years of probation. Lorenzo Perez and Estevez Gonzalez corroborated Crump's statements after their capture by U.S. authorities. Their testimony allowed the United States to try four Cuban officials in absentia: René Rodríguez Cruz, Vice Admiral Aldo Santamaría Cuadrado, Ambassador Fernando Ravelo Renedo and First Secretary Gonzalo Bassols Suárez. [71]

Guillot Lara's Cuba enterprise was over, but the U.S. government now addressed allegations that directly tied Castro to the drug trade. In particular, Castro was accused of acting as the Medellín cartel's mediator in its disputes with various entities, including the M-19 and Panama's military strongman, Manuel Noriega. José Blandón, an intelligence aide to Manuel Noriega who defected to the United States, reported that Castro believed that he needed "to have an influence over Colombia's drug trafficking world" if he was going "to have influence over Colombia's political world."[72] Thus, maintaining a relationship between the Medellín cartel and the various Colombian guerrilla groups was a significant policy goal for Cuba, which Manuel Noriega helped to fulfill.[73]

Manuel Noriega led the intelligence branch (G2) of the Panama National Guard for Omar Torrijos. In this position, Noriega cultivated relationships with the CIA, Cuba, and the Medellín cartel during the mid-1970s.[74] He often served as a go-between for the CIA and the Cuban DGI. Nevertheless, in 1980, while working under Torrijos, Noriega significantly aided Cuba by providing weapons and an active sanctuary for the Cuban-backed Colombian guerrillas, the M-19.[75] As described in chapter 3, the kidnapping of Medellín cartel kingpin Fabio Ochoa's daughter in 1981 by the M-19 precipitated a war between the Medellín-backed paramilitary force, the MAS, and the M-19. The M-19 was forced to sue for peace, and Noriega was asked to mediate. Part of the deal he brokered gave responsibility for managing the relationship between the cartel and the M-19 to the Cuban Ambassador to Colombia, Ravelo Renedo—the same Cuban ambassador who had participated in the Lara operation.[76]

After Noriega seized power in August 1982, the Medellín cartel decided to diversify its center of operations into Panama. Since the cartel had developed a close relationship with Noriega in the 1970s, it set up a processing plant in La Palma, on the border of Colombia in the province of Darién.[77] In order to get this facility underway, the cartel gave four million dollars to Lieutenant Julián Melo Borbua to pay off Noriega. While Noriega was out of the country, the Panamanian Defense Forces (PDF) moved in and shut down the facility on May 29, 1984. Later, Noriega explained that the PDF had conducted this raid because he was under pressure from Colombia to act against the Medellín cartel's presence in Panama after the April 1984 assassination of Colombian Minister of Justice Rodrigo Lara Bonilla.[78] Moreover, Noriega was constantly fighting off charges by opposition groups in Panama that he was involved in the drug trade. He saw the raid against the La Palma plant as a way to allay these charges, as well as to divert the DEA from investigating money laundering and other narcotics-related activities.[79]

The Medellín cartel felt betrayed by Noriega. At the time of this incident, cartel representatives were in Panama proposing to former Colombian president López Michelsen (1974–1978) that they would end their operations in exchange for an end to extradition. Noriega feared for his life.[80] Fortunately for him, Castro intervened by using his preestablished ties with the Medellín cartel. Castro chose to help Noriega because he feared that if "Noriega were replaced [or] eliminated," his own "illegal dealings in Panama" (his Central American and Colombian operations) would be terminated as well.[81]

Noriega flew to Cuba to meet personally with Castro. They agreed that Noriega would return the four million dollars to the Medellín cartel, along with the machinery and raw materials seized at the plant, and release the twenty-three men taken prisoner by the PDF. At the conclusion of this meeting, Noriega informed Blandón "that everything had been arranged and they were going to proceed according to Castro's approval."[82] However, Noriega still felt that his life was in danger, so Castro sent a twenty-five-soldier unit to fly back with him to ensure his safety until the terms of the deal were carried out.[83]

Some questions remain regarding the veracity of Blandón's testimony, because no one could corroborate his story and because he confused some of the dates he cited in his statements.[84] However, if the allegations made by Blandón were true, then clearly Castro used his connection with the Medellín cartel to advance his political agenda. His involvement with the Medellín cartel, the M-19, and Noriega meant that in one form or another, he was cooperating with reputed narcotics traffickers, making him guilty by association.

The Reagan administration's accusations against Castro's government did not end there. In 1988 the United States filed an indictment against seventeen of Castro's agents who were using Cuba as a transshipment station to smuggle cocaine from Colombia to Florida. The indictment charged that a ton of cocaine was moved through Cuba with the aid of Cuban military and government officials, who even provided a MiG fighter escort for the cargo plane carrying the narcotics.[85] On March 23, 1988, Major Florentino Aspillaga, Cuba's chief intelligence officer in Prague, defected to Austria. In Vienna, he testified that Cayo Largo, the island south of Cuba, had been used as a transshipment port for narcotics from South America to the United States since early 1978.

The case against General Arnaldo Ochoa and Colonel Antonio de la Guardia confirmed Cuba's role in the narcotics trade. On June 12, 1989, General Ochoa, Colonel de la Guardia, and twelve subordinates were rounded up and placed in jail. On the evening of June 15, Raúl Castro gave a rambling speech to discredit Ochoa, and on June 16, the government charged de la Guardia and Ochoa with corruption and drug trafficking in Cuba's Communist Party newspaper, *Granma*.[86]

Ochoa was a veteran of the Cuban revolution who had fought in the Sierra Maestra with Castro. He had also taken part in Cuba's military venture in Angola (1967–1969 and 1976) and the 1978 Ethiopian operation. In addition, Ochoa had served as a military advisor to the Sandinistas between 1985 and 1986, and completed another tour in Angola between 1987 and 1988.[87] De la Guardia was a commander of Cuba's Special Forces, part of the Ministry of the Interior's MC Department. The MC Department ran covert ventures to circumvent the U.S. embargo and to obtain hard currency for the Cuban government and the Ministry of the Interior's intelligence section, the DGI.[88] In particular, de la Guardia was in charge of smuggling medical and computer technology from Florida to Cuba.[89] He was also reported to have a close relationship with Castro's son.[90] For many in Cuba, it was hard to fathom that a national hero like Ochoa and a close associate of Castro like de la Guardia were involved in such nefarious activities.

The charges against both officials amounted to accusations of treason. Those against de la Guardia were more extensive than those against Ochoa. The government accused de la Guardia of smuggling six tons of Colombian cocaine, worth $3.4 million, through Cuba to the United States over roughly a two-year period that began in April 1987.[91] At his trial, de la Guardia testified that he had conducted nineteen different operations between 1987 and 1988.[92] In addition, de la Guardia was linked with two Cuban Americans, Reinaldo Ruiz and his son Ruben, who had been indicted and arrested in Miami for narcotics smuggling. At their trial in Miami, the father-and-son team confessed that they had worked with Cuban officials. They never specifically mentioned de la Guardia, but during his trial in Cuba, de la Guardia confirmed that he had been involved with the Ruiz family.[93]

Ochoa, who had not been involved with de la Guardia, was charged on three counts.[94] The first was neglect of his military duties and trading in the black market for ivory and diamonds for personal profit when he was in Angola. The second was the theft of $161,000 from the Nicaraguan army in a failed arms procurement deal attempted while he served as an advisor to Nicaragua. The third charge was for conspiring with Pablo Escobar to build coca refineries in Cuba in order to send cocaine shipments to the United States. Both Ochoa and de la Guardia faced potential death sentences, while the rest of the accused faced long prison terms.

Much of the evidence against Ochoa and de la Guardia was circumstantial; any allegations that implicated the Castro brothers or the Cuban government were blocked. Many of the accused believed that they had been acting on standing orders from the regime. An assistant of Ochoa's who was also on trial asserted that Ochoa became involved in the drug business because "he had discussed it at the highest levels."[95] De la Guardia told his brother, Patricio, that "smuggling narcotics had become an integral function [of] the DGI." When evidence identified Luben Petkoff as Ochoa's connection to Escobar, the government removed Petkoff's name from the public record, because Petkoff had a business association with Fidel Castro. Cuban authorities promptly dismissed all assertions against the government, and many people believed that Fidel and Raúl manipulated de la Guardia and Ochoa into admitting guilt by threatening their families' safety.[96]

The trial looked even more like the proceedings of a kangaroo court when it became known that one of the forty-seven presiding judges was Vice Admiral Aldo Santamaría Cuadrado, who was among the accused Cuban officials tried in absentia by the United States for narcotics trafficking in the Guillot Lara case.[97] It appeared as though justice was not the real motivation, and critics of Cuba alleged that Castro had a hidden agenda: the trial was a scheme to remove the Castro brothers' potential rivals and at the same time make them appear as if they were cooperating with the United States in the War on Drugs.

According to Huberto Matos, a prominent Cuban exile, Cuba held the trial to "demoralize and destroy the most valuable men in the army whom Castro [saw as] dangerous enemies because of their valor and influence in the military."[98] Ochoa had proven himself on the battlefield for thirty years. Intelligence officials believed that he openly questioned Castro's conduct of the war in Angola, a war that many Cuban military officers were also beginning to question. In addition, Ochoa had trained at the Frunze Military Academy in the USSR and appeared to favor détente and an economic liberalization platform. Castro, on the other hand, opposed détente with the United States and distanced himself from Gorbachev's *glasnost* (opening) and *perestroika* (liberalization) policies in the late 1980s.[99] For example, Castro abolished the free peasant markets in Cuba that were emerging in other communist countries, deriding them for creating liberal bourgeois tendencies.

Castro's refusal to withdraw from Angola and Nicaragua and his unwillingness to compromise his vision of socialism made Ochoa, the military hero, a potential threat to the Castro brothers' hold on power. By abandoning de la Guardia, Castro deflected preexisting accusations of high-level Cuban involvement in narcotics trafficking onto one or two corrupt elements within the Cuban government. On July 13, 1989, a firing squad executed Ochoa and de la Guardia.

The trial revelations and the perception that Cuba was coming clean led several members of the U.S. Congress, including Charles Rangel, chairman of the House Narcotics Committee, to discuss the possibility of renewing cooperation with the Castro government. Rangel chafed at the State Department's skepticism about these arrests and accused them of "playing anti-Communist politics," adding that "drugs, not Communists, were killing our kids."[100]

If this was a show trial, Castro had killed two birds with one stone. However, if he were actually coming clean, then he could no longer maintain his previous contention that "Cuba had an unimpeachable record on drugs."[101] Nevertheless, after the de la Guardia and Ochoa trials, Cuban authorities maintained that no evidence of narcotics-related corruption by government officials existed. When reports about Cuban officials' direct or indirect involvement in trafficking continued to surface, Cuba denied them, but speculation remained that narcotics were shipped through Cuba with Castro's personal approval.[102] Many U.S. government sources provided a long history of Cuban complicity in narcotics trafficking, although much of the evidence depended on the testimony of convicted drug dealers and intelligence agents who had defected from Cuba.

Irrespective of the continuing allegations, the existing evidence was enough for the Reagan administration to justify its belief that the narcotics explosion in the United States was part of a communist conspiracy to undermine America. Cumulative evidence against the Sandinista government in Nicaragua, a government the Reagan administration bitterly opposed, reinforced this conviction.

The Sandinistas and Central America

During the 1980s, the Sandinista government was accused of facilitating narco-trafficking. The Sandinistas were fighting a brutal civil war against the U.S.-financed Contra forces; allegedly they became involved in the narcotics industry to finance hemispheric revolution and to destabilize the West. According to Antonio Farach, a former minister and counselor to the Nicaraguan embassies in Venezuela and Honduras, the Sandinista government wanted to use drugs as a "political weapon [to] destroy the youth of their enemies," particularly those of the United States. Farach added that the drug trade's profitability was an additional justification since the Sandinistas needed money "for their revolution."[103] The Sandinistas were clients of Cuba, a fact that reinforced the notion of a communist conspiracy to destabilize the West by any means necessary, including the use of drugs.

In the mid-1980s, as the civil war in Nicaragua wore on and the Medellín cartel expanded its operations, hard evidence surfaced that pointed to Sandinista facilitation of narcotics trafficking. The first piece of evidence against Nicaragua appeared in 1983. Palacios Talavera, first secretary of the Nicaraguan embassy in Canada, was arrested for possessing cocaine with an estimated street value of ten thousand dollars. According to a Canadian police informant, Talavera was a part of a major drug ring that included Interior Minister Tomás Borge and other high-ranking Sandinistas. Canada deported Talavera and declared him persona non grata.[104] Talavera's operation, however, was just the tip of the iceberg. Allegations against the Sandinista government became ever deeper.

In his testimony to the U.S. Senate, Antonio Farach stated that the Cuban and Nicaraguan governments conspired to smuggle narcotics, implicating some of the highest members in both governments. Farach claimed that Cuba's minister of defense, Raúl Castro, visited Nicaragua in September 1981, where he met with his Nicaraguan counterpart Humberto Ortega, who was President Daniel Ortega's brother. Farach stated that he learned from unnamed sources that at this meeting, the Cuban government offered a "reasonable and a safe way" for the Nicaraguan government to engage in the narcotics business using Cuban "connections with international traffickers." Farach also testified that he was instructed to provide support and cover to men from guerrilla organizations, including the M-19 and the FARC, when they traveled in countries where Nicaraguan diplomatic officials resided. For Farach, this included following the orders of Cuban officials in charge of Nicaragua's Office of Immigration and Naturalization to provide passports to people who were not Nicaraguan citizens.[105] Although damaging, Farach's testimony on the Sandinistas' drug involvement was limited and inconclusive. Moreover, Farach's statements were criticized for containing secondhand hearsay information. Yet, shortly after, the most convincing evidence against the Sandinista government appeared.

In 1984, the same year that Farach shared evidence against the Sandinista government, an undercover CIA operation presented photographs showing that Federico Vaughan, an aide to Interior Minister Tomás Borge, had been working with the Medellín cartel to smuggle cocaine out of Nicaragua. The CIA obtained this information using Adler Berriman Seal (also known as Barry Seal), a former Green Beret turned drug runner and then DEA/CIA informer.

Around 1984, when the Colombian government was cracking down on the Medellín cartel, Pablo Escobar and Jorge Ochoa started operating out of Nicaragua.[106] Previously, Escobar had sent Floyd Carlton, a pilot for Noriega and the Medellín cartel, to Nicaragua to locate airstrips that could handle flights carrying cocaine paste from Bolivia to Nicaragua.[107] According to Seal, the Medellín organization also sought to move its cocaine-processing laboratories to Nicaragua, and the Sandinista government was helping the cartel develop an airfield and hangar.[108] To manage this operation, Vaughn gave the cartel access to Los Brasiles Airport, a military airfield northwest of Managua.[109]

The sting operation to set up Vaughn was a complicated process by which Seal lured Vaughn and Escobar into exposing their operation in Nicaragua. The DEA had captured Seal in February 1984 for smuggling cocaine into the United States by air, but the cartel did not know this. To escape jail time, Seal, released on bond, went to Vice President Bush's office and told members of Bush's South Florida Task Force what he knew. He then became an undercover informant for the DEA and CIA, although it is alleged that Seal had been secretly transporting weapons from Mena, Arkansas to CIA operatives in Central America since 1982, and that he had been smuggling cocaine for the Medellín cartel on his return trips back to the United States.[110] To provide intelligence for the DEA and CIA, Seal went undercover and renewed his former business association with Carlos Bustamante, a smuggler for the Medellín cartel. The cartel flew Seal to Managua, where he met with Vaughn, who told Seal how the cartel expected the Los Brasiles operation to work.

On May 20, 1984, Seal rendezvoused with Carlos Lehder and picked up a load of cocaine in Colombia; but the plane Seal was flying was overloaded, and it crashed. The next day the cartel outfitted Seal with a new plane that he flew to Los Brasiles to refuel. After refueling and taking off, Seal flew off course and was hit by anti-aircraft fire coming from an oil refinery near the airport. Forced to make a crash landing, Seal had to leave the cocaine behind.[111] Vaughn promised to protect the cargo, and the cartel sent Seal to the United States to acquire a new plane.

These circumstances presented the DEA and the CIA with an opportunity to devise a plan that would confirm the Sandinistas' involvement with the Medellín cartel and narcotics smuggling. With DEA and CIA help, Seal purchased a C-123, which they outfitted with special cameras to film the drugs being loaded onto the plane. On June 24, 1984, Seal landed at Los Brasiles, unloaded some electronic equipment, and handed over $450,000 in cash to pay off Nicaraguan workers at the airfield. The camera filmed Escobar and Vaughn at Los Brasiles putting the cocaine on the plane.[112] Seal then flew back to the United States, where he turned over the cocaine to the DEA. He flew to Nicaragua one more time, carrying precursor chemicals for a new cocaine laboratory and $1.5 million to pay Escobar and Vaughn. When Seal arrived, Vaughn told him that the new cocaine processing laboratory was ready for use; the conversation was taped.[113]

News of this sting soon became public. The Reagan administration had a vote on Contra funding coming up, and they likely released this information to influence Congress.[114] The Sandinista government denied the accusations and claimed that Vaughn had not worked for the Sandinista government for at least two years prior to the sting, although they admitted that he had at one point worked for Borge and the Interior Ministry. The Sandinistas also claimed that this was a black propaganda operation run by the CIA to defame Sandinista political figures.[115]

Even if some doubt surrounded the photos of Vaughn and Escobar, the Robert Vesco case provided more evidence connecting Frederico Vaughn and the Nicaraguan government with the drug industry. The Robert Vesco case stemmed from testimony presented by James Herring, a former narcotics trafficker, who voluntarily came forward to work as a U.S. government operative in 1983.[116] Herring reported that he had worked with Cuban government officials and Robert Vesco, a known narcotics trafficker, to help the Nicaraguan government build a cocaine processing laboratory near Managua.[117] Herring had met Vesco through Jitze Kooistra, a fugitive drug dealer from Europe. Kooistra was a client of Herring's business (Everything Goes, Inc.), which procured hard-to-find items. Herring's usefulness to Kooistra led Kooistra to introduce Herring to Vesco. Herring slowly developed an association with Vesco, who eventually brought him to Nicaragua. On his first trip to Nicaragua, Herring met Vaughn, who asked him for advice about developing a cocaine-cutting lab.[118] Herring then made several additional trips to Nicaragua to provide assistance and equipment to Vaughn and Vesco.

Herring testified that an unnamed Colombian guerrilla organization brought cocaine directly to Vaughn, who used diplomatic immunity to transport money and the drugs. According to Herring, Vesco supplied "the money to purchase" the cocaine, and the Sandinistas provided "the security in the form of gun carrying soldiers." Vesco, Kooistra, and Vaughn divided the proceeds from the sale. Herring quoted Vaughn as saying that the money that the "Nicaraguans were getting out of this sale" of cocaine would "go back into their economy." Moreover, Herring was introduced to Tomás Borge who told Herring, "[W]e appreciate your help." In the same hearing against Vesco, another witness with the code name Dekker testified that Nicaragua used drug profits to generate hard currency.[119]

In addition to helping with the cocaine smuggling operation, Herring made repeated trips to Cuba from Florida for Vesco. He sailed to Cuba carrying high-tech equipment, guns, radios, and various things that Vesco needed. Herring's involvement with Vesco was "no longer just a drug operation." He became concerned that the contraband he was carrying could be "utilized against the United States." Herring stated at the end of his testimony that "at all times he was escorted and treated very well by dignitaries from both governments."[120] If Herring's testimony was true, it constituted major evidence against the Nicaraguan and Cuban governments. He passed a polygraph test. Any denial that narcotics trafficking occurred inside Nicaragua at this time seemed doubtful.

The testimony of José Baldizón provided the last bit of evidence that the Reagan administration needed to accuse top officials in the Sandinista government of being narco-communists. José Baldizón was a Nicaraguan lieutenant, serving as chief of the special investigations commission run by Tomás Borge in the Ministry of the Interior. Baldizón defected to the United States from Nicaragua in 1985, when he provided information that implicated Borge and the Ministry of the Interior. In 1982 the ministry had ordered Baldizón to send all "cocaine, U.S. dollars, and precious metals seized by the police" to them.[121] This aroused Baldizón's suspicions about Nicaragua's involvement in narcotics trafficking, but he viewed them as hearsay.

Baldizón reported in 1983 that a woman named Jacqueline Lyons Pastora was arrested by Nicaraguan customs agents for possession of four ounces of cocaine. Pastora claimed that she worked for the Nicaraguan government, and that was why, she explained, she had the cocaine. According to Baldizón, Borge ordered Pastora to be freed. Baldizón looked into the charges against Pastora and discovered that she was part of a Managua-to-Miami cocaine smuggling ring that included the Nicaraguan minister of transportation, Carlos Zarruk, and the head of the Nicaraguan Air Force, Raúl Venerio. Baldizón also learned that a domestic network, following Borge's orders, sold drugs and received money from corrupt diplomats in Nicaragua, including representatives from France, Spain, and Venezuela and a U.S. Marine working at the U.S. embassy.[122]

Baldizón forwarded his investigation to Borge, who sent him a strong reprimand. Borge then issued an order to send any further cocaine-related investigations to his office. Baldizón stated that in 1984 Borge's office directed him to investigate Second Lieutenant David Miranda, head of information and analysis at the Ministry of the Interior. Miranda's reputed crime was leaking state secrets. Miranda had told friends that Borge was involved in cocaine trafficking with the Colombian Mafia, and Baldizón was expected to find out how Miranda had obtained this information. Baldizón claimed that he was shocked when he learned that the investigation was a tacit admission that the Nicaraguan government was involved in narcotics trafficking. When Baldizón expressed his concern, Borge's assistant, Captain Franco Montealegre, told him that the government of Nicaragua was indeed engaged in cocaine trafficking—but only to "obtain dollars needed to finance espionage activities [and] operational expenses" for the Ministry of the Interior (MININT). Baldizón accepted this explanation and claimed that he was not disillusioned with the Nicaraguan revolution. However, according to his testimony, doubts about his loyalty to the revolution grew after he received this admission. [123]

At a 1984 luncheon that included members of the Cuban MININT and a Cuban military advisor, Baldizón was given further justification for the revolution's use of narcotics. A member of the MININT, Commander Omar Cabezas, declared that the United States was going to destroy itself "from within by ideological differences and by the drug traffic." Moreover, drug trafficking served three functions: (1) it damaged America's future generations by corrupting its youth; (2) income from drug sales to America's youth would finance liberation movements; and (3) the cocaine networks transferred weapons to the leftist liberation movements. That same year Baldizón learned of an instance in which Borge personally removed "two large bags containing drugs" after anti-aircraft artillery at the Los Brasiles airport attacked a "Colombian mafia" plane.[124] Clearly, Baldizón's testimony referred to the Barry Seal operation. In the end, Baldizón became disenchanted with the Sandinista leadership, and he defected. Baldizón's testimony presented a convincing and a credible case against the Nicaraguan government.

The evidence provided by all of the congressional witnesses incriminated Nicaragua's Ministry of the Interior and further incriminated Cuba. Although not much of the evidence pointed directly at Castro or Ortega, it showed that many people around them were involved in narcotics smuggling.

Overall, the main motivation for narcotics smuggling in these countries appeared twofold. First, government officials wanted to destabilize the United States by facilitating the availability of drugs; and second, members of the intelligence services needed ways to finance revolution throughout the Western Hemisphere as well as the war against the Contras in Nicaragua. Cocaine provided a simple solution to money problems. Drug dealing retained no ideological boundaries, which created a complex situation for the United States. Although it seemed clear that the Cubans and Nicaraguans were engaged in the drug trade, the Sandinistas' opponents, the Contras, also took advantage of the narcotics trade to finance their counterrevolution.

The Contras

The Contras were a counterrevolutionary organization backed by the CIA. They emerged in response to the imposition of an authoritarian Marxist government by the Sandinistas, who took control of Nicaragua in 1979 after defeating the dictator, Anastasio Somoza Debayle. The Contras were composed of *Somocistas* (supporters of the former dictator), members of the private business sector, leading church officials, conservative Catholics, elements of the farming and peasant community, Miskito Indians, and disillusioned Sandinistas, who felt that the principles of the revolution had been betrayed. They operated within Nicaragua and from bases in Honduras and Costa Rica.

The Reagan administration began providing aid to the Contra rebels in late 1981. Reagan and his advisors believed that the Sandinistas were turning Nicaragua into another Cuba and supporting communist guerrillas throughout Central America. Reagan reasoned that "the national security of all of the Americas was at stake . . . [I]f we cannot defend ourselves there, we cannot expect to prevail elsewhere . . . and the safety of our homeland would be put at jeopardy."[125] Reagan decided that the best way to defeat the Sandinistas was to support a CIA plan to back the Contras. In National Security Decision Directive 17, Reagan requested nineteen million dollars from Congress for the Contras to stop the flow of arms from Cuba and Nicaragua to the rest of Central America, particularly El Salvador.

However, the development of Contra forces soon took on a broader purpose, for they directly challenged the Sandinista government. Reagan defended this policy, arguing that "if the Soviet Union can aid and abet subversion in our hemisphere, then the United States has a legal right and a moral duty to help resist it."[126] Reagan's determination to help the Contras became one of the main themes of U.S. foreign policy throughout his presidency. His administration believed that "continuous pressure on the Sandinista leadership via the Contras [was] an essential element of U.S. strategy for establishing the democratic process in Nicaragua and for countering Soviet/Cuban strategy in the Western Hemisphere."[127]

Many of Reagan's critics charged that he was seeking a military solution in Central America and that he was creating another Vietnam. Reagan flatly denied these accusations, maintaining that "we have no intention of that kind of involvement."[128] Reagan's Contra strategy incited a tremendous uproar in Congress.[129] His critics there charged Reagan with supporting the overthrow of an internationally recognized and democratically elected government. When certain Democratic members of the House of Representatives heard about U.S.-Contra activities, they sought to limit U.S. support. In December 1982, Edward Boland, chairperson of the House Intelligence Committee, offered an amendment to replace a proposal made by Tom Harkin to end all aid to the Contras. Boland's amendment allowed funds to go to the Contras, but prohibited the CIA's use of funds "for the purpose of overthrowing the government of Nicaragua."[130]

The growing rift between the Reagan administration and Congress over the Contras' anti-Sandinista activities decreased the amount of aid flowing into the Contras' coffers: Congress set a cap of twenty-four million dollars for Contra funding. In October 1984, Congress set a moratorium on all direct or indirect aid to the Contras from any U.S. intelligence agency. As a result, elements within the Contra organization began to look for alternative means to fund their revolution, while the Reagan administration set up private covert networks to assist them.

The first real accusations against the Contras for narcotics smuggling emerged in 1986. Senator John Kerry began to investigate reports that the Honduran arm of the Contra movement, the Fuerza Democratica Nicaragüense (FDN), had been involved in gunrunning, drug trafficking, and terrorist activity. The head of the FDN, Adolfo Calero, denied these allegations, stating that there was "not one single element of truth to them." [131] Kerry's investigation came at a time when questions were arising about the Contras' effectiveness. The FDN was considered corrupt and full of former Somocistas who were unable to mobilize the Nicaraguans against the Sandinistas. [132] In 1984 the CIA wanted to unite the FDN with the Alianza Revolucionaria Democratica (ARDE) fighting on the Costa Rican border, but ARDE leaders—notably the former Sandinista Edén Pastora—refused, citing the presence of too many former national guardsmen commanding the FDN.

After the ARDE's rejection of the FDN in 1984 and the consequent CIA threat to cut off their aid, the ARDE broke up and many members joined the FDN. The remains of the ARDE, led by Pastora, experienced financial difficulties for their counterrevolution, which caused them to turn to drug trafficking. Consequently, in the midst of Kerry's investigation, Costa Rican security forces arrested a member of the ARDE, known as Adolfo "Popo" Chamorro, for smuggling cocaine. [133] Chamorro was the ARDE's second in command. This event undermined the Reagan administration's effort to renew funding for all Contra forces. According to an ARDE officer, drug traffickers approached "political groups like ARDE trying to make deals that would somehow camouflage or cover up their activities." The ARDE's operational mode was to use pilots to ferry weapons from the United States to northern Costa Rica, exchange the weapons for narcotics, and send the narcotics to the United States. [134] Thus, the lack of funds resulting from the splintering of the ARDE led to its participation in a guns-for-drugs program and the eventual capture of Chamorro.

Senator Kerry's investigation into the FDN Contras did not turn up any "substantial or credible evidence" against Contra leaders.[135] In 1986, as the Contra movement grew, the FDN re-formed itself into the United Nicaraguan Opposition (UNO), which included former ARDE members. Reagan officials declared that the people involved in drug trafficking were members of a "discredited faction" (the ARDE) and not the leadership of the main rebel alliance.[136] Thus, when the Justice Department reported on its inquiry into allegations against the Contras, it stated that "individual members of the Contras may have engaged in such activities, but it was, in so far as [they could] determine, without the authorization of resistance leaders."[137] Nevertheless, critics of the Contras such as Senator Kerry urged that Congress continue investigating Contra activities.

In 1986, Sandinista forces shot down a C-123 cargo plane piloted by CIA operative Eugene Hasenfus. Hasenfus confessed that he worked for the CIA and was secretly delivering military supplies to the Contras.[138] At the same time, a Lebanese newspaper reported that the United States had been conducting secret arms deals with Iran. By selling weapons to Iran, the United States was supposedly trying to improve its negotiating position with Hezbollah, the Lebanese guerrilla organization. Iran supported Hezbollah, which was holding U.S. hostages in Lebanon.[139] While probing the question of the arms-for-hostages deal, Attorney General Edwin Meese discovered that only twelve million of the thirty million dollars the Iranians reportedly paid had reached government coffers. Thus, Hasenfus's capture and the reports of U.S. arms sales to Iran led directly to the Iran-Contra investigation.

The investigators learned that the CIA had set up the Iran-Contra operation to fund and supply the Contras through weapons sales to Iran between 1984 and 1986, when the ban to limit all military equipment for the Contras was in effect. National Security Council member Lieutenant Colonel Oliver North explained that he had diverted funds from the Iranian arms sales to the Contras with the full knowledge of National Security Adviser Admiral John Poindexter and with the tacit approval of President Reagan.

The information provided by the Iran-Contra investigation led Senator Kerry to reopen his inquiry into drug trafficking charges against the Contra leadership and the CIA's role in helping them finance their counterrevolution. Kerry's investigation alleged that the Contra supply network had developed a connection with the Medellín cartel, which had funneled nearly ten million dollars in seed money to the Contras between

1983 and 1985 to curry favor with the CIA.[140] Richard Brenneke, an arms dealer and former CIA/Mossad agent with a questionable reputation, corroborated the information. He reported that the Medellín cartel initially put up the money to fund the private Contra arms network.[141] The cartel's accountant, Ramon Milian Rodríguez, passed this money to Felix Rodríguez, a CIA Contra supply officer who directed operations from Ilopango Air Force Base in El Salvador.[142] Donald Gregg, Vice President Bush's national security aide and the "Washington contact" for the Contras' arms network, supposedly oversaw the fundraising actions for the Contras.[143] Gregg was a close associate of both Felix Rodríguez and retired Air Force General Richard Secord, a corporate officer for Corporate Air Services.[144]

Corporate Air Services was a subsidiary of Southern Air Transport, a Miami firm once owned by the CIA.[145] Corporate Air Services had contracted with Southern Air Transport for the plane flown by Hasenfus when he was shot down over Nicaragua.[146] The investigation into the Iran-Contra scandal revealed that the Corporate Air–Southern Air network operated out of Ilopango Air Force Base in El Salvador and ran guns to the Contras in Honduras, Nicaragua, and Costa Rica. Drugs were reputedly loaded onto the planes on their return flights to Ilopango from Contra bases, where the drugs were stored and then shipped back to the United States.[147] Unnamed sources from the Customs Bureau contended that the CIA planes took off and landed at U.S. airports without undergoing customs inspections.[148]

As the Kerry inquiry continued, investigators learned that General Secord, the corporate officer for Corporate Air Services, had worked directly with Oliver North on Project Democracy, the CIA-directed private Contra-supply operation that had employed Felix Rodríguez—the CIA Contra-supply officer who had allegedly received ten million dollars in start-up money from the Medellín cartel.[149] It turned out that the World Anti-Communist League, directed by General John Singlaub, also used Corporate Air Services/Southern Air Transport, employing them to run supplies out of Miami for Contra forces in Nicaragua.[150] Both Secord and Singlaub had been implicated in the Nugan Hand Bank scandal in 1980. This scandal alleged that the CIA had used the bank to launder profits from heroin sales in the Golden Triangle with its Air America operation, which had supported covert activities in Laos.[151] Hasenfus stated that when the CIA hired him, they told him that the Corporate Air Services/Southern Air Transportation operation would be run "just like Air-America."[152]

As the Kerry investigation probed deeper, it uncovered that the CIA and the Contras had utilized other front companies to run drugs-for-guns operations.[153] Between 1983 and 1985, the Honduran Contras (the FDN) and the CIA employed Servicios Ejecutivos Turistas Commander (SETCO), a Honduran airline run by known cocaine smuggler Juan Ramón Matta Ballesteros, to transport supplies.[154] In 1985 the CIA replaced SETCO due to mounting public allegations that Matta Ballesteros was a narcotics trafficker. As a result, a former SETCO pilot and CIA operative named Frank Moss formed his own air-supply company, called Hondu Carib, to supply the Contras.[155] However, Hondu Carib was implicated in a drugs-for-guns operation, as were two CIA officers whose names and telephone numbers were included in papers confiscated by the DEA when they seized a drug-running plane owned by Hondu Carib in 1987.[156] Further evidence of a Contra-CIA drug link with Hondu Carib came from Oliver North's diary. In the diary, North speculated that Mario Calero, the FDN's supply officer and brother of Contra leader Adolfo Calero, had worked with Frank Moss to smuggle narcotics on a DC-6 supply plane that operated out of Honduras and New Orleans.[157] Oliver North also wrote in his diary that General Secord had told him that a cache of weapons worth fourteen million dollars stored in a Honduran warehouse for Contra use "came from drugs"; Hondu Carib had supposedly transported them for an arms firm called RM Equipment.[158]

Other informants in the Kerry inquiry stated that CIA and other U.S. officials helped the Contras run the drugs-for-guns operation from Costa Rica.[159] One of the convicted smugglers who testified before Congress, Gary Betzner, testified that he flew Contra weapons and drugs from the ranch of John Hull in northern Costa Rica. Hull was a reputed CIA asset and confederate of Oliver North.[160] Although Hull admitted to taking money from the CIA, he denied that he was an agent.[161] Nevertheless, Betzner stated that he had made several trips to Hull's ranch to exchange weapons from Florida or Ilopango Air Force Base in El Salvador for drugs that came from Colombia and Panama. Betzner transported the drugs back to Ilopango Air Force Base or directly to Florida, using CIA cover. He stated that he did this with the "full knowledge and assistance of the DEA and the CIA."[162]

The CIA denied these accusations and sought to discredit the witnesses who provided information against them. CIA spokesperson Sharon Foster called the allegations absurd. She added that if anyone in the CIA was "found to be involved in drug trafficking," the CIA fired that person, and the relevant information was "turned over to the appropriate law enforcement organization."[163] Vice President Bush's office dismissed the claims against Gregg as "just rumors, the same old regurgitated stories we thought we'd put to rest long ago."[164] William Yout, from the DEA, stated that "these individuals" who claimed CIA and DEA complicity in drug trafficking were selling a story to Congress and the media "to have their sentences reduced or to have their cases dismissed." According to members of the U.S. attorney's office in Miami, the allegations presented by Kerry Commission witnesses were the normal tactics of Miami cocaine traffickers, who commonly used an "I was working for the CIA" defense. [165]

Ironically, the government readily accepted accusations against Cuba and Nicaragua by convicted drug dealers and other nefarious characters. But when evidence from similar or the same sources put the Reagan administration and U.S. intelligence agencies on the hot seat, it was not considered credible. Although the Kerry Commission believed its witnesses were truthful and went out of its way to ascertain the veracity of their statements, the systematic effort to discredit those witnesses was enough to raise doubts about the CIA's role in drug trafficking.

At the end of his investigation in 1989, Senator Kerry's conclusions severely criticized the Reagan administration, but they did not provide conclusive proof that high-level Contra leaders or CIA operatives were engaged in narcotics trafficking. Kerry's report stated that the Reagan administration undercut law enforcement efforts against the Medellín cartel at a time when it was becoming the most dangerous criminal enterprise in U.S. history.[166] The Kerry report also concluded that foreign policy priorities in Nicaragua and Panama at times delayed, halted, or interfered with U.S. law enforcement efforts to keep narcotics out of the United States. In particular, U.S. officials involved in Central America failed to address the drug issue for fear of jeopardizing the war effort against Nicaragua. The lack of effort to address this problem weakened an already inadequate law enforcement capability in the region, which a variety of mercenaries, pilots, and others involved in the drug trade easily exploited. Finally, the Kerry report concluded that, though there was substantial evidence of drug smuggling through the war zones by individual Contras, as well as Contra suppliers, pilots, and supporters, none of the Contra leadership was personally involved in drug trafficking. [167]

The Kerry Report did not end the allegations against the CIA and the Contras. In 1989, as a result of the Huanchaca case, the CIA was accused of running its own HCL production facility in Bolivia to finance the Contras. Spanish biologist Vicente Castelló was the only survivor of a scientific team that was murdered after it discovered a coca processing center and an airfield in the jungle in Huanchaca. During its investigation, the Bolivian government contended that the CIA ran the processing center to generate money for the Contras and that Oliver North had visited this region several times.[168] The situation heated up further when Roberto Suárez Levy, son of Bolivian kingpin Roberto Suárez—in hiding since his father's capture in 1988—told the press that an unnamed minister of information for García Meza had proposed the CIA's plan to the Suárez cartel. Suárez Levy stated that the CIA had offered to provide protection for the distribution of cocaine from Huanchaca so that it could generate revenue to purchase arms for the Contras. Moreover, Suárez Levy reported that the CIA had asked Manuel Noriega to channel the operation through Panama.[169]

In the end, Washington blocked the inquiry, declaring that it would not allow an investigation of U.S. government employees involved in either the Huanchaca case or narcotics trafficking through Bolivia.[170] No definitive proof about this case has ever been found; the Huanchaca case remains one of the unresolved mysteries surrounding the Contras and the CIA.

Allegations against the CIA and the FDN resurfaced in 1996, when reporter Gary Webb released his "Dark Alliance" series in the *San Jose Mercury News*. Webb reported that a high-ranking FDN leader Oscar Danilo Blandon Reyes testified for the U.S. Department of Justice, that he sold cocaine to a Los Angeles drug dealer named Ricky Donnell Ross, also known as "Freeway Rick." According to Webb, this operation initiated the crack cocaine boom in Los Angeles. Blandon testified that the profits from the operation were for "the Contra revolution" and that he took orders from Juan Norwin Meneses Cantarero, a previously convicted drug dealer, who was a known associate of Adolfo Calero, the head of the FDN and UNO. Webb's attempts to delve deeper into the case were blocked, and federal prosecutors obtained a court order preventing defense lawyers from delving into Cantarero's ties with the CIA.[171] Moreover, Webb's story was quickly discredited for failing to provide any substantial proof of a CIA link.[172] In response to the allegations brought up by Webb's story, the CIA's inspector general's office conducted its own internal investigation, which concluded that there was "no information to indicate that the CIA coordinated or condoned drug trafficking."

A Summary of Cuban, Nicaraguan, and Contra Involvement in Drug Trafficking

If narcotics smuggling was indeed an official policy of Nicaragua, Cuba, or the Contra leadership, no one was able to prove it conclusively. Much of the evidence against the Cuban and Nicaraguan governments and the Contras rested on allegations and speculation; nothing confirmed beyond doubt that they condoned or were involved in narcotics operations. However, if the same standards of evidence used against Cuba and Nicaragua were applied to the United States, both President Nixon and CIA Director Richard Helms could be accused of approving the CIA-directed Air America operation that smuggled heroin to pay for the Hmong insurgency in Laos. Moreover, if the logic that linked Castro to the M-19 were utilized, the assertions that the Contras smuggled cocaine or ran HCL production facilities would have meant that Ronald Reagan, who directed the War on Drugs, also had a national policy to support a guerrilla organization covertly through drug sales.

In many respects, the accusations against the Cuban, Nicaraguan, and Contra-CIA leadership reflect those made against the governments of Bolivia, Peru, and Colombia for officially condoning money laundering. Nevertheless, elements in both the Cuban and Nicaraguan governments, as well as in the Contra-CIA leadership, were linked to narcotics traffickers, and narco-dollars directly influenced the northern Andean governments' macroeconomic policies.

Substantial proof exists that certain members of the Cuban and Nicaraguan intelligence services, as well as the CIA, ran operations that served each nation's covert political aims. Evidence shows that some Cuban and Nicaraguan intelligence officers trafficked cocaine to undermine the United States and finance revolution. The intentions of these intelligence networks clearly presented a national security threat to the United States. Yet evidence also confirms that some members of the Contras, and possibly U.S. government officials, used drugs to finance counterrevolution at a time when funding for the Contra cause was scarce. Although drug trafficking served varied purposes for each country and organization, it provided an easy source of revenue for all.

To prevent public exposure, the governments employed plausible deniability to prevent confirmation of any evidence that these operations were matters of national policy. David L. Westrate, the deputy assistant administrator of the DEA in 1985, reported that when the Reagan administration requested information regarding Sandinista involvement in narcotics, he had told them that if he shared this information, "both the good guys and the bad guys were going to get splashed equally."[174] This is exactly what happened as covert operations to prosecute the civil wars in Central America and finance revolution in South America were exposed.

Government responses to the revelations about the smuggling operations took different directions. To give the impression that they were not rogue nations that trafficked in narcotics, both the United States and Cuba found scapegoats. However, their approach to exposing drug-related crimes highlighted the differences between a communist authoritarian state and a bureaucratic capitalist democracy. In Cuba, Ochoa and de la Guardia had questionable trials and were shot for treason. In the United States, Senator Kerry's congressional investigation consisted of a deep and lengthy inquiry. The investigation presented substantial evidence against the Contras, and possibly against members of the U.S. intelligence services as well, but not enough to prove a conspiracy. In the end, regardless of who was involved in the smuggling operations in Central America and the Caribbean, the allegations against Cuba and Nicaragua remained the principal explanation for the Reagan administration's belief in a narco-communist nexus. This belief became the basis for the policy formula they employed against guerrilla insurgencies in Colombia and Peru.

5

Northern Andean Guerrillas, Drug Trafficking, and Cold War Politics

The United States recognized that turmoil in South America, both socio-economic and political, prolonged "existing patterns of insurgency [that] assumed terrorist dimensions."[1] Prior to 1980, South American guerrillas had depended on "bank robberies, kidnap for ransom, and similar crimes for the money needed to buy weapons and sustain operations." By the early 1980s, narcotics began to serve that purpose. Secretary of State George Shultz considered this a "modern form of piracy" because "money from drug smuggling supported terrorists [while] terrorists provided assistance to drug traffickers."[2] In Colombia and Peru, this was most definitely true, although many Andean experts believed that the relationship between traffickers and guerrillas was primarily opportunistic rather than ideological.[3] Social crises and the consequent coca boom in both countries opened the door for guerrillas to use narcotics as a means to fuel their uprisings.

As the 1980s wore on, evidence that guerrillas were cooperating with drug traffickers became incontrovertible. Narcotics profits made it possible for northern Andean guerrillas to create serious challenges for the governments they opposed. For the Reagan administration, the possibility that other nations in the Western Hemisphere might join the ranks of Cuba and Nicaragua, because they could not defend themselves against narcotics-financed Marxist insurgencies, was a danger too great to ignore.

However, U.S. counternarcotics efforts only deepened guerrilla involvement in narcotics production and trafficking. U.S. policymakers chose to emphasize military force to defeat the guerrillas and narcotics traffickers simultaneously. The decision to attack guerrillas and traffickers at the same time strengthened the bond between the guerrillas and campesino coca growers. The U.S. government's conflation of the guerrillas with the drug industry, its increasingly militaristic antinarcotics policy, and its inability to grapple with the economic side of the drug equation developed into a dangerous situation for the northern Andes.

Colombian Guerrillas

As early as 1979, the Colombian government vehemently asserted that Colombian guerrillas were trafficking in narcotics. In 1980 the U.S. embassy in Bogotá began debating whether the FARC and the ELN were "dealing marijuana to obtain weapons."[4] Evidence from FARC deserters indicated that the organization either "grew its own marijuana" on the land it controlled or that it exempted local farmers from "periodic extortion payments in return for their promise to cultivate marijuana." According to other reports, the guerrillas traded "harvested marijuana to local drug traffickers in exchange for weapons." The U.S. embassy believed that the FARC dealt only in marijuana. Colombian government officials, however, thought that FARC units in Cauca, Antioquia, and parts of southern Colombia had an agreement with narcotics traffickers to prohibit the destruction of coca "in exchange for payment of tribute, either in cash or weapons."[5]

In 1981 President Turbay publicly stated that "guerrillas were helping to transport drugs." Turbay described this as the "most dangerous aspect of narcotics trafficking" because the "druggers and the subversives challenged" Colombia's democratic institutions. The government saw both groups testing its ability to maintain political stability; thus, it was politically beneficial for the government to present the two groups as one by linking narcotics with Marxist guerrillas.

In 1981 the U.S. embassy in Bogotá was still unaware of any "hard evidence" of a narco-FARC connection.[6] U.S. embassy analysts in Bogotá did not see any clear sign that the FARC's leaders were "promoting the involvement of its adherents with narcotics traffickers, whose long term goals" differed "significantly from those of the subversive groups." The main distinction between the Colombian Mafia and the guerrillas was that the traffickers preferred "to cozy up to the government," while the guerrillas sought to overthrow it. To further illustrate the long-term divisions between guerrillas and traffickers, the embassy report stated that "some subversive organizations . . . denounced the involvement of corrupt" Colombian officials who were involved in the drug trade but who publicly maintained "a puritanical attitude towards such issues as narcotics."[7]

However, the Colombian Mafia felt "no compunction about using the FARC to harass the military" and deflect government attention. The Mafia also worked with the guerrillas to "prevent the subversives from moving in on *traditional* mafia-controlled areas." The FARC, on the other hand, collaborated with the Colombian Mafia to obtain weapons to help achieve the "eventual realization of its political aims." In the end, embassy analysts concluded that "direct contact between the traffickers and the guerrillas [was] almost inevitable."[8]

As a narc-FARC relationship solidified and the War on Drugs intensified in Colombia, the lingering civil war between the Colombian government and guerrilla organizations increasingly alienated campesinos. At the turn of the decade, the U.S. embassy in Colombia noted that the FARC's "efforts to enlist campesinos" in areas such as Antioquia had failed partly because the campesinos were "enjoying the good life" from marijuana profits.[9] Embassy officials felt that if a "recession in the marijuana industry" occurred, the campesinos might open up to the FARC.

According to an article sanctioned by the FARC, their Marxist-Leninist strategy was designed to help the campesinos find a means to survive. This strategy included regulating coca production in their zones of control, while looking for alternative development possibilities.[10] Notably, in the rural areas that they dominated, the FARC and the M-19 were "providing protection to the campesino *coqueros'* fields in exchange for cash contributions."[11]

The U.S. embassy in Bogotá observed that, although the Colombian army was "winning the military fight," the insurgents were "winning the battle for the hearts and minds of the populace." Since southern and eastern Colombia were so sparsely populated, the government had made "little effort to integrate" the rural population into the "social and economic life of the country."[12] The campesinos had "no real prospects before them." Profits from narcotics production, along with the protection offered by the guerrillas, created a marriage of convenience between coca-growing campesinos and guerrillas.

Up to that point, Colombian guerrillas had not had any real ideological reason to engage in the drug trade. The allegations of a narco-terrorist nexus seemed hard to sustain because the guerrillas' long-term objectives differed from those of the traffickers. Even President Turbay admitted that the guerrillas had not turned to narcotics *production* to finance their operations.[13] Instead, they protected narcotics producers and associated with traffickers as a practical way to finance their revolution. Conversely, the economically marginalized campesinos cultivated narcotics in order to live.[14]

The United States placed so much emphasis on narcotics control in Colombia in the early 1980s that its policy actually strengthened ties between guerrillas and campesinos.[15] The U.S. counternarcotics policy also exacerbated the country's civil war because it failed to address the campesinos' economic desperation. Colombia's long-standing economic and political problems left its remote areas ripe for revolution. The government had to confront the growing power of the narcotics traffickers, as well as the guerrillas, or face the collapse of its central authority. As the United States pressed Colombia to do more about the drug trade, the government began to lose control of the campesinos, who were directly affected by both the government's civil war with the guerrillas and its antinarcotics campaign. Within a few years, the interlocking of Colombia's civil war with the War on Drugs had become almost complete.

After U.S. Ambassador Lewis Tambs arrived in Colombia to confront the perceived narco-guerrilla nexus, more evidence began to turn up against the guerrillas. In 1983 the U.S. embassy in Bogotá stated that the "coca boom in the llanos created . . . something of a bonanza for the guerrillas." The embassy reported that subversives benefited in two important ways: first, they "generated considerable revenue for their war chests by taxing the coca industry," and second, they successfully recruited "transient laborers attracted to the coca zones." Guerrilla patrols were able to move freely in the coca-growing regions as the Colombian government's authority waned. The taxes that guerrillas placed on narcotics cultivation did not hurt campesinos because their profits were "still sufficiently high." Moreover, the campesino coca growers could "hardly turn towards the authorities for protection," unless they desired to jeopardize their livelihood.[16] The benefit that the coca growers received from the guerrillas was clearly protection.

Emerging volatility in southern and eastern Colombia, marked by the "twin incentives of increased revenues and recruitment," clearly drove up the number of subversives and their degree of preparation. Reporters who visited a FARC camp observed that the rebels increasingly appeared armed with "modern light infantry weapons, mortars, and rockets." The U.S. embassy believed that drug money was "probably being used to finance some" of those purchases.[17] Guerrillas such as the FARC increasingly controlled strategic points of entry into Colombia's interior, which rendered law enforcement in those regions ineffective and freed both guerrillas and traffickers to operate with impunity.

Narcotics were clearly expanding Colombia's civil war. The situation demanded a plan that separated the guerrilla insurgency from its base of support, but this was not forthcoming. The region required substantial economic investment through USAID to encourage campesinos and transient workers to stop growing narcotics. The Colombian government also needed to address its own macroeconomic activities, including high tariffs and the ventanilla siniestra, which encouraged narcotics trafficking. In addition, the government needed to make a serious attempt to establish a lasting peace with the guerrillas rather than initiate a dirty war disguised as a truce. To move the guerrillas away from armed insurgency, this peace would have to be devoid of the Cold War's polarizing ideologies and reflective of Colombia's political reality. Instead, U.S. and Colombian counternarcotics activities focused increasingly on the idea of an "unholy" alliance and expanded military operations against the narco-guerrilla nexus.[18]

In 1984, based on information it received from a FARC deserter, the U.S. embassy reported that the "relationship of the FARC and the narcotics traffickers" appeared to be "sanctioned by the FARC's national directorate."[19] Jacobo Arenas, the FARC's ideological leader, had developed a functional agreement with Medellín cartel member Gonzalo Rodríguez Gacha, also known as "the Mexican." The Medellín cartel paid a fee to the FARC for each ton of cocaine processed in FARC territory. In exchange, the FARC provided security services to the cartel.[20] According to the U.S. embassy, this working relationship was "part of the FARC's plan to take over the country."

Each FARC front had a responsibility to cooperate with specific narcotics traffickers for "money and arms." The embassy believed that the FARC was earning roughly "$3.38 million per month" taxing the coca and marijuana industries. They also believed that the FARC was engaging in coca cultivation. In return, the FARC warned the coca growers and traffickers of the arrival of antinarcotics police or military patrols.[21]

The FARC used the revenue earned from drug-related activity to bolster the political representation and position of the Partido Comunista de Colombia (PCC) in the Colombian Congress. Moreover, the embassy speculated that the FARC employed drug profits to supply "their Marxist/Leninist sympathizers" in neighboring countries with "financial aid" or "volunteers who fight and train troops." The embassy concluded that "it would not be surprising" if the FARC, "which controlled those areas where coca was principally produced, dealt directly or indirectly" with Cuba. However, the embassy had no conclusive proof other than the evidence against the M-19. The embassy also thought that the FARC was beginning to use the drug trade as an ideological method to "subvert, corrupt, and undermine the American public and other democratic countries," just as Cuba and Nicaragua had done.[22]

The 1984 raid on the Medellín cartel's coca-processing center at Tranquilandia and the guerrillas' association with it, as well as the Colombian government's preoccupation with the cartel, were the final bits of proof that Colombia's guerrillas were trafficking in narcotics. During the raid, the Colombian police found a "FARC camp a half a mile away from the laboratory."[23] They also captured two FARC members at Tranquilandia and discovered an internal FARC document showing that the group collected taxes from coca processing in their areas of control.[24] Although analysts argued that the Tranquilandia foray did not confirm FARC participation in cocaine refinement, they felt it did "indicate some form of coexistence agreement with the traffickers."[25] For the State Department and Ambassador Tambs, this meant only one thing: the "FARC . . . the EPL . . . and the ELN" were actively engaged in illicit drug production.

Around 1986, weak government authority and the collapse of the FARC-Medellín cooperative agreement created the impression in the State Department that the FARC was consolidating its control over coca growing in rural areas. The State Department believed that the FARC had taken "over the large farms" abandoned by "the major narcotics traffickers" after the Colombian government declared war on the cartel in 1984.[26] When the Medellín cartel joined forces with conservative landholders, chaos erupted in Colombia's interior as the "traffickers and insurgents [vied] for control over the same territory."[27]

President Betancur's 1984 announcement of a "moral peace" in Colombia, the subsequent cease-fire between the government and the FARC, and the all-out war against the Medellín cartel made the government reluctant to move into the country's interior to reestablish its authority over guerrilla-held territory. In the State Department's view, Colombia did not want to "jeopardize the cease-fire" while it battled the cartel.[28] However, for Washington, the truce "gave the rebels additional capability to build up their forces and make them even more dangerous to the government." The power vacuum in the narcotics-producing regions enabled the guerrillas to consolidate their power.[29]

Soon the United States used the perception that the guerrillas were becoming too powerful to justify increased military assistance to the Colombian government. Prior to the M-19 attack on the Palace of Justice, the State Department believed that the "M-19 was moving towards closer coordination with the FARC."[30] Following the attack, in early 1986, the M-19 supposedly attempted to establish a "common guerrilla front" with the Sendero Luminoso and the MRTA in Peru.[31] The M-19's actions during the attack and their close association with Cuba, along with previously obtained information on cooperation among traffickers, the FARC, and other guerrilla organizations, led the United States to define the crisis in Colombia as narco-terrorism: drug criminals, political terrorists, and guerrillas working together to overthrow the Colombian government.

Even though the FARC had agreed to support the government's anti-drug campaign along the Venezuelan border in 1987, Tranquilandia, the FARC's presence in coca-growing areas, and the FARC's alleged relationship with the M-19 made the FARC narco-terrorists in the eyes of U.S. policymakers.[32] According to Assistant Secretary of the INM Jon Thomas, the truce with the FARC and their strength necessitated counternarcotics operations based on "firepower" and "getting in and conducting raids."[33] The State Department argued that it had made it clear to the "highest levels of the Colombian government that attacking major drug labs, FARC-protected or otherwise, [was] critical to their joint war against traffickers." For the State Department, remedying the "firepower imbalance" was the only way to regain control of remote coca-growing areas. Therefore, in 1988 the State Department recommended strengthening military assistance to "enhance the Colombian military's ability to counter both the insurgents and traffickers."[34]

At that point, the FARC's growing power, the battle in the countryside between the FARC and the Medellín cartel, and mounting U.S. pressure to pursue counternarcotics activities in FARC-held territory motivated the Colombian military and the right-wing, drug-financed paramilitaries to find common ground.[35] They launched a dirty war against the Union Patriotica that eventually led to the breakdown of the government's 1984 truce with the FARC.

The truth, however, was that guerrilla participation in the narcotics trade had followed opportunity and initially could have been prevented or at least controlled. Cocaine profits began to drive FARC expansion in the early 1980s, when the organization was trying to enter legitimate politics through the Union Patriotica. An accord between the government and the FARC was still possible then—but too many chances to preempt the insurgents' connection with the drug business were lost. U.S. determination to focus on military force pushed Colombia away from reaching an agreement with the guerrillas. When the Barco administration called for the FARC's complete demobilization, trafficking became their modus operandi, and their goal became the overthrow of the Colombian government. It was another ten years before serious peace talks resumed.

Peruvian Guerrillas

The Sendero Luminoso's armed strategy made the situation in Peru more complicated than the one in Colombia. The Sendero Luminoso was the primary guerrilla organization in Peru using narcotics to finance its insurgency. Spreading sheer terror, the Sendero sought to create a political vacuum in which it could use narcotics profits to facilitate its takeover of the government. The Sendero's interpretation of Maoist doctrine prepared it to move from a "people's revolution," called *petardismo* by the Sendero, to a "guerrilla revolution" that was a "prelude to the final stage" of revolution, which would be characterized by a "general offensive" against the government.[36]

The Sendero designed its operations to terrorize the Peruvian people, assuming that this would force the "government of Peru to be more aggressive in combating the terrorist menace."[37] The Sendero's attacks included random bombings of government buildings and public meeting places as well as attacks on Peru's infrastructure, for example on high-tension towers to cause blackouts. U.S. embassy analysts believed that the Sendero was trying to heighten the mystery behind its movement by creating a situation where almost any "untoward event was seen as a possible terrorist incident."[38] In a separate report, the State Department remarked that the Peruvian government was unprepared to deal with the Sendero's attacks because it "underestimated the threat" and did not have a "workable counterinsurgency strategy."[39] According to a CIA report, military intervention could demonstrate police inefficiency and make the terrorists appear more dangerous than they were.[40]

Initially, the Peruvian military's primary strategy was to drive a wedge between the Sendero Luminoso and the coca growers by allowing the growers to cultivate coca unimpeded, while vigorously combating the Sendero support network. As noted previously, the Sendero had "presented the anti-coca issue as an example" of the central government's attempt to "take away the livelihood of the Indian population."[41] By giving the coca growers free reign, the military's strategy of concentrating on the Sendero encountered considerable success.

When Alan García became president in 1985, he ordered the military to respect human rights while at the same time reinvigorating counternarcotics activities.[42] The government then moved in on both the Sendero and narco-traffickers located within the UHV.[43] This shift in military strategy combined with the renewed counternarcotics operations created what the Sendero called "internal contradictions," which enabled the group to consolidate its presence in the UHV and gain the support of the cocaleros.[44] The United States supported Peru's tactics, even though the embassy had previously argued that confronting the "cocaine industry" weakened the government's "institutional ability to cope with terrorism."[45] But as a consequence of the decision to conduct counternarcotics programs while taking on the Sendero, the Peruvian government had lost control over the UHV by the end of 1986.[46]

The Sendero Luminoso's battle against the Peruvian military in the UHV was peripheral to its overall plan. The organization sought to create so much chaos in the rest of the country that areas such as the UHV became active sanctuaries or *bases de apoyo* (bases of support).[47] As the Sendero started to consolidate its foothold in the UHV, it also moved to take advantage of growing dissension in the cities. The Peruvian army's incursion in the UHV against the Sendero caused hundreds of thousands of refugees to flood Peru's cities, and the Sendero responded by establishing an integrated rural-urban front against the government. Since the army and police were busy confronting urban terrorism, the Sendero anticipated that "government pressure would ease elsewhere," enabling them "to consolidate their grip on the countryside."[48] The strategy worked. By 1986 the Sendero had absolute control of the UHV. This allowed it to dominate the narcotics trade, which in turn financed its insurgency.

The mystery surrounding the Sendero's structure and identity fostered rumors and yielded many allegations of disreputable activity after it became militarily active in 1980. Initial accusations of Sendero narcotics trafficking appeared in 1982, when President Belaunde coined the phrase "narco-terrorism." At this time, the U.S. embassy received reports that the Sendero was "shaking down the drug traffickers [to] obtain operating funds."[49] The embassy also believed that the Sendero had a mechanism in Lima to launder money. Yet none of these possibilities were ever confirmed. In fact, logic suggested that the Sendero's radical "ideology and doctrine discouraged such involvement" because the drug industry was capitalist in nature and therefore repugnant to the Sendero.[50]

In addition to suspicions about the Sendero's drug activities, there were widespread claims that the Sendero was "receiving support from foreign countries," including Cuba.[51] However, according to U.S. embassy officials, "no evidence of significant . . . links [between] local terrorists and other Communist or radical countries" could be discovered.[52] The U.S. embassy was also dubious about the claim that Cuba conducted "discoverable subversive actions" in Peru, because this would have jeopardized "the position of the Soviets," who enjoyed a "military supply relationship" with Peru.[53]

In 1986 and 1987, as the Sendero's campaign in the urban centers heated up and as political and military instability in the UHV intensified, "growing ties between insurgents and narcotics traffickers . . . provided the guerrillas with new opportunities to expand" their control and firm up their financial base.[54] Although relations between traffickers and insurgents occasionally broke down—the Sendero overran and destroyed narco-trafficker Maximo Perez-Salas's private army, Movimiento Anti-Terrorista (MAT), and compound—cooperation increased around 1987.[55] This became possible as the Sendero abandoned some of its anticapitalist ideology and started to traffic in narcotics in order to bolster its military strength.[56] One study theorized that the Sendero justified narcotics trafficking by pointing to its corrosive and demoralizing influence on the Yankee imperialists.[57]

A 1987 report from several journalists who entered the UHV confirmed Sendero cooperation with the narco-traffickers. The reporters witnessed Colombian narco-traffickers working and living in association with Sendero Luminoso militants in the town of Uchiza in the UHV.[58] Statements taken from campesinos later backed allegations about the Sendero's drug-related activities. A campesino in Moyobamba, a province next to the UHV in the department of San Martín, stated that the "Sendero benefited from coca." Another campesino in the Province of Picota, also in the department of San Martín, maintained that the "subversives" were "involved" with the production of coca, because it "sustained" their "subversive" program.[59] It often appeared that narco-traffickers and the Sendero defended the same cause: coca leaf production.[60]

About 1989, Major Erwin Montero, a member of Peru's antidrug police, observed a change in relationship between the Sendero and the traffickers. Whereas once they "seemed to work in parallel," it appeared they had begun to work in "unison."[61] The Sendero, by that time in control of the UHV, ordered the cocaleros to grow coca for the insurgency; in return, it "promised to give the campesinos a fair price for their product."[62]

Researchers differ on the quality and degree of campesino support for the Sendero. The authors of a study on the department of San Martín determined that the Sendero forced the majority of cocaleros to submit to its directives on coca cultivation.[63] The campesinos obeyed the Sendero because they feared execution—the traffickers' policy—if they did not meet their quotas. Alternatively, they faced economic hardship if government counternarcotics operatives destroyed their crops.[64] But others argued that campesino support for the Sendero was "soft; they tolerated the Sendero only as long as its interference did not adversely affect their economic interests or personal safety."[65] Campesinos in the UHV were generally more interested in coca profits than in the Sendero's orthodox Maoist philosophy.[66] Whether or not the Sendero received full backing from the UHV's campesinos, Sendero power protected the cocaleros against traffickers and against government eradication efforts, creating, at the very least, a tacit alliance.[67]

With the cocaleros bowing to Sendero authority, the Sendero increased coca production in the UHV. The Sendero's strict code of conduct ended what it described as the campesinos' pursuit of a hedonistic lifestyle from the coca dollars they earned. The Sendero enforced a rigorous work ethic, eliminated the use of alcohol, and closed discos and brothels—and coca production grew.[68] Sendero control guaranteed the traffickers a source of coca leaves and gave the Sendero the power to charge the drug Mafias, also known as *firmas*, for the right to export coca from the UHV and elsewhere in the department of San Martín.[69]

The Sendero received a 10- to 15-percent cut from the traffickers for their services, and it charged the traffickers fees up to fifteen thousand dollars per aircraft landing in the UHV.[70] Reports from the UHV claimed that "two Colombian flights a day" were carrying out coca leaves and/or paste.[71] The Sendero's estimated annual revenue ranged from fifteen million to thirty-five million dollars; one Pentagon assessment thought the amount exceeded one hundred million dollars.[72]

The Peruvian government was extremely concerned that the Sendero was using narco-dollars to finance attacks on the rest of Peru's economy.[73] Through its terrorist activity, the Sendero created an enclave for itself in the UHV. The military's counternarcotics program and repressive actions in the UHV had weakened the government's legitimacy and strengthened the Sendero's link among coca growers. Once it secured this enclave, the Sendero used its coca profits to finance attacks on Peru's economic infrastructure. Through these actions, the Sendero hoped to propel the internal collapse of the government by causing it to lose all economic and military control.

In light of the situation, the U.S. State Department believed that it needed to go after the Sendero as well as the traffickers. In one cable, the State Department argued that "military tactics can be used against both narcotics traffickers and insurgents"; but Peru was in an economic and political crisis, and narcotics were a "secondary priority."[74] The U.S. embassy in Lima contended that the policy of separating "drugs" from "subversion" had failed and needed to be changed. The embassy analysts added that unless Washington paid "attention to Peru's problems" by dedicating "resources to solving them," counternarcotics efforts would come to nothing.[75]

The "deteriorating . . . security situation" forced the United States to shut down the air fleet that supported Peruvian CORAH and UMOPAR forces in February 1989.[76] The U.S. embassy concluded that the "increasingly violent [and] hostile environment" in the UHV made it imperative for the U.S. to "work with the [Peruvian] military."[77] As in Colombia, the security situation in Peru led the United States to see military assistance as the only viable option for pursuing its antinarcotics objective.

The U.S. embassy's strategy for restoring security in the UHV seemed to disregard previous events and instead played into the hands of the Sendero.[78] The embassy proposal emphasized attacking the guerrillas while conducting counternarcotics programs—the same plan that had precipitated the Peruvian government's loss of control in the UHV in the first place. Peru's General Alberto Arciniega knew that "U.S.-Peruvian eradication efforts [had] alienated the people of the UHV." The general argued for a plan that clearly distinguished drug traffickers from coca growers, and he maintained that the only way to regain control in the UHV was "to support the campesinos against the subversives."[79] Arciniega pointed out that it was a "mistake to drive the coca growers into the hands of the Sendero." To split the narco-terrorist connection, he called for a "suspension of involuntary eradication programs," the purchase of "coca grown in the zone," and CORAH participation in "civic action programs," just as had been done in the 1960s.[80] Arciniega wanted Peruvian efforts to defeat the Sendero to use all the strategies that brought the army limited success prior to 1984.

Arciniega's proposals to the United States received a cool reception. U.S. Ambassador to Peru Anthony Quainton told Arciniega that "coca cultivation in the UHV was illegal under Peruvian law and . . . must be destroyed."[81] The U.S. government believed that the purchase of excess coca leaf would "merely stimulate further production." Moreover, a "temporary alliance with drug growers or traffickers" would have "a devastating impact on Peru's image as a good partner in the anti-narcotics struggle."[82] The State Department insisted that Peru's suspension of eradication operations "would torpedo any chances of obtaining aid" from Congress for military operations in the UHV. It also thought that the UHV did not have the infrastructure to develop a workable alternative crop program. Thus, using diplomatic double-talk, the U.S. ambassador informed Arciniega that "development" could not begin before "there was security" and that Peru could "not generate security" until there was "development."[83] The U.S. position, therefore, constrained the Peruvian military's ability to deal with the insurgency, because it tied the issue of security to the issue of economic development for the campesinos.

Corruption and Arciniega's opposition to the U.S. program proved to be his downfall. After Melvyn Levitsky, the U.S. assistant secretary of state for narcotics matters, accused Arciniega of narcotics trafficking, Peru removed the general from his position only seven months after his appointment.[84] Levitsky asserted that Arciniega had occasionally looked the other way when he had become aware of drug offenses in the military; he had needed to raise money for the troops combating the Sendero threat, and Peru's economy under Alan García had been bankrupt.[85]

U.S. policymakers were obviously unable to understand that security and economic issues needed separate treatment. It was almost as if all the lessons from Vietnam and Latin America during the 1960s—as well as CIA Director William Colby's belief that an effective counterinsurgency program had to be fought at the village level—were lost on the U.S. government.[86] When the United States pressured Peru to conduct simultaneous campaigns against narcotics production and the narco-terrorist connection in the UHV, they shackled Peru's government with a no-win strategy. In fact, the U.S. approach created greater difficulties for Peru: antidrug efforts drove the peasants into the protective arms of the guerrillas, while attacks against the guerrillas gave drug producers a free hand to pursue their business.[87] If the government had given the campesinos even a slight respite from coca eradication, Arciniega and the military might have won some support from the UHV populace, as they did prior to 1984. Instead, U.S. plans simply played into the hands of the Sendero Luminoso and bolstered its long-term strategy.

Carlton Turner, a White House drug policy advisor, admitted that it "took a long time to realize what was happening." He added that "no one looked at the big picture," and ultimately the United States was stuck "playing catch-up."[88] In many ways, the U.S. counternarcotics program and the actions of the Peruvian and Colombian governments reinforced the guerrillas' position in the countryside, which in turn allowed the guerrillas to dominate the narcotics industry. In both countries, the guerrillas filled a political vacuum in the rural areas while they developed a plan to ally themselves with the campesino coca growers. At the same time, they taxed the traffickers in their zones of control, while allowing them to continue operating freely. When the government tried to carry out counternarcotics programs, they not only lost the backing of coca-growing campesinos but also increased the guerrillas' base of support, revenue, and recruits for insurgency.

Watching the collapse of security in the rural areas of Peru and Colombia, the United States looked for immediate solutions. Although they knew of no clear connection between the Andean guerrillas and Communist countries such as Cuba and Nicaragua, the guerrillas' past relationship with Cuba as well as their Marxist/Maoist ideologies concerned U.S. policymakers far more than the macroeconomic problems of the northern

Andes. The United States saw military force as the only viable way to attack the drug-financed military strength of the guerrillas and narcotics producers head-on. However, as one DEA helicopter pilot explained, "as long as antidrug efforts ignore the economic realities underlying the drug trade, law enforcement [will] prove futile."[89]

U.S. counternarcotics planners prioritized security over the economy, which flew in the face of the macroeconomic problems in the northern Andes. They also ignored the socioeconomic and political complexities within each nation that had given rise to rural instability, the coca boom, and subversive movements. The ability to preempt the insurgencies was lost as the United States called for more reinforcement measures to fight the guerrillas and traffickers simultaneously.

The subsequent militarization made it harder to separate the guerrillas from the campesino coca growers who supported them. Melvyn Levitsky believed that it was politically impossible for U.S. planners to recommend that the United States go after the guerrillas before attacking the narcotics problem.[90] Such a decision would have made the War on Drugs in the northern Andes look like a farce and would have called into question the legality of U.S. participation in the region's internal conflicts.

Campesino resistance grew as militarization of the War on Drugs expanded. Resistance generated more chaos, which made more room for the narco-traffickers to operate with impunity. The chaos also enlarged support for the guerrillas and justified their growing domination over the narcotics trade. Inadvertently or not, the United States' response to the narco-guerrilla nexus benefited the guerrillas, destabilized the governments of the northern Andes, and amplified the potential for more narcotics-related violence.

6

The Militarization of the Drug War: Bush, Panama, and the Andean Strategy

When George H. W. Bush became president in 1989, he advocated a counternarcotics program for the northern Andes that emphasized military aid, and the Department of Defense (DOD) became the lead agency in the battle with illegal drugs. The Bush administration's Andean Strategy increased U.S. funding for Andean military forces and also deepened U.S. military participation in counternarcotics operations, although some military leaders continued to oppose military involvement in the War on Drugs. Nevertheless, with the end of the Cold War and the rise of narco-terrorism in the northern Andes, Bush officials insisted on this new role for the Andean and U.S. armed forces.

When the administration ruled that the armed forces could join in law enforcement operations, the commitment of the U.S. military to the War on Drugs was complete. The 1989 invasion of Panama clearly demonstrated the new policy. One of the primary justifications for the invasion was Noriega's alleged association with the Medellín cartel and the M-19. Noriega's posturing with the United States in the war against Nicaragua and his Machiavellian manipulation of Panamanian politics hastened his fall from power. While Noriega fought off U.S. accusations of drug trafficking by distancing himself from the Medellín cartel, his control of Panama unraveled. Consequently, his authoritarianism intensified, and he moved closer to Cuba and Nicaragua politically. When the Bush administration declared that the military could go after international fugitives, the United States invaded Panama, justifying it on the basis of Noriega's association with the narcotics trade.

The invasion of Panama and the Andean Strategy's focus on force angered the northern Andean governments, who threatened to break with the United States in the War on Drugs. In order to allay criticism of the Andean Strategy, President Bush agreed to hold a summit in Cartagena, Colombia, where his representatives reexamined the economic aspect of the narcotics trade. At Cartagena, the United States offered to support alternative development programs, and more important, it proposed the Andean Trade Preference Act (ATPA), an economic liberalization program that the administration believed would generate enough revenue for the Andean governments to overcome their economic crises. The Bush administration expected that the combination of alternative development and economic liberalization programs would eliminate the economic incentive for narcotics cultivation.

Steps to Militarization: The Origin of the Andean Strategy

The 1986 Anti-Drug Abuse Act had produced disappointing results. In 1986, six months after President Reagan called for "a national crusade against drugs," pressure to reduce spending had forced him to cut federal funding for the act.[1] The government cut $225 million from state and local drug enforcement programs and reduced the drug education budget from the promised $200–250 million to $100 million.

In 1987 Congressman Charles Rangel pointed out that Reagan's proposed budget cuts for 1988 would have a "chilling effect on new drug abuse programs."[2] In the words of Senator Alfonse D'Amato, the 1986 bill was "a sham."[3] Calling for a "total war" against the drug epidemic,

Senator Bob Dole pronounced that it was "time to bring the full force" of the U.S. "military and intelligence communities into this war."[4]

The Reagan administration denied that it was "soft on drugs," and in 1988, an election year, Reagan reinvigorated the debate on narcotics. Calling narcotics "public enemy number one," Reagan declared that it was necessary to send a "loud, clear message to drug kingpins and cop-killers."[5] Reagan also called for a high-level commission to look into increased use of the armed forces in the War on Drugs.

As the debate on U.S. drug policy heated up, Congress passed the 1988 Anti-Drug Abuse Act. The bill provided $2.8 billion to combat drug crime and abuse and created stiffer penalties for drug offenses, including the death penalty for narcotics kingpins and those who committed drug-related murders.[6] The 1988 bill also formed the Office of National Drug Control Policy (ONDCP), which was expected to submit an annual national drug-control policy report to Congress. In conjunction with the formation of the ONDCP, the bill established a cabinet-level position: national drug czar.[7] However, the bill's most significant measure, and the one with the greatest consequences for the northern Andes, was the congressional request for the U.S. military to step up its participation in the fight against narcotics.[8]

In 1989, at the start of his presidency, George Bush was faced with gloomy evaluations of the War on Drugs. An NSC document reported that Bolivia, Colombia, and Peru were the cause of the cocaine problem, because cocaine poured out of those countries.[9] A Department of State audit by the inspector general stated that INM programs had not "resulted in significant reductions of coca cultivation or cocaine trafficking in host countries."[10] James Baker, Bush's secretary of state, told Congress that the international War on Drugs was "clearly not being won." Moreover, he stated that in "some areas" the United States "appeared to be slipping backwards."[11]

While Baker was making this assessment, the House Armed Services Committee called for the U.S. military to "take the lead" in the war against drugs.[12] In a memorandum to the Joint Chiefs of Staff, Secretary of Defense Richard Cheney asserted that "detecting and countering the production, trafficking, and use of illegal drugs" was a "high priority, national security mission of the Department of Defense."[13] President Bush declared that "the violence and corruption of the drug traffickers and their alliance with insurgent groups had a destabilizing effect" that "must be dealt with aggressively."[14] The administration believed that "a concerted effort to suppress trafficking in the Andes" would collapse efforts to "expand [the] industry into Brazil, the Southern Cone, Central America, and Mexico."[15]

In August 1989, Bush authorized National Security Decision Directive 18 (NSDD 18), which had two parts: (1) enhanced involvement by the Pentagon and U.S. intelligence agencies in the antidrug effort, and (2) the Andean Strategy.[16] The first was an outgrowth of the Defense Authorization Act of 1989, which made the DOD the lead agency for detecting and monitoring the aerial and maritime transit of illegal drugs into the United States. The act also gave the DOD the task of centralizing all drug intelligence and operations information into a single communications network.[17]

On September 18, 1989, acting on President Bush's NSDD 18, Defense Secretary Cheney ordered the Pentagon to embrace its primary role in drug operations. Simultaneously, he ordered each branch of the military to develop a detailed plan by October 15 for cutting the flow of drugs.[18] The DOD would now not only collect intelligence, detect and monitor narcotics activity, and provide assistance to law enforcement agencies, but it would also cooperate with "foreign countries in their own counternarcotics efforts."[19] The NSDD further defined the DOD mission to include expanded assistance for "U.S. counternarcotics efforts" and "training for host-government personnel and operational support activities anywhere in the Andean region."[20]

Cheney acknowledged that some military officers were reluctant to jump into counternarcotics, and he claimed that he did not want to turn the Defense Department into a law enforcement agency.[21] However, the defense secretary added that he "set the policy for the department" and that military leadership responded favorably when he gave "firm guidance" on the administration's "objectives and policies." Cheney concluded by saying that the Department of Defense was an "enthusiastic participant" in the War on Drugs.[22]

Despite Cheney's assurances that the military supported his objectives, not everyone in the DOD agreed with him. Frank Carlucci, former secretary of defense, had maintained, right up to Cheney's nomination as secretary of defense, that manning the front line of the country's drug war was "not the function of the military."[23] Like his predecessor Caspar Weinberger, Carlucci believed that the "primary role" of the Defense Department was to "protect and defend the United States from armed aggression." Nothing should stand in the way of the military's "readiness or preparedness to perform this task."[24] Meanwhile, Representative Larry

Hopkins from Kentucky explained "that just because the Secretary of Defense" had "signed on," that did not "necessarily mean" the "institutional and cultural bias against the drug mission" was going to "disappear overnight."[25] Within the DOD, many officers opposed Cheney's directive behind closed doors. According to one flag officer for the U.S. Navy, it was "a no-win situation" for the military.[26]

However, as the Cold War wound down, a fear of budget cuts encouraged many officers to approve the military's new role in counternarcotics programs. The military had enjoyed eight years of surging defense budgets under Reagan, and Pentagon officials grew concerned when Congress started to talk about cutting military spending. Some economic analysts feared that a recession might set in if military expenditures were reduced.[27] Lieutenant Colonel Juan Orama described a sudden scramble to prove the military's ability to "conduct special operations and/or counternarcotics operations in order to justify military funding."[28] William Taylor, a military expert at Washington's Center for Strategic and International Studies, believed that both the military and the country were best served by the military's enhanced function in the War on Drugs. Taylor added that "the Department of Defense" needed to "develop some social-utility arguments" since the "Soviet threat" was gone. Third World problems, such as "insurgency, terrorism, and narcotics interdiction," could fill that void.[29]

Still, many officers remained wary of committing to counternarcotics operations in the northern Andes. They feared that the United States would be drawn into a Vietnam-like quagmire of regional guerrilla wars.[30] A 1989 State Department Inspector General's report noted that the DOD's "more direct and visible role" in the War on Drugs—which included military assistance advisory group (MAAG) training—was similar to the country's early actions in Vietnam.[31] Describing the military's new narcotics role, an officer in the Special Operations Command at McDill Air Force Base stated that "we deal with the ghosts of Vietnam . . . every day."[32]

Some military officers also feared that their enhanced responsibility for the War on Drugs could undermine democracy in the Andes: assigning law enforcement actions to the military could open the door to martial law in those countries.[33] General Alfred Gray, the commandant of the Marine Corps and a member of the Joint Chiefs of Staff, warned that winning the hearts and minds of the campesinos was of primary importance. A military solution alone could not win any type of "revolutionary warfare environment, insurgency war, [or] counternarcotics type warfare."[34] Other military experts argued that a stronger armed forces presence in counternarcotics efforts simply "raised the cost of smuggling activities, thus increasing the profit incentives for future smugglers to engage in drug trafficking."[35] In the end, reports pointed to a consensus group within the DOD who believed that the U.S. military was "ultimately going to end up holding the can for the failure to stop the flow of drugs."[36]

The second part of NSDD 18 was the Andean Strategy, designed to provide military assistance, training, and logistical support to the northern Andean governments to help them "regain control of their countries from an insidious combination of insurgents and drug traffickers, and to stop the flow of narcotics to the United States."[37] According to Melvyn Levitsky, assistant secretary of state for narcotics matters, the failure to curb coca cultivation had created an excess supply, which in turn had increased demand: the excess supply had made narcotics cheaper and more accessible to all economic classes.[38] The Andean Strategy aimed to reduce coca and cocaine cultivation in the region by "isolating major coca-growing areas, blocking the delivery of chemicals used for coca processing, destroying cocaine hydrochloride-processing laboratories, and dismantling trafficking organizations."[39]

Bush officials determined that military assistance was the best way "to get a handle on the security situation."[40] Once security was reestablished in the coca-growing regions, the administration reasoned, the regional governments could conduct counternarcotics activities safely.[41] Thus, the budget for fiscal year 1989 allotted $234 million to the northern Andean nations: $86 million to Colombia, $85.1 million to Bolivia, and $63.2 million to Peru. In 1990, the plan increased spending to $359 million, with $154.6 million going to Bolivia, $123 million to Colombia, and $81.6 million to Peru.[42]

All of the money poured into the Andean Strategy took the form of military assistance. There were few restrictions on its use, which meant that the money could be utilized to fight guerrilla insurgencies to achieve the security necessary for counternarcotics activities. Peter Borromeo, deputy assistant secretary to the INM, reported to Congress that 72 percent of the aid went directly to the Andean militaries, with no questions asked about what they did with it. Counternarcotics programs absorbed the rest of the funds, although the Andean governments could redirect these funds to the fight against the guerrilla insurgencies if counternarcotics activities were necessary in guerrilla-held territory.[43]

Policymakers tied the Andean Strategy's economic component to progress on the military front. The Bush administration did not want to send economic aid until the Andean militaries restored order.[44] They felt that they could not "legitimately invest money in economic capabilities until [rural areas] were made more secure" and therefore "more capable of accepting economic aid." Crop eradication and substitution could not begin until protection for Andean crop substitution personnel, such as the Bolivian and Peruvian CORAH teams, could be assured.[45]

Up to this point, the 1961 Foreign Assistance Act had banned using ESF (economic support funds) for military operations. However, in 1989 Congress decided to allow their use to aid the armed forces.[46] The new rules made all funds going to the northern Andean governments available to their armed forces, with no questions asked, as long as they used them to establish "secure" conditions for counternarcotics programs.

The decision to give the Andean militaries such an important role in counternarcotics activities was highly problematic, especially considering the history of narcotics-related corruption.[47] In Colombia, where the armed forces worked in conjunction with the Medellín cartel's paramilitaries, the determination to apply a military strategy was dubious at best. In Bolivia, the military and UMOPAR police had tipped off many traffickers prior to Blast Furnace operations, while in Peru, the military was trying to create a form of détente with the traffickers as they pursued the Sendero. Donald J. Mabry, an expert on the U.S. military, argued that deploying northern Andean special operation units in counternarcotics work could lead them into a "dirty war" against the campesino populations.[48] Mabry's assertion proved true in all three countries, as militarization opened the door to human rights abuses. Yet, rather than change direction, policymakers ignored all the cautionary signals along the road.

The Andean Strategy not only multiplied military aid in the northern Andes, but it also sent U.S. Special Forces to take part in counternarcotics activities. Initially, the Special Forces served as advisors to the Colombian, Peruvian, and Bolivian armed forces. They offered training, reconnaissance, planning, logistics, and medical and civic services.[49] Their teams were assigned to three areas: the mountains near Cochabamba in Bolivia, the UHV in Peru, and the territory between the Japura and Putumayo Rivers in Colombia. The Bush administration claimed that it had no plan to place U.S. military personnel in "direct contact with either insurgents or the drug traffickers" and that U.S. forces would "observe peace time rules of engagement."[50] The U.S. military would not get "directly involved" or "do anything proactive."[51]

However, a general debate about the rules of engagement for the Special Forces caused the Bush administration to seek a legal ruling on its participation in counternarcotics operations. The administration determined that the armed forces had the legal authority to arrest drug traffickers, international terrorists, and other fugitives overseas. It justified this ruling by concluding that the Posse Comitatus Act, which prohibited the military from arresting criminal suspects and conducting law enforcement actions, did not apply outside U.S. borders. The judgment also gave U.S. troops permission to accompany Andean military forces on training missions. In addition, groups such as the Green Berets and Special Forces could now conduct military operations designated as law enforcement operations without congressional consultation.[52]

The ruling meant that U.S. forces could wind up fighting Andean guerrillas while conducting counternarcotics operations. Most important, it provided the pretext for U.S. forces to apprehend international drug traffickers, including Manuel Noriega. Despite the administration's denial, the Andean Strategy created a law enforcement role for the U.S. military, along with broadened exposure to the War on Drugs. It also increased the potential for U.S. troops to lose their lives in counternarcotics operations.

The Bush government had opened the door for the armed forces' entanglement in the civil conflicts of the northern Andes. Moreover, they had implemented a strategy that was counterproductive to fighting a guerrilla war because it placed security above economic considerations. However, the new role for the military and the reinterpretation of the Posse Comitatus Act gave the Bush administration the pretext it needed to invade Panama and remove Manuel Noriega from power.

Noriega and the Panama Invasion

Manuel Noriega's career as the head of the Panamanian Defense Forces (PDF) was central to events surrounding the war in Central America and the expansion of the narcotics industry during the 1980s. Noriega ruthlessly manipulated Panamanian politics to ensure his political domination while also serving as a liaison between the CIA and the Cuban DGI. He supported the CIA's efforts against Nicaragua's Sandinista government while helping Cuba supply the M-19 and the Salvadorian guerrilla organization, the Farabundo Martí para la Liberacion Nacional (FMLN). Most important, Noriega facilitated and profited from drug smuggling through Panama. His narcotics-related crimes, combined with his Machiavellian manipulation of foreign and domestic politics, eventually brought about his demise.

In 1970 his loyalty to Panamanian military leader Omar Torrijos led to Noriega's promotion to lieutenant colonel and his designation as head of Panama's intelligence service, the G2.[53] As noted previously, Torrijos was a military reformer who took power in 1968.[54] Torrijos argued that the Panamanian military, also known as La Guardia Nacional (the National Guard), should pave the way for reform and democracy, and he derived his power from his effort to renegotiate the Panama Canal Treaties.[55] After renegotiating the treaties, Torrijos permitted the return to traditional electoral politics in Panama. However, while he was overseeing the transition to democracy, Torrijos died in a plane crash on July 31, 1981.[56] Torrijos's death created a power vacuum that turned into a test of power between the National Guard and President Aristides Royo, who was plagued with accusations of corruption and mismanagement.[57]

Immediately following Torrijos's death, Colonel Florencio Flores Aguilar assumed command over the National Guard. His command was short-lived; in March 1982 General Rubén Paredes ousted Flores in a coup. To secure his power, Paredes replaced President Royo with Vice President Ricardo de la Espriella and changed the constitution, giving the military a governing role equal to that of other political institutions running Panama.[58] Noriega was promoted to colonel in April 1982 and to chief of staff for the National Guard on December 15, 1982.[59] Following Noriega's appointment, Paredes declared his intention to run for president in the 1984 election, the first real democratic election in Panama since Torrijos had taken power.[60] Panamanian law required that Paredes resign his command before he could run. Consequently, on August 12, 1983, Noriega rose to brigadier general and assumed command of the Panamanian National Guard, which he reorganized into the Panamanian Defense Forces (PDF) that same year.[61]

Noriega had cultivated ties with the CIA since his rise to power as head of the Panamanian G2. Noriega stated that he had served as the CIA's "contact person throughout the 1970s." If the CIA "sought a channel of communications with the Russians," they knew they could rely on Noriega for a "clean and reliable transmission of information." Significantly, Noriega also served as "a reliable conduit of messages from the United States to the Cubans." In 1981, Noriega, still head of the G2, traveled to the United States and met with CIA Director William Casey at CIA headquarters in Langley, Virginia. At this meeting, Casey told Noriega that the United

States was "concerned about the Cuba–Grenada–Nicaragua triangle" and that the United States planned to meet the challenge by using covert action and guerrilla insurgencies to block Cuban- and Soviet-inspired designs. According to Noriega, this meeting was the start of a "cozier relationship with the CIA." For example, Noriega provided Panamanian passports and visas for CIA operatives on specific intelligence missions. [62] In addition, he oversaw the use of Howard Air Force Base as a center for resupplying the Contras.[63] As Noriega maintained, Panama, under his command, gave the United States "help and more."[64]

Noriega's problems started with Panama's 1984 elections. When Noriega withdrew the support of the PDF from Paredes, the election of 1984 boiled down to two men: Nicolás Ardito Barletta was the Partido Revolucionario Democrático (PRD) and PDF candidate, as well as a former World Bank economist and Torrijos's planning minister. The opposition candidate, Arnulfo Arias, was the former three-time president of Panama prior to Torrijos and was vehemently anti-military.[65]

Voting irregularities during the election made it difficult to determine the winner. Rumors spread that the PDF had rigged the vote. Arias supporters, who had believed that their candidate was going to win by a landslide, started street protests. Noriega retorted that the PDF would respond "with clubs" if "partisan action" undermined Panamanian stability.[66] In the end, the election results showed that Barletta had won the election by 1,713 votes. The Reagan administration promptly recognized Barletta's victory, and opposition to the allegedly fraudulent election soon died out.

However, in 1985, one year after Barletta's election, Noriega forced him to resign and placed Vice President Eric Arturo Delvalle in the presidency. Barletta had instituted liberalization policies and austere economic measures to deal with Panama's debt, and consequently, he had grown extremely unpopular with the military and trade unions as well as with his own party, the PRD. Barletta explained his departure from office as the result of the PRD and PDF's inability to work with him and "carry out [the] government actions" necessary at that time "to pull the country out of the difficult circumstances."[67]

Following Barletta's dismissal, speculation circulated that Noriega had removed Barletta in order to cover up the murder of Hugo Spadafora. Spadafora had served in the Sandinista Panamanian brigade against Anastasio Somoza Debayle until he became disillusioned with the Sandinistas and joined Edén Pastora's southern Contra front, ARDE. In

1984 Spadafora turned into a vociferous critic of Noriega, accusing him of being a narcotics trafficker who had corrupted Panama. Spadafora was found beheaded in September 1985 where he had tried to enter Panama along the Costa Rican border. [68] Noriega was instantly suspected of ordering the crime. In a cable to the State Department, the U.S. embassy in Costa Rica stated that informants had told them that Spadafora was "killed by drug dealers connected with Noriega."[69]

Theories about the murder multiplied. Some political analysts thought that, because the murder directly implicated Noriega, Spadafora's blatant killing might have been a ploy to embarrass Noriega and force him out of power.[70] On a more conspiratorial note, Ramón Lamboglia, a member of the Arnulfo Arias anti-Noriega resistance, alleged that Noriega had killed Spadafora because the CIA had told him to do so. According to Lamboglia, the CIA had ordered Spadafora's murder because his denunciation of Noriega had the potential to expose CIA activities in Central America and the Contra narcotics smuggling operation in Costa Rica.[71]

In his own defense, Noriega wrote in his memoirs that Spadafora turned against him because the Panamanian controller general's office cut off Spadafora's cost-of-living allowance. Spadafora had received two thousand dollars a month since his days as the leader of the Sandinista Panamanian brigade.[72] In addition, Noriega's trial proceedings included evidence that Spadafora had been called back to Panama to support a coup led by Colonel Roberto Diaz Herrera, Torrijos's cousin and Noriega's rival in the PDF.[73]

The controversy prompted President Barletta to consider appointing a commission to look into Spadafora's murder. If Noriega were indeed guilty, the commission would pose a serious threat to his power. Noriega was warned that removing Barletta from power would look suspicious and tarnish his reputation. Attributing Barletta's forced resignation to strong legislative, labor, and military opposition only further incriminated Noriega.[74] Following Barletta's removal from office, Panamanian popular support for Noriega declined drastically.[75]

The most damaging evidence against Noriega appeared in two forms in 1986. The first was a *New York Times* article by Seymour Hersh, published on June 12. North Carolina Senator Jesse Helms later corroborated the article's claims, following a set of hearings he conducted on Noriega and Panama. Hersh's article laid out a series of charges against Noriega. Using leaked classified documents and statements from Reagan officials, Hersh accused Noriega of selling weapons to Colombia's M-19—which, by this point, was linked to the Medellín cartel and the attack on the Colombian Palace of Justice. The article also accused Noriega of helping the Cuban DGI and supplying contraband to Cuba through the Colón Free Trade Zone. Hersh's most serious accusations covered Noriega's extensive illegal money laundering for guerrillas and drug dealers alike and his active engagement in drug trafficking.[76]

On June 22, 1986, Jesse Helms publicly confirmed Hersh's information on the television show *Meet the Press*. Helms, who had held hearings on Panama in April, was the first public official to verify on record that Noriega was the "head of the biggest drug trafficking operation in the Western Hemisphere."[77] Noriega's spokesman denied the allegations, saying that "Noriega and the military were victims of a campaign of slander that had no basis in fact"; these were "political attacks" to "damage" the PDF.[78] Noriega claimed that the charges were part of a campaign to keep Panama from taking charge of the Panama Canal.[79]

Why this information was made public was a matter of some debate. When asked if the United States should reassert its power over the Canal Zone, Helms, noted for his extreme Republican partisanship, stated that "it might be entirely necessary down the road" to remove Noriega from power forcibly. Helms's decision to broadcast his denouncement of Noriega and his statement on the canal raised international speculation over U.S. intentions in Panama. A subsequent congressional investigation added to the speculation on the motive behind the release of the negative findings on Noriega. The inquiry examined the possibility that the allegations were publicized to undermine Noriega and Panama's support for the Contadora peace process, which sought to end the conflict in Nicaragua.[80]

U.S. government officials had long known about Noriega's illicit activities. U.S. Ambassador to Costa Rica Francis McNeil described Noriega as a "rent a colonel" who developed a "cozy" relationship with U.S. intelligence agencies.[81] Noriega's questionable involvement in the drug industry dated back to 1972, when U.S. officials passed information about him to Torrijos.[82] The Senate's review of the Panama Canal Treaties in 1978 again incriminated Noriega. Senator Birch Bayh reported to Congress that he had information that a "high official in the Guardia Naciónal" had "overall operational control" of officially sanctioned drug trafficking in Panama. Bayh added that this official "directed narcotics operations between Panama and Cuba."[83] In 1985 the House Foreign Affairs Committee alleged that Noriega had a major financial interest in a narcotics processing plant along the Panama-Colombia border.[84]

The 1984 raid on the Medellín cocaine processing plant at La Palma in Darién raised deep suspicions about Noriega in the State Department. Although Castro's role in mediating a deal between Noriega and the Medellín cartel was still unknown at the time, Lieutenant Julio Melo Borbua's arrest as a result of the raid raised State Department suspicion that Melo was "acting as an agent of Noriega." The State Department found it hard to believe that Melo was "playing a lone hand" and speculated that Noriega had traveled out of Panama at the time of the raid in order to "put some distance between himself and the inevitable revelations." [85] In another cable, the U.S. embassy in Panama wrote that the Medellín organization had given Melo four million dollars to "pass around to the general staff" of the PDF and Noriega had been "one of the intended beneficiaries."[86] The same cable noted that Noriega had supposedly "refused the offer" and denied any association with the Medellín cartel.[87]

Even with all the information available against Noriega, the "Reagan administration and past administrations . . . overlooked Noriega's illegal activities, because of his cooperation with American intelligence and his willingness" to give "the American military extensive leeway" in Panama.[88] Moreover, high government officials, including CIA director William Casey, NSC director John Poindexter, and NSC-Contra liaison Lieutenant Colonel Oliver North, failed to bring up the issue of narcotics with Noriega because he was "providing valuable support for U.S. policies in Central America, especially Nicaragua."[89]

As public accusations against Noriega grew, the relationship between the United States and Panama began to sour. Noriega became less cooperative with the CIA at a critical time, just when the CIA's efforts to support the Contras were running into severe logistical and political difficulties. Noriega, despite his permission to use Panama as a base to train and support the Contras, publicly maintained opposition to U.S. policy in Central America.[90] In addition, he fed information about the Contras to the Cubans and supported the Contadora peace process.[91] Noriega claimed that he was growing weary of the swelling U.S. military presence throughout the region, especially when he considered Panama's sovereignty and future control over the Panama Canal. According to Noriega, the United States started to make "more demands" on him that Panama "could not meet," and applied "more pressure" than Noriega "could tolerate."[92]

The Reagan administration leaned on Noriega to support the Contras. In June 1985 Oliver North asked Noriega for Panamanian support to expand the Contras' southern front in Costa Rica. According to *Wall Street*

Journal reporter Frederick Kempe, Noriega thought that this plan was "stupid" because the southern front did not exist. In Noriega's opinion, the southern-front Contras were "more interested in conducting negotiations and sleeping with prostitutes" than they were with the "struggle." [93] Noriega believed that the CIA's "Central American plans" were going "too far" and that it was not in Panama's "strategic national interest" to be drawn into the Central American war.[94] However, Noriega could not control U.S. actions in the Canal Zone and did not want to break openly with North.[95] Noriega asserted that Panama supported "the Sandinista revolution," and he understood "the nationalist aspirations of the FMLN" in El Salvador. He did not believe that communism was "about to overrun Latin America."[96]

In November 1985, NSC chief John Poindexter flew to Panama to meet with Noriega. Investigative journalist John Dinges described this meeting as one of the most closely guarded secrets of the Reagan administration.[97] During their encounter, Poindexter informed Noriega that Barletta had to be returned to power and that Panama had to terminate its peacemaking role in Central America and diminish its relations with Cuba.[98] According to Frederick Kempe, Poindexter and Elliott Abrams, the assistant secretary of state for Latin American affairs, also told Noriega that he had to democratize Panama because, under his leadership, Panama's political direction was contrary to the U.S. effort to promote democracy in Latin America.[99] Noriega balked at these demands and said that Poindexter threatened him with "consequences for Panama."[100]

Noriega worked with the United States up to a point, but he was not going to allow the United States to dictate Panama's national policy. Noriega believed that Abrams and Poindexter "were grasping for anything that could work; the Contras were not making any progress; the Honduras front was visible and weak; the southern front was collapsing; there was limited money to finance the war." Noriega claimed that when he refused to cooperate, "the real reaction was vindictive, angry, and filled with calls for revenge against a pawn who would not play along."[101]

Further evidence of the breakdown in relations between Noriega and the CIA/NSC came in June 1986 when Noriega seized the ship *Pia Vesta*.[102] The *Pia Vesta*, headed for Peru, was loaded with East German weapons worth about six million dollars. Prior to the ship's arrival in Peru, the CIA tipped off Alan Garcia, who ordered its seizure. Washington sources alleged that the weapons were going to the Sendero Luminoso, although Miami arms dealer David Duncan claimed they were for the Peruvian navy. As the ship entered Peruvian waters, the Peruvian navy failed to capture it, and it turned back toward Panama. There, acting on the wishes of Alan García, Noriega seized the ship. [103] The boat's papers had been revised to state that it was heading to Acajutla, El Salvador, to deliver its cargo to Adolfo Blandón, chief of staff of El Salvador's army.[104] Duncan stated that he turned to the Salvadorian military as an alternate buyer when the Peruvian navy failed to carry out the purchase.[105]

Both Peru's navy and the Salvadorian military denied any knowledge of the shipment, creating suspicions that the cargo was part of a CIA covert operation, either to deliver the weapons to the Contras or to show that East Germany was sending weapons to the Sendero.[106] In 1988, in an unsubstantiated charge, Jose Blandón, one of Noriega's chief advisors, claimed that Noriega was behind Duncan's shipment. The weapons were scheduled for delivery to cocaine organizations in Peru through corrupt elements in its navy. However, when the mission was exposed and the boat turned back toward Panama, Blandón contended that Richard Secord and Oliver North had proposed to Noriega that they purchase the weapons from Duncan and then secretly redirect the arms shipment to El Salvador. According to Blandón, their plan had been to seize the shipment en route in order to show the world that East German weapons were going to the Marxist rebels in El Salvador. Once the scandal had died down, they would funnel the weapons to the Contras. [107]

Blandón testified that this plan was never carried out. Luis Murillo pointed out that Seymour Hersh's article on Noriega came out on June 12, 1986, just as the *Pia Vesta* case was unfolding. Two days later, Noriega confiscated the ship and kept the weapons because he discovered that NSC members were behind the leaks to Hersh.[108]

In 1987, in an attempt to show that the CIA was working to discredit him, Noriega provided the *Miami Herald* with taped conversations between Miami arms dealer David Duncan and Panamanian authorities. Duncan could be heard on these tapes stating that the *Pia Vesta* weapons were headed to El Salvador all along and that the Salvadorians had promised to hold the weapons for "third parties" (the Contras).[109] The recorded conversations provoked several questions: Who really owned the weapons on the ship? Did the CIA thwart the arms shipment for its own purposes? Were the weapons always intended for the Contras, and was the Peruvian manifest the fake one?

While no concrete proof of what really happened has yet been found, the incident does afford circumstantial evidence that the relationship between Noriega and the CIA had gone bad. It also leads to conjecture that Noriega's decreased cooperation with anti-Sandinista operations was part of this breakdown, particularly since he retained the weapons for the PDF. Nevertheless, prior to William Casey's death in 1987, Noriega tried to maintain a loose relationship with the CIA in the hopes that Casey would clean up his standing with the U.S. government.

A Defense Intelligence Agency analysis confirmed that the "unfavorable U.S. press reports" pointing to Noriega's involvement "in weapons and drug trafficking . . . provoked a political tempest in Panama."[110] Consequently, Noriega sought to use his CIA contacts to improve his image with U.S. officialdom. He agreed to meet Oliver North, the NSC-CIA liaison with the Contras, while on a trip to England in August 1986.[111] North noted in a memo to Poindexter that, at this meeting, Noriega proposed to "take care" of the Sandinista leadership in exchange for help with cleaning up his image and a removal of the ban on foreign military sales to Panama. Noriega asserted that he had "numerous assets in place" in Nicaragua and that, without his help, "a Contra victory" was out of the question. In his memo on the meeting, North stated that "if as in the past" Noriega refused "to work" directly "with the CIA," permitting Noriega to use his own Panamanian operatives against the Sandinistas was a "very effective, very secure means of doing some of the things which must be done if the Nicaragua project [was] going to succeed." [112] Although the CIA rejected the plan—the assassination of the entire Sandinista leadership was out of the question—Noriega's willingness to renew his relationship with the CIA on his own terms demonstrated his desperation to hold onto power.

Noriega then went on the attack, accusing Jesse Helms of being a right-wing fanatic and making veiled threats in the press that he would expose the CIA's activities in Central America.[113] Clearly, the relationship between Noriega and the CIA had fallen apart over the Contra program and his unwillingness to bend to U.S. demands. His break with the CIA provides an explanation for the public revelations about his illegal activities as well as for the U.S. invasion of Panama.

In 1987 Colonel Roberto Diaz Herrera denounced Noriega on Panamanian national television, severely weakening his political power. Diaz Herrera had attempted an unsuccessful coup against Noriega at the time of Spadafora's murder. In the aftermath of the coup attempt, Diaz Herrera remained the PDF's second in command, although his power was basically sidelined. In June 1987, to prevent any future threat from Diaz Herrera, Noriega forced him to retire from the PDF. Diaz Herrera responded by confessing both his own crimes and Noriega's to Panamanian journalists. Diaz Herrera accused Noriega of rigging the 1984 elections, trafficking narcotics, being involved in Hugo Spadafora's death, and conspiring with the CIA to kill Omar Torrijos.[114] Diaz Herrera also claimed that U.S. SOUTHCOM's commander, John Galvin, was aware of these actions: the United States had been unwilling to act against Noriega because it "was afraid to alienate" Noriega, when the "General was constantly flirting with Soviet bloc nations, notably Cuba."[115]

Noriega called these statements high treason. Diaz Herrera responded by encircling his house with loyal soldiers. He assumed the persona of a martyr-prophet, dressing in white and carrying a Bible to all of his public appearances.[116] The PDF spokesperson for Noriega called Diaz Herrera mentally unstable. Noriega sent troops to surround the house, but backed off because Diaz Herrera had turned his house into a center of opposition against him. Among the Panamanian people, nothing could stop the rioting that followed these accusations. The massive street demonstrations lasted for a week. The government imposed a state of emergency and shut down opposition newspapers. Noriega placed a chokehold on Panama.

The initial U.S. reaction to Panama's crisis was a call for circumspect calm. The U.S. Senate passed a resolution that called on Noriega to step down from power, but the State Department rejected it, fearing that this position could jeopardize the safety of the Canal.[117] Noriega continued to collaborate with the DEA throughout 1987. For instance, he assisted with Operation Pisces, an anti-money laundering operation that targeted Panama's banking system.

Money laundering in Panama had declined as a result of the country's 1982 economic crisis. The crisis was closely associated with Latin America's financial troubles and decreased lending, which had reduced Panama's role as a dollar-based center.[118] Around 1985, money laundering in Panama resumed.[119] In response, the United States launched Operation Pisces to investigate money laundering between New York, Miami, Los Angeles, and Panama. By its conclusion, Noriega had helped the DEA freeze fifty-four accounts worth more than fourteen million dollars in Panama's banks.[120] However, some of Noriega critics claimed that Noriega had cooperated with the United States to deflect attention from his purported drug activities. Others argued that Noriega had worked with the DEA to "eliminate" the Medellín cartel's "competitors."[121] Nevertheless, the DEA affirmed its "deep appreciation" for Noriega's "anti-drug trafficking policy." Noriega also received praise from Attorney General Edwin Meese.[122]

Following the June 1987 death of his CIA benefactor, William Casey, relations between Noriega and the United States deteriorated. Noriega declared that Diaz Herrera's accusations and the subsequent public demonstrations against him were part of a U.S. plot to retain control of the Panama Canal. Noriega denounced Yankee intervention, and in mid-June 1987, he brought Daniel Ortega, the Sandinista president of Nicaragua, to Panama City to defy the United States.[123] In late June 1987, U.S. Ambassador Arthur Davis pleaded for an end to censorship of the local press, and the U.S. Senate voted for an investigation into Noriega's rule. Noriega countered by organizing a protest march against the United States for meddling in Panama's affairs. His supporters attacked the U.S. embassy, causing superficial damage with stones and paint.[124] In response, Elliot Abrams delivered a scathing speech against Noriega, while the Reagan administration called on him to step down from power to allow Panama to move toward democracy. The administration also cut off all economic aid to Panama.[125]

Undeterred, Noriega initiated more demonstrations against the United States while proclaiming, "Not one step back," a reference to the Panama Canal Treaties. Some political observers believed that Noriega was trying to divert attention from his domestic crisis by rallying supporters against the United States and appearing to defy "the gringos."[126] Noriega declared U.S. intervention in Panama an "unpardonable affront"; any further comments by the United States on Panama's domestic affairs would be considered an "action hostile to the government of Panama."[127] The growing discord between Noriega and the Reagan administration encouraged Noriega to exploit anti-American sentiment as a way to hold on to power. How much would the United States tolerate before it saw Noriega as a serious threat to its security?

Investigations into Noriega's activities by the U.S. Senate and a Miami grand jury led to further allegations against him. In particular, the testimonies of Floyd Carlton (one of Noriega's personal pilots), Steven Kalish (a convicted drug dealer and Noriega associate), and José Blandón (Noriega's intelligence/political advisor) were extremely damaging. As mentioned earlier, Floyd Carlton, convicted in 1987 of drug smuggling, testified before a Miami grand jury and the U.S. Senate that he started smuggling cocaine for the Medellín cartel while he worked as Noriega's personal pilot. Carlton claimed that as an intermediary between Noriega and the cartel, he had delivered cash payments of $250,000 to Noriega for moving cocaine through Panama into the United States. The planes that delivered the cocaine to Panama often belonged to traffickers who were rivals of the Medellín organization and whose assets had been seized by Noriega. Carlton also stated that in 1980, while Noriega headed the Panamanian G2, he had used PDF planes to transport surplus weapons to the FMLN with Noriega's permission[128]

Steven Kalish, another convicted drug smuggler, told the Senate that in 1983, after he learned that Noriega had made Panama available to drug traffickers, he approached Noriega and offered him a three-hundred-thousand-dollar bribe to run narcotics through the country.[129] Kalish also testified that Noriega later invited him to become a partner in Servicios Turísticos as a way to launder drug payments to him. Finally, Kalish contended that he attempted to purchase a Boeing 737 airplane on Noriega's behalf and that Noriega had intended to use this plane for a money laundering operation.[130]

The testimony of José Blandón was the most damaging because he was a former Noriega loyalist. After Diaz Herrera's public denouncement of Noriega, Blandón had encouraged Noriega to seek a negotiated settlement with his political opposition to end Panama's crisis. However, this would have meant Noriega's forced retirement from the PDF.[131] Noriega refused this advice and fired Blandón. Blandón then defected to the United States, where he accused Noriega of protecting the Medellín cartel following the murder of Lara Bonilla, the Colombian minister of justice. Blandón also testified that Noriega had gone to Fidel Castro to negotiate a settlement with the cartel after the raid on the Darién cocaine processing center and had participated in the *Pia Vesta* incident.[132] Noriega was convicted in the United States without a trial or a word in his defense. Noriega, the de facto leader of Panama, became public enemy number one.

Two indictments were filed against Noriega in the United States on February 4, 1988. In the first, a federal grand jury in Miami charged Noriega, along with Medellín cartel members Pablo Escobar, Fabio Ochoa, and Jorge Ochoa, with multiple counts of narcotics trafficking and other related offenses. In particular, Noriega was charged with money laundering, facilitating the distribution of narcotics through Panama, and aiding and abetting the Medellín cartel by using the PDF to ship precursor chemicals to its HCL-processing facilities in Colombia and Panama.[133] The second indictment came from a federal grand jury in Tampa, Florida.

The Tampa indictment accused Noriega of working with Steven Kalish to smuggle more than one million pounds of marijuana into the United States.[134]

Noriega declared the indictments part of an effort to undermine the 1977 Panama Canal Treaties. He asserted that the Reagan administration was seeking an excuse to keep U.S. military bases in Panama after the treaties expired. Noriega also pointed out that the testimony against him came from "two convicts, who in order to shorten their sentences, lend themselves to a process against the dignity of a leader, only because he has demanded respect for his country."[135] In his memoir, Noriega wrote that the evidence provided by Blandón was flimsy. For example, Blandón had a photograph of Castro, Noriega, and himself together, which was used as evidence in the Senate hearings to prove that Noriega and Castro had conspired to traffic in narcotics. Noriega claimed that Blandón turned against him for spite and that a photo of the three men together proved nothing, since Noriega had at one point served as an open channel to Castro for the CIA.[136] Other sources argued that Blandón got the dates of Noriega's trip to Cuba wrong in his testimony.[137]

Plainly, Noriega saw the indictments as politically motivated. He claimed that he was charged because of his nationalist stance and unwillingness to cooperate with the CIA against the Sandinistas. Noriega also maintained that the indictments gave the United States an excuse to invade Panama and quell Panamanian nationalism if it challenged U.S. hegemony over Central America and the Canal.

Responding to the indictments, Noriega drummed up more anti-American sentiment. He declared that the U.S. SOUTHCOM "constituted a national security threat" and was "another point of aggression against Panama." Noriega added that U.S. bases in Panama were an impediment to the country's "social, economic, political, and jurisdictional development" and called on the U.S. SOUTHCOM to withdraw from Panama.[138] The United States responded that the canal treaties sanctioned its presence in the country until 1999.[139] As tension grew between Noriega and the U.S. SOUTHCOM, the State Department wrote that if Noriega's inability to control Panama continued, his need to use anti-Americanism to hold on to power could lead to the "harassment of U.S. military personnel."[140] The relationship between Noriega and the United States was a marriage of convenience that had become inconvenient for both. Noriega and the United States backed themselves into corners from which they could not extricate themselves.

The showdown between Noriega and the U.S. government became even more serious when Noriega turned to Cuba, Nicaragua, and Libya for support. Writing on Noriega, Ela Navarrete Talavera argued that Noreiga tried to accelerate communism in Panama to protect himself against the United States. Talavera believed that the communists exploited this sentiment to turn the Panamanian people against the United States and gain control over the canal.[141]

Cuba began a seven-month airlift during which it delivered two hundred tons of material and supplies to Panama after the indictments.[142] As Noriega became friendlier with Cuba and Nicaragua, the Reagan administration's sworn enemies, Cuba and Nicaragua started to funnel weapons and instructors into Panama. In addition, they helped Noriega form civilian defense committees, called Dignity Battalions, which he used to gather intelligence and keep a firm hold over the population. A DIA study reported that Noriega also received twenty million dollars from Libya in 1989 in return for permission to use Panama as a base to coordinate terrorist and insurgency groups throughout Latin America.[143]

While he flirted with Cuba, Nicaragua, and Libya, Noriega announced that it was "extremely dangerous to challenge the tolerance, patience, and good faith" of Panama's "people with campaigns that can engender unpredictable reactions."[144] This did not seem like an idle threat, especially considering the presence of the Dignity Battalions. The U.S. embassy in Panama started to worry that Noriega would "unleash" and "orchestrate the use of weapons-bearing goon squads" to "move against the U.S. embassy and its personnel" or "the U.S. military." The embassy also feared that Colombian narco-traffickers were a potential threat. Embassy staff wrote that the "Medellín cartel . . . either on its own or prompted by Noriega . . . could choose to displace its attention to the U.S. mission in Panama." They also reported that as long as "Pax Noriega" remained, no major threat would arise. If Noriega let it be known that Americans were "fair game," the "threat" to U.S. interests "would be critical."[145]

The United States and Noriega were on a collision course, but Panama's presidential election in May 1989 strengthened Noriega's control over the country. Noriega used his Dignity Battalions to intimidate voters in the May election, despite the presence of former President Jimmy Carter as an election observer. Nevertheless, the opposition candidate Guillermo Endara won. His victory over Noriega's candidate, Carlos Duque, was a triumph for Noriega's opponents. In the aftermath of the election, Noriega annulled the results, alleging foreign interference. He had the Dignity

Battalions attack the opposition candidates, forcing them into hiding and leaving Noriega in complete control of Panama.

A military coup against Noriega in October 1989 further buttressed Noriega's power. Moisés Giroldi, a former Torrijista PDF officer, led the coup. Giroldi, who had helped suppress an abortive coup against Noriega in March 1988, staged the 1989 rebellion with the full knowledge of the U.S. SOUTHCOM. However, General Maxwell Thurman, the commander of SOUTHCOM, did not trust Giroldi. He feared that Giroldi might be setting the United States up to intervene blindly on behalf of a nonexistent coup as a ploy to revive anti-American sentiment and bolster Noriega's popularity.[146] Consequently, when Giroldi launched the coup, he did so without the support he expected and needed from U.S. forces. The rebellion's failure strengthened Noriega's grip over the PDF: in Panama, Noriega's power was absolute.

When Bush became president in 1989, he moved against Noriega. As vice president, Bush had opposed the Reagan administration's attempt to negotiate with Noriega, and during his campaign, Bush had promised that he would not make deals with narco-traffickers.[147] With the support of Secretary of Defense Richard Cheney, Bush issued National Security Decision Directive 17 (NSDD 17). The directive intensified media and psychological operations and increased the United States' military presence in the Canal Zone.[148]

Bush decided that the armed forces should begin preparations for a surprise invasion of Panama rather than follow the course of pressure and intimidation used by the Reagan government. Hostility between the United States and Panama mounted when the Panamanian National Assembly passed a resolution declaring, "[O]wing to U.S. aggression . . . a state of war exists with the United States." [149] Noriega made the situation even worse when he named himself "maximum leader" and publicly speculated that the "bodies of our enemies" would float down the Canal.

When four U.S. officers took a wrong turn and ran into a PDF checkpoint outside the Canal Zone on the night of December 16, 1989, the tension between the United States and Panama boiled over. The army's official story asserted that the four officers refused to get out of their vehicle at the checkpoint and sped off, fearing for their lives. The PDF forces then opened fire on the car. Three of the men were wounded, and one of them subsequently died from the attack. The checkpoint incident gave the Bush administration the pretext it needed to attack Panama.[150] On December

19, 1989, the United States launched Operation Just Cause, the invasion of Panama to overthrow Manuel Noriega.

The invasion of Panama was motivated by complex conditions, including Noriega's criminal activity, nationalism, and failed covert operations with the CIA. On first inspection, it appeared the United States attacked Panama to overthrow a rogue leader involved in illegal activities that threatened U.S. security interests. Noriega's nationalistic aspiration to separate Panama and himself from U.S. hegemony provided a deeper justification. However, Noriega's dealings with the CIA, combined with his desire to manipulate the political situation in Central America to his benefit, were the final straw, a situation the United States could not tolerate.

Noriega saw his troubled position in Panama as part of a U.S. plot to weaken his regime because he refused to let the CIA drag him into the Central American war. Even so, Noriega had kept his channels to the CIA open, although, after William Casey's death, he had few friends left in Washington. An underlying antagonism between Noriega and the United States began to build, while political opposition in Panama pushed for his ouster. Noriega's alleged association with the Medellín cartel, or with Cuba and the M-19, as well as his decision to play the United States off enemies such as Nicaragua, were his final undoing. Using the pretext of the War on Drugs, the United States removed Noriega from power.

Political pundits have contended that Bush launched this war to overcome the "wimp factor." Yet, in the overall scheme of U.S. policy in Latin America, Noriega played a crucial role in the War on Drugs. Although Panama was an easy target, the invasion of Panama demonstrated the United States' determination to stop the flow of narcotics from Latin America and its willingness to use military might to do so. President Bush declared that Noriega's "apprehension and return to the United States" sent "a clear signal that the United States" was seriously committed to ensuring "that those charged with promoting the distribution of drugs cannot escape this scrutiny of justice."[151]

In the aftermath of the invasion, the United States turned Panama into its center of operations for the U.S. SOUTHCOM's coordination of counternarcotics operations throughout Latin America.[152] According to military expert Donald J. Mabry, following Operation Just Cause, General Thurman began planning a low-intensity conflict, directed from Panama, in which Colombian, Bolivian, and Peruvian military forces, aided by the U.S. military, would launch strikes against drug traffickers.[153] Panama had become a key area of interest for the Bush administration as it ratcheted up U.S. military involvement in the War on Drugs.

The Cartagena Summit and the Andean Trade Preference Act

The northern Andean governments criticized the Andean Strategy's emphasis on military solutions and its lack of economic incentives. The Bush administration took the position that, if it "ceded . . . the Andean ridge countries" to the "cartels and traffickers," they would become "permanent powers" there, as "Noriega" had been "in Panama."[154] Therefore, military and INM counternarcotics assistance remained high, at $187.9 million in 1990, $166.6 million in 1991, and a requested $195.8 million in 1992.[155] On the other hand, the Andean Strategy based economic aid on each country's performance in curbing narcotics production, a policy that the regional governments severely condemned.[156] To placate them, President Bush agreed to hold a summit in Cartagena, Colombia; however, the invasion of Panama just prior to the summit led the northern Andean countries to threaten to end their cooperation with the United States in the War on Drugs.

The invasion of Panama put the Bush administration on the defensive. When the Cartagena Summit convened in February 1990, the Bush administration agreed to reexamine the Andean Strategy's economic aspect. Accordingly, the Bush administration agreed to help create alternative development programs and to participate in the Andean Trade Preference Act (ATPA). The ATPA was a plan to liberalize the regional economy by reducing tariffs and taxes between the United States and the Andean nations. Cartagena Summit members saw the ATPA as a step in the right direction; but the U.S. commitment to alternative development programs was weak, and the ATPA drew sharp condemnations from domestic critics in the United States. The ATPA also drew disapproval because many of the products made by the Andean campesinos were not even included in the agreement. In many respects, the economic focus of the Andean Strategy was too little, too late.

The lack of alternative development programs was a cause of concern for the northern Andean countries, particularly Bolivia and Peru. Eradicating the coca crops without supplying compensatory sources of economic revenue for the growers threatened political stability; it drove a wedge between the governments and the campesinos. Prior to the

Cartagena Summit, Jaime Paz Zamora, the Bolivian president elected in 1989, was strongly opposed to "military involvement" unless the United States was "willing to ante-up" millions of dollars for "alternative development" and other "types of cooperation in the interdiction and eradication areas." Unfortunately, the U.S. embassy believed that unless Bolivia showed up with "concrete results in interdiction and eradication," Paz Zamora's request for alternative development financing would "almost certainly be refused."[157]

The Peruvian government argued that its efforts to control the "production, smuggling, and the processing of coca derivatives" was not going to be successful until "the foreign demand for illicit coca products" decreased and the "consumer/developed countries" contributed "their share of assistance to the Peruvian effort."[158] In the last year of his presidency, Alan García was highly critical of the level of U.S. funding for Peru. Guillermo Larco Cox, Peru's foreign minister, proposed legalizing the personal use of cocaine and argued that Peru should use its debt payments to the United States to purchase the country's entire coca leaf crop. The State Department's response was that these comments made "cooperation difficult" and reinforced "the impression in Washington" that the United States could "not work constructively with the García administration."[159] The State Department rejected Peru's proposal, claiming that it would encourage more coca production. They would base all assistance only on active efforts to decrease narcotics cultivation and trafficking, as well as the institution of sound economic policies.[160]

Just prior to the Cartagena Summit, the ambassadors of Bolivia and Peru spoke before the U.S. Congress to drive home the need for more economic support to pursue antinarcotics activities. Peru's Ambassador Cesar Atala called on the U.S. government to "exonerate Peru, Bolivia, and Colombia from their obligations of interest and principal on the credits" they received for USAID programs and military purchases. Atala called for the legal purchase of coca leaf and its destruction by the United States, adding that the cost of purchasing and destroying coca would be a "fraction" of what was "spent on interdiction, eradication, and antidrug prevention programs."[161] Finally, Atala called for a crop substitution program that could create an agro-industrial infrastructure to encourage higher, value-added prices for items grown in the UHV.

Bolivia's Ambassador Jorge Crespo-Velasco also supported crop substitution. Crespo-Velasco added that Bolivia's efforts to counter coca production would depend on the continued support for its orthodox stabilization program, the NEP, even though the program had many negative side effects in the short-term—including driving people into the illegal economy when they could not find jobs. Therefore, Crespo-Velasco called for increased investment in the Bolivian economy to supplant foreign exchange, income, and employment derived from "illicit activity." The country needed debt relief, crop substitution, and investment in the agro-industrial sector to "mitigate the terrible social costs" from the adoption of the NEP. The ambassador concluded that Bolivia had upheld its part in "international partnerships" involving "debt, drugs or the environment"; however, the commitment to end illegal coca production was a "two-way street" that the United States would have to fully match with "deeds and words." [162]

The attack on Panama nearly sabotaged all hopes of developing a working agreement for the region. The invasion sparked fears through-out Latin America that Washington intended to embark on a new era of gunboat diplomacy.[163] Political analysts reported that Latin Americans believed that the War on Drugs was replacing communism as the United States' excuse to intervene in the Southern Hemisphere.[164]

Peruvian president Alan García suspended antinarcotics operations with U.S. drug agents to protest the invasion. García also called on the governments of Colombia and Bolivia to cancel or postpone the summit.[165] García asked, "How can I meet with a president that comes to crush Latin America?"[166] Colombia became extremely hostile to U.S. operations in the Caribbean. In January 1990, after the invasion, the United States prepared to deploy the aircraft carrier USS *Kennedy* and the cruiser USS *Virginia* off the Colombian coast to step up naval radar surveillance. The deployment looked like a military intervention and a blockade of Colombia's territorial waters.[167] Since 1990 was an election year in Colombia and Barco was a lame-duck president, the U.S. deploy-ment became a political football. Barco's party and cabinet forced him to denounce the deployment. Barco stated that Colombia could in "no way accept armed intervention or blockade . . . under the oblique premise of patrolling international waters."[168]

To improve its image, the United States sent Vice President Dan Quayle to mollify Latin American agitation. Quayle emphasized that the United States had no intention of intervening anywhere else.[169] Quayle had pre-dicted that no long-term negative repercussions would arise from the U.S. invasion, but anti-American sentiment throughout the region curtailed his trip.[170] Quayle's journey seemed to be a failure, but both the Colombian and Bolivian governments remained committed to the summit, regardless of their criticism of the United States.[171] When Bush announced that he was going to withdraw U.S. forces from Panama by the end of February 1990, García ended his opposition to the Cartagena Summit.[172]

The Cartagena Summit began on February 15, 1990. At the meeting, the presidents of Bolivia, Colombia, Peru, and the United States put together a multilateral agreement to strengthen their counternarcotics programs. The four nations concurred that a coordinated approach to counternarcotics had to address the issues of demand, consumption, and supply. The summit agreement stated that all four countries had to accept certain understandings on "economic cooperation, alternative development, and the encouragement of trade and investment." Moreover, these policies could not be effective unless they were accompanied by "concomitant dynamic programs attacking the production of, trafficking in, and demand for illicit drugs."[173] The strategy was interconnected: failure in any one of these areas jeopardized progress in the others.

President Bush stated that the Cartagena Summit created "the first anti-drug cartel." William Bennett, the U.S. drug czar, who accompanied Bush to the summit, commented that although there was no "magic bullet, no simple solution to the drug problem," the act provided a "comprehensive effort that put pressure on every point of the spectrum."[174]

Colombia's President Barco noted that progress was made at the summit because the participants agreed "not only to a well-defined path" but also to the "need to adopt trade measures to strengthen [their] economies to face the drug problem in all its scope and magnitude."[175] Julio Londoño Paredes, Colombia's foreign minister, explained that the Cartagena agreement went beyond an approach based solely on "repressive actions" and recognized the need for adequate economic cooperation. Paredes also noted that the summit defined economic cooperation as "a reasonable and favorable attitude towards products derived from the soil and subsoil of our respective states."[176]

García remarked that he spoke frankly to Bush, pointing out that the United States had a "military budget of $400 billion," yet Bush had offered the nations of the northern Andes only "a millesimal part of that budget to solve a problem" that the United States described "as its most serious." García also told Bush that he had to become an "ally" of Peru's peasants by "lending them money, buying their products and guaranteeing them that their products" would "go out to a consumer market."[177] García concluded that the summit was positive because it created a multilateral atmosphere.

The United States adopted several resolutions after Cartagena to address the Andean nations' concerns. In addition to the crop eradication, interdiction, and cooperative military programs that the Bush administration sought, the United States limited the export of assault weapons and precursor chemicals to make cocaine. It had become apparent to the DEA and the INM that U.S. corporations were shipping the precursor chemicals used in the production of cocaine hydrochloride, such as acetone and ether, to Latin America. The shipments were routinely seized in the jungles of Colombia.[178] The 1988 UN Convention against Illicit Traffic in Narcotics Drugs and Psychotropic Substances set controls over commercial chemical transactions to identify and stop those used for illegal drug manufacturing.[179] Since Bolivia, Colombia, and Peru, as well as the United States, were signatories to the convention, the United States could not expect the Andean nations to combat narcotics production while its own companies openly sold and distributed precursor chemicals abroad. The emphasis on developing a multilateral system to track the domestic and international movement of essential chemicals soon became a central method to control the refinement of coca leaves into cocaine.[180]

The United States also agreed to crack down on money laundering. This included efforts to identify, trace, freeze, seize, and apply other legal procedures to drug crime proceeds. The crackdown included the sharing of forfeited assets when Bolivia, Colombia, and Peru helped the United States in counternarcotics operations.[181] Finally, the Bush administration's acknowledgment that consumer demand was equally responsible for the drug epidemic led Bush to propose $7.6 billion for demand-and-supply reduction programs in the United States.[182]

The Cartagena summit clarified the need for regional development assistance, including help with foreign exchange problems.[183] As a result, the United States increased ESF support funds from $16 million in 1989 to $38 million in 1990 and $185 million in 1991, with a request for $422.3 million in 1992.[184] However, the release of this money was contingent on counternarcotics efforts and the adoption of sound economic policies; and this meant accepting Washington's plans for economic liberalization, which were expected to lift the Andean nations out of their economic malaise.

The ATPA, a significant outgrowth of the Cartagena Summit, was created to expand economic alternatives for the northern Andean countries.[185] It was designed to liberalize the region's economies by opening its markets to free trade. Bush made the ATPA a part of his Enterprise for the Americas Initiative, which envisioned hemispheric free trade as a long-term goal.[186] By opening up trade between the United States and the northern Andes, the administration hoped that the Andean economies would grow, thereby offering financial incentives for farmers to abandon coca production. Policymakers expected the ATPA to generate economic growth by providing new markets for alternative crops and gainful employment for people who cultivated coca out of necessity.[187]

The ATPA was a ten-year enactment that allowed Andean goods to enter the United States duty-free and vice versa, and it faced a great deal of opposition in the United States. Domestic interests, from tomato farmers to ceramic tile makers and garment manufacturers, worried that low-cost Andean producers would undercut them.[188] The American Soybean Association, for instance, lobbied Congress to prevent any funding to support Bolivian soybean production between 1988 and 1990, although USAID argued that this was detrimental to America's counternarcotics policy in Bolivia.[189] U.S. producers also argued that tariff reductions made it too costly for them to compete against foreign companies and that U.S. businesses and jobs would relocate outside of the United States as a result of the ATPA.[190]

Nevertheless, both houses of Congress passed the ATPA in December 1991.[191] Its supporters contended that Andean exports to the United States were not large enough to have a major impact on trade.[192] The administration also argued that U.S. exports would increase as the country's neighbors grew more prosperous. The ATPA allowed flowers, minerals such as copper, semiprecious stones, precious metals, crustaceans, tobacco, fruits, nuts, and vegetables to enter the United States duty-free.[193] Textiles made without Andean yarn, canned tuna, petroleum, watches, and footwear were excluded from the act.[194]

Unfortunately, the ATPA's ability to assist the coca-growing campesinos had one serious flaw: many imports that the United States purchased were sophisticated manufactures. The ATPA hoped to encourage this kind of industry in the Andean countries, but the coca farmers could not produce these kinds of goods. Consequently, economic experts believed that the ATPA's ability to reduce coca production would succeed or fail depending on its ability to promote agricultural exports. The Bush administration soon sent experts to Latin America to determine which crops had the greatest potential to expand in the global market.[195]

The northern Andean nations had high hopes that a concerted plan to lower trade barriers would remove the need to grow coca. All four participants at the Cartagena summit also believed that the ATPA would increase the demand for higher-paying alternative crops, another spur to a downward shift in coca cultivation. Bush officials agreed in principle to the development of alternative crop programs—accompanied, of course, by the Andean Strategy's military pressure on guerrillas and traffickers—because it believed that the combination of these two approaches could eliminate the perceived main sources of instability in the northern Andes: guerrilla insurgencies and narcotics production.

7

The Failure of the Andean Strategy

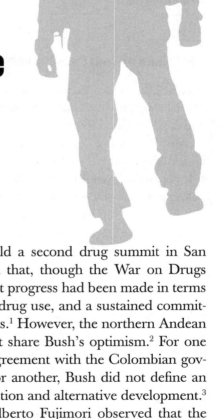

In February 1992, President Bush held a second drug summit in San Antonio, Texas. There he announced that, though the War on Drugs could not be won overnight," significant progress had been made in terms of increased cocaine seizures, reduced drug use, and a sustained commitment to challenging narcotics traffickers.[1] However, the northern Andean representatives at San Antonio did not share Bush's optimism.[2] For one thing, the summit failed to reach an agreement with the Colombian government to cut cocaine production. For another, Bush did not define an economic aid package for crop substitution and alternative development.[3] At the summit, Peruvian president Alberto Fujimori observed that the United States simply "did not understand the poverty and problems of the coca growers."[4]

By 1993, the last year of the George H. W. Bush presidency, there was a general consensus among Latin American and many U.S. officials that the Andean Strategy was not working. Complex circumstances hampered its implementation: disagreements between the Andean nations and the United States over how to stop narcotics trafficking, the upheaval caused by economic liberalization, the narcotics industry's ability to adapt its operations to circumvent counternarcotics measures, and continued campesino resistance to eradication programs. These conditions spurred coca cultivation, while the plan's emphasis on a military solution resulted in corruption and human rights abuses. Its proscriptive and punitive approach to narcotics control undermined its stated goal of creating the secure conditions necessary for effective counternarcotics operations. Rather than curing political instability in the northern Andes, the Andean Strategy fostered it.

The Failure of Crop Substitution

Perhaps the most contradictory policy within the Andean Strategy was that of crop substitution. U.S. policy linked economic assistance for alternative crop development to coca eradication. By destroying coca plantations, disrupting coca paste production, and stopping cocaine exports, U.S. policymakers hoped to drive the price of cocaine so high that stateside consumers would not purchase it, while at the same time making coca cultivation so risky for campesinos that the price of coca would ultimately fall. However, reducing the supply of coca leaf drove up its price, encouraged more coca production, and made the switch to alternative crops less and less attractive for coca growers. Meanwhile, Andean nations found it extremely difficult to earn the eradication credits they needed to develop an infrastructure that could provide real alternatives to growing coca, even supposing that such alternate crops existed or could be developed.[5]

It was far from clear that viable markets existed for alternative crops.[6] The most competitive traditional crops required several years to mature and were expensive to handle and transport.[7] In Bolivia and Peru, citrus, bananas, pineapples, and palm hearts had little economic allure for the campesinos because the international market for tropical produce was saturated.[8] In Bolivia nontraditional crops that could compete against coca—for example, macadamias, which paid $4,600 per hectare, and black pepper, which paid $3,360 per hectare—were discouraged because they were not eligible for economic credit, while traditional crops were.[9]

Transport costs were another problem. Profitable crops were those with a high value per pound or cubic foot. This made coca the cheapest product to transport to market. However, the United States would not support the construction of the new roads so vital to agricultural marketing for fear of facilitating the transport of coca and cocaine.[10] Evo Morales, executive secretary of the Bolivian coca growers' union, described alternative crop development as a "trick" because those who had experimented with crops other than coca soon realized that there were "no alternative markets"—or none that could be reached.[11]

Another unanswered question was whether farmers would plant alternative crops in *place* of coca or in *addition* to it. USAID pointed out one aspect of the answer: the soils in the UHV and the Chapare were "very poor," and those regions were "very wet in climate," making the land best suited for forestry, not traditional agriculture.[12] Cash flow was the other major factor. Most alternative crops produced a profit only after three or more years, compared to two years or less for coca. Moreover, alternative crops "required large investments in the first year," followed by "lesser but still significant expenses for several more years until there was any production to sell."[13] The most profitable alternative crops, macadamia nuts and black pepper, took nine years and five years, respectively, to reach full production.[14]

Few farmers could "afford to give up their source of income for two-to-five years, while waiting for a replacement crop to come on line."[15] Coca offered guaranteed returns and a guaranteed market.[16] No coca producer was willing to "eradicate his entire coca plantation in one felling in order to make room for alternative crops."[17] In the UHV, for example, many "legitimate farmers subdivided their land," which they rented or sold to the cocaleros, or cultivated their own coca on the side to provide "income insurance against the vagaries of legitimate agricultural markets." The ONDCP study on crop substitution concluded that legitimate farmers might be willing to diversify production, but only while continuing to cultivate coca.[18]

U.S. insistence on repressive counternarcotics tactics to reduce the price of coca leaf also strongly influenced the crop substitution program. The United States believed that driving down coca's price through eradication and interdiction would make alternative crops competitive with it. For example, in January 1987, around the time of the Blast Furnace operation in Bolivia, the price of coca leaf fell to $50 per one hundred pounds. However, as Blast Furnace wound down, the demand for coca drove the cost back up to $120 per one hundred pounds by July 1988. It fell again to $70 per one hundred pounds as supply stabilized in October 1988. Even with these fluctuations, coca's price in Bolivia made it more valuable than most alternative crops. In 1990 the USAID estimated that, with the exception of pineapples, macadamia nuts, and black pepper, coca—at $50 per one hundred pounds—far surpassed the prices earned by alternative crops, including palm hearts, oranges, coffee, cacao, corn, and bananas.[19]

The annual volume of coca leaf cultivation corresponded with flux in its value. In 1987, during Blast Furnace, only 41,400 hectares of coca were planted. When Blast Furnace ended, the temporary lack of supply it had produced drove up demand. As a result, coca leaf cultivation rose to 50,400 hectares in 1988.[20]

U.S. policymakers deduced from this that repressive actions such as Blast Furnace drove down the price of coca, while the lack of a vigorous eradication campaign allowed coca leaf production to increase. The U.S. government now made the case that a sustained, vigorous interdiction and enforcement program had depressed the price of coca. In particular, policymakers were certain that the price of coca fell due to the increased pressure that the Andean Strategy placed on traffickers.[21] As a result, the United States stepped up its cooperative eradication and interdiction programs with the Andean governments. Between December 1989 and May 1990, the INM argued that renewed pressure on the drug industry had reduced the price of coca leaf in Bolivia to ten dollars per one hundred pounds.[22]

The State Department touted the stabilization or decline of hectares dedicated to coca farming in the northern Andes between 1989 and 1990 and attributed the improvement to the Andean Strategy. In particular, the State Department estimated that Peru's coca leaf production remained steady at 121,000 hectares, while it declined from 52,900 to 50,300 hectares in Bolivia, and from 42,400 to 40,100 hectares in Colombia.[23]

But the claim that a vigorous narcotics enforcement program had cut the price of coca was open to doubt. The 1990 decline in coca leaf production was an aberration, not the result of counternarcotics efforts. From 1986 onward, coca leaf prices had fluctuated on a massive scale. The major disruption in the value of coca leaf in 1986 was overproduction. While the 1986–1987 Blast Furnace and Operation Condor programs affected coca prices, Operation Snowcap, which replaced these operations in 1987 and continued for the duration of the Bush administration, had little influence on price and production.[24]

Between 1989 and 1992, an increase in coca farming and a decline in the street value of cocaine caused the price of coca leaf to continue fluctuating. With the exception of the 1989–1990 growing season, the DEA estimated that overall coca leaf production in the northern Andes rose from 293,700 metric tons in 1988 to 333,900 metric tons in 1992.[25] In Peru the number of cultivated hectares increased from 109,155 in 1987 to 121,300 hectares in 1991, while in Bolivia, the figure grew from 41,400 in 1987 to 55,600 in 1991. In Colombia, the number of cultivated hectares jumped from 22,960 in 1987 to 40,900 in 1991 (see chart 7.1).[26]

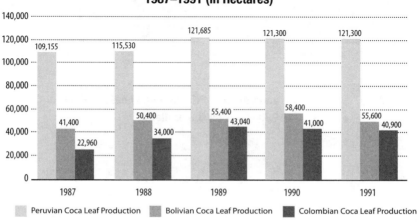

Chart 7.1 | **Coca Leaf Production in the Northern Andes, 1987–1991 (in Hectares)**

While coca cultivation was expanding, cocaine's street value declined. In 1987, cocaine cost $120 per gram. According to DEA estimates, between 1988 and 1989, the street price of cocaine fell to $105, only to jump to $159 in 1990; however, this price steadily dropped to $92 by 1994 (see chart 7.2).[27] At the same time, the price of coca leaf continued to fluctuate (see chart 7.3). In Bolivia, the price of coca leaf rose to an estimated $1.10 per kilogram in September 1990 and then climbed to $1.60 per kilogram by June 1991. Following this, coca leaf's value moved between approximately $0.75 and $1.20, until it rose to $1.75 per kilogram in June 1993. The price then dipped below roughly $1.00 in June 1994 but started rising again to $1.40 in 1995.

In Peru, coca leaf value moved steadily, with minor shifts, from an approximate $0.40 a kilogram in 1990 to $1.60 a kilogram in June 1991. From there, it shot up to a high of roughly $4.30 per kilogram in June 1992, but collapsed to $1.00 per kilogram in June 1993. The price rose again to almost $3.00 a kilogram in June 1994 and peaked at $4.30 in

Chart 7.2 | **Price Per Pure Gram of Cocaine, 1987–1994 (in U.S. Dollars)**

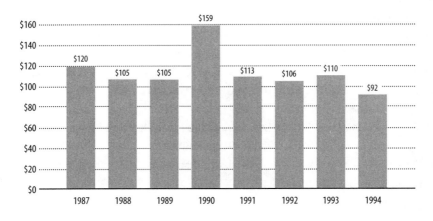

Chart 7.3 | **Bolivian and Peruvian Price of Coca Leaf Per Kilogram,
1990–1994 (in U.S. Dollars)**

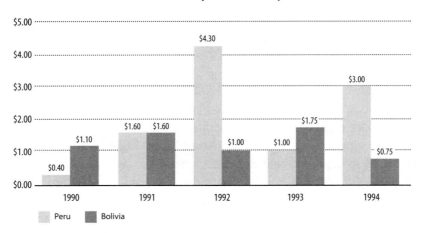

December 1994.[28] Only after this period did coca's value in Peru fall: between 1995 and 1996, the appearance of a fungus called *Fusarium oxysporum* brought prices down.

These figures show that coca leaf production was cyclical.[29] Regardless of interdiction and eradication programs, the price of coca leaf varied with supply and demand. A State Department cable noted that the depressed "farmgate coca leaf prices" in the late 1980s were the result of "larger leaf supplies." Thus, an oversupply of coca planted two years earlier caused a decline in coca cultivation in 1990, the same year the State

Department argued that vigorous eradication programs had depressed prices.[30] After the initial crackdown in Colombia in 1990, the price of coca leaf began to stabilize as traffickers and growers adjusted to new conditions. The economic incentive to grow coca continued, regardless of the risks involved.

This ongoing economic incentive, combined with price oscillations, also explains why campesinos continued to grow *both* coca and legitimate crops. The Bolivian government estimated that the cost of redirecting farmers into the legal agricultural economy would be seven thousand dollars per hectare, while the Peruvian government estimated an overall cost of eight hundred million dollars to develop an alternative crop program. Yet the prices that the alternative crop programs offered were roughly three hundred dollars per hectare in Peru and two thousand dollars per hectare in Bolivia.[31] According to Alberto Zamiro, an officer from DIRECO, "only those in absolute necessity" were eradicating.[32] A USAID study on the UHV stated that "project resources were not adequate and probably would never be adequate to carry out a comprehensive, integrated rural development effort."[33]

Since the United States released funding based on eradication results, expanded coca leaf production led to a decline in aid for developing long-term crop substitution programs. Chairman of the House Committee on Western Hemisphere Affairs George Crockett Jr. felt that the aid strategy for alternative crop programs "put the cart before the horse." Crockett believed that these countries needed "increased economic resources in order to attack the narcotics problem," rather than aid after the fact, received "as a reward for attacking it."[34]

Crisis in Colombia: The Drug Cartels

The Medellín cartel's assassination of Colombian presidential candidate Luis Carlos Galán in 1989 led the government to declare an all-out war against the cartel. Even prior to the assassination, the Barco government had been under strong domestic and international pressure to rein in the cartel, which was growing extremely powerful politically. In 1989, backed by the paramilitaries, the cartel had tried to form a political movement, called the Movimiento de Restauración Nacional (MORENA), to protect its interests.[35] One of the domestic leaders who had pressed the Barco government to challenge the cartel was Luis Carlos Galán, a senator described as the Colombian Liberal Party's great hope.[36] The Medellín cartel killed Galán because he had pushed for a renewal of extradition and because the government had directed the military and police to attack Medellín farms, airfields, and HCL refineries.[37]

In response to the assassination, the Colombian government declared a state of siege, made the state of Antioquia an emergency zone, and announced a major crackdown against the cartel. The government detained more than eleven thousand people for three days as Colombian forces made sweeping raids to capture cartel members.[38] In addition, and most important, immediately following the assassination, the Barco government announced a renewal of Colombia's extradition treaty with the United States. The Medellín organization then issued a public letter to the government, in which it declared that it was prepared to "fight with blood" against the government and extradition. They added that they wanted peace but were not willing to beg for it. Signing the letter as "Los Extraditables," in reference to their opposition to extradition, the cartel prepared for a second war over extradition.[39]

With the help of the United States, Colombia designed a kingpin strategy to bring down the Medellín cartel. It aimed to wipe out the cartel by "attacking and destroying those organizations that produce, transport, and distribute" cocaine and other drugs. The DEA believed that if they neutralized the cartel's kingpin and his leadership, the cartel would implode.[40] Instead, the kingpin policy boosted narcotics-related violence throughout the country as the cartel fought back. Bombings of public and government institutions, including the partial destruction of the Departamento Administrativo de Seguridad (DAS) headquarters in December 1989 and soft targets that represented U.S. political and economic influence, became everyday occurrences. The cartel negotiated through intimidation. In one particularly egregious incident, it allegedly bombed Avianca Flight 203 in November 1989, killing all 107 people on board. Pablo Escobar was thought to have directed the bombing, in retaliation for government efforts to capture him. Speculation circulated that "Escobar and other leaders of the Medellín cartel had decided" that their previous efforts to deter extradition had been ineffective, and consequently, they had resolved to "escalate the war to demonstrate their powers and capabilities."[41]

Nevertheless, Colombia's relentless pursuit of the Medellín cartel led to the near capture of both Jorge Ochoa and Pablo Escobar, while raids on Escobar's properties provided information that led government forces to Gonzalo Rodriguez Gacha. Consequently, the CNP raided Gacha's hacienda at the port of Coveñas in northern Colombia in December 1989, leading to the death of Gacha, his son, and five of his bodyguards in a bloody shootout.[42] Stunned by this act, the Medellín cartel admitted defeat. The cartel issued a communiqué stating that its members accepted "the triumph of the state" and indicated that they were willing to "lay down their arms." The remaining members of the Medellín organization offered to end their involvement in the drug business and surrender, in return for the government's promise not to extradite its members to the United States.[43]

A group of powerful politicians and leaders, known as the Notables, and including former presidents Turbay and Michelsen and Roman Catholic Cardinal Mario Revollo Bravo, announced that they approved of the "spirit" of the communiqué. The Barco administration remained reserved about the cartel's eleven-point proposal but noted that it created a "new situation."[44] In the end, Barco refused to let the cartel intimidate him and rejected the proposal, although the government continued to bargain with the Medellín cartel over the terms of surrender.

Barco's successor, César Gaviria (1990–1994), eventually accepted the cartel's peace offer. He believed that by applying strong police pressure, he could induce the cartel to surrender.[45] In the end, he also agreed, in return for the cartel's submission, not to extradite its members to the United States.[46] For Gaviria, "extradition was an imperfect second choice."[47] Gaviria believed that by allowing the cartel to plea bargain, Colombia could strengthen its judicial system and end the bloody conflict. Fabio and Jorge Ochoa then turned themselves in, and Pablo Escobar negotiated favorable terms for his surrender in 1991.[48]

As a part of the cartel's surrender, the Colombian Congress made the extradition of Colombian nationals illegal.[49] The United States met Gaviria's proposal with skepticism but recognized that the important issue was putting the cartel "behind bars," whether those bars were "manu-factured in the U.S. or Colombia."[50] It appeared as though the Medellín cartel's days were over.

Following the surrender of the Medellín organization, the Cali cartel emerged as the dominant narcotics force in Colombia. Run by Miguel and Gilberto Rodríguez Orejuela and their associates José Santacruz Londoño and Helmer "Pacho" Herrera, the Cali group was more businesslike than the flamboyant Medellín cartel and sought to draw less attention to itself. The Cali cartel ran their operations like a franchise. They used "on site representatives" to distribute coca to individual cells that were "independent" of each other.[51] Moreover, rather than openly challenging the government—a Medellín tactic—the Cali cartel sought to corrupt the government from within.

Despite their differences, the Cali and Medellín cartels recognized each other and had often cooperated throughout the 1980s. Between them, they smuggled roughly 80 percent of the cocaine entering the United States for most of that decade.[52] They developed a tacit agreement in which the Cali cartel controlled the New York City market and the Medellín cartel controlled the Florida market. California was up for grabs between the two.[53] The Cali organization also helped the Medellín cartel with the formation of the paramilitary organization Muerte a Secuestradores following the kidnapping of Fabio Ochoa's daughter. The alliance between the Medellín and Cali cartels made them almost invincible until it fell apart in 1988.

Journalist Ron Chepesiuk believed that the cartels broke apart as the Cali group grew more powerful and refused to form a supercartel with the Medellín group.[54] Alternately, Gustavo Veloza argued that the alliance collapsed due to growing differences over how to manage political affairs with the government.[55] Regardless of the reason for the antagonism between the cartels, the Medellín started to move in on the Cali organization's New York market in 1988.[56] When a bomb exploded outside of Escobar's apartment building on January 13, 1988, he concluded that the Cali cartel was responsible, thus starting the hostilities.

The conflict between the cartels did not end when Escobar turned himself in to Colombian authorities. He continued to run the Medellín cartel from his prison, known as La Catedral, which he had built to his personal specifications.[57] Because of lax security and Escobar's corruption of the guards, he was free to come and go as he pleased and to exact revenge against his enemies, notably the Cali cartel. When the government tried to rein in Escobar by moving him to a military prison, he escaped and continued his attacks on the Cali cartel and the government.[58]

To capture Escobar, the military and police, as well as a special unit known as the Bloque de Busqueda, made extensive use of intelligence provided by the Cali-funded paramilitary organization, Perseguidos por Pablo Escobar (PEPES), which committed acts of violence against Escobar and his family for attacks against them on a "one for one basis."[59] In 1993, following leads from the Cali cartel, the CNP raided Escobar's hideout in Medellín and killed him in a shootout as he fled for safety.[60] The Medellín cartel was effectively defeated. On the other hand, the Cali cartel was stronger than ever.

Crisis in Colombia: La Apertura, Economic Collapse, and Civil War

In the late 1980s, Colombia liberalized its troubled economy in a series of policy changes known as "La Apertura" (the opening). The government expected liberalization to boost tax revenues by raising imports and to stimulate growth in the export market by devaluing the Colombian peso and relaxing exchange controls.[61] Initially, the tariff reductions and loosened restrictions on capital did not bring in the expected imports. Instead, imports dropped, while massive amounts of money flooded the economy. To prevent inflation, the government kept interest rates high, but this only served to attract more money to the economy because Colombian banks provided better returns than U.S. banks.[62]

To create an outflow of cash reserves that would help keep inflation in check, Colombia reduced its tariff rate from 44 percent in 1989 to less than 12 percent by 1993. Yet the lowering of tariffs became a destructive force as imports began to surpass exports (see chart 7.4). Although the Colombian government originally wanted to increase imports and thereby increase tax revenues from those imports, in actuality, reductions in its tariff rate meant that the flood of imports provided minimal tax revenues. Consequently, exports began a downward shift, from 21 percent in 1991 to 15 percent in 1994, where they remained for the rest of the decade. At the same time, imports steadily rose, from 14 percent in 1991 to 21 percent in 1994 [63]

Chart 7.4 | **Colombian Imports vs. Exports, 1991–1994 (as a Percentage of GDP)**

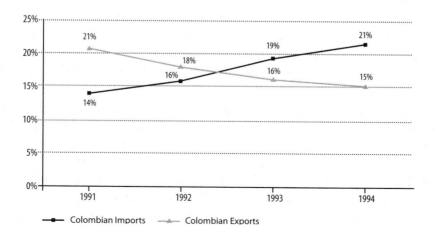

La Apertura damaged many different sectors of the Colombian economy. The campesinos were hurt the most, as tariffs on agricultural commodities such as wheat, corn, barley, sorghum, soy, rice, sugar, and powdered milk were phased out in 1994. Products such as electrical appliances, tobacco, and liquor were also made duty-free, which hurt local industries.[64] La Apertura started the Colombian GDP on a slow but steady downward trend: export revenues declined, and cheap imports destroyed the country's economic infrastructure. For instance, in 1991 the GDP's annual growth was an estimated 2 percent. In 1992 it climbed to 5 percent, only to fall back down to 2 percent in 1993 (see chart 7.5). In addition, unemployment remained relatively high, ranging between 8 percent and 10 percent, from 1988 to 1993 (see chart 7.6).[65] Clearly, the fluctuating GDP, high unemployment, and unequal import-to-export ratio demonstrated that La Apertura had not yielded the expected benefits. The collapsing economy, particularly the agricultural sector, corresponded with an increase in narcotics production and a new interest in poppy cultivation.[66]

Poppy cultivation began to rise in the late 1980s (see map 3).[67] The Mexican cartels were earning massive profits from poppies, and the U.S. demand for cocaine was leveling off.[68] Through their contacts with the Mexican cartels, Colombian organizations began experimenting with poppy production. By 1991, poppy farming was reported in twelve of Colombia's departments, including Caquetá, Cauca, Cundinamarca, Huila, and Tolima. Meanwhile, the Colombian groups, including the Cali cartel, developed the capability to produce white heroin with a purity concentration of 80 to 90 percent.[69]

The State Department understood that the weakening economy turned Colombia's campesinos toward planting poppies. A State Department cable stated that an "important factor contributing to the rapid growth of the poppy crop is the outstanding debt of many small farmers." The cable added that the "devaluation of the Colombian peso, inflation, and the relatively low prices for local agricultural products (coffee, corn, beans)" forced "many peasant farmers to turn to the quick profits from growing opium poppies," which had "a three to four month cycle."[70] Another cable cited that "once the opium poppy gets a foothold in an area, agricultural production declines further, because of the high profit yielded by the poppy."[71] For Colombia, this meant that the profitability associated with opium-poppy production exacerbated Colombia's bleak economic picture. As more campesinos dedicated more land to plant-

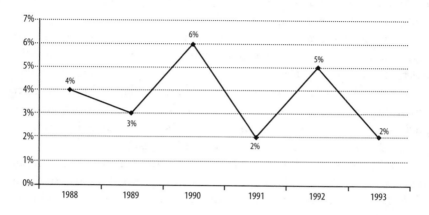

Chart 7.5 | **Colombian Gross Domestic Product, 1988–1993 (Annual Percentage)**

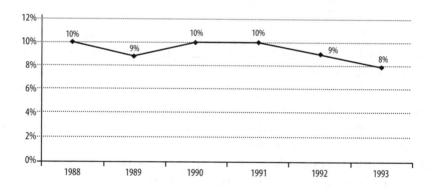

Chart 7.6 | **Colombian Unemployment, 1988–1993 (Annual Percentage)**

ing poppies, agricultural productivity for domestic and export markets sank.

As the United States and Colombia moved against the Medellín cartel, narcotics traffickers looked for new and safer—but often less efficient—smuggling routes.[72] The crackdown following Luis Carlos Galán's assassination escalated the trend. The cartels relocated processing plants to Brazil, Bolivia, Ecuador, and Peru, while the distribution network shifted operations to Central America and Mexico.[73] Mexican corruption and the porosity of the United States' southwestern border helped the Colombians capitalize on the long-standing routes and distribution networks established by Mexican groups.[74] By the mid-1990s, the Colombians had created solid partnerships with Mexican syndicates. The chief of the Mexican narcotics investigations unit, Javier Coello Trejo, succinctly described Mexico as a "trampoline for Colombian cocaine."[75]

When the Mexican government tried to shut down the Mexican–Colombian connection, the Colombians found new routes and used Central America as a storage and transshipment point. In Guatemala the cartels moved their cocaine up the rivers into Chiapas and then distributed it to the various Mexican cartels.[76] The Colombian government's attack on the cartels forced them to adjust their operations but in no way stopped the flow of cocaine into the United States.

In 1992 the Colombian government mounted a vigorous campaign against growing coca and opium poppies that included the use of the herbicide glyphosate. The government decided to employ herbicides because the CNP declared that it could not eradicate coca and poppy plants by hand.[77] The eradication program provoked resistance among campesinos and widespread criticism of the Gaviria government, which quickly translated into angry sentiment against narcotics control.

Many in Colombia felt that U.S. narcotics policy was counterproductive. Carlos Holguín Sardi, governor of the state of Valle de Cauca, declared, "We don't need the DEA here."[78] The Colombian government tried to reach an accord with the campesinos on poppy production. It promised to give them "money and resources to facilitate a crop substitution program" in exchange for their cooperation in poppy eradication.[79] However, the campesinos felt that the government did not fulfill "their end of the bargain" and threatened to go back to "poppy cultivation" because of the "serious misery" in which they lived. By the end of 1994, the government was forced to suspend herbicide use temporarily when campesinos protested that coca and poppy farming were their only means of supporting themselves.[80]

Although the Andean Strategy funneled millions of U.S. dollars into eradication and interdiction programs, opium production skyrocketed, and coca leaf supplies remained high well into the 1990s.[81] Moreover, drug seizures remained low, and eradication efforts failed to match production. The hectares under opium poppy cultivation leaped, from zero in 1990 to 32,858 in 1992. Eradication barely dented production, and seizures were nonexistent (see chart 7.7).

At the same time, coca leaf production expanded, from 34,230 hectares in 1988 to 38,059 hectares in 1992, although production spiked at 43,000

Chart 7.7 | **Colombian Opium Production and Eradication, 1990–1992**

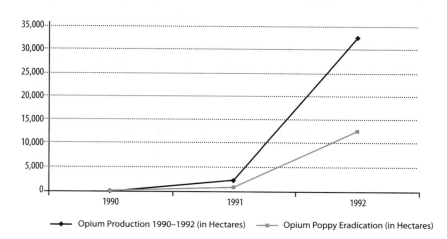

—◆— Opium Production 1990–1992 (in Hectares)   —■— Opium Poppy Eradication (in Hectares)

hectares in 1989. Coca eradication programs ranged from 230 to 952 hectares between 1987 and 1991, but this only made a small difference in overall production (see chart 7.8). Meanwhile, HCL seizures between 1988 and 1992 remained low, except in 1991, when they surpassed the estimated potential HCL from coca leaf production (see chart 7.9).[82]

However, these problems became the least of U.S. and Colombian worries when Colombia's civil war became entangled with America's War on Drugs.

After 1989 the Colombian government made an effort to negotiate peace with the guerrillas. The M-19 joined the political process in 1990, following negotiations with the Barco and Gaviria administrations. Weary of the war against the Medellín cartel, the Colombian government allowed the M-19 to participate in the 1990 elections, where it made a strong showing, although it suffered from political persecution by paramilitary forces.[83] In the aftermath of the election, the newly elected president, César Gaviria, solidified the M-19's participation in politics by naming the M-19's presidential candidate, Antonio Navarro Wolff, minister of agriculture.[84]

The Gaviria government also made overtures to the FARC and the ELN.[85] However, those efforts were unsuccessful, and the Medellín cartel continued to wage its own war against the FARC-backed Union Patriotica (UP).[86] By 1990 the UP was politically defunct. The political alienation of the FARC and the ELN soon made them two of the most powerful guerrilla forces in Colombia, and they deepened their involvement in the drug industry to finance their war against the government.

By 1991 the FARC and ELN had moved beyond their previous modus operandi of protecting campesino coca growers and extorting money from traffickers. They stepped up their involvement in production and trafficking and became the most dangerous and problematic factor in the U.S.–Colombian War on Drugs. A DEA report stated that "changing economic and social conditions" and the "collapse of communism . . . deprived

Chart 7.8 | Colombian Coca Leaf Production vs. Eradication, 1987–1991

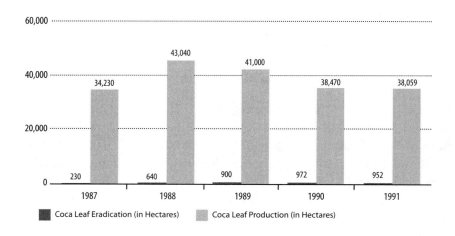

Chart 7.9 | Colombian Cocaine Seizures vs. Potential Production from Coca Leaf Harvest, 1988–1992

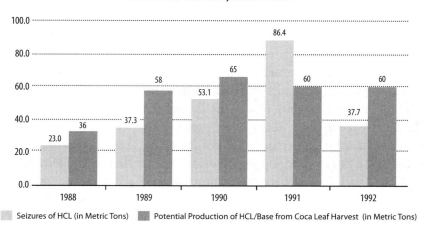

insurgents of outside financial and ideological support," which may have "heightened insurgent involvement in the domestic drug trade."[87]

In November 1991 the State Department alleged that the FARC controlled "clandestine air fields" owned by Colombian "narco-trafficking gangs," including the "Medellín and Cali cartels." In addition, the FARC Sixth Front commander, with the nom de guerre Fernando, boasted to reporters that he "financed his column's war chest from cocaine laboratories."[88] The State Department reported that Colombia's General Manuel Sanmiguel Buenaventura discovered five thousand hectares of coca that was used to finance the ELN.[89] More important, FARC deserters revealed that the FARC earned roughly "$1.6 million a month" from a "cocaine collection center" and that its high command had decided to turn the province of "Caquetá into a poppy emporium."[90] The FARC also increased military operations in strongholds such as Tolima, where the poppy boom was thriving, to make them "important poppy growing areas."[91] Furthermore, a DIA cable noted that the guerrillas were demanding a 30-percent cut from the gross profit of the opium crops in return for not destroying poppy crops or killing the campesino poppy growers.[92]

President Gaviria explained that guerrilla groups used their "millions in earnings" to "buy armaments and advanced communications and information equipment." Gaviria added that, with the Cold War winding down, the guerrillas had abandoned all "ideological and political justification and wanted to convert themselves into the new drug barons."[93] In the opinion of José Serrano, the former head of the Colombian CNP, the guerrillas lost their moral authority once they abandoned their ideologies and converted themselves into narco-trafficking organizations.[94]

Despite mounting evidence against the guerrillas, some U.S. officials still believed that their involvement in the narcotics trade was limited. In a 1994 report, *Insurgent Involvement in the Colombian Drug Trade*, the DEA stated that no credible evidence indicated that the national leadership of the FARC or ELN had, as a matter of policy, engaged in independent drug production or distribution, although some insurgents had assisted trafficking organizations and engaged in trafficking. The report went on to say that the DEA had "no evidence that the FARC or ELN" was involved in the "transportation, distribution, or marketing of illegal drugs to the United States or Europe."[95]

FARC statements also denied allegations that it engaged in narco-trafficking.[96] The FARC claimed that the accusations against it were part of the military's ongoing disinformation campaign to delegitimize its struggle and justify U.S. military aid. The FARC also contended that it did not serve the hypocritical antidrug policy by running over the campesinos and then enriching itself from the benefits of the business. In particular, the FARC derided the use of narcotics profits to promote industrial and financial centers in Colombia.[97] Adding to the doubt about the guerrillas' association with the drug trade, some observers stated that the guerrillas "rarely had their own cultivations or labs" because "mobility was essential to their security."[98] Despite these doubts, however, the Colombian government was convinced that the guerrillas were Colombia's "third cartel."[99]

As the Andean Strategy enhanced Colombia's military participation in the War on Drugs, military interests began to mesh with those of the cartels. Although the armed forces were supposed to run counternarcotics operations, they were reluctant to join the fight against narcotics. The army and air force did not want to transfer their resources to the fight against drugs because their main priority was to defeat the guerrillas.[100] Moreover, military leaders feared that active involvement in the War on Drugs would open the door to narcotics-related corruption.[101]

By 1993 the cartels had bought up nearly three million acres of land using narco-dollars they had purchased and laundered in financial institutions as a result of Colombia's relaxation of exchange controls. In doing so, the narco-traffickers displaced many campesinos, who moved deeper into Colombia's interior where the guerrilla presence was strong. When the Colombian military moved into the rural areas they had abandoned during the 1960s and 1970s to conduct counternarcotics and counterinsurgency operations, the landless campesinos "organized in defense of their livelihoods" and supported the guerrillas.[102] Consequently, the narco-capitalist cartels, aided by the large landholders, recognized that they had a common interest with the military—annihilation of the guerrillas.

Some sectors of the Colombian military, frustrated by the government's inability to defeat the guerrillas, opposed peace with the guerrillas and supported the cartel-backed self-defense forces.[103] A CIA report observed that many officers blamed the military's shortcomings on the government's failure to support the armed forces adequately.[104] As a result, many middle- and low-ranking soldiers and police officers joined the paramilitaries to defeat the leftist insurgencies.[105] Furthermore, in 1992 claims surfaced alleging that the military tacitly permitted the paramilitaries to operate freely in areas under its control.[106] A State Department cable explained that the alliance between the military and the cartels was more of a "businesslike, situational pragmatism on the part of some military commanders" than a "steadfast alliance." The cable added that "military dealings with the cartels" represented "transitory correlations of interests as both organizations pursued their separate agendas." This created a kind of "expedient behavior" that "both complicates and impedes the Colombian military's commitment to the counter-drug war."[107]

All three factions committed human rights violations as they fought for control over the countryside.[108] When the FARC won significant ground in Colombia from drug financing, the paramilitaries, assisted by the military, took matters into their own hands. Defending the large landowners and the nouveau-riche drug lords, the paramilitaries terrorized the country-side, killing any peasant whom they thought was loyal to the guerrillas.[109] In many respects, the military and paramilitaries saw the campesinos as the guerrillas' auxiliary forces, and their demands for land reform and protests against government eradication activities were considered a part of the FARC's plan to destabilize rural areas.[110] As early as 1991, reports emerged that military and paramilitary units attacked civilians indiscriminately, kidnapped and murdered young people, and engaged in torture; political enemies often simply disappeared. The paramilitaries' behavior was no different than the guerrillas'. Rebel movements also engaged in "violations of the laws of war." The guerrillas collected war taxes by taking hostages for ransom. They murdered civilians suspected of spying for the government or belonging to paramilitary organizations.[111]

Throughout the 1990s, human rights abuses continued to escalate as the United States placed more and more pressure on the Colombian government to reduce narcotics production in rural areas and as the socio-economic and political realities on the ground countermanded U.S. efforts. In the U.S. Congress, the "Vietnam syndrome" provoked fears that the country was getting bogged down in an ugly civil war. By the mid-1990s, Colombia appeared to be on the verge of becoming a failed narco-state.

Crisis in Peru: Alberto Fujimori and the War on Drugs

The election of Alberto Fujimori (1990–2000) to the Peruvian presidency in June 1990 complicated the agreements the United States had reached with Alan García at the Cartagena Summit. Upon his election, Fujimori stated that the United States was "fooling itself" with its military approach. He also declared that the peasants needed "an alternative" or else they would "die of hunger and join the ranks of the guerrillas."

Fujimori blamed the two preceding presidents of Peru, Belaúnde Terry and Alan García, for the guerrilla war, saying, "[I]n the mountains, people were dying of hunger, children were not going to school, but everything looked fine from the Presidential Palace."[112] Moreover, "repression had not produced any results in the fight against drug trafficking."[113]

Fujimori decided not to accept $37.5 million in U.S. military aid for fiscal year 1991.[114] He explained that "since the military aid was destined only for the fight against drug trafficking," accepting this assistance was "inconvenient" to Peru's interests.[115] The decision to refuse this aid seriously weakened counternarcotics operations in the UHV for 1991, thus complicating efforts to control coca cultivation.

In rejecting the U.S. offer, Fujimori introduced the Fujimori Doctrine.[116] This plan covered both military and economic assistance and was an attempt to renegotiate the terms of use for counternarcotics assistance. Fujimori wanted to use counternarcotics aid to fight the Sendero Luminoso, not to attack the narco-traffickers.[117] More important, he believed that defeating the guerrillas and wiping out coca production depended on improving economic assistance to Peru's campesino population.

Fujimori argued that the country needed assistance for building highways, railroads, and schools. He favored a rural economic development model in which coca farming would dry up with the construction of a 350-mile railroad to connect the coca-growing regions to markets for conventional crops.[118] Fujimori also called for a land registry and titling program that would give campesinos legal ownership of their land, and in turn, enable them to receive mortgage credit. With the ability to earn credit, Fujimori believed that the campesinos would be able to finance the capital investment projects required to develop alternative crops.[119]

The Bush administration publicly supported Fujimori's plans. On a state visit to Peru in August 1990, Vice President Dan Quayle affirmed that the U.S. government backed Fujimori on the "tough decisions" that he had to make and recognized that his goals would not be achieved "overnight." Quayle stressed that the United States did not want to "militarize the effort against Andean drugs" and added that, in order to have the economic development necessary to halt the production of narcotics, the country needed more "privatization . . . international lending . . . agricultural reform," and support for the "tough economic reform" that needed to take place in Peru. Quayle was tying economic liberalization to success in the War on Drugs while downplaying the role of military involvement in counternarcotics operations.

However, Peru's sluggish economy, combined with the fact that U.S. aid did not match Quayle's rhetoric, translated into continued incentive to grow coca throughout the country. On the positive side of Peru's economic equation, inflation fell, from 2,928 percent in 1989 to 47 percent in 1993 (see chart 7.10).[120] Additionally, annual GDP growth increased, from

Chart 7.10 | **Peruvian Inflation, 1989–1993**

Chart 7.11 | **Peruvian Annual GDP, 1989–1993**

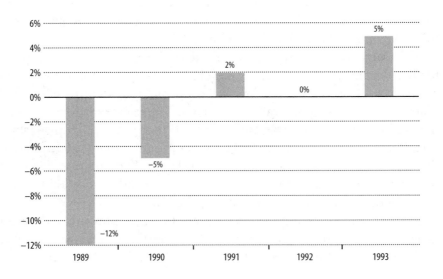

−12 percent in 1989 to 5 percent in 1993, although the GAO argued that the cocaine industry had provided $640 million to Peru's GDP in 1993 (see chart 7.11).[121] Other estimates stated that in 1989, 2 to 11 percent of Peru's GDP and 14 to 78 percent of Peru's export income were derived from the coca economy.[122]

On the negative side, from 1989 to 1993, unemployment ranged between 8 and 10 percent (see chart 7.12). By 1992, only 20 percent of

Chart 7.12 | **Peruvian Unemployment, 1989–1993**

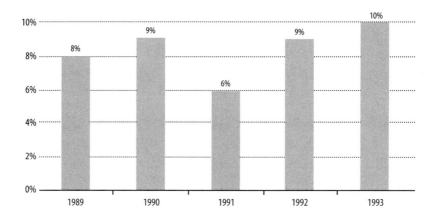

Peru's workforce had what "economists called an adequate job."[123] In addition, foreign direct investment remained stagnant at 0 to 2 percent between 1989 and 1993, and Peru's foreign debt continued to grow, from $18.6 billion in 1989 to $23.6 billion in 1993 (see chart 7.13).

This same period saw a trend in which imports surpassed exports for the remainder of the decade (see chart 7.14).[124] Adding to these economic woes, U.S. certification laws for cooperation in antidrug efforts left Fujimori's land titling program in the lurch. The release of aid to conduct the land titling program was contingent on the success of crop substitution. But since the campesinos had no economic incentive to plant alternative crops, Fujimori had no money for his land titling program. His only remaining option was to pursue coca interdiction and eradication to force campesinos to accept crop substitution programs.

In 1989 the Peruvian government bowed to U.S. pressure and began experimenting with herbicides such as Tebuthiuron, also known as Spike, in the UHV.[125] Assistant Secretary of State Ann Wrobleski stated that

Chart 7.13 | **Peruvian External Debt, 1989–1993 (in Billions of U.S. Dollars)**

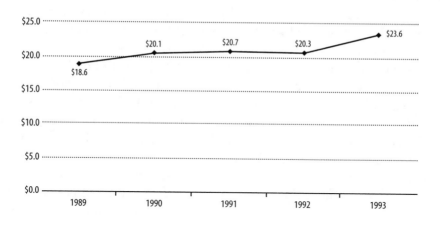

Chart 7.14 | **Peruvian Exports vs. Imports, 1989–1993
(as a Percentage of the GDP)**

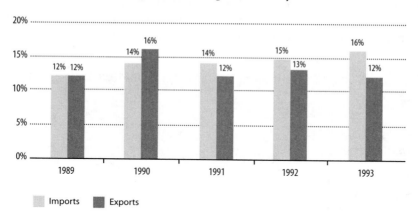

aerial spraying was "the safest, most efficient way" to control coca growing in Peru.[126] Coca-spraying operations worked out of the Santa Lucia
base in the UHV, using U.S.-supplied helicopters. Opponents of herbicide
spraying claimed that it supported the guerrillas' cause and destroyed food
crops.[127]

Starting around 1990, this is exactly what happened. Campesinos near
the Santa Lucia base complained that U.S. helicopters were spraying
something that killed their coca bushes and made their animals sick. The
UHV peasants called the spreading disease *seca-seca*; more formally, it was

the fungus *Fusarium oxysporum*.[128] The fungus had first appeared in Hawaii during the 1970s on the Coca-Cola Corporation's coca research farm. Seeing the fungus's devastating effects, the U.S. government launched a two-decade, fourteen-million-dollar research program to investigate the use of the fungus as a mycoherbicide.[129]

Herbicidal coca eradication, combined with the spread of *Fusarium oxysporum*, had a ruinous effect on Peru's legal crops, such as cassava and banana, and thereby stimulated coca farming.[130] By 1991 the fungus had destroyed nearly fifteen thousand acres of coca and fifty thousand acres of legitimate crops.[131] Many farmers in the UHV were forced to move deep into the jungle to secure land that was uncontaminated and out of range of the herbicide-spraying helicopters.[132] The destruction of traditional crops and the threat of herbicide dispersal strictly limited the campesinos' willingness to participate in crop substitution programs. Moreover, the use of herbicides and the spread of the fungus became major motivators for expanded coca cultivation, since sowing more plants served as a form of insurance against both threats.[133] The guerrilla presence in the UHV, the undermining of the Fujimori Doctrine, and the herbicide program all contributed to a rise in coca cultivation, which climbed from 110,400 hectares in 1988 to 129,100 hectares in 1992 (see chart 7.15).[134]

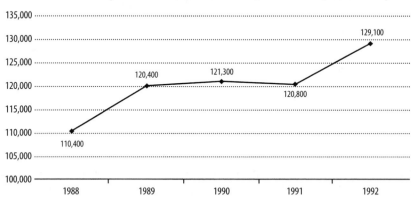

Chart 7.15 | **Peruvian Coca Production, 1988–1992 (in Hectares)**

The Andean Strategy placed Fujimori in a catch-22. To receive aid for land titling, he had to pursue rigorous interdiction, which would force the campesinos to adopt alternative crops. This approach, however, alienated the campesinos and gave little incentive to switch to other crops. U.S. counternarcotics policy also complicated Peru's ability to liberalize its economy: Washington would not provide aid to develop alternative crops until Peru brought coca production under control. Consequently, liberalization, which was intended to create new markets, was stifled by the constraints on the release of aid. As a result of U.S. economic manipulation, Peru could support few alternative development programs that could ameliorate the economic plight of the coca-growing campesinos.

In addition to undermining Fujimori's reforms, U.S. policy forced his administration to recommit itself to go after the traffickers as well as the Sendero Luminoso. U.S. officials believed that corruption was behind Peru's reluctance to pursue traffickers militarily.[135] Fujimori's perceived unwillingness to cooperate led the Bush administration to cite Peru for a lack of commitment to combat "cocaine processing" and "coca cultivation." The Bush administration ultimately decided to certify the Fujimori government in 1991, but at the same time, it withheld $94.9 million in aid. Thirty-five million dollars of this assistance was for the military, and the other sixty million dollars was for economic support programs.

Facing the loss of this aid, Fujimori proposed to work with the United States and go after traffickers. His new plan called for U.S. assistance to feed, equip, train, outfit, and adequately remunerate the police and armed forces to fight drug traffickers and those who supported them, including the Sendero Luminoso. Peru also proposed developing an elite force to intercept airplanes loaded with cocaine, blow up cocaine laboratories, and seize traffickers' assets.[136] A State Department cable described Peru's decision to "intercept trafficker" flights as "an earnest sign of Peru's commitment" to fight the drug trade. The cable also reported that a "successful implementation of Peru's current anti-narcotics strategy" depended "to a large extent on its success in repressing terrorism."[137] Thus, on May 14, 1991, Fujimori signed a formal bilateral agreement with the United States, which promised assistance in the fight against narcotics.[138]

Fujimori then seized extralegal constitutional powers in order to comply with the new security agreement and obtain help to defeat the Sendero Luminoso. In June 1991, following the ratification of the agreement, he asked Peru's Congress for special powers to legislate economic issues and deal with insurgencies and drug traffickers. Thirty decrees out of 126 placed before the Congress gave unlimited power to the military to defeat the terrorists in designated emergency zones such as the UHV. Five decrees were anti-narcotics laws, including two that made it a crime to assist traffickers or launder money. The Congress struck down many of the anti-narcotics laws, including those that forbade money laundering and complicity with traffickers. Consequently, Fujimori declared the Congress incompetent and unwilling to bring traffickers to trial.[139] On April 5, 1992, he suspended the Peruvian constitution, dissolved Congress, and disbanded the judiciary. Fujimori insisted that a suspension of democracy was essential to revamp the government and attack both terrorism and Peru's economic problems.[140] Fujimori's critics countered that he had suspended the constitution to prevent Peru's Congress from investigating human rights abuses committed by his government.[141] Regardless of the reason for his takeover, Fujimori reinstated the laws rejected by Congress and gave the air force the authority to shoot down planes loaded with narcotics.[142]

Fujimori's government takeover strained U.S.–Peru relations. The United States called on Fujimori to restore democracy, reestablish civil liberties and a free and independent press, and reinstate the legislative and judicial branches.[143] Moreover, Vladimiro Montesinos's appointment as the head of the Servicio de Inteligencia Nacional (SIN) was a serious concern. Montesinos, a former CIA informant and defense lawyer for traffickers, was said to run the Fujimori government behind the scenes. As the head of the SIN, Montesinos took control of Peru's antinarcotics activities. Although there was no proof that Montesinos sponsored illegal narcotics activities, his past ties to the drug underworld placed him under deep suspicion. In particular, Peru's former army inspector general, General Luis Palomino Rodríguez, warned the U.S. embassy that Montesinos intended to "frustrate joint U.S.-Peruvian counter-drug efforts."[144] Several Peruvian generals alleged that Montesinos' SIN was "in effect running the state."[145] Finally, coupled with Montesinos' appointment, Fujimori's insistence on attacking the Sendero Luminoso and any traffickers associated with them convinced U.S. officials that the Peruvian military was corrupt and only worked with the United States on counternarcotics issues with the goal of defeating the guerrillas.

Despite these differences and despite the U.S. decision to withdraw the Green Berets from Peru, the Bush administration finally decided that it had no choice but to work with Fujimori. The administration hoped that the Peruvian military's unrestrained role and Fujimori's authoritarianism would bring about the necessary resolve to disrupt narcotics traffic.[146]

Not surprisingly, the decision to fight the insurgencies and the drug industry at the same time provoked human rights violations. When the government sent the military into areas such as the UHV to attack the insurgents, both the military and the insurgents committed human rights abuses to keep control over their areas of operation. A State Department memorandum noted that these abuses occurred because officers in the field believed "that the civil justice system" could not "effectively restrain or punish captured terrorists or drug traffickers." State Department analysts concluded that "under the stress of a near combat situation, human rights standards were neglected."[147] A State Department embassy report in 1990 called the violations a demonstration of the "no holds barred manner" in which "control for the Peruvian countryside was being fought."[148]

The Peruvian military was accused of killing campesinos at random and placing them in mass graves.[149] It was alleged that they added anyone they killed, including innocent civilians, to the Sendero body count.[150] For example, in 1991, Peruvian armed forces entered the town of Huancavelica and threatened to kill the residents if they did not give them food and livestock. When the campesinos resisted, fourteen people accused of being Sendero sympathizers disappeared from the village. Crimes like this were common. Peruvian authorities were unable to rein in the officers responsible for these atrocities because Fujimori gave the military free reign.[151]

Rondas, civilian auto-defense committees that worked in conjunction with the armed forces, committed many of the atrocities. The military recognized that repression had been counterproductive in previous efforts to quell the insurgency, so they began adopting a paternalistic attitude toward the campesinos. As a result, the military supported the rondas, which were composed of campesinos who opposed the Sendero's terrorist methods.[152] According to Carlos Tapia, the Sendero's strict authoritarian rule reestablished the old system of exploitation. Campesinos not yet fully dominated by the Sendero resisted it.[153] The military used the rondas to protect "infrastructure" and serve as defensive organs against the Sendero's "ability to attack all but remote and lightly defended villages." However, in fighting Sendero terror, the rondas became equally violent, and people often disappeared if they did not cooperate. In one instance, the rondas captured thirteen suspected Senderistas and beheaded them.[154]

The Sendero was not above committing human rights violations either. Abimael Guzmán repudiated human rights, calling them an individualistic bourgeois construction. According to Guzmán, human rights were a counterrevolutionary method used by the bourgeoisie to implement social conformity, which in turn prevented the creation of a new social order.[155] The U.S. embassy believed that the Sendero was trying to replicate Spanish colonial violence against the Incas and therefore made torture a part of its executions. Drawing connections to the death of Atahualpa, the

Incan leader killed by the Spanish in 1533, the Sendero used beheading and garroting to demonstrate "cultural links between the peasants of the twentieth century and their forefathers."[156] David L. Westrate, the deputy administrator for the DEA, called the Sendero the Khmer Rouge of Latin America.[157]

The U.S. Department of State noted that the Sendero was "inhumanly brutal in its administration of 'popular justice.'" For example, the Sendero took campesinos who refused to cooperate with them, brought them into the town square, held a people's trial, tied the accused up, and then made every member of the village cut a piece of flesh from the victims.[158] In one instance, the Sendero singled out eighteen youths at a roadblock in the Ayacucho province, accused them of working for the rondas, held a quick "popular trial," and subsequently shot them.[159] Headless bodies attributed to Sendero killings were often seen floating down the Huallaga River.[160] In many cases, to win more support, the Sendero conducted targeted assassinations and psychological propaganda campaigns, hoping to incite the military to slaughter innocent civilians whom they suspected of being "terrorist sympathizers."[161]

Joseph P. Kelly, director of security and international relations issues at the Department of State's National Security and International Affairs Division, said that such human rights violations became a "great concern for the United States."[162] Between May 1988 and July 1991, the Peruvian military was held responsible for nine incidents of extrajudicial killings.[163] In 1991 alone, nearly three thousand Peruvians civilians were murdered in extrajudicial killings.[164] The State Department saw the military's increasing abuse of human rights as a "critical problem in dealing with Congress on the anti-narcotics issue."[165] This assessment was correct, and it seriously affected the U.S. Congress's willingness to fund Peru's armed forces. Fearing that human rights violations would continue, Congress reduced military aid to Peru from $34.5 million to $24.5 million for fiscal year 1992.[166]

The ten million dollars that Congress denied had been budgeted to train three army battalions to provide security for counternarcotics operations. According to Melvyn Levitsky, the U.S. assistant secretary of state for narcotics matters, the aid reduction hampered efforts to "make a significant impact on narcotics trafficking" because of the "alliance between traffickers and the Shining Path." Levitsky, however, was unwilling to admit that Peru was diverting money from fighting the drug industry to finance "counterinsurgency operations independent of counternarcotics purposes."[167] Either the Andean Strategy failed to consider the nature of the conflict in Peru or policymakers were unwilling to understand the predicament in which the U.S. government had placed the Fujimori administration. By failing to separate Peru's counternarcotics program from its antiterrorist campaign, as Fujimori initially desired, the Bush administration helped foster political instability and human rights abuses.

The surprise capture of Abimael Guzmán Reynoso, leader of the Sendero Luminoso, in September 1992 was a dramatic victory for the Fujimori government and significantly improved its relations with the United States. Guzmán was taken without resistance in an apartment in the center of Lima. Fujimori declared that he had defeated an "evil genius."[168] According to Bernard W. Aronson, the assistant secretary of state for inter-American affairs, Guzmán's arrest provided the "Peruvian government and people with what they need most, [a] sense of hope and confidence."[169]

Although Guzmán made an appeal for his followers to lay down their arms, the Sendero was not totally defeated, and it quietly regrouped. The Sendero still operated in the UHV and Ayacucho provinces and relied heavily on drug trafficking to finance its operations.[170] Nevertheless, Guzmán's capture helped heal relations between the United States and Peru. Fujimori's commitment to hold democratic elections in November 1992 also bolstered relations with the United States.

Regardless of the Sendero's strategic retreat, the MRTA continued to function in Peru, although the government did not consider it a serious threat. The CIA claimed that the MRTA sustained contacts with other guerrilla organizations that aligned ideologically with Cuba, such as Colombia's ELN and Bolivia's Comisión Nestor Paz Zamora. However, the CIA believed that the MRTA no longer received support from the Soviet Union, Cuba, or Nicaragua as the Cold War wound down. In addition, the CIA concluded that the MRTA was not getting "enough support from narcotics traffickers to cover the MRTA's expenses."[171]

Clashes over the coca trade with the Sendero Luminoso threw the MRTA on the defensive after it entered the UHV in 1987. The MRTA was no match for the Sendero, which kicked the group out of the department of San Martín's principle coca-growing areas.[172] As a result, the MRTA lost a source of income and popular support. By 1992 the organization's failure to develop a rural front forced it to return to its initial strategy of waging insurrection in urban centers.[173] The group stepped up a campaign of extortion and kidnapping to finance its activities, but once Fujimori gave the order to "annihilate" the MRTA, it appeared as though subversive activity in Peru was near its end.[174]

Between 1989 and 1992, U.S. drug policy in Peru did not gain much ground. It became clear that, with or without the presence of narco-guerrillas, narcotics production was going to continue: the Sendero's defeat had not ended drug cultivation. Fujimori knew that he had to destroy the guerrillas before attacking the narcotics trade, or face the loss of his overall objective—political stability. He wanted to focus on the narcotics problem only after stability was restored and economic development reestablished. However, the United States connected his reluctance to take on the traffickers with the well-known corruption in Peru's military and government. When the Bush administration forced Fujimori to abandon his doctrine and insisted on an active role for the Peruvian military in counternarcotics programs, it invited corruption and human rights abuses. If the United States had addressed narcotics and terrorism separately, Peru could have dealt better with the socioeconomic forces driving narcotics cultivation, weakened the base of support for the guerrillas, and controlled the spread of military corruption.

Crisis in Bolivia: The Andean Strategy and Coca Nationalism

In 1989, as the War on Drugs intensified and militarized, Bolivia tottered on the brink of collapse. The Paz Zamora government (1989–1993) strove to maintain a delicate balance between U.S. demands and the demands of Bolivian campesinos. Although the country's economic outlook had vastly improved, many Bolivians opposed the government's economic reforms because they failed to address rural poverty—a situation that provoked the beginning of a serious crisis for the Bolivian government.

Bolivia had become a hub for the transshipment of narcotics following the crackdown on the Colombian cartels and the violent guerrilla war in Peru. The Paz Zamora government tried to resist the militarization of the War on Drugs but found that it had to cooperate with U.S. policy for Bolivia to receive badly needed economic aid. Yet Paz Zamora's decision to work with the United States increased political opposition and instability. As the United States enlarged its military presence in the country, some campesinos rebelled, and several nationalist, anti-U.S. guerrilla organizations appeared. Accompanied by these events, human rights abuses multiplied as the Bolivian military deepened its involvement in the War on Drugs. At the same time, the specter of corruption loomed within the Bolivian Congress over the issue of extradition. By the end of the Bush administration, the Andean Strategy had made little headway in Bolivia.

In 1988, in order to adhere to U.S. demands for an interdiction and eradication policy, Bolivia passed a new law: Ley del Régimen de la Coca y Sustancias Controladas 1008.[175] This law allowed the government to regulate coca farming and distinguish between legal coca production for religious and cultural purposes and coca production for making HCL.[176] In accordance with U.S. demands to eradicate excess coca, the law required the annual eradication of increments of five thousand to eight thousand hectares of coca. It also set a cap for the legal cultivation of coca at twelve thousand hectares (30,000 acres) in the traditional coca-growing areas, meaning the Yungas region, not the Chapare. In addition, the law set up zones for traditional, transitory, and illicit coca farming, and was accompanied by Plan Integral de Desarollo y Sustitución (PIDYS), an alternative development program initiated in 1987.[177] For the Bolivian government, Law 1008 was an attempt to meet its international obligations to reduce illegal narcotics production. However, the law incited resistance among Bolivia's campesino coca growers, who rejected the idea of subjecting coca to regulation.[178] The Bolivian government's adherence to U.S. demands and the advancement of Law 1008 opened the door for a massive struggle between the Bolivian government and its campesino coca growers as Bolivia moved into the 1990s.

Although Bolivia's prohibition of herbicides caused tensions with the United States, its coca eradication and interdiction efforts improved between 1989 and 1990.[179] Both governments agreed to add Annexes I and II to Plan Trienal in May 1990. The annexes enhanced coca control efforts by delineating each country's responsibilities related to reducing coca cultivation and trafficking.[180] Coca eradication jumped from 2,500 hectares in 1989 to 8,100 hectares in 1990. To demonstrate their commitment to disrupting narcotics trafficking further, the Bolivian government also broke up the Meco Domínguez organization.[181] Yet, following this benchmark year, the Bolivian government failed to live up to expectations.[182] Their failure evoked a question: why couldn't the government maintain the same level of coca control that it had in 1990?

Political opposition to the government's economic reform package complicated U.S.–Bolivian coca control efforts. Paz Zamora promised a crusade against poverty, but many Bolivians never emerged from indigence. The government did create economic stability, though; inflation decreased from 18 percent in 1988 to 7 percent in 1993 (see chart 7.16). During that same period, Bolivia's external debt remained constant, between $4.9 and $4.0 billion, although some estimated that the coca economy financed 7 to 25 percent of that debt.[183] Still, even with these successes, economic growth did not match population growth, and economic activity failed to trickle down to Bolivia's poor.[184]

Bolivia's annual gross domestic product hovered between 1 and 3 percent between 1989 and 1993; some calculations showed that the coca economy contributed roughly 6 to 19 percent to the GDP (see chart 7.17). Unemployment ranged from 10 to 6 percent between 1989 and 1993, and the coca economy was believed to employ between 207,000 and 463,000 people.[185] The "government and banks" widely applauded Zamora's free-market policies, but they were widely perceived as being initiated "at the expense of the poor."[186] Specifically, Bolivians strongly opposed Paz Zamora's decision to privatize sixty-six state companies in order to liberalize the economy and attract foreign investors, because Bolivians associated privatization with the loss of national sovereignty and corruption.[187]

In 1992 the State Department concluded that the Bolivian government's economic stabilization program had "increased social unrest" and was "seen by the populace" as the primary cause "of massive unemployment and increased corruption." [188] Bolivia's implementation of the Washington Consensus liberalization policies created hostility among sectors of society that were not even associated with the coca economy. Consequently, the government's privatization and counternarcotics policies became associated with U.S. imperialism.[189] This perception married Bolivia's poor to its coca growers. Confrontations between the government and the majority population of poor Indians began to cripple the government and provoked the possibility of civil war as Bolivia moved into the 1990s.

U.S.–Bolivian coca control programs inadvertently turned Bolivia into a hub for the trafficking and refining of cocaine. Coinciding with the Colombian crackdown on the Medellín cartel, Operation Safehaven (launched in June 1991) and Operation Ghost Zone (launched in January 1992) significantly affected Colombian traffickers' access to Bolivian coca leaves. Operation Safehaven was directed at seizing assets, for example, aircraft that belonged to Bolivian traffickers associated with the Colombians. Operation Ghost Zone sought to cut off the Colombian cartels from their sources of coca and cocaine base by severing transportation routes out of the Chapare. The State Department noted that these operations followed

Chart 7.16 | **Bolivian Inflation, 1988–1993**

Chart 7.17 | **Bolivian Annual GDP, 1988–1993**

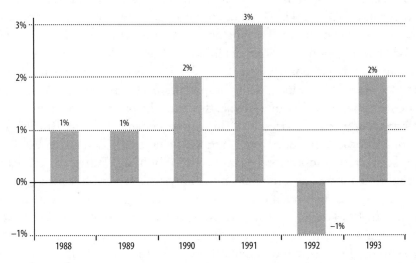

the kingpin strategy and primarily targeted "Colombian cartel operations in Bolivia and cartel-controlled Bolivian trafficking groups."[190]

In many respects, the operations were successful. For instance, in 1992 Operation Ghost Zone dismantled a major Colombian trafficking organization in Bolivia, known as the Celimo Andrade, that was associated with the Cali cartel.[191] However, as joint U.S.–Bolivian operations shut off Colombian operations, Bolivian traffickers moved beyond their normal role—producing coca leaves and paste—and started to refine coca paste into HCL. At the same time, they developed new trafficking routes to the United States and Europe. Moreover, unlike the highly organized Colombian networks, many Bolivian enterprises were "mom and pop" operations that were decentralized and therefore harder to control.[192]

From Bolivia, narcotics networks were reestablished in Argentina, Paraguay, Chile, and Brazil. Frequently, the networks used old routes from the 1970s that they reopened as the United States tried to shut down smuggling routes through Colombia and Panama. A State Department communiqué observed that "Bolivians would continue to compensate for the decline in Colombian interest by seeking direct lines to the U.S. and Europe."[193] Bolivian cocaine bound for Europe and the United States frequently traveled through Argentina. Cocaine in Europe brought in roughly $150 to $250 per gram, whereas prices in the United States had declined to roughly $100 per gram.[194] In other instances, cocaine was shipped from Bolivia to Argentina through Europe and then sent to the United States.

Bolivia's Law 1008 made precursor chemicals such as kerosene, as well as items like toilet paper, illegal in coca-growing areas since they could be used to refine coca paste. This inspired new smuggling networks between Bolivia and its Southern Cone neighbors. Thus, while cocaine flowed out of Bolivia into Argentina, Brazil, or Chile, precursor chemicals flowed into Bolivia.[195] In addition, because precursor chemicals were banned in the coca-growing areas of Bolivia, the State Department explained that Bolivian enterprises started to "ship more cocaine base to Brazil," and Brazilian cocaine buyers were "frequently entering Bolivia to establish new sources of supply for cocaine base." Similarly, Peruvian traffickers started to transport cocaine base into Bolivia from Peru because the border was so porous and the price of base was higher in Bolivia than in Peru.[196] In 1993 the U.S. SOUTHCOM determined that narco-traffickers were "flying cocaine base" out of the "Chapare valley with impunity."[197] By 1996 the DEA concluded that "Bolivian trafficking organizations" had become "increasingly independent of their Colombian counterparts, and most Bolivian groups were now smuggling refined cocaine hydrochloride to Brazil, Paraguay, Argentina and/or Chile."[198]

Coca production in Bolivia continued at a steady pace between 1988 and 1993 as Bolivia became a center of cocaine trafficking and manufacturing. Although coca cultivation peaked in 1990 at 58,400 hectares, between 1988 and 1993, it remained constant at roughly 50,000 hectares.

Chart 7.18 | **Bolivian Coca Cultivation vs. Eradication, 1988–1993 (in Hectares)**

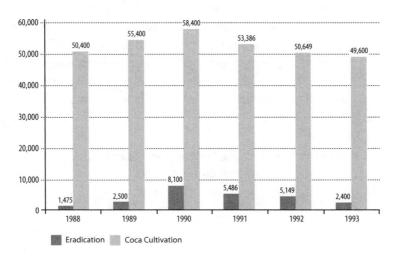

Coca eradication on the other hand steadily declined after 1990, from 8,100 hectares to 2,400 hectares in 1993 (see chart 7.18).

At the same time, the potential amount of cocaine produced from Bolivian harvests increased from 110 metric tons in 1988, to 240 metric tons in 1993, while cocaine seizures remained scant, reaching barely 0.31 metric tons in 1993. Charts 7.19 and 7.20 indicate the vast disparity between HCL production potential and actual seizures.[199] Bolivia, could not meet the demands of Law 1008. The goal of eliminating eight thousand hectares of coca was impossible to achieve as economic forces and the side effects of the War on Drugs in Colombia drove up coca production and cocaine processing in Bolivia.

The Andean Strategy's plan to use the Bolivian military and U.S. Special Forces to conduct counternarcotics operations complicated the government's ability to maintain political strength and cut narcotics production. The addition of Annex III to Plan Trienal sent Bolivia's armed forces into antinarcotics operations, militarizing the War on Drugs and destabilizing the government.[200]

Significantly, Bolivian military involvement was not "clearly delineated."[201] The Bolivian government agreed to use the military in counternarcotics operations, but the exact degree of the cooperation was unclear. As a result, a rivalry arose between the military and the UMOPAR over who would receive the lion's share of assistance.[202] The United States considered the problem symptomatic of Paz Zamora's mismanagement and lack of clear leadership.[203] A State Department report on Bolivia described Zamora's preference for supporting the UMOPAR as a sign of the government's "denial" of virtually any "aspect of the drug problem in Bolivia other than coca cultivation" and the belief that it was "a problem of only economic development and poverty." Moreover, Zamora and the Bolivian government were "long on rhetoric and demanding additional assistance, but short on implementing the tougher provisions of their own laws and agreements."[204]

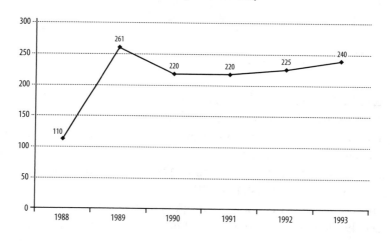

Chart 7.19 | **Potential HCL Produced from Bolivian Harvest, 1988–1993 (in Metric Tons)**

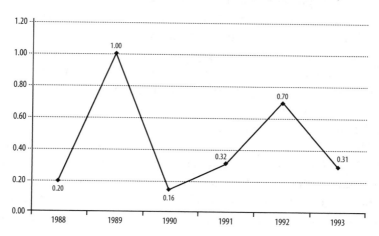

Chart 7.20 | **Bolivian HCL Seizures, 1988–1993 (in Metric Tons)**

Zamora preferred to direct a limited counternarcotics program, using the UMOPAR, to avoid confrontation with the campesinos and because national law prevented the army from taking part in domestic operations.[205] The State Department claimed that the "degree of military support to the overall effort" was a "Bolivian decision" and asserted that it did not want to force a "military option on the Bolivians."[206] However, U.S. insistence on Andean military participation forced Zamora to make the unpopular decision to use the Bolivian army to prevent coca production. Zamora's capitulation planted the seeds of political instability and corruption that diminished the government's ability to pursue an effective counternarcotics program after 1990.

Once the Bolivian armed forces jumped into counternarcotics operations, they opened themselves to corruption. The results became obvious in 1991, when General Faustino Rico Toro was appointed head of the military's antinarcotics effort.[207] Rico Toro had worked as chief of the army's intelligence unit, Section 2, during the García Meza regime, and was a known associate of Klaus Barbie.[208] This information did not help his drug-fighting credentials, and Washington accused him of cocaine trafficking.[209] But Toro was not the only official involved in the drug business: evidence indicated that the entire Interior Ministry was taking payoffs from traffickers. Following Rico Toro's appointment, U.S. Ambassador Robert Gelbard cut off nearly one hundred million dollars in aid to Bolivia.[210] The U.S. action compelled the Zamora government to fire Toro and several members of the Interior Ministry to stem the perceived corruption.

U.S. economic pressure also forced Zamora's government to authorize the use of U.S. troops to provide the Bolivian military with counternarcotics operational training. In April 1991, Bolivia's Congress passed a resolution that allowed six hundred U.S. military advisors to enter the country and assist in counternarcotics actions. U.S. and Bolivian officials considered the approval of U.S. advisors an important advancement in the relationship between the two countries.[211]

The U.S. contingent included 132 trainers, eighty-four officers and enlisted men to participate in joint maneuvers with Bolivian troops, 250 noncommissioned officers specializing in road construction, and two medical teams with up to sixty-five men in each group. Much of the training consisted of jungle survival, military operations, and small-unit tactics. The need for this type of training to control coca production was unclear and thus raised questions about the political implications of U.S.

troop presence. As María Teresa Paz, the deputy of the opposition party, Movimiento Nacionalista Revolucionario (MNR), declared, "a resolution has been approved which will lead to violence in this country. [212] This sentiment became even more apparent when the Cinco Federaciones del Trópico de Cochabamba wrote an open letter to President Paz Zamora stating that the presence of U.S. troops undermined the sovereignty of Bolivia. They added that they would not be responsible if acts of violence occurred when U.S. forces or the Bolivian military entered the Chapare. [213]

U.S. troops on Bolivian soil also amplified concerns about extradition. Prior to the 1991 deployment, the Bolivian government arrested and extradited General Arce Gómez to the United States, a definite signal that it was willing to cooperate. [214] However, political pressure following the arrival of U.S. Special Forces created a political backlash in the Bolivian Congress. Congressional members announced that they would no longer extradite drug traffickers, if the traffickers surrendered and agreed to end their involvement in the cocaine trade. [215] This decision mirrored the Colombian government's decision not to extradite the Medellín cartel. Meanwhile, President Zamora decided that he was not going to sign the extradition treaty until the United States accepted Bolivia's requests for aid to support alternatives to a cocaine-based economy. [216]

The United States saw this decision as a setback. Bolivia's refusal to extradite traffickers led to speculation that Bolivia's government was corrupt. [217] Bolivia opposed extradition because it believed that submission to U.S. demands for extradition weakened the credibility of the state, which in turn made it difficult to control the population. [218] The government delayed extradition of Asunta Roca Suárez to the United States until 1992. Suárez was the niece of notorious Bolivian kingpin Roberto Suárez. She took over the coca business with her brother, Jorge Roca Suárez, after Bolivian authorities arrested their uncle in 1988. [219]

Bolivia also declined to turn over either Roberto Suárez after his capture or General García-Meza, who was extradited from Brazil to Bolivia in 1993. [220] The United States felt that this reflected continued corruption in the military and police and was further proof that the Paz Zamora government aided narco-trafficking networks in Bolivia. [221] Both men remained in Bolivian jails (Suárez was released in 1996 after serving seven years of his fifteen-year sentence), protected by Bolivian authorities, while the U.S. Justice Department continued to press for trials in the United States. Bolivian nationalism clearly repudiated extradition, and the country's

Supreme Court determined that narcotics violations were not extraditable offenses. Extradition remained a continuous source of diplomatic wrangling between the U.S. government and Bolivia.[222]

The introduction of U.S. Special Forces into Bolivia further exacerbated political problems, especially with the campesinos. The quasi-military operations conducted by the Bolivian military and the UMOPAR, such as blowing up airstrips, raiding jungle laboratories, searching village markets, and destroying coca crops, led one campesino to comment that "the Americans were like invaders"; they arrived in Bolivia and did "what they want[ed] in a country that [was] not theirs."[223] Socialist leader Roger Cortéz Hurtado argued that the U.S. military came to Bolivia to practice guerrilla warfare techniques, with the intention of breaking up popular movements such as the Bolivian coca growers' syndicate.[224] A document issued by coca producers, university organizations, and members of the Catholic Church stated their belief that the United States replaced the struggle against communism with the War on Drugs to provide a pretext for intervention in Latin America.[225]

To protest the deployment of two U.S.-trained Bolivian infantry battalions and the overall militarization of the War on Drugs, the CSUTCB voted in 1991 for a national road and rail strike.[226] The campesinos wanted guarantees that the armed forces would only go after traffickers and not enter coca cultivation zones, because they believed that the military's presence increased the risk of violent interactions.

In response to the UMOPAR's gross violations of human rights, several peasant organizations promised to form self-defense groups to protect themselves against military incursions.[227] The "massacre" at Villa Tunari in June 1988, following the seizure and detention of USAID workers at the offices of the subsecretary of rural alternative development, was an explicit example of such abuse.[228] The UMOPAR troops in the Chapare commonly used elaborate forms of torture and also confiscated private property. The enactment of Law 1008 further enhanced UMOPAR abuse and corruption because it permitted detention of innocent people on charges of narco-trafficking. Whether guilty or not, detainees faced a possible sentence of three years in jail if they were sent to the Bolivian Court of Controlled Substances. To obtain release and avoid jail time in what were probably some of the worst jails in the world, the alleged detainees had to pay bribes to the UMOPAR. Moreover, the UMOPAR used roadblocks and the threat of detention to extort money from travelers.[229]

Despite these dangers, many campesinos pledged that they would grow coca in open defiance of Law 1008.[230] According to German Portanda, a member of the coca-growing federation, "alternative crops such as black pepper and pineapples" were a "failure." Farmers could not earn a profit on any of those crops and therefore had to "return to growing coca as the only profitable crop available."[231] By 1994 the U.S. State Department noted that "violent confrontation between the government and coca-growing campesinos was a visible sign of an eradication program that had fallen on hard times."[232]

Guerrilla activity in Bolivia also increased at this time. The guerrillas were anti-U.S. coca nationalists who showed a "greater willingness to use violence to resist coca enforcement."[233] In 1984 the possibility arose for "a major Cuban-supported effort by a coalition of Communist and far-left elements to take power through clandestine means, including the arming of paramilitary forces."[234] Although no "compelling evidence" for this conspiracy appeared, the discovery of a plot to murder Ambassador Edwin Corr in December 1984 signaled that all was not well in Bolivia.[235]

In 1987, following Blast Furnace and the subsequent Operation Snowcap, guerrilla activity intensified. Between 1987 and 1988, guerrillas launched several bombing attacks against western targets, including the U.S. embassy, the Mormon church in La Paz, Citibank, and the Bolivian Ministry of Mines.[236] Although the assailants in these attacks were not always identified, one group, known as the Fuerzas Armadas de Liberación Zárate Willka, claimed responsibility for many of the incidents. Another organization, known as Ejército Guerrillero Túpac Katari (EGTK), was suspected of other attacks, in particular the bombing of the La Paz Mormon church.

The Zárate Willka and the EGTK had similar ideologies with indigenous roots that reflected ideas espoused by the Sendero Luminoso and the MRTA. The Zárate Willka took its name from a Bolivian Indian who fought against the Spanish at the end of the nineteenth century. The Zárate Willka believed that the Spanish conquest and the introduction of Christianity had marginalized Bolivia's Indian population. Thus, their philosophy, known as Katarismo, combined revolutionary Marxism with the idea of Indian revalidation. The Zárate Willka claimed to fight for the rights of the poor and against U.S. intervention in Bolivia, often focusing on the Mormons, since Mormonism originated in, and was associated with, the United States.[237]

Like the Zárate Willka, the EGTK believed that Bolivia should return to its precolonial status in terms of its government, economic system, and social structure. The EGTK hoped to decrease Western influence and promote indigenous people's power over Bolivia's culture and priorities.[238] Notably, the group concentrated its guerrilla activities in the Chapare, where most of Bolivia's illegal coca was grown.

In mid-1988 the terrorist situation in Bolivia became more serious, manifesting as both coca nationalism and anti-American imperialism. In August 1988 the Zárate Willka conducted a bombing attack that damaged three vehicles in a motorcade carrying U.S. Secretary of State George Schultz, who was visiting La Paz to discuss narcotics matters. In May 1989 the Zárate Willka murdered two Mormon missionaries in response to the arrival of U.S. military engineers and troops, who had come to build an airport for the city of Potosí. The Zárate Willka released a statement declaring: "[T]he violation of our national sovereignty cannot remain unpunished." They added: "[T]his is a warning to the Yankee invaders who come here to massacre our peasant brothers."[239] The two Mormon missionaries were pawns in the War on Drugs.

As the campesinos struggled to survive, they resisted U.S. counternarcotics policies that threatened their livelihood. Consequently, guerrilla insurgencies that saw the presence of all Westerners as a threat to their existence throve. Anti-Americanism was reaching a crescendo, and assaults on U.S. targets and Bolivian governmental institutions became almost monthly occurrences between 1989 and 1990.

In October 1990 a new guerrilla organization called the Comisión Nestor Paz Zamora (CNPZ) suddenly appeared; its debut was a bombing attack on a U.S. Marine house that killed a Bolivian guard. The CNPZ took its name from President Paz Zamora's brother, who was a leftist radical killed by Bolivian security forces in 1970. The CNPZ claimed to be a splinter group of Che Guevara's ELN, which the Bolivian police forced into dormancy in the mid-1970s.[240] The CNPZ based their philosophy on *foquismo*, or revolution by means of guerrilla warfare, and they directed their efforts against U.S. military, diplomatic, and commercial interests. After the assault on the Marine barracks, the CNPZ issued a manifesto that "denounced imperialism, trans-nationals, and the Bolivian government." It described its objective as "political and revolutionary." The CNPZ claimed to have no connection to the drug trade, but promised to "continue operations until Yankee troops" were "out of Bolivian political and territorial sovereignty."[241] Though denying a link to narcotics, the

CNPZ was determined to drive the "Yankee imperialists" out of Bolivia, which could only mean that its opposition to U.S. troop presence was narcotics-related. Narcotics were, after all, the central reason for sending the U.S. military to Bolivia. The Bolivian newspaper, *Ultima Hora*, summed up the situation when it wrote: "[T]he stated rationale of the terrorists speaks of anti-imperialism that has been recently revived, because of the militarization of the war against narco-trafficking in the coca producing regions."[242]

Following the bombing of the Marine barracks, the U.S. embassy remarked that this event provided Bolivia with "concrete evidence that they do have a terrorist problem, a fact that many, including government officials, recently did their utmost to ignore or deny."[243] The embassy never considered, in any of its reports, that the introduction of U.S. forces and U.S. narcotics policy were responsible for the reappearance of guerrilla organizations in Bolivia. However, the embassy in La Paz did note that the underlying socioeconomic factors behind the EGTK's emergence remained, despite several setbacks for the organization in 1992.[244] In that same year, another narcotics guerrilla organization, the Jóvenes Cocaleros, appeared in the Chapare. They passed out leaflets declaring that the Chapare would "not become a military base"; it would be the "trench of national liberation." The leaflets ended with the exclamation "coca or death," and, in Quechua, "*Wañuchun yanquis*" (Death to the Yankees).[245]

The U.S. government never recognized that its narcotics policy in Peru caused the Sendero Luminoso to spill over into Bolivia. In late 1988 the war in Peru entered Bolivia when the Sendero Luminoso assassinated Peru's naval attaché in downtown La Paz.[246] By 1992 the Sendero used the Bolivian border as an active sanctuary to develop campesino political networks in association with the EGTK and to refit units. Reacting to these events, the U.S. embassy stated that the Bolivian government had played down hints of narco-terrorist links and was in denial about narco-guerrillismo's existence in the Chapare.[247] The United States appeared to place the onus for the appearance of guerrilla insurgencies on the Bolivian government, which was basically helpless to do anything about their presence. Washington never acknowledged that its strategy had stirred up guerrillismo in Bolivia.

Many of Bolivia's political problems emerged from the Andean Strategy's insistence on sending U.S. Special Forces into Bolivia's counternarcotics operations. The Andean Strategy's vigorous interdiction and eradication policies also had many negative consequences: military-

UMOPAR competition, corruption, campesino opposition, and the emergence of coca-nationalist/anti-U.S. guerrilla organizations, all of which significantly weakened Bolivia's ability to fulfill eradication quotas. U.S. efforts to shut down the Colombian connection to Bolivia inadvertently turned Bolivia into a hub for trafficking and refining cocaine, while the intensification of counternarcotics operations in the Chapare increased human rights abuses.

Moreover, a vast number of Bolivians rejected the economic liberalization programs associated with the Andean Initiative and saw these policies as forms of U.S. neo-imperialism. According to Fernando Garcia Argañarás, most people in Bolivia believed that their government only benefited the wealthy. For many Bolivians, the government was a system dedicated to enlarging markets, rather than expressing the will of the governed.[248]

U.S. limitations on aid and the weakening of the agricultural sector as the result of liberalization created a permanent army of the unemployed who relied on coca to exist. Coca was a powerful economic force, and a strategy that emphasized its elimination before providing an alternative could not work. As long as Bolivia was caught in a catch-22, where money for economic development was tied to eradication, and as long as the nation's military was employed in counternarcotics programs, resistance to coca control efforts would remain. Rather than modernizing Bolivia and curbing its coca production, the Andean Strategy kicked up coca-nationalist sentiment that limited the government's ability to regulate coca farming and initiate economic reform.

The Andean Strategy stirred up a multitude of problems for the northern Andes that undermined its overall goal of achieving the political and military security required to conduct effective counternarcotics programs. It provided little stimulus to participate in alternative crop programs while there remained continued economic incentive for the northern Andean campesinos to grow coca. Moreover, the plan destabilized the northern Andean governments, forcing them into confrontations with their own people over issues such as extradition, herbicide spraying, and the commitment of military forces to counternarcotics operations. Finally, the Andean Strategy's interdiction and eradication programs were unable to halt narcotics production or the traffickers, who opened up new distribution networks to circumvent coca-control efforts.

A 1992 CIA memorandum concluded that the use of "antidrug aid for counterinsurgency purposes" would provide "little payoff against trafficking."[249] The expanded role of the Andean militaries in the War on Drugs not only increased corruption but also generated rural instability as human rights abuses abounded. The strategy's emphasis on a military solution drove the campesinos away from their governments. In 1988 Juan Gabriel Tokatlián warned that identifying the "narco-guerrilla" as the new enemy in the War on Drugs would overextend the function of the armed forces and create a new type of intervention that would have a negative impact on constitutional governments.[250] Although Tokatlián was writing about Colombia, his assertion applied to the northern Andes as a whole and was proven true by the end of the Bush administration in 1992.

In Colombia, the three-way war among the guerrillas, the paramilitaries, and the Colombian military for control over rural coca cultivation areas generated so much instability that coca production skyrocketed. In Bolivia the Andean Strategy's military focus inadvertently fostered the appearance of narcotics-related guerrilla insurgencies. In Peru, even though the Andean Strategy witnessed the defeat of the Sendero Luminoso, narcotics production continued, and military corruption grew. The Andean Strategy, through its militarization of the War on Drugs, undermined political stability in all three nations, which in turn destroyed any chance for its own success.

8

Clinton: From the Andean Strategy to Plan Colombia

When President Bill Clinton took office in 1993, he attempted to distance himself from the Andean Strategy's failure to halt narcotics proliferation. He shifted U.S. domestic policy toward the reduction of demand while at the same time decreasing U.S. foreign counternarcotics assistance. Nevertheless, President Clinton continued to apply many of the Reagan-Bush diplomatic tools to compel northern Andean nations to cut production of narcotics. In essence, the Clinton administration expected the Andean governments to do more with less. When combined with the region's mounting socioeconomic and criminal problems (corruption, cartel violence, disparity caused by liberalization, government clashes with campesino coca growers, entrenchment of guerrillas in coca-growing areas—particularly in Colombia), this approach created an environment in which narcotics control efforts stagnated.[1] Clinton's coercive supply-side strategy for the northern Andes weakened each government's ability to respond to its mounting domestic troubles.

Domestically, the Clinton administration considered drug use a social-health problem.[2] It reduced spending on supply-side programs to 59 percent from Bush's high of 70 percent, while increasing programs to curtail demand.[3] Most important, Clinton officials sought to shift U.S. drug policy away from the "drug war" rhetoric initiated by Reagan and Bush.[4] President Clinton moved the War on Drugs from number three to number twenty-nine on the White House list of national security priorities.[5] Attorney General Janet Reno expressed the administration's view that continuing the Reagan–Bush policies was "economically prohibitive."[6] Clinton officials argued that "for every $1 dollar invested in treatment programs, the government would save $7 from its eradication policies."[7]

Clinton did consider narcotics a national security threat, albeit a lesser one than Reagan and Bush had believed. His Presidential Decision Directive 14 (PDD 14) instructed U.S. counternarcotics agencies to put more emphasis on stopping drugs in Latin American source countries than in transit routes to the United States.[8] The NSC proposed a "controlled shift" that redirected Pentagon resources away from interdiction. Instead, military aid supported operations aimed at dismantling cocaine labs and disrupting trafficking organizations.[9] The Clinton administration also supported coca eradication in Colombia and Peru on the assumption that this would impact the availability of cocaine in the United States. Carrying out the new directive was another matter, however, especially when in 1993 the government slashed antidrug aid to the northern Andes from $387 million to $174 million and cut $47 million from a State Department program that supported U.S.–Andean raids on cocaine traffickers in Peru and Bolivia.[10] The drop in assistance resulted in a dramatic decline in AWAC counternarcotics flights from President Bush's high of 5,265 flights in 1991 to 1,448 in 1996.[11]

Colombia's Descent into the Abyss

In Colombia the sagging economy caused by liberalization (La Apertura), the need to redirect government resources toward poppy control, and the fact that interdiction efforts had cut off Colombian traffickers from Peru and Bolivia led to a significant increase in coca production during the first half of the Clinton years. The lowering of trade barriers brought a flood of U.S. dollars into the country. To counter inflation, the Colombian government raised its interest rates. Then Colombia could not expand

Chart 8.1 | **Annual Growth of Colombian GDP and Unemployment, 1994–1999 (in Percentages)**

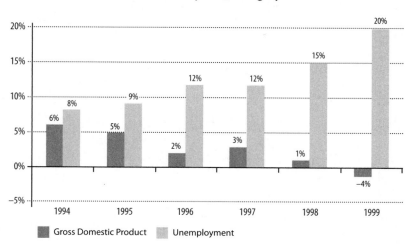

its traditional export market because high interest rates made its exports uncompetitive. In 1994, Colombia's GDP topped out at 6 percent and began a downward spiral, reaching –4 percent in 1999. Unemployment soared, from 8 percent in 1994 to 20 percent in 1999 (see chart 8.1).

Meanwhile, imports continued to surpass exports, and government expenses from the ongoing civil war and drug war as well as the imploding

Chart 8.2 | **Colombian Imports vs. Exports, 1994–1999 (in Percentages)**

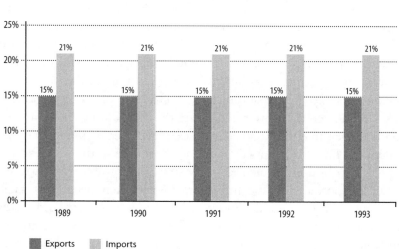

Chart 8.3 | **Colombian National Debt, 1993–1998 (in Billions of U.S. Dollars)**

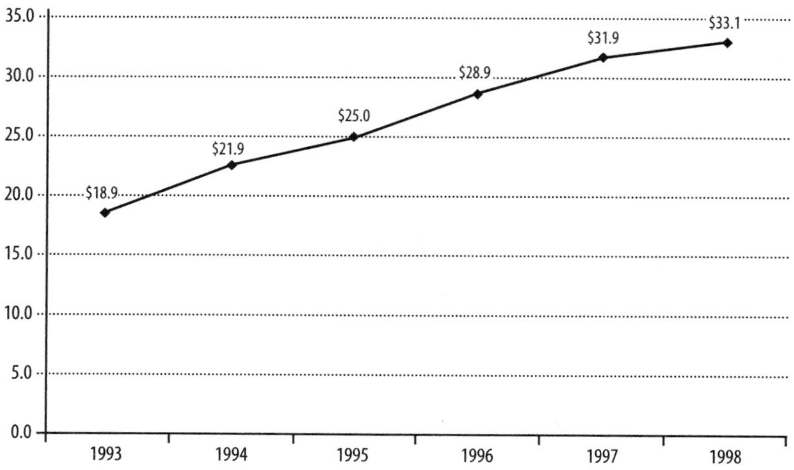

economy caused Colombian debt to rise steadily, from roughly nineteen billion dollars in 1993 to thirty-three billion dollars in 1998 (see charts 8.2 and 8.3).[12]

According to the Colombian government, nearly seven hundred thousand hectares of agricultural production were lost due to the rise in imports during the 1990s.[13] The campesinos were devastated. "[We] do not want to die of hunger," one leader in Putumayo declared. "[If] we continue to plant yucca and corn we are ruined."[14] The bleak economic picture made coca the only crop from which many Colombian campesinos could earn a living.

Colombia's diversion of resources from controlling coca to controlling opium poppy production had the effect of making coca more available to the market.[15] According to the 1993 International Narcotics Control Strategy Report, "because the (Colombian) government had to shift resources from coca and cocaine control operations to the destruction of the country's rapidly expanding poppy crop . . . coca and cocaine seizures were lower than projected."[16] At the same time, Colombian traffickers "moved to consolidate all phases of the cocaine industry up to the moment the finished product" could be "delivered to the Mexican cartels for final distribution," which also boosted coca production.[17] Moreover, the DEA reported that the traffickers moved their processing facilities deeper into the Colombian jungle, where it was difficult and costly to mount counternarcotics operations.[18] The consolidation was motivated by stepped-up U.S. eradication operations in Bolivia and Peru, which severed the air bridge among the three northern Andean nations. Cut off from their primary source of coca leaf, Colombian cartels began to look more seriously at domestic production to meet demand.[19]

Herbicide spraying and a weak alternative development program also debilitated Colombia's narcotics control program. Displaced campesinos joined mass demonstrations against herbicide spraying in 1994 and forced the government to halt it temporarily. The campesinos also attempted to reach an accord with the government on coca farming, alternative development, and herbicide use. In 1995 the government responded to campesino demands by creating Plan Nacional de Desarrollo Alternativo (PNDA or PLANTE), an alternative development program.[20] At the same time, President Ernesto Samper's administration renewed the herbicide campaign by launching Operation Splendor, using U.S.-supplied planes and U.S.-trained pilots to spray coca and poppy crops. Samper pronounced the program nonnegotiable.[21] Coca- and poppy-growing campesinos reacted by multiplying the number of hectares of coca or poppy they cultivated.[22] They claimed that they were going hungry since the government "fumigated everything" and made "little effort to avoid legal crops."[23] PLANTE made little headway with Colombia's narcotics-producing campesinos.

In 1996 the campesinos launched another mass strike.[24] Ricardo Vargas Meza, an expert on herbicidal fumigation, explained that the lack of an agreement on herbicide use, along with the size of campesino demonstrations, made it appear that these problems coincided with an increase in the political and military power of the Colombian guerrillas.[25] PLANTE's director claimed that the "mobilization of thousands of people," their "capacity of resistance," and their "lack of interest in negotiating options of development" with the government was a clear demonstration of the "invisible hand" of the "narco-traffickers and the guerrillas."[26] Retrospectively, the governor of the department of Putumayo, Jorge Devia, explained that besides poisoning legitimate crops, the herbicide-spraying campaign forced the campesinos deeper into the jungles to grow coca and opium poppies. It also made the campesinos resentful and more likely to favor the politics of the leftist guerrillas.[27]

Coca leaf and opium poppy cultivation in Colombia steadily increased, while eradication and seizures failed to approach production levels. Between 1993 and 1998, the estimated coca leaf production rose from 39,700 hectares to 101,800 hectares (see chart 8.4). Opium production remained high at roughly 13,572 hectares in 1997, although this was a decline from 29,821 hectares in 1993 (see chart 8.5).[28]

For the Clinton administration, it was evident that the eradication of coca and opium did not match cultivation levels. Moreover, while production increased, total seizures of cocaine and opium were minimal. Chart 8.6 illustrates the startling disparity between actual seizures of cocaine, which reached fifty-four metric tons in 1998, and the 165 metric tons of HCL available that year.[29]

Chart 8.4 | **Potential Colombian Coca Leaf Cultivation vs. Eradication, 1993–1998 (in Hectares)**

Chart 8.5 | **Colombian Opium Cultivation vs. Eradication, 1993–1997**

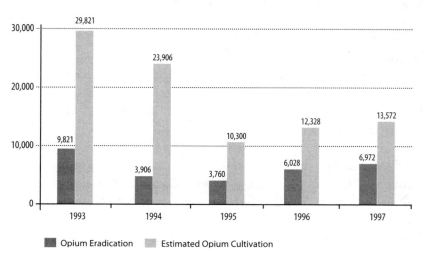

Chart 8.6 | **Colombian HCL Seized vs. Potential HCL Available, 1993–1998**

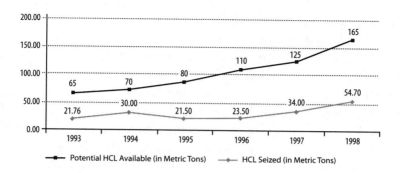

Chart 8.7 | **Potential Opium Available, 1993–1998 (in Metric Tons)**

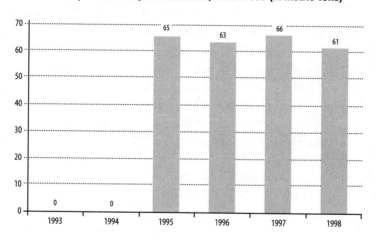

Chart 8.8 | **Opium Seized, 1993–1998 (in Metric Tons)**

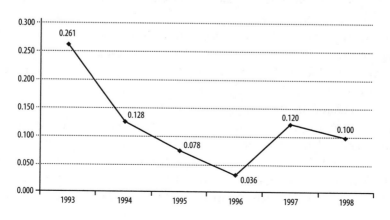

Opium seizures were even less significant: only 0.12 metric tons in 1997, compared to the sixty-six metric tons of opium gum available for conversion to heroin (see charts 8.7 and 8.8).[30]

The U.S. claim that it was winning the War on Drugs in Colombia was a farce. The U.S.-sponsored Colombian antinarcotics program only served to intensify political instability in the volatile rural areas of Colombia.

Corruption and U.S.–Colombian differences on how to defeat the Cali cartel also complicated the Clinton administration's drug policy.[31] The extradition issue seriously upset relations between the two nations. The United States objected to any form of negotiation with the Cali cartel, while Colombian Attorney General Gustavo de Greiff offered favorable terms to cartel members for their surrender in the belief that negotiations would reduce "violence" from "cartel elements," including members of the PEPES who helped bring down the Medellín cartel.[32] U.S. policymakers responded by accusing members of de Greiff's staff of corruption and having links to drug traffickers.

Following the election of Ernesto Samper (1994–1998), the United States renewed pressure on Colombia to crack down on the Cali organization.[33] Samper told U.S. ambassador Myles Frechette that the Cali cartel was more dangerous than the Medellín cartel because it had penetrated "Colombian society at virtually all levels."[34] The Colombian government directed the head of the Colombian National Police (CNP), General José Serrano, whose antinarcotics credentials were impeccable, to form an elite police squad to take on the cartel in 1994.[35] Serrano cleared out corrupt members of the CNP and worked with the U.S. Special Forces to create professional units trained to fight narco-traffickers, paramilitaries, and subversives in jungle areas.[36] Modeled on the Bloque de Busqueda that brought down Pablo Escobar, Serrano's CNP worked closely with U.S. authorities to break up the Cali cartel.[37]

The Clinton administration also pushed for a change in Colombia's extradition policy, setting off a wave of assassinations directed by the Cali cartel against influential pro-extradition people. The growing violence and U.S. pressure led the Colombian Congress to rewrite the extradition law. The new version made it legal to extradite narcotics traffickers but prevented the retroactive extradition of cartel members arrested in 1995.[38]

The eventual destruction of the Cali cartel was a significant victory for the United States. However, learning from the demise of the Medellín and Cali cartels, other narcotics groups such as the Valle de Cauca cartel "democratized" as a consequence.[39] They organized themselves into small, decentralized groups that worked together quietly to expand the market for drugs instead of displaying their political power.[40] The ability of smaller cartels to fill the void created by the destruction of the Medellín and Cali cartels demonstrated that the kingpin strategy had serious flaws. Although the U.S. and Colombian governments had to confront the cartels, the kingpin strategy always left another person or organization ready to fill the vacuum. Some theorists argued that these smaller and (presumably) weaker groups posed less of a threat to the Colombian government than the big cartels.[41] Nevertheless the economic and political power derived from cocaine and heroin was not eliminated, nor was the violence and corruption associated with narcotics production. Moreover, the democratization of the industry made it harder to break up trafficking networks.

Although the Samper administration took several measures to counter the drug trade and the Cali cartel, narcotics corruption at the highest levels of the government undermined U.S.-Colombian counternarcotics efforts. Military officers and police were charged with trafficking in controlled chemicals and narcotics, and even President Samper was accused of taking bribes from the Cali cartel.[42] The discovery that Samper and members of his cabinet (most notably, Defense Minister Fernando Botero) had accepted six million dollars from the cartel for Samper's 1994 presidential campaign seriously disrupted U.S.-Colombian relations and cooperation over narcotics matters.[43]

In an attempt to delegitimize the Samper administration, the Clinton administration decided to decertify Colombia in 1996 and 1997. Secretary of State Madeleine Albright stated that decertification "was aimed at the senior levels of the Colombian government, as heroin and cocaine" flooded "unabated into the U.S."[44] Although decertification did not completely cut off aid for the CNP led by General Serrano, the Colombian government responded to this act by temporarily suspending its aerial eradication program.[45] Most important, decertification enabled narcotics producers and traffickers to take advantage of the divide created between the United States and Colombia.

By the mid-1990s, allegations of human rights abuses by the Colombian military and paramilitaries provoked U.S. congressional disapproval of Colombia's conduct of the War on Drugs. Human rights organizations reported that the paramilitaries were responsible for nearly 76 percent of Colombia's human rights violations, in comparison to 21 percent attributed to the guerrillas and 3 percent attributed to the military.[46] Although the military had a relatively clean record, its known association with the paramilitaries made it an accomplice to the paramilitaries' abuses.

In 1994, when Colombia issued Decree 356, which allowed the legal formation of self-defense units, serious concerns arose concerning the government's commitment to human rights. Originating in Antioquia, these units were called Servicios de Vigilancia y Seguridad Privada, later known as CONVIVIR. The CONVIVIR units were private security services that provided intelligence for the military. Although sidearms were the only weapons they could carry, the CONVIVIR units supposedly committed human rights abuses against suspected guerrilla sympathizers.[47] In response to growing allegations of abuses committed by government forces or their associates, Senator Patrick Leahy introduced a law in 1995 that withheld U.S. military assistance from foreign security units credibly accused of human rights violations.[48] The resulting Leahy Amendment, along with the decertification decisions in 1996 and 1997, crippled U.S. counternarcotics efforts in Colombia.

Significantly, decertification and the withdrawal of military assistance undermined the Colombian military's cohesion. These policies reversed the Andean Strategy, which had thrown a reluctant Colombian military into the War on Drugs. Withholding military aid placed the country's armed forces at a serious disadvantage because the guerrillas continued to finance their efforts through narcotics.[49] The FARC, using their drug windfalls, began to win significant military victories against the Colombian military and the CNP, bringing counternarcotics operations to a near halt by the mid-1990s.[50] The Clinton administration was walking a fine line by trying to combat drug trafficking while avoiding involvement in Colombia's counterinsurgency efforts.[51] In the end, the negative response to the military's ostensible association with the paramilitaries together with fears that U.S. policy was fostering human rights abuses led to a withdrawal of support for Colombia's armed forces, which in turn undermined government control over rural areas.

Withholding aid from the Colombian Army inevitably expanded paramilitary ranks. By 1996, CONVIVIR units were more important in the fight against guerrilla forces than the military. In 1997 the Colombian government ruled several of these units illegal because their activities had gone beyond the limits set by the national Congress, and subsequently, the illegal CONVIVIR units incorporated themselves into paramilitary forces.[52] That same year, the major paramilitary organizations united under one banner and formed the Autodefensas Unidas de Colombia (AUC) with the objective of fighting the guerrillas.[53] A 1997 CIA report on the paramilitaries found "scant indications" that the Colombian military was making an effort to confront paramilitary groups. In the eyes of the CIA, the "growth of paramilitary violence was likely to complicate U.S. interests in Colombia in the areas of human rights and counternarcotics."[54]

Following the defeat of the Medellín and Cali cartels, the paramilitaries became more independent of the narco-traffickers and moved into the coca market themselves to finance their operations against the FARC and ELN.[55] By the late 1990s, U.S. counternarcotics programs in Colombia had ground to a halt due to the declining security situation and the growing power of Colombia's paramilitary and guerrilla organizations.

Fujimori's Folly

In Peru, despite the defeat of the guerrillas and the government's aerial eradication program, coca cultivation continued to increase owing to factors including the mixed economic forecast, the temporary suspension of U.S. assistance to the air-interdiction operation, the Peruvian–Ecuadorian border war, and the corruption of the military and SIN under Vladimiro Montesinos. Coca-control programs began to experience some success only after 1996, when *Fusarium oxysporum* spread in the UHV.

The mixed economic forecast for Peru significantly supported continued narcotics production. Unemployment hovered at 8 to 10 percent between

Chart 8.9 | **Peruvian Unemployment, 1993–1998**

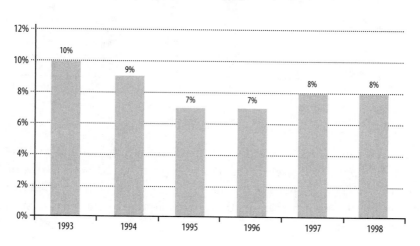

Chart 8.10 | **Peruvian National Debt, 1993–1998 (in U.S. Dollars)**

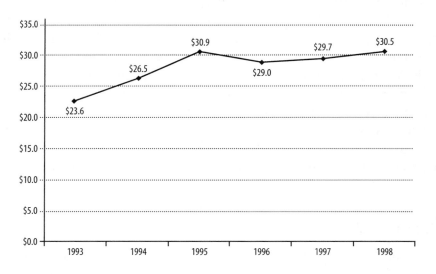

Chart 8.11 | **Peruvian Exports vs. Imports, 1993–1998**
(as a Percentage of the GDP)

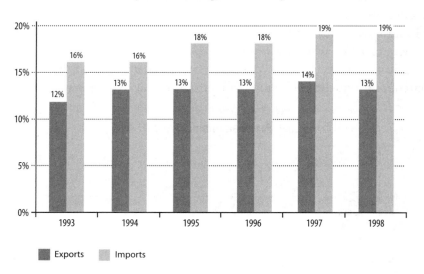

1993 and 1998. Peru's external debt rose, from $26.5 billion in 1994 to $30.5 billion in 1998 (see charts 8.9 and 8.10). GDP declined from 13 percent in 1994 to –1 percent in 1998. Foreign investment dropped from 7 percent in 1994 to 3 percent in 1998, while imports continued to surpass exports (see chart 8.11).

On the positive side, inflation remained in check, declining from 26 percent in 1994 to 6 percent in 1998. However, coca remained a powerful economic force because alternative development programs and economic liberalization failed to improve the campesinos' financial condition. Prior to 1996, the Peruvian coca economy employed 5 to 10 percent of the rural population, or roughly 169,000 to 178,000 people.[56] Coca brought in an annual income of $1,036 to $1,585 in rural areas where average income was roughly $420 to $720. Throughout the mid-1990s, the sluggish economy provided room for the coca economy to grow, although not at the same pace as in the1980s.

Clinton's May 1994 restriction on access to counternarcotics intelligence created new difficulties for U.S.–Peruvian narcotics-control efforts. The administration was concerned about the Peruvian government's use of U.S. intelligence to shoot down suspected drug planes.[57] In 1993, Peru implemented Peruvian Decree Law Number 25426, allowing it to shoot down any plane believed to be carrying narcotics.[58] With an estimated one thousand flights a year heading north to Colombia, this decision represented a dramatic shift.[59] U.S. policy opposed the use of weapons against civilian aircraft, fearing that this could endanger innocent U.S. citizens and make U.S. officials liable under international law.[60] Peru responded by banning AWACS surveillance planes from its airspace.

Although Clinton's constraint on intelligence sharing appeared to cause a rift between the United States and Peru, it only lasted until December 8, 1994.[61] Clinton officials resolved the issue by proposing an amendment that made it legal for foreign officials to destroy aircraft involved in drug trafficking and for U.S. officials to assist them. The government also promised to consult with Peru, Colombia, and the rest of Latin America to accept the shootdown policy as a "narrow exception to international law."[62] If the estimate of one thousand flights per year was accurate, the suspension of intelligence sharing had a devastating effect on U.S. narcotics control efforts in 1994. Furthermore, when intelligence sharing started again, many of the traffickers adapted to the shootdown policy by using river and land routes to traffic coca leaves and coca base to Colombia and Brazil.[63]

On January 26, 1995, one month after the shootdown policy resumed, Peru launched an attack against Ecuador's border. The month-long hot war devolved into brief skirmishes between the two countries that continued until July 1995. The conflict revolved around their shared border, the limits of which had never been settled, even after both countries had agreed to the 1942 Rio Protocol.[64] The 1995 war forced Peru to pull many of its troops away from areas such as the Upper Huallaga Valley. This allowed the remnants of the Sendero to move back into the UHV and temporarily reestablish its authority.[65] In 1995, reports from the UHV stated that the Sendero was running narcotics operations and paying campesinos to smuggle coca to Brazil as the renewed air-interdiction program kicked in.[66] A great deal of room exists for more research on the effect of the border war on counternarcotics operations, but the diminished presence of the Peruvian army in the UHV must have contributed to the rise in coca production in 1995.

Chart 8.12 | **Peruvian Coca Cultivation, 1992–1998 (in Hectares)**

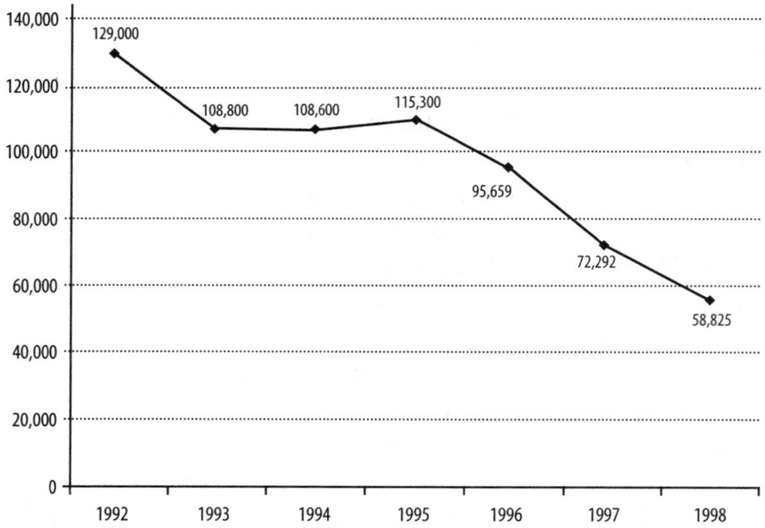

Coca control in Peru was a dismal failure until 1996, when production fell off due to the proliferation of *Fusarium oxysporum* throughout the UHV. Between 1993 and 1994, coca cultivation dropped to 108,000 hectares, and then rose above 115,000 hectares in 1995 (see chart 8.12).[67]

After 1996, coca leaf prices in the UHV started to decrease because of *Fusarium oxysporum* and the Peruvian Air Force's renewed ability to sever the air-bridge between Peru and Colombia. Nevertheless, the destruction of the coca crop in the UHV only served to displace narcotics production to other zones in southern and central areas of Peru, where production estimates were not available.[68] Moreover, Peru continued to produce large quantities of HCL in comparison to the number of government seizures. Between 1993 and 1996, estimates for potential HCL production hovered between 410 and 435 metric tons. At the same time, seizures of HCL and cocaine base between 1993 and 1997 remained inconsistent. They ranged from a low of 5.77 metric tons in 1993 to a high of 22.65 in 1995 (see charts 8.13 and 8.14).[69] Only the advent of *Fusarium oxysporum* cut the potential availability of HCL to 325 metric tons in 1997 (see chart 8.14). The DEA and the State Department were hard-pressed to explain how

Chart 8.13 | **Total Peruvian HCL and Base Seizures, 1993–1998 (in Metric Tons)**

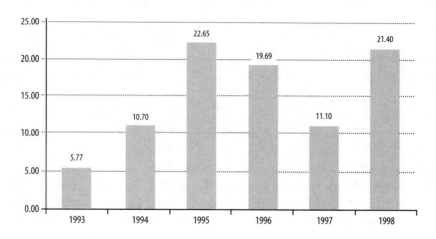

Chart 8.14 | **Potential Peruvian HCL Availability, 1993–1998 (in Metric Tons)**

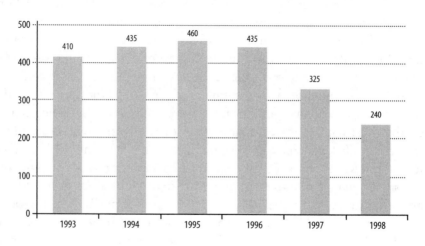

their efforts had slowed the production of coca; ignoring the role *Fusarium oxysporum* in the UHV was impossible.[70]

Peru's military corruption also fostered the coca industry in the UHV. Ties between the military and traffickers grew after the strategic defeat of the Sendero, and their relationship consolidated coca trafficking operations in the UHV. Only four planes carrying narcotics were shot down between April 1992 and February 1993. After 1996, as *Fusarium oxysporum* spread into areas run by the insurgents, coca farming moved into military-controlled land in the UHV, just outside the barbed-wire fences around the bases.[71]

Statements accumulated by researchers in the department of San Martín showed that a significant portion of the campesino population perceived corruption in sectors of the "forces of order."[72] According to one campesino in Moyobamba, a province next to the UHV, the authorities "planted coca." Another campesino explained the reason for military involvement in the drug business: the military had "entered the region not to combat narcotics trafficking" or "coca leaf" production, but rather "to combat subversion."[73] Given the Fujimori government's preoccupation with the insurgencies, this final statement may clarify why the Peruvian military often looked the other way when it came to drugs. These allegations reinforce the likelihood that the armed forces in one way or another facilitated Peru's narcotics industry. In 1996, as if in proof, certain members of Peru's navy were accused of smuggling narcotics on board Peruvian vessels, and six air force members, as well as Fujimori's pilot, were charged with smuggling narcotics onto Fujimori's personal plane.[74]

As the head of the SIN, Vladimiro Montesinos became the most visible symbol of military corruption. Montesinos forced Hernando de Soto, head of Fujimori's alternative development plan, out of power and took control of Peru's counternarcotics program. Montesinos controlled a faction of the military that was Fujimori's base of support. Fujimori had to accept Montesinos' enlarged role in the government because he could not afford a confrontation with the military.[75] In 1996, the same year that members of Peru's navy and air force were accused of smuggling narcotics, the most damaging accusation against the government was made. A narcotics trafficker named Demetrio Chavez Peñaherrera ("El Vaticano") denounced Montesinos. El Vaticano accused Montesinos of accepting fifty thousand dollars a month from him. In return, Montesinos provided military protection for El Vaticano's smuggling operation, which he ran out of an airstrip called La Campanilla that was protected by the military in the Huallaga Valley.[76] El Vaticano made this claim from jail because he feared for his life following his arrest. Purportedly, the partnership between the two soured when Montesinos raised the price for protection to one hundred thousand dollars.

The claim against Montesinos further damaged his questionable reputation. He needed to show results; the United States was considering decertifying Peru due to the country's poor performance in 1995. To cover his tracks, Montesinos launched a full investigation into the navy and air force following the revelations of their illicit activities in 1996.[77]

In 2000 Montesinos' corruption reached new heights when he was accused of masterminding a drugs-for-guns operation with the FARC. Officials discovered the operation when Fujimori publicly disclosed an arms deal called Plan Siberia.[78] Two brothers, Frank and Luis Aybar Cancho, both ex-military officers, were held responsible for the deal. The Aybar brothers had purportedly falsified papers to purchase East German weapons from the Jordanian military on behalf of the Peruvian government in 1999.[79] They then ostensibly parachute-dropped the weapons to the FARC in Colombia as the planes headed to the city of Iquitos in northeast Peru.[80] Fujimori revealed this information to show that his administration was working against corruption, after rumors started to appear in the Peruvian press that Montesinos had fixed Fujimori's reelection victory over Alejandro Toledo (2001–2006).[81]

Fujimori's revelation created more problems than it solved. Sarkis Soghanalian, an arms dealer known as the "merchant of death," with offices in the United States as well as ties to the CIA, had put the deal together.[82] Both Soghanalian and the Jordanian government claimed that they had acted through legal channels, sold the weapons to legal representatives of Peru's military, and received the green light from the CIA to conduct the transaction. Soghanalian stated that he had negotiated the arms deal with Montesinos.[83] He explained that Montesinos had ordered fifty thousand AK-47s but in the end only paid seven hundred thousand dollars for ten thousand rifles.[84] Further complicating the situation, the Aybar brothers were purportedly both former members of the SIN, although Montesinos denied knowing them.[85] The questions surrounding this issue, combined with the election scandal, caused the Fujimori government to collapse. Fujimori sought exile in Japan and resigned from the presidency. Montesinos fled to Panama and then to Venezuela, where he was captured and returned to Peru for trial.[86]

During Montesinos' trial, questions arose about why he had aided the FARC. Montesinos had been on record for opposing the FARC and considered the Peruvian counterinsurgency model the best way to deal with guerrillas in Latin America.[87] For some, the operation appeared to be a CIA black propaganda operation since both Soghanalian and Montesinos were CIA assets. The Peruvian prosecutor against Montesinos, Ronald Gamarra, believed that Montesinos had CIA support in this operation, although he did not have any proof.[88]

In 2001 Frank Aybar told a Colombian magazine that Montesinos had trafficked in weapons with the CIA. The goal was to demonstrate the FARC's threat to the U.S. Congress and incite confrontations between Peru's armed forces and the FARC, which would justify an invasion of Colombia to combat the FARC. However, he added that the CIA also used this venture to set up Montesinos, who had become a liability.[89] Although the CIA denied these allegations, its reputation was once again tarnished by its alleged involvement in criminal enterprises.[90]

Accusations of corruption against Montesinos persisted following Fujimori's downfall. Pablo Escobar's brother Roberto announced from his prison cell that Fujimori and Montesinos had received up to forty-five million dollars from Escobar for military protection of landing strips used by the Medellín cartel.[91] In 2001 a Peruvian informant claimed that Montesinos had helped ship eighteen tons of cocaine to the Arellano Félix cartel (based in Tijuana, Mexico) between 1995 and 1998.[92] While evidence against Montesinos aired publicly, claims persisted that the CIA, with full knowledge of Montesinos' activities, had continued to give him one million dollars annually between 1990 and 2000 for his assistance.[93] Montesinos' corruption of Peru's military and intelligence forces clearly damaged U.S. counternarcotics efforts throughout the Fujimori presidency. Speculation that the CIA removed Montesinos from power when he became a liability does not erase the CIA's previous association with him. This connection served as another indictment against the CIA and its activities in Latin America. The War on Drugs in Peru may have looked successful on paper, but closer inspection puts that success in doubt.

The Bolivian Divide: Coca Control and Liberalization

In Bolivia, economic liberalization did not reduce poverty levels. Economic reform brought inflation under control, and annual growth in GDP remained steady at 4 to 5 percent between 1993 and 1998 (see chart 8.15). Yet the continuation of liberalization policies by Paz Zamora's successor, Gonzalo Sanchez de Lozada (1993–1997), polarized Bolivian soci-

Chart 8.15 | **Bolivian Annual GDP and Inflation, 1993–1998**

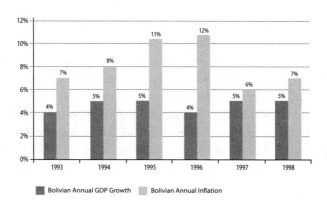

■ Bolivian Annual GDP Growth   ▨ Bolivian Annual Inflation

Chart 8.16 | **Bolivian Imports vs. Exports, 1993–1998**

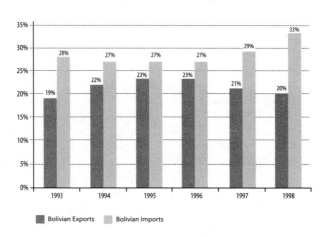

■ Bolivian Exports   ▨ Bolivian Imports

Chart 8.17 | **Bolivian External Debt, 1993–1998 (in Billions of U.S. Dollars)**

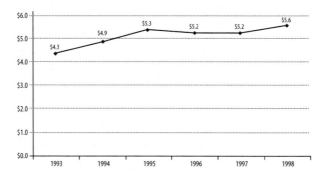

ety. Opponents of coca control and economic liberalization joined forces against what they perceived as elite-backed U.S. imperialism.[94]

Between 1993 and 1998, imports outpaced exports while the Bolivian national debt moved up to $5.6 billion in 1998 (see charts 8.16 and 8.17). IMF demands for economic reform plus stark economic reality forced Sanchez de Lozada to maintain Zamora's liberalization policies, but he presented them with a different spin, calling them "capitalization" instead of "liberalization." Capitalization allowed foreign investors to purchase 50 percent of state-run enterprises, and the government promised to distribute the other 50 percent of ownership equally among Bolivia's adult population. As a result, foreign direct investment climbed from 2 percent in 1993 to 11 percent in 1998 (see chart 8.18).[95]

Chart 8.18 | **Foreign Direct Investment, 1993–1998 (as a Percentage of GDP)**

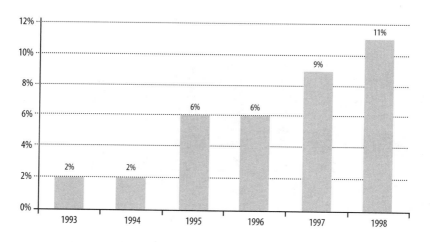

Bolivia's labor sector and campesino population opposed capitalization, however, because it paid no dividends to finance programs for the poor. Moreover, coca remained an important part of the Bolivian economy. In 1996 it made up 21.5 percent of Bolivia's exports and 6 percent of its annual GDP.[96] The COB, Bolivia's main workers union, took up the coca farmers' cause.[97] Strikes against coca control and liberalization became commonplace. Farmers marched through the streets of La Paz denouncing liberalization and shouting pro-coca slogans, while Sanchez de Lozada "swore to God" that he would see through his reforms.[98]According to the UN Economic Commission for Latin America and the Caribbean, Bolivia's ability to address social problems such as poverty and unemployment was "insufficient" because the country was limited "by tight monetary policies." The report added that "frustration" over the economic model was one of the principal causes of "civic unrest" in Latin America.[99] By 1995, Bolivian coca-growers, led by Evo Morales, had taken over leadership positions in the COB.[100] In 1996 Morales formed his own party, Asamblea por la Soberanía de los Pueblos (ASP), which took political control of Cochabamba away from the CSUTCB.[101] Sandro Calvani, the director for the UN International Drug Control Program (UNDCP), explained that Bolivians saw the coca growers as representative of all that "was pure and radical," in contrast with "modernization and the tyranny of whites."[102]

U.S. pressure on the Bolivian government to pursue stringent eradication measures incited angry coca demonstrations, weakened government authority, and undermined narcotics control. In 1993, to earn U.S. certification, Lozada proposed Option Zero. Working in conjunction with Law 1008, another policy based on U.S. rather than Bolivian national interest, Option Zero was designed to eliminate all excess coca production, provide alternative development, and relocate cocalero producers from the Chapare to other parts of Bolivia. The cocaleros responded to Option Zero by proposing Option Uno, which called for the expulsion of all U.S. military forces, the DEA, and a change in Law 1008.[103] Opposition to Option Zero grew so strong that in March 1994 the government agreed not to forcefully destroy coca in transition zones. It also agreed to respect the cocaleros' human rights and consult with them on how to proceed with alternative development programs.[104]

In 1995 U.S. pressure continued to weaken the Lozada administration's position among Bolivia's cocaleros. Though Bolivia failed to achieve coca reduction targets, the United States certified the country in 1994, but once again, only on the basis of national interest. This was the second year that Bolivia fell short of full certification, so the Clinton administration cut assistance to $87.4 million.[105] Cabinet member Carlos Sánchez Berzaín responded that Bolivia found itself caught between the need to "apply the law with one hand and a socio-economic program with the other." Berzaín added that the United States "needed to give more aid" to economic development.[106]

President Lozada also was critical of U.S. policy toward Bolivia. He declared that his country needed at least two billion dollars in foreign aid to develop crop substitution programs that could halt coca production. Lozada felt that Bolivia "could not wait for the demand side of cocaine to be resolved."[107] But, in 1995, when the United States delivered threats to cut more nonhumanitarian aid, Lozada started a mass eradication program that triggered protests in the Chapare. Though Lozada declared a state of siege, violence continued. Bolivian campesinos replanted coca crops in previously eradicated areas and took over new protected areas as well.[108] Evo Morales maintained that without sufficient infrastructure and access to investment funds to make alternative crops viable, crop eradication programs could provoke "civil war."[109]

Throughout the 1990s, coca cultivation remained at constant levels in Bolivia, and eradication stayed weak. Between 1993 and 1998, coca farming was constant at 49,000 hectares, although production spiked to 55,612 hectares in 1996, and eradication eliminated only a small portion of the coca harvest (see chart 8.19). Combined HCL and coca base seizures barely dented the estimated HCL availability.

Chart 8.19 | **Bolivian Coca Production vs. Eradication, 1993–1998 (in Hectares)**

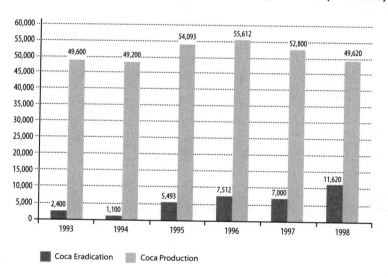

For instance, in 1997 the government seized only 10.39 metric tons of the two hundred metric tons of potential HCL produced (see chart 8.20).[110]

Since coca cultivation employed more than 10 percent of the population and economic liberalization had not improved the conditions of the poor, coca production and anti-liberalization became synonymous in Bolivian politics.[111]

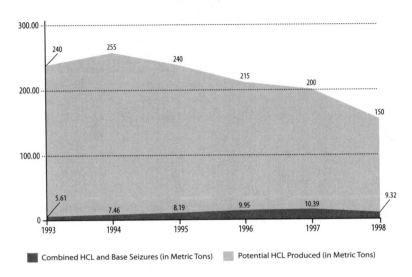

Chart 8.20 | **Bolivian HCL Seizures vs. Potential HCL Production from Bolivian Harvest, 1993–1998**

Combined HCL and Base Seizures (in Metric Tons)   Potential HCL Produced (in Metric Tons)

Clinton Rethinks His Narcotics Control Strategy

As narcotics production surged and instability increased in the northern Andes, the Clinton administration was forced to reconsider its approach to narcotics control. Drug seizures were steadily declining or stagnant, while drug availability remained high. More important, congressional Republicans declared that Clinton's demand-reduction policy did not work. As early as 1994, Republican Senate Majority Leader Bob Dole and Senator Orrin Hatch wrote to the director of the ONDCP, Lee Brown, that "the Clinton administration's drug policy was failing."[112] In 1996, a mid-term election year for Congress, criticism of Clinton's policy mounted as drug use trends in the United States climbed (see charts 8.21 and 8.22).[113]

The rise in the number of emergency room admissions for cocaine and heroin abuse reinforced the perception that Clinton's demand-reduction policy had failed (see chart 8.23).[114]

The House Republican Policy Committee condemned the Clinton administration for ignoring the narcotics problem. They called for "an examination" of what went "wrong under Bill Clinton" and an examination of what "worked from 1980–1992."[115] In 1996, in response to

Chart 8.21 | **Number of U.S. Cocaine Users, 1992–1996 (in Millions)**

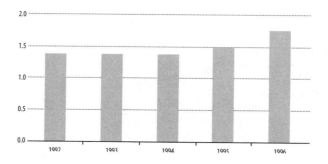

Chart 8.22 | **Number of U.S. Heroin Users, 1992–1996 (in Thousands)**

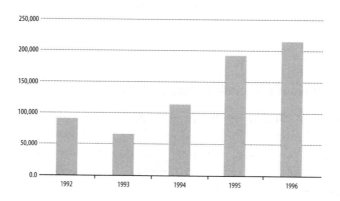

Chart 8.23 | **Cocaine and Heroin Emergency Room Admissions,
1992–1998 (in Thousands)**

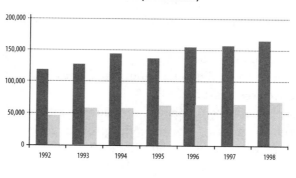

Republican criticism, the Clinton administration nominated General Barry McCaffrey, the former general of U.S. SOUTHCOM in Panama, to head the ONDCP. McCaffrey was firmly behind a tougher drug policy, commenting soon after his appointment, "[W]e must not allow drug use by young Americans to return to the disastrous levels of the 1970s and early 1980s."[116]

Bob Dole and Orrin Hatch's 1994 letter further claimed that U.S. resources were "focused on stopping the flow of drugs at the gram or the kilo level on the street, rather than on stopping the tonnage coming in over our borders."[117] By 1998, Republican Benjamin Gilman, Chair of the House Committee on International Relations, accused the Clinton government of "trying to fight the war on drugs on the cheap."[118] For many in Washington, the inadequacies of the country's counternarcotics policy in the northern Andes had become self-evident. Clinton's policy had led to political instability and rural violence in all three countries, had created breathing room for narcotics traffickers to increase production and trafficking, and had destabilized relations between the United States and the governments of the northern Andes as they bickered over counternarcotics strategy. Alberto Fujimori, speaking for himself and other Andean leaders, declared that the War on Drugs had been a "disaster."[119]

And so Clinton reversed course. In 1998, supported by Congress, he signed the Western Hemisphere Drug Elimination Act. Congress then appropriated $232,600,000 to the INM in the Department of State to carry out the Act's counternarcotics objectives. This money was supplemental to regular INM funding and was meant to help stem the flow of northern Andean cocaine and heroin into the country. According to Rand Beers, the State Department's assistant secretary of international narcotics and law enforcement affairs, it was "evident that eradication and alternative development programs, combined with strong law enforcement efforts," were the most effective means of "reducing the cultivation of coca in Bolivia and Peru."[120] Moreover, U.S. policymakers believed that the continuation of the ATPA would help encourage alternative development while offsetting the influence of the drug industry on the Bolivian and Peruvian economies.[121] The new U.S. strategy was to make alternative development more attractive to coca growers by supporting aggressive eradication and law enforcement efforts that sought to disrupt narcotics organizations.

At first the new strategy seemed to work. Between 1998 and 2000, coca production in Peru and Bolivia tapered off. Coca production in Bolivia dropped off from 38,000 hectares in 1998 to 14,600 hectares in 2000. In Peru coca production dropped from 51,000 hectares in 1998 to 43,400 hectares in 2000.[122] U.S. officials attributed Peru's success to alternative crop development, eradication, and aggressive air-interception.[123] Bolivia, under former dictator Hugo Banzer (1998–2002), also achieved some success using alternative development programs. Banzer's Plan Dignidad offered the cocaleros in the Chapare and the Yungas regions credits, such as roads and technical help, in exchange for promises not to grow coca, convincing some farmers to terminate coca farming in favor of other crops.[124] Nevertheless, persistent opposition to eradication and economic pressures associated with liberalization encouraged more confrontations over coca.[125] Campesinos repeatedly complained that they had no markets for their products and that alternative development projects such as schools and medical posts did little to generate income.[126]

In Peru the eradication program and the destruction of legitimate crops by *Fusarium oxysporum* created havoc. As a result, Fujimori issued a presidential decree that prohibited the use of any chemical or biological agent to eliminate coca, although herbicidal eradication on public lands was renewed during Alejandro Toledo's presidency.[127] After the year 2000, coca cultivation in both Bolivia and Peru began to rise again. By 2002, coca production had surpassed 2000 figures: Peru was producing 46,700 hectares, and Bolivia was producing 21,600 hectares.[128]

Nowhere was the rearticulation of U.S. policy more pronounced than in Colombia. Elected president in 1998, Andrés Pastrana believed that the Colombian government had experienced a "crisis of credibility" over the ability of the "armed forces, police and judicial system" to guarantee "order and security."[129] Drugs had caused "distortions within the Colombian economy." They had "reversed achievements in the redistribution of land." They were "a source of corruption," a "multiplier of violence," and a "negative factor in the climate of investment." Most of all, they served as a growing source of "resources for armed groups."[130] In 1998, coca production in Colombia reached roughly 101,800 hectares. That same year, following his election, Pastrana announced his counternarcotics agenda, called Plan Colombia. The lack of a peace accord with the guerrillas and rising levels of narcotics production motivated Clinton officials to adopt Pastrana's plan.

Plan Colombia's ultimate goal was to "consolidate the central responsibilities of the state" and reestablish "confidence" between the government and its citizens. Backed by the Clinton administration, Pastrana announced his ten-point plan, which included the development of alternative crop programs and open access for foreign investment; modernization of the armed forces so they could provide security for the whole nation; improvement in human rights and a judicial system that protected those rights; a narcotics strategy that partnered with other nations to combat all components of illegal drug traffic; and a peace process with the country's guerrillas to strengthen the state.[131]

A permanent peace agreement with the guerrillas was a major priority for Pastrana. He recognized that the government's problems with the guerrillas stemmed from agrarian movements and the Cold War. Like Betancur, Pastrana believed that he needed a political solution to end the conflict. Moreover, he expected a successful peace agreement to have a positive impact on the struggle against drugs. According to the Pastrana administration, the guerrillas' objectives differed from those of the traffickers. Pastrana argued that the guerrillas' revolutionary ideology would facilitate the ability to negotiate with them, whereas no settlement could be reached with the narco-traffickers.[132] To initiate the peace process, Pastrana agreed to a truce with the FARC in 1999. He withdrew the military from an area the size of Switzerland, the Zona de Distensión, although this agreement did not completely end the fighting between the government and the FARC in other parts of the country (see map 3).[133] In addition, Pastrana agreed to negotiate with the ELN, although he refused to offer them their own demilitarized zone.[134]

Although the Colombian government took the FARC's word that it would help eliminate coca production, peace talks were sporadic, and each side contended that the other was not keeping its promise to maintain the peace.[135] Raúl Reyes, a FARC commander, told a U.S. fact-finding delegation that "the FARC was the best ally the United States could have against drugs" and that the FARC supported alternative development.[136] However, many U.S. policymakers viewed the Zona de Distensión as a FARC refuge where it could expand narcotics production and, ultimately, power.[137]

In 1998, ONDCP head Barry McCaffrey asserted that a major shift in coca cultivation, from Peru and Bolivia to guerrilla-controlled territory in Colombia, had occurred.[138] According to Undersecretary of State Thomas R. Pickering, "Colombia's national sovereignty" was "increasingly threatened by well-armed and ruthless guerrillas, paramilitaries, and narcotrafficking interests which [were] inextricably linked" and which had taken control over Colombia's rural areas.[139] General Charles Wilhelm, the commander of U.S. forces in Latin America, felt that for the negotiations to succeed, the Colombian government had to "strengthen its negotiating position" with the guerrillas by making gains "on the battlefield."[140]

Pastrana's negotiations with the guerrillas stalled when he went to the United States to seek foreign assistance for his version of Plan Colombia. U.S. officials believed that Pastrana had to be more aggressive in meeting the combined guerrilla/drug challenge. Washington's insistence that Pastrana combat the "narco-guerrillas" undermined his peace efforts.[141] A FARC statement illustrated the problem when it accused the Pastrana administration of a "warlike attitude" because it had requested U.S. assistance. The FARC communiqué added that the "alliance of Pastrana and the United States to augment the war in Colombia against the FARC with the distractive sophism of jointly combating drug trafficking" put in doubt the Pastrana government's "peace intentions."[142]

The FARC also believed that the United States was using Plan Colombia to protect its economic interests in Colombia since the plan allowed the U.S. military to extend its presence in Latin America after having pulled out of Panama.[143] The problem, as described by Jaime Ruiz, the Colombian minister in charge of Plan Colombia, was that the United States "saw Colombia's problems through the prism of El Salvador, or human rights, or guerrillas, or left versus right, or through the prism of drugs—that the guerrillas are narco-traffickers and the problem is drugs."[144]

The stalled peace talks and the perception that the FARC was growing more powerful within the Zona de Distensión led the U.S. Congress to pass its own version of Plan Colombia in 1999. It was different from Pastrana's initial proposal in that, like Bush's Andean Strategy, it reinvigorated the Colombian military's participation in the War on Drugs.[145] The Clinton administration had already provided $289 million in 1999 for Colombia to develop a joint military/police antinarcotics battalion. However, to conduct counternarcotics operations and allow small aircraft to spray herbicides over coca and poppy fields, the military had to move into guerrilla-controlled territory where herbicide spraying was opposed.[146] As a result, Plan Colombia became a two-year, $7.5-billion-dollar plan to attack narcotics production and any organization associated with it for fiscal years 2000–2001.[147] Of the $7.5 billion, the Colombian government provided $4 billion, the U.S. government provided $1.3 billion, and European nations provided the rest. Roughly 70 percent of the United States' $1.3 billion went to the military. Washington committed sixty-one combat helicopters and five hundred military advisors to aid Colombian police and military units.[148] The plan also included $115 million for the Colombian National Police and added $68 million to upgrade U.S. radar systems.[149] Support for Plan Colombia was scheduled for renewal in 2002, with the objective of reducing narcotics production 50 percent by 2005.[150]

Following the passage of this more aggressive Plan Colombia, Pastrana's government still hoped to negotiate peace with the FARC and ELN. On October 16, 2000, renewed peace talks were held with the FARC in Costa Rica, but they were complicated by Plan Colombia's military component and by the FARC's claim that the paramilitaries, aided by the Colombian military, had entered the Zona de Distensión to soften up the guerrillas.[151] By November 2000, Pastrana's negotiations with the FARC had temporarily ceased because of the paramilitaries' ongoing assaults on the FARC and the rising number of assassinations against local government authorities in the Zona de Distensión.[152] The peace process was clearly in jeopardy, and Pastrana threatened to end his recognition of the Zona de Distensión in January 2001.

Meanwhile, the ELN, without its own demilitarized zone, began a wave of mass kidnappings in 1999. In April of that year, the ELN hijacked an Avianca flight and took all passengers hostage after forcing the plane to land in the remote San Lucas mountain range. In May, members of the ELN, disguised as police, kidnapped many wealthy Colombians from a Catholic church service in Cali.[153] Bowing to ELN pressure and his own desire for peace, Pastrana agreed in principle to negotiate with them.[154] In April 2000, Pastrana offered the ELN its own demilitarized zone in the states of Antioquia and Bolívar, where the ELN was already the de facto power.[155] The military withdrawal was set to begin in March 2001, but the Colombian armed forces and the U.S. government disapproved of the deal. They contended that the ELN was paying small farmers as much as $2,500 to grow coca that the guerrillas then sold to drug cartels operating in the region. Campesinos who were members of the legally sanctioned self-defense forces (CONVIVIR) feared ELN reprisals and called on the government to reestablish its authority over Antioquia and Bolívar.[156] By August 2001, as the violence spiraled out of control, all talks with the ELN terminated.

In January 2001, when it appeared that Pastrana would soon end his support for the FARC's Zona de Distensión, the military began to build up its forces around the zone to demonstrate its authority.[157] U.S. helicopters began carrying U.S.-trained counterinsurgency units into coca-growing areas outside of the Zona de Distensión to launch attacks against coca labs and any guerrillas who protected them. For instance, in the Push into Southern Columbia operation, the Colombian units moved into rebel-held areas such as Putumayo to support counternarcotics activities. Assistant Secretary of State Phillip Chicola expressed Washington's support for these attacks when he said, "[C]rop substitution and rural development will only work if there is adequate security on the ground." According to Chicola, this meant "that the umbilical link between the guerrillas and the cocaine business must be broken."[158] Violence escalated, and by March 2001, nearly ten thousand campesinos were displaced as guerrillas, paramilitaries, and the Colombian military fought for control over the coca-growing region.[159]

Even as talks broke down, Pastrana vainly held out hopes for peace. The Zona de Distensión was extended after the January 31 deadline, when the FARC promised (as part of El Acuerdo de los Pozos) not to kidnap innocent civilians on Colombian highways. In June 2001, the government and the FARC agreed to a prisoner exchange.[160] The government continued to extend the Zona de Distensión periodically throughout 2001, hoping for a major breakthrough in peace negotiations.[161] Yet Pastrana remained under constant pressure from elements within the military and the government to end the zone because they believed that the FARC was using it as a staging area for kidnappings and assassinations as well as strikes against army units.[162] Accusations persisted that the FARC used the Zona de Distensión to profit from narcotics trafficking.[163]

Following the September 2001 attacks against the United States by al Qaeda, Washington was quick to identify the FARC as a multinational terrorist network linked to the overall War on Terror.[164] In October 2001 the FARC froze further talks, complaining of aerial overflights and the military's presence around the zone. In November of that same year, President Bush issued Executive Order 13224, designating the FARC as a Specially Designated Global Terrorist organization.[165] By January 2002, President Pastrana had ended all hopes for peace by discontinuing recognition of the Zona de Distensión.[166] In Colombia the War on Terror made the narco-guerrilla/narco-terrorist image complete. In order to win the War on Drugs as well as the new War on Terror, the Colombian government had to defeat the guerrillas militarily.

To help curb coca production, Plan Colombia proposed an herbicide-spraying program accompanied by crop substitution. Aerial fumigation in provinces including Putumayo, Guaviare, and Cauqetá began in December 2000 but ran into several complications. President Pastrana argued that aerial fumigation of drug crops was "useless without providing coca grow-ers a legal alternative."[167] However, out of the $1.3 billion appropriated for Plan Colombia, Washington earmarked a meager eighty million dollars for crop substitution programs.[168]

In any case, crop substitution had little chance of success. Nearly 60 percent of Colombia's coca-producing land was too far from potential markets for legal crops to be profitable.[169] Colombia's weak economy forced its government to cut funding sharply for its alternative develop-ment program, which then failed to grant aid to more than half the fam-ilies who joined.[170] Funding dropped from seventy-one billion pesos in 1997 to eighteen billion pesos in 2000.[171] A UN report cited evidence that the herbicides used for crop eradication were mistakenly sprayed on small farmers' legal food plots. As a result, they lost motivation for developing alternative crops, or they planted coca alongside their legitimate crops as a form of insurance against spraying.[172] As Colonel Roberto Trujillo explained, "[T]here seemed to be a gap between the fumigation of the fields and the delivery of alternative aid."[173] The leader of the Puerto Asís campesino association in Putumayo observed that they "fumigated the crops" but the "promised help has not arrived."[174]

Colombian campesinos were understandably reluctant to give up a crop that tripled the amount they could make by growing legal crops.[175] The eight hundred dollars in assistance from the government was too little for the campesinos. Two hectares of coca yielded a kilogram of coca base worth about eight hundred dollars, and they could harvest coca at least four times a year. A 2002 U.S. embassy study detailed the breakdown of crop substitution when it determined that few of the thirty-seven thousand campesinos in Putumayo who signed up for government aid intended to abandon coca farming completely.[176] The USAID laid the alternative crop program's problems at the Colombian government's door: the govern-ment did not control many coca-growing areas, had limited capacity to carry out sustained interdiction operations, and maintained a question-able capacity to coordinate eradication and alternative development effec-tively.[177] Two years after its inception, the alternative crop program ended. The State Department concluded that crop substitution in Colombia was a failure but decided to continue spraying herbicides.[178]

The Clinton administration's disengagement from the Andean Strategy and its support for the Western Hemisphere Drug Elimination Act and Plan Colombia represented a complete policy flip-flop. Like the Andean Strategy, Plan Colombia significantly increased military spending to fight drug production and drew the United States deeper into Colombia's civil conflict, which the administration conflated with the War on Drugs. Plan Colombia left both the United States and Colombia with only one option: a military victory over guerrillas and drug traffickers. The Clinton administration's new policy intensified violence in Colombia and threatened to destabilize the security of its neighbors—Ecuador, Bolivia, Panama, Venezuela, and Brazil—as war, refugees, and narcotics spilled across their borders.[179] Guerrillas, cartels, campesino opposition, and economic disparity made it impossible for northern Andean nations to control the narcotics industry. Like every other government program to date, Plan Colombia failed to halt narcotics production in the northern Andes.

Conclusion

U.S. Drug Policy Comes Full Circle

In the mid-1970s, the War on Drugs moved to the northern Andes with the goal of blocking South American marijuana, heroin, and cocaine from reaching markets in the United States. The region is so vast and so remote that narcotics production there is almost impossible to control. As demand grew, the production and distribution of narcotics in the northern Andes accelerated; lawlessness and corruption escalated; and the drug trade metamorphosed into a major source of political instability. The United States was unable to respond to this mounting crisis because policymakers had not developed viable programs to curb narcotics production. By the late 1970s and early 1980s, political factors such as the cocaine coup in Bolivia and the rise of the Medellín and Cali cartels in Colombia enabled narcotics traffickers to function for the most part with impunity. The United States' ability to counter the spread of drug production in the northern Andes declined, and narcotics became an entrenched industry that had cultural, economic, and political ramifications for the whole region.

In the early 1980s, the collapse of the northern Andean economies further accelerated narcotics production and trafficking in the region.

Narcotics cultivation became an increasingly important source of income for the campesinos, while drug profits provided desperately needed foreign exchange for Bolivia, Colombia, and Peru. But trafficking profits had a negative impact overall on the region's economies, damaging each country's ability to manage inflation, while multiplying reliance on narco-dollars for revenue. Ultimately, the profits derived from narcotics became so essential to these economies that it was nearly impossible for the Andean countries to wean themselves from dependence on them.

Since the United States remained incapable of putting together an effective counternarcotics policy through the early 1980s, regional problems escalated. The campesinos' growing reliance on narco-dollars fostered opposition to U.S.-backed efforts to control narcotics. U.S.-designed alternative development and crop-substitution programs failed to provide a feasible economic replacement for coca farming. Violence in coca-growing regions erupted in reaction to mandatory eradication and crop-substitution programs. Narcotics traffickers and guerrilla organizations took over coca-growing regions where there was little government authority and attacked northern Andean antinarcotics forces conducting eradication and crop-substitution programs. By the mid-1980s, lack of security and the inability to solve the economic equation driving narcotics production severely weakened narcotics control throughout the Andes.

The Reagan administration attributed the failure of its counternarcotics policy to a communist conspiracy driven by narco-terrorist networks. Reagan believed that Cuba and Nicaragua were communist narco-states that were trying to destabilize the United States with drugs, and Reagan officials collected evidence that implicated members of the Cuban and Nicaraguan governments in the drug business. However, conflict in Central America and the difficulties faced by the Reagan administration in its attempt to support the Contras generated allegations of narcotics trafficking by CIA-backed Contra forces. War in Central America facilitated narcotics trafficking throughout the region as each side in the conflict sought ways to fund its particular cause. The situation paved the way for narcotics organizations, especially the Medellín cartel, to funnel narcotics through Central America to the United States. Throughout the conflict, the Reagan administration continued to insist on the existence of links between the Cuban and Nicaraguan governments and guerrilla movements in the northern Andes.

There was some truth in this analysis, but the strategies devised by the Reagan and Bush administrations did not address the political and socioeconomic factors that lay behind the narcotics trade and guerrilla insurgencies. In dealing with the narco-terrorist connection in coca-growing regions, the United States always gave precedence to security over economic development. This flew in the face of the socioeconomic and political complexities that had given rise to the coca boom and subversive movements in each nation. To be successful, the United States needed to design a policy that separated guerrilla insurgencies from narcotics instead of conflating them.

Step by step, the Cold War objective of defeating leftist guerrillas merged with the goal of the War on Drugs. Militarization of U.S. policy made it harder to split guerrillas from campesino coca farmers, who increasingly supported the guerrillas to protect their livelihoods. The symbiosis between narcotics trafficking and guerrilla insurgencies yielded a political vacuum that bred more chaos, which in turn made more room for the narco-traffickers to operate freely. The political void stemming from U.S. policies helped the guerrillas to dominate the narcotics industry. Inadvertently or not, U.S. strategy played into the hands of guerrillas as well as narco-traffickers.

After Reagan identified narcotics as a national security threat, the military role in the War on Drugs steadily expanded in spite of Pentagon resistance. Military leaders considered narcotics control a civilian law enforcement issue and feared being drawn into a Vietnam-like quagmire. Nevertheless, in 1989 the Bush administration's Andean Strategy finalized the commitment of U.S. armed forces to the War on Drugs and boosted funding and military assistance to combat narcotics production. The Andean Strategy intensified the military's direct engagement in northern Andean counternarcotics operations, a role the military accepted with reservations and which many northern Andean people deeply resented.

The invasion of Panama in 1989 became the first overt example of increased U.S. military involvement in narcotics control. The story of Manuel Noriega exposed the dirty underbelly of the War on Drugs and U.S. policy in Central America. Noriega had been a CIA asset throughout the 1970s and had served as a CIA liaison to Castro. When Noriega became head of the PDF, the U.S. intelligence services intentionally overlooked his illegal activities because he helped the Contra program. When Noriega stopped cooperating with the CIA, his illegal activities were made public. Noriega lost control over Panama as both foreign and domestic pressure mounted against his rule. When the United States indicted Noriega, he used anti-American sentiment in Central America to deflect attention from the allegations. Noriega and the United States were unable to maintain diplomatic relations, and Noriega moved closer to Cuba and Nicaragua, which caused the United States to see him as a growing national security threat. Heightened tensions eventually led to the U.S. invasion of Panama in order to remove the "drug-dealing" dictator from power. The Panamanian invasion was a mixture of criminal activity, nationalism, and covert operations gone awry, and it virtually ended U.S.–Andean cooperative efforts to control narcotics.

To improve relations, President Bush met with northern Andean leaders at the Cartagena Summit in February 1990. The summit produced the Andean Initiative, a program designed to address the economic side of the narcotics problem with economic liberalization and an expanded emphasis on alternative development. By opening up new markets and supporting crop substitution, the Andean Initiative, through the ATPA, was expected to generate economic alternatives that would give Andean campesinos viable alternatives to narcotics cultivation.

However, liberalization did not benefit the Andean coca growers because they had few markets for their alternative crops. Moreover, the provision of alternative development assistance depended on coca crop eradication, while the fluctuating price of coca caused coca production to rise and fall according to demand. Hence, the campesinos had little incentive to plant other crops. Additionally, extradition of drug traffickers and U.S. military involvement in counternarcotics efforts severely disrupted relations between the United States and northern Andean governments. U.S. pressure on the northern Andean countries to move against coca farming incited violence and anti-U.S. coca nationalism. When the United States applied military force, the coca industry simply found new outlets for transporting and distributing narcotics. Finally, the use of northern Andean armed forces in counternarcotics operations escalated corruption, human rights abuses, and rural instability. Coca cultivation moved deep into the jungles, where government authority was minimal to nonexistent.

The United States made security the key to its antinarcotics strategy, when in reality, winning the support of the coca-growing campesinos was the core requirement for success. Even the defeat of the Sendero Luminoso did not slow down the rise of coca production in Peru. Promoting and financing the military to combat the drug trade and the guerrillas at the same time, while failing to provide sufficient alternative development options, alienated the coca-growing campesinos from their governments and caused them to defend their economic interests against counternarcotics operations.

When Clinton took over from Bush, he tried to distance himself from the Andean Strategy while continuing to pursue a supply-side approach with reduced funding. By 1998, narcotics cultivation in the northern Andes had reached epidemic proportions. Clinton then reversed direction and adopted a policy similar to the Andean Strategy, increasing U.S. military assistance to the northern Andean governments for counternarcotics operations. The Clinton administration's Western Hemisphere Drug Elimination Act in Bolivia and Peru was met with continued campesino resistance and had no long-term impact on the drug business. The U.S. version of Plan Colombia remilitarized the War on Drugs in that country and never achieved a successful crop-substitution program. While the economy stagnated and the military carried out counternarcotics actions, the bond between the campesino coca farmers and guerrilla forces solidified. Rather than ending the War on Drugs, Plan Colombia intensified it.

Even today, the United States follows a supply-side rubric to resolve the drug problem. The George W. Bush administration devised the Andean Regional Initiative (ARI) and the Andean Counterdrug Initiative (ACI) in 2001 to counter narcotics production in Colombia and the Andean region.[1] Like the Andean Initiative and the ATPA, the ARI was designed to promote democracy, economic development, and regional stability, while the ACI was designed to sustain Plan Colombia and other regional counternarcotics programs.[2] Funding for these programs clearly leaned toward military solutions. For fiscal year 2002, $625 million of the $782.82 million appropriated for the ARI was designated for the ACI; for fiscal year 2003, $700 million of the $835.5 million appropriated for the ARI went to the ACI.[3] In addition to increased military funding, in July 2002, as part of an emergency supplemental spending bill, the U.S. Congress removed all restrictions on Colombia's use of U.S. counternarcotics aid so that it could support a "unified campaign against narcotics trafficking, terrorist activities, and other threats to its national security."[4]

Nearly thirty-five years into the War on Drugs, the United States continues to recycle the same narcotics control policies under different names. Cocaine use among the U.S. public remained at a constant level between 2002 and 2006 (see chart C.1). In 2006, the DEA reported that potential coca cultivation in South America had climbed back up to 970 metric tons from its previous high in 2002 of 975 metric tons (see chart C.2.)[5] Despite

U.S. counternarcotics efforts, demand and the cultivation and trafficking of coca in the northern Andes remain constant.

In Colombia the guerrilla war, along with the War on Drugs, continues in the form of Plan Colombia. The election of Alvaro Uribe Vélez as pres-

Chart C.1 | **Percentage of Past Year Drug Use (Cocaine Any Form), 2002–2006**

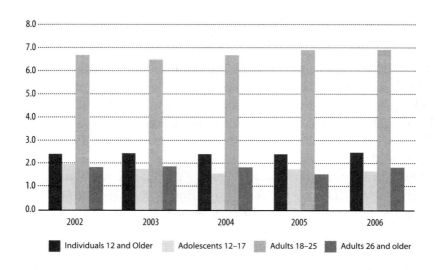

Chart C.2 | **Potential Coca Production in Metric Tons, 2002–2006**

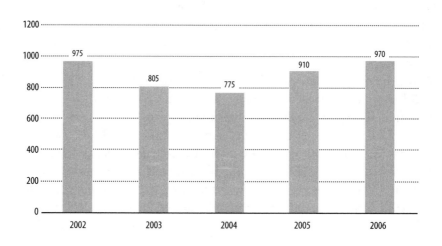

ident of Colombia in May 2002 indicated that the Colombian government was going to take a more hard-line stance against Colombia's guerrillas. In coordination with the Uribe administration, the Bush administration renewed Plan Colombia in return for Colombia's support in the United Nations for its campaign against Iraq in December 2002. At the time, Colombia held the temporary presidency of the UN Security Council. In exchange for renewed aid, the Colombian ambassador to the United Nations gave the Bush administration an unedited report on Iraqi weapons of mass destruction prior to its circulation within the United Nations. Originally this report was to be given to all members of the United Nations at the same time; however, by giving the Bush administration the report beforehand, the Colombian ambassador made sure that the Bush administration could disseminate the information to the other four permanent Security Council members as it saw fit.[6]

Although Plan Colombia was renewed, serious questions persisted about Uribe's relationship with Colombia's paramilitaries and the Medellín cartel. Alvaro Uribe comes from a prominent landholding family in Colombia; his father was assassinated by the FARC in 1983. Uribe campaigned for the presidency in 2002 on a platform that promised the destruction of the FARC and ELN.[7] However, as governor of Antioquia between 1995 and 1997, Uribe was rumored to have allowed the formation of the CONVIVIR units alleged to have worked with Colombian paramilitaries.[8] A 1991 DIA report cited Uribe for assisting the Medellín cartel in the late 1980s and early 1990s. Other reports linked him to a narcotics business in the United States and referred to him as "a friend of Pablo Escobar." The State Department claimed that this information had not been fully evaluated and could be neither confirmed nor denied.[9] Obviously, these associations should have raised questions about Uribe's drug-fighting credentials and his interest in preventing Colombia from becoming a narcocracy.

In 2005 President Uribe initiated the demobilization of paramilitary organizations. This effort was criticized by international organizations for offering favorable terms to the paramilitaries, allowing them to remain intact and protecting their leaders from prosecution on charges of drug trafficking or human rights abuses.[10] According to a 2008 GAO report on Plan Colombia, the Autodefensas Unidas de Colombia (AUC) demobilized, but many mid-level AUC officers re-formed their units into new individual paramilitary drug-trafficking gangs such as the Aguilas Negras and the Organizacíon Nueva Generacíon.[11]

In 2007 the Uribe presidency found itself mired in several scandals that tied many members of its administration to the paramilitaries, including the secretary of state, María Consuelo Araújo, and the chief of the DAN, Jorge Noguera.[12] Further complicating matters, thirty-three members from pro-Uribe parties within the Colombian Congress, including Partido Social de Unidad Nacional (PSUN) leader Senator Carlos García, have been arrested, and another thirty members are under investigation for their ties to paramilitary organizations.[13] In June 2008 it was revealed that Uribe had bribed Congresswoman Yidis Medina for her vote to change the Colombian Constitution, allowing him to run and win a second term as president in 2004.[14]

In addition to the parapolitics scandal, the DAS found itself caught in a wiretapping scandal in February 2009, when its director, María del Pilar Hurtado, was replaced by Felipe Muñoz. Allegations appeared in Colombian papers that Hurtado, who had replaced Jorge Noguera in 2007, directed the DAS to eavesdrop on Supreme Court justices, journalists, and opposition leaders.[15] According to the reports, Uribe was the primary beneficiary of the wiretapping. Uribe denied the allegations and blamed the illicit recordings on corrupt agents in the pay of drug lords, adding that they were a threat to national security.[16]

To overcome allegations of bribery and corruption, Uribe, riding on his successes against the FARC, called for a third referendum that would allow him to extend his presidency until 2014. Opposition legislators decried this move and accused him of acting like a "dictator," a caudillo who was disguising dictatorship by manipulating the constitution and providing a false sense of democracy.[17] Because of these scandals and political obstacles in changing the constitution, Uribe has not committed himself to running for a third consecutive term. Latin American analysts pointed out that it would have been "difficult for the United States to recognize a third term for Uribe" when it had objected "to reelection attempts" by Chavez, Morales, and Correa.[18] Still, Uribe remains widely popular, with a 70 percent to 80 percent approval rating among the war-weary Colombian people, who appreciate his hard-line stance and his military successes against the guerrillas, which have allowed him to restore a semblance of order within urban centers such as Bogotá and Medellín.[19] In February 2008 there was a spontaneous and massive nationwide demonstration in the cities of Colombia against the FARC.[20] In response, demonstrations against all violence, including state and paramilitary violence, were held in March, but these marches were marked by intimidation and government criticism that they had been organized by the FARC.[21]

New marches against the FARC and kidnapping were held in late July 2008, indicating growing public opposition.[22] However, the nation remains divided between urban centers and rural areas populated by campesinos, indigenous people, and Afro-Colombians, who have been the primary victims of paramilitary violence.[23] By 2009 more than one thousand extra-judicial killings were being investigated in Colombia. The military used them to inflate their body count of defeated guerrilla and paramilitary forces. The most widely publicized incident was the cashiering of twenty-five soldiers, four colonels, and three generals for the extrajudicial killings of eleven innocent civilians. Human rights groups allege that at least six indigenous groups have been pushed to the brink of extinction as they find themselves caught in the crossfire.[24]

Related to these human rights abuses is the issue of a free trade deal between Colombia and the United States. U.S. Democrats oppose the deal on the basis that it undermines U.S. workers and gives support to a government that has done little to combat human rights abuses. Yet Colombia's trade unions favor the free trade act because it benefits the industries in which they are employed. While the Democrats' concerns regarding paramilitary violence against labor unionists were justified, denying Colombia the free trade deal presented another set of problems. The Colombian people ask how the United States can close the door on Colombia when it has been such a staunch ally of the United States and has sacrificed its own blood and treasure to fight the U.S. War on Drugs.

Uribe's attempts to negotiate peace with the guerrillas have been unsuccessful because of paramilitarism and human rights abuses committed by all sides in the conflict. Peace talks started with the ELN in 2005 collapsed in 2007 over the Colombian government's demand that they concentrate all of their troops in one area.[25] Negotiations between the Colombian government and the FARC stalled as they traded accusations of paramilitarism and the penetration of drug money into all levels of politics and state security.[26]

The Colombian military scored several important victories against the FARC in 2008. In March 2008, the cross-border attack on a FARC safe haven in Ecuador killed the spokesperson and second in command of the FARC, Raúl Reyes.[27] The assassination of Iván Ríos, another FARC commander, also in March 2008, was a second blow to the FARC's organization. The FARC picked up small-scale attacks after these events, but the death of the FARC leader Manuel Marulanda on May 24, 2008, left the FARC hierarchy in disarray.[28] Owing to desertions, the FARC's operational capacity was reduced from sixteen thousand men in uniform in 2001 to an estimated nine thousand men in uniform in 2008. Alfonso Cano is now thought to be in control of the FARC, although some analysts believe that there is infighting among its leadership for control.[29] The Colombian military's success in freeing former presidential candidate Ingrid Betancourt, kidnapped in 2002, and three U.S. counternarcotics contractors for the Pentagon captured in 2003 has demonstrated the FARC's weakness.

The freeing of Betancourt stiffened Uribe's position against the FARC. Nevertheless, the whole story about the rescue operation is not known. There were reports from the Swiss radio station Radio Suisse Romande that the Colombian government paid twenty million dollars to the guerrilla in charge of guarding the hostages and then exploited a decision already reached by the FARC's central command to release the hostages by staging the rescue mission.[30] The Colombian government denied that this report was true on the basis that it refuses to deal with terrorists. To admit complicity in dealing with the FARC would have undermined Uribe's hard-line stance against them. Further clouding the situation was the use of the Red Cross symbol as a cover for the rescue mission. Observers believed that the misuse of the Red Cross symbol endangered all nongovernmental workers who work in rural areas dominated by the FARC and could undermine third-party peace negotiations.[31]

Even under Plan Colombia and the FARC's recent setbacks, Colombia's capacity to produce large quantities of cocaine remains undiminished. Between 2003 and 2006, coca production increased from 114,100 hectares to 157,000 hectares.[32] The DEA reported in 2007 that coca growing had expanded into areas where it was not previously reported and that the campesinos were learning to adapt to eradication efforts.[33] According to the United Nations, Colombian coca growers expanded the amount of land under cultivation by 27 percent in 2007.[34] In 2008, a GAO report criticized Plan Colombia for failing to reduce narcotics cultivation by 50 percent since 2003, when it was renewed. It did credit U.S. military assistance for improving the security situation throughout Colombia, but the report also stated that the United States had no "alternative development projects in areas where the majority of coca is grown," that little infrastructure in these areas existed, and that the Colombian government did not permit any alternative development "projects in areas where illicit crops" were grown.[35] U.S. support for alternative development projects remains weak.

The Colombian military, however, has continued to eradicate coca in some areas, emphasizing manual eradication over aerial fumigation because it is believed to produce better results. Manual eradication is more dangerous because it threatens to bring the military into direct contact with traffickers and guerrillas and can result in the negative side effects that were seen with Peruvian and Bolivian manual eradication programs in the 1980s.[36] Significantly, herbicide-resistant coca plants grown at higher altitudes have undermined the effect of herbicide campaigns.[37]

Venezuelan President Hugo Chávez's involvement in the hostage negotiating process and his alleged relationship with the FARC has been a source of international scandal and cross-border tension.[38] Chávez leads the Socialist Bolivarian Revolution in Venezuela and shares political ground with the FARC, which has its own urban political front, the Movimiento Bolivariano. Adding fuel to the fire, Chávez has supported Fidel Castro and has strengthened his ties with the Iranian government, which the United States considers a state sponsor of terrorism.[39]

Documents retrieved from Raúl Reyes's computer after he was killed have revealed a deep relationship between Chávez and the FARC. Captured documents show that Chávez provided the guerrillas with three hundred million dollars. The documents also alleged that Ecuadorian president Rafael Correa, who shares ideology with Chávez, received money from the FARC to finance his political campaign for the presidency in 2006. Chávez claims that the documents, whose validity was verified by Interpol, were part of a disinformation campaign.[40] Of even greater concern, the documents exposed an attempt by the FARC to sell fifty kilograms of uranium, although the amount was not enough to make an atomic bomb or even a dirty bomb. The ties between Chávez and Iran fuel speculation that the uranium was intended for sale to the Iranian government, which is suspected of having a secret nuclear weapons program.[41]

Tensions on both sides of the Colombian border remain high. Venezuela and Ecuador have restored low-level political ties with Colombia, but this has not eased Colombia's concern that the FARC operates with impunity along both borders.[42] Ecuador does not consider the FARC a terrorist organization, and its growing hostility toward the War on Drugs has led it to terminate the U.S. contract to use Manta Air Base for drug interdiction flights in 2009. Still, Ecuadorian officials expressed concern over the FARC's presence along the San Miguel River separating Colombia and

Ecuador and have made attempts to prevent its infiltration.[43] On the other hand, Chávez has threatened war if the Colombian military, in pursuit of the FARC or drug traffickers, crosses over into Venezuelan territory.[44] Venezuela and Colombia have promised more cooperation along their shared border, and in the recent wake of FARC setbacks, Chávez has repeatedly called for the FARC to lay down its arms.[45]

In the meantime, FARC deserters have reported that the group has found a secure refuge in Venezuela in return for bribes and has formed a nonaggression pact with the Venezuelan military. The Venezuelan border has become a FARC operational area where FARC commanders such as German Briceño and José Felipe Rizo plan operations and traffic in narcotics across the Colombian border.[46] More than 30 percent of Colombian cocaine now transits through Venezuela. Estimates claim that the FARC trafficked nearly five tons of cocaine a month across the Venezuelan border.[47] Chávez claims that these allegations are an attempt to "demonize" his government. He adds that his government "landed the strongest blows against drug trafficking in Venezuelan history" by seizing 142 tons of cocaine since 2004.[48] In light of the events in Ecuador that exposed the Chávez government, Venezuela has signaled that it is willing to reinvigorate stalled antidrug efforts with the United States.[49] Yet the 2009 State Department INCSR maintained that drug trafficking through Venezuela has increased fivefold since 2002. Chavez criticized this report and the incoming administration of Barack Obama, inaugurated as president of the United States in January 2009, declaring that "Bush was still in charge."[50] Obama has signaled that he would like to open up a dialogue with Chavez, but at the Summit of the Americas in April 2009, these issues remained untouched.

Chávez's alienation from the United States and the increase in U.S. military aid to Colombia pushed him to seek arms deals with Russia. Russia agreed to cooperate because of its concerns about NATO pushing along its border. In 2006 Chávez purchased one hundred thousand Kalashnikov rifles and a license from Moscow to make Kalashnikovs and ammunition to bolster its defenses and those of other Latin American nations such as Bolivia and Cuba.[51] In 2008 Chávez purchased twenty-four Sukhoi fighter jets, which he claims are for use in defense against "imperialist" aggression. Chávez also made deals for four diesel-powered submarines and twenty Tor-M1 air defense systems, and there were rumors that he was going to allow the Russians to open a military base in Venezuela.[52] In December 2008, Venezuela held naval exercises with Russia, and Cuba has offered to allow Russia military access to its territorial waters and airspace. According to Andrei Klimov, deputy chairman of the Russian State Duma's Committee for International Affairs, "Cuba's location has geopolitical importance," and a "presence in both economic and military affairs must be built in America."[53] Considering the political situation in the Andean region, a strengthening of the Russian military position in the Americas and a military buildup in Colombia and Venezuela bodes ill for regional peace and stability. Tensions along Colombia's borders remain high and will persist if military actions and destabilization efforts continue there.

Since 2000, Cuba has given the appearance of wishing to cooperate more openly with the United States. The U.S. government has remained uneasy, concerned that Cuba has become a refuge for Colombian guerrillas, that commerce with Venezuela has increased the flow of drugs through Cuba, and that tourism has expanded drug smuggling via Cuba to Europe.[54] Although Cuba has made several attempts to reduce the flow of narcotics through its territory, the State Department believes that Cuba conducted these operations and maintained a policy of transparency for purely political reasons.[55] According to a report published by *El Nuevo Herald*, the Cuban government used a tourism company as a front to establish guerrilla training camps along the Venezuelan border in 2008.[56] Given the close association between Chávez and Castro, recent information indicating that Chávez actively supported the FARC, and the fact that Cuba has been a safe haven for guerrillas, speculation continues on the extent of Castro's involvement in Colombia. The June 2009 revelation that a State Department employee with access to top-secret documents was spying for Cuba until 2007 further prejudices the idea that Cuba is seeking to cooperate more fully with the United States.[57]

President Obama's attempt to reset relations with Cuba and Venezuela likewise raises many questions. The biggest is whether his policy of opening dialogue with Cuba and Venezuela without preconditions is naive in light of recent events in the northern Andes. Obama must determine whether Chavez is actually a caudillo trying to subvert his neighbors by supporting Marxist guerrillas and facilitating the drug trade. The Obama administration must decide if the growing ties between Venezuela, Russia, and Iran pose a real threat to U.S. security in the Caribbean and whether Cuba will move toward democracy and end its support for subversion, given its current backing of Chavez, the FARC, and the ELN. Does Obama's policy give Venezuela and Cuba the upper hand in implementing the final phase of their Gramscian–Marxist strategy for achieving international socialism, whereby they destroy American youth through fostering addiction to cheap and available narcotics? Does greater openness toward Venezuela and Cuba undermine U.S. relations with Colombia, jeopardizing its political and economic interests, and complicating its efforts for self-defense? Finally, can a constructive peace be created within these larger ideological and geopolitical issues that have such enormous impact for the world?

In 2006 the Sandinistas returned to power in Nicaragua under the leadership of Daniel Ortega. Ortega's government pledged cooperation with the United States.[58] Although the government does not officially sanction narcotics trafficking or production, corruption is rife throughout Nicaragua, particularly within its law enforcement agencies and judicial system.[59] Following the killing of Raúl Reyes in 2008, Ortega condemned the Colombian government's action as an illegal violation of Ecuador's sovereignty and broke off relations with Colombia for a month.[60] In light of its setbacks, the FARC approached Ortega in June 2008 to discuss "issues of war and peace." Ortega responded by declaring his willingness to meet with FARC rebels to reach a negotiated solution to their conflict. Ortega also used the Nicaraguan Air Force to pick up three survivors (including two guerrillas) from Reyes' camp in Ecuador, offering them asylum in Nicaragua. These events created a diplomatic row between the two countries, with Colombia threatening to bring charges against Nicaragua for harboring terrorists.[61] Colombia added that it did not authorize any negotiation with terrorist organizations, and it called for the FARC's demobilization before peace talks can begin.[62] In late 2008, Nicaragua remained a significant sea and land transshipment point for cocaine and heroin.[63]

In the rest of Central America, the drug war is becoming a regional problem as drugs are trafficked north. Current estimates indicate that three-quarters of all cocaine reaching the United States from Mexico has at one point transited through Central America by land, air, or sea.[64] Once the cocaine arrives in Mexico, the Tijuana, Juárez, Michoacán, Zetas, Sinaloa, and Gulf cartels battle among themselves and with the Mexican government over the distribution of cocaine and other narcotics into the United States. Guatemala and El Salvador are seeing Mexican violence spill over their borders as Mexican and transnational gangs vie for control of drug routes through Central America.[65] In Guatemala, a gang that calls itself the Kabiles is especially notorious. Composed of deserters from Guatemala's Special Forces, the Kabiles have converted themselves into hired guns for the cartels, particularly for the Zetas cartel, which was fighting for control over Acapulco.[66]

In Panama, "major Colombian and Mexican drug cartels" as well as "Colombian" guerrillas continue their "drug trafficking and money laundering." Poorly paid police and judges in Central America are easily bought off by the gangs. To respond to this growing crisis, the United States has launched the Mérida Initiative in Central America and Mexico to fund programs that "strengthen the institutional capabilities of Central American governments to prevent corruption within law enforcement agencies"; facilitate the "transfer of information between regional governments"; and "fund equipment, training, economic and social development programs."[67] As of 2009, the results of this program have yet to be seen.

In Bolivia, campesino opposition to narcotics control and liberalization policies brought about the election of Evo Morales. Morales, a former coca grower, proposed a counternarcotics policy of "zero cocaine" and the "revalidation" of the coca leaf by making it an industrialized product.[68] Morales has aligned his government with Chávez but has tried to maintain a balance between coca control and the promotion of coca for legal usage.[69] During his presidency, Morales has tried to adhere to U.S.-backed eradication demands despite President Bush's 2006 budget, which reduced spending on alternative development projects by 10 percent.[70] Bolivia destroyed roughly 12,350 hectares in the Chapare region in 2007, with the result that coca farming has shifted away from the Chapare and increased significantly in the Yungas region.[71] Cultivation in the Yungas has risen to 45,700 acres, well beyond the twelve thousand hectares (30,000 acres) legally permitted by the 1988 Ley del Régimen de la Coca y Sustancias Controladas 1008. Bolivian coca paste is flowing through Brazil in ever greater quantities, where it is refined into cocaine for domestic and European consumption.[72]

Divisions over economic liberalization threaten to disrupt counternarcotics operations in Bolivia. Morales's nationalization and land reform policies benefiting Bolivia's Indian highland majority are meeting opposition from Bolivia's lowland elites. His attempt to rewrite the Bolivian constitution to favor the indigenous population stirred up calls for autonomy in the lowlands. Morales alleged that the United States was behind the autonomy movement.[73] In 2007, Bolivian coca growers loyal to Morales drove USAID workers from the Cochabamba region in central Bolivia, accusing them of aiding government opponents.[74] The initial threat of sending the Bolivian army into the lowlands to resolve the political crisis led to rumors of civil war throughout 2007 and 2008.[75] Despite these rumors, in early July 2008 the four eastern lowland states of Santa Cruz, Beni, Pando, and Tarija moved forward with their autonomy movement by declaring their independence from the Bolivian government. By early January 2009, Morales had pushed through a vote to rewrite Bolivia's constitution. This was a major victory for Bolivia's indigenous population, although all four autonomous states opposed it. The new constitution gave the autonomous states limited authority to direct local affairs; but the differences between the indigenous highlands and the autonomous lowlands on a national level remain great, and divisions over the nationalization of land and resources persist.[76] The discovery of a plot to assassinate Morales in April 2009 underscored the tension in Bolivia. Suspicion was cast upon Morales's political opposition, which was alleged to have been supporting "mercenary cells" to overthrow the government. The opposition responded by saying this was black propaganda to delegitimize the opposition movement.[77]

Throughout 2008 and 2009, Morales reiterated his belief that the lowland effort to declare autonomy was directed by the U.S. government in an attempt to cripple his administration.[78] In June 2008, leaders in Cochabamba officially expelled all USAID personnel from the region; and in July 2008 Morales held meetings with U.S. officials to repair diplomatic ties. However, after these meetings Morales restated his charge that the United States was conspiring against his government. Morales pointed to well-substantiated evidence that USAID had given $4.5 million in funding to opposition groups as part of its "political party reform project" and that U.S. embassy representative Vincent Cooper had attempted to recruit members of the Peace Corps and a Fulbright scholar to spy on Cuban and Venezuelan activities in Bolivia.[79] By September 2008, relations between the United States and Bolivia had deteriorated so badly, the Bolivian government expelled the U.S. ambassador. The United States retaliated by cutting trade with Bolivia and expelling its ambassador from the United States. The Bolivian government then kicked out the DEA, indefinitely suspending all U.S. antidrug operations, and declared that the DEA was spying and also supporting Morales's opponents.[80] With the inauguration of Barack Obama, the United States attempted to improve relations with Bolivia by sending U.S. Assistant Secretary of State for Western Hemisphere Affairs Thomas Shannon Jr. to speak with Morales. While tensions have cooled, the DEA remains unwelcome, and Morales continues to believe that the United States is conspiring against his government.[81]

In Peru, Ollanto Humala, a leader who advocated policies similar to Morales's, won the first round of elections in April 2006, and coca production rose from twenty-seven thousand hectares in 2003 to thirty-seven thousand hectares in 2006.[82] Although Humala ultimately lost the runoff election to Alan García, García is extremely unpopular in Peru's highlands, where Humala's political strength is the greatest. Following the adoption of free trade policies and the signing of a trade pact with the United States, the Peruvian economy, driven by mining and natural gas, has achieved 6.5 percent annual growth since 2003. However, this growth has not reduced poverty for Peru's campesinos, and few markets for alternative crops have opened up.[83] According to Peruvian economist Carlos Gonzalez, Peru has two economies: "one developed and competitive, another depressed and lost in poverty."[84] Adding to the complications, voluntary eradication has declined while forced eradication has increased.[85] The 2006 U.S. budget reduced spending on alternative development projects by 20 percent.[86] In April 2007 President Garcia called for the "bombing" of cocaine labs and for an increase in eradication.[87] Peruvian campesinos have declared that coca is their only "option" and that black market sales of coca have helped fund schools and infrastructure in areas where the police rarely patrol.[88] Clashes in the UHV between UMOPAR and CORAH teams and coca-growing campesinos have become more frequent; violent demonstrations against García's government occurred in 2007.[89] The situation in the rural parts of Peru has given Humala room to renew his bid for the presidency in 2011.

Since 2006, powerful Colombian and Mexican criminal organizations have reestablished their foothold in Peru. The Sendero Luminoso remains active, with two columns still operating (one in the Upper Huallaga Valley, the other in the Ene River Valley).[90] Skirmishes with Peruvian military and police forces are more frequent, and accusations persist that the Sendero provides protection for coca growers and traffickers.[91] The Peruvian government responded to the Sendero resurgence by declaring that "they continue to kill soldiers and police, but they will not defeat the army, the police or much less our democracy."[92]

Another significant development in Peru recently is the growing FARC presence along its border with Colombia. According to an independent study on the FARC's international presence, the FARC uses the Peruvian border as an active sanctuary and has been operating coca plantations there on a limited scale. The FARC recruits poor indigenous Peruvians along the border, often paying them $250 per month to work the plantations or join its military cadres. According to the same article, the Peruvian newspaper *El Comercio* cited the head of FARC's southern bloc, Pedro Rivera Crisancho, also known as Tiberio, claiming that the FARC remains along the border region to "help the many who are dying of hunger and for lack of medicines whether they are Peruvians or Colombians." The Peruvian government recognized this problem and in 2006 implemented Plan Putumayo, which increased development programs and reinforced the military presence in the Putumayo region along the border. While the FARC's presence in Peru is limited, it has developed a significant intelligence network within Peru, which could allow it to continue operating along the border region for some time to come.[93]

Confronted with this four-decade losing battle to control narcotics production in the northern Andes and to halt trafficking into the United States, some experts have advised that the narcotics trade be legalized so that it can be controlled.[94] However, legalizing narcotics is politically out of reach at the moment in the United States, and in the northern Andes, it could spawn more problems than it solves. Who would control the profits earned from legalization? Would campesinos see the economic rewards, or would multinational corporations and/or national bureaucracies like ENACO, which fix ceilings on prices and production, exploit their labor? Would legalization counter land reform efforts (as the Medellín cartel's narco-wealth did) and reestablish a semi-feudal system in which coca-growing areas become more valuable—but only the wealthiest landowners or corporations can afford to own and pay taxes on the land? These questions go unanswered when the issue of legalization arises, and thus, as a solution, it remains in dispute.

To prevail in the War on Drugs, the United States must develop a comprehensive counternarcotics strategy that addresses the economic factors underlying continued narcotics production and regional political instability. Domestically, it needs to look at issues such as decriminalization to reduce the financial incentives that drive up the price and production of narcotics. At the same time, the United States needs a strategy for the northern Andes that tackles narcotics cultivation at the village level while simultaneously limiting U.S. military presence in the region.

The United States must also separate narcotics from internal security concerns. In particular, the Andean militaries should cease involvement in counternarcotics operations and return to their traditional role of maintaining national security. Both the U.S. and Andean governments must give the coca-growing campesinos a political voice, offering them the opportunity to participate directly in their economic development. This solution prevents the recruitment of future cadres for the insurgents and brings the campesinos closer to their governments. Finally, regional governments must offer guerrilla movements political incentives to lay down their arms without threats of retribution or dirty wars. Only when the United States adopts a comprehensive policy of this nature will it have a chance of halting narcotics production and trafficking in the northern Andes.

Within these recommendations, a lingering concern remains about the possibility of cooperation between the northern Andes and the United States on narcotics control. In general, the northern Andean nations have seen U.S. demand as the foundation of the drug dilemma, while the United States has perceived narcotics largely as a problem of uncontrolled supply. This difference in perspective has ignited decades of confrontation over how to conduct the War on Drugs. U.S. coercion has complicated Andean governments' ability to maintain political stability, forcing them to make unpopular decisions regardless of the political fallout. Some have argued that only the Andean nations can design effective counternarcotics plans, because their policies will gain public support. While this may be true, many factors could challenge their success, including the corruption and lack of results that, in the past, have provoked the United States' heavy-handed approach in putting together its counternarcotics strategies. The U.S. approach has its own flaws, notably, that it has bred conflict with both campesinos and guerrillas while ignoring the demand side of the drug business at home.

The unequal relationship between the United States and the northern Andean nations lies at the heart of the difficulties surrounding cooperation. The United States insists on input into northern Andean domestic and foreign policies while maintaining the attitude that Andean opinions concerning U.S. policies are irrelevant at best. The political imbalance calls into question whether the United States and the northern Andean nations will ever take the necessary steps to reduce narcotics demand and production.

Even if the issue of cooperation could be resolved, other serious questions remain. Has the War on Drugs become institutionalized in all the nations concerned? Do bureaucrats in the United States and in the northern Andes benefit from it as a source of both employment and huge budgets to allocate as they see fit? Will the military defeat of the Colombian guerrillas end narcotics production there, or will new criminal organizations and corrupt elements step in to fill the continuing demand for coca and cocaine?

Over the long term, U.S. narcotics policy has prevented a successful outcome to the War on Drugs and may have prolonged it. The very concept of a "war" on drugs highlights how policymakers have muddled Cold War objectives with the problem of domestic narcotics control. Today, in early 2009, U.S. military commitments in other parts of the world, especially in the Middle East, have left the United States with a counternarcotics policy that it cannot afford. While the drug industry thrives, the War on Drugs continues with no end in sight.

Notes

Introduction: U.S. Drug Policy in the Northern Andes and Latin America

1. Sarita Kendall, "Colombia Rules Out Negotiations with Rebels Holding Hostages," *Financial Times*, 8 November 1985, sec. 1, p. 5.

2. *Christian Science Monitor*, "Troops Storm Bogotá Court Building," 8 November 1985, 2.

3. Senate Subcommittee on Terrorism, Narcotics, and International Operation of the Committee on Foreign Relations, *Drugs, Law Enforcement, and Foreign Policy*, 100th Cong., 2nd sess., December 1988, 31.

4. Ibid.

5. United Press International, "Nicaragua Denies Charge by Reagan," *New York Times*, 16 December 1985, sec. A, p. 3. The Colombian newspaper *El Tiempo* claimed that five Sandinistas helped plan the raid. In addition, ten rifles belonging to the guerrillas had been supplied in 1976 to the Nicaraguan National Guard, which was overthrown by the Sandinistas in 1979. Significantly, two other rifles, of Belgian manufacture, were part of a lot that the Venezuelan government had given to the Sandinistas early in 1979. The Sandinistas responded by explaining that only one third of the Venezuelan arms shipment had ever arrived in their hands, and the whereabouts of the remainder were unknown. See: Tim Coone, "Nicaragua and Colombia Defuse Row on M-19 Attack," *Financial Times*, 9 January 1986, sec. 1, p. 4; *Globe and Mail*, "Around the World: Envoy Recalled by Colombia," 23 December 1985.

6. Richard B. Craig, "Illicit Drug Traffic: Implications for South American Source Countries" (Prepared for the Conference on International Drugs, Washington, DC, Defense Intelligence College, 2-3 June 1987), 52.

Chapter 1: The Growth of the Narcotics Industry in the Northern Andes, 1971–1980

1. Associated Press, "Armed Forces Seize Control of Bolivia," *New York Times*, 18 July 1980, sec. A, p. 3; Michael Levine, *The Big White Lie: The CIA and the Cocaine/Crack Epidemic an Undercover Odyssey* (New York: Thunder's Mouth Press, 1993), 55–60. The coup started in the northern city of Trinidad.
2. Ibid.
3. Ibid.
4. Jacqueline E. Sharkey, "U.S. Terminates Drug Enforcement Programs in Bolivia," *Washington Post*, 14 August 1980, sec. A, p. 29.
5. U.S. Department of State, Office of the Historian Bureau of Public Affairs, *Chronology on International Narcotics Control 1833–1980* (December 1981), 5, National Security Archive, Narcotics Collection, U.S. Policy/ Military: Especially DEA Reports, box 23.
6. Senate Committee on the Judiciary of the United States Senate, *World Drug Traffic and Its Impact on U.S. Security: Hearings Before the Subcommittee to Investigate the Administration of the Internal Security Act and Other Internal Security Laws*, 92nd Cong., 2nd sess., 14 August, 1972, 1–2. Opening remarks by James O. Eastland, chairman of the Subcommittee to Investigate the Administration of the Internal Security Act and Other Internal Security Laws.
7. Richard M. Nixon, "Special Message to the Congress on Drug Abuse Prevention and Control" (17 June 1971), *Public Papers of the Presidents of the United States* (Washington, DC: Office of the Federal Register, National Archives and Records Service, 1972), 739.
8. Melvin R. Laird to Richard M. Nixon, "Memorandum for the President: Drugs" (2 May 1970), 1, National Archives, Nixon Presidential Materials Project, National Security Council Staff Files (1969–1973), box 357.
9. House of Representatives Committee on Armed Services, *Alleged Drug Abuse in the Armed Services: Hearings Before the Special Subcommittee on Marijuana and Dangerous Drugs*, 91st Cong., 2nd sess., 30 September 1970, 1247–1272.
10. Egil Krogh, Jr., "Heroin Politics and Policy under President Nixon," in *One Hundred Years of Heroin*, ed. David F. Musto (London: Westport House, 2002), 39–42.
11. Senate Committee on the Judiciary, *World Drug Traffic and Its Impact on U.S. Security*, 1, 54–58. Testimony of General Walt. See: Joseph D. Douglass, *Red Cocaine: The Drugging of America and the West*, 2nd ed. (London: Edward Harle, 1999), 60–61. Allegations of a communist plot to hook U.S. servicemen and civilians on drugs were rife among military and other governmental agencies. However, those charges ignore the allegations that the CIA was running narcotics through its Air America operation in Laos. See: Alfred W. McCoy, *The Politics of Heroin: CIA Complicity in the Global Drug Trade*, 2nd ed. (New York: Lawrence Hill Books, 1991).
12. Senate Committee on the Judiciary, *World Drug Traffic and Its Impact on U.S. Security*, 1, 54–58. Testimony of John E. Ingersoll, director of the Bureau of Narcotics and Dangerous Drugs, Department of Justice.
13. Richard M. Nixon, "Special Message to the Congress on Control of Narcotics and Dangerous Drugs" (17 June 1971), *Public Papers of the Presidents of the United States*, 513.
14. Ibid.
15. Ibid.; Abstract, *New York Times*, 30 December 1970, sec. A, p. 32.
16. Richard M. Nixon, "Remarks at the Opening Session of the Governors' Conference at the Department of State" (3 December 1969), *Public Papers of the Presidents of the United States* (Washington, DC: Office of the Federal Register, National Archives and Records Service, 1971), 1986; Drug Enforcement Administration, *DEA History Book 1970–1975*, http://www.usdoj.gov/dea/pubs/history/deahistory_01.htm (accessed 9 July 2004). The act was passed fifteen months after it was proposed.

17. Richard M. Nixon, "Statement on Establishing the Office for Drug Abuse and Law Enforcement" (28 January 1972), *Public Papers of the Presidents of the United States*, (Washington, DC: Office of the Federal Register, National Archives and Records Service, 1971), 115.

18. Drug Enforcement Administration, *DEA History Book 1970–1975*, http://www.usdoj.gov/dea/pubs/history/deahistory_01.htm (accessed 9 July 2004).

19. Richard M. Nixon, "Special Message to the Congress on Drug Abuse Prevention and Control" (17 June 1971), *Public Papers of the Presidents of the United States*, 740.

20. United Nations, *The Single Convention on Narcotic Drugs 1961: Treaty Obligations of the United States Relating to Marihuana*, (New York: United Nations, 1961), 1, from the Files of Geoffrey C. Shepard, National Archives, Nixon Presidential Materials Project, White House Special Files, Staff and Member Files (1969–1973).

21. U.S. Department of State, "Memorandum for the President: Request for a Recommendation on the Heroin Problem" (20 October 1969), 3, National Archives, Nixon Presidential Materials Project, National Security Council Staff Files (1969–1973), box 357.

22. Commission on Marijuana and Drug Abuse, "Public Hearings Held at New York City" (February 23, 1972), 200, National Security Archive, Narcotics: Drug Documents, Presidential Libraries, box 54; Fabio Castillo, *La Coca Nostra*, (Bogotá: Editorial Documentos Periodisticos, 1991), 44–49. Castillo also implies that members of the French Connection, who conspired with North America's Italian mafia to assassinate John F. Kennedy, sought refuge in Medellín, where they established a smuggling base.

23. Commission on Marijuana and Drug Abuse, "Public Hearings Held at New York City," 200.

24. House of Representatives Select Committee on Narcotics Abuse and Control, *South American Study Mission August 9–23, 1977*, 95th Cong., 1st sess., November 1977, 9. Members of a U.S. South American study mission believed that poppy growth in the border region between Colombia and Ecuador was the result of eradication programs conducted in Mexico. See: House of Representatives Committee on Foreign Affairs, *The World Narcotics Problem: The Latin American Perspective: Report of Special Study Mission to Latin America and the Federal Republic of Germany*, 93rd Cong., 1st sess., 21 March 1973, 5; Drug Enforcement Administration, "A Study of the Illicit Opium, Morphine, and Heroin Traffic in South America 1973–1976" (1 April 1977), 49, National Security Archive, Narcotics Collection, Colombia: Cartels, U.S. Operations, Corruption, box 8.

25. Drug Enforcement Administration, "A Study of the Illicit Opium, Morphine, and Heroin Traffic in South America 1973–1976," 13. Demonstrating their lack of creative vision, U.S. officials thought it was "illogical" for heroin to be shipped from Europe to the United States though South America.

26. Comptroller General of the United States, "Problems in Slowing the Flow of Cocaine and Heroin from and through South America" (30 May 1975), Washington, DC: General Accounting Office, 2.

27. House of Representatives Committee on Foreign Affairs, *The World Narcotics Problem*, 3. This figure excludes Mexico.

28. House of Representatives Committee on International Relations, *The Shifting Pattern of Narcotics Trafficking: Latin America: Report of a Study Mission to Mexico, Costa Rica, Panama, and Colombia*, 94th Cong., 2nd sess., 6–18 January 1976, 2.

29. Drug Enforcement Administration, "South American Narcotics Traffic" (January 1975), 3, National Security Archive, Narcotics Collection, U.S. Policy/Military: Latin America General Issues, box 22, 287.

30. Drug Enforcement Administration, "South American Narcotics Traffic" (January 1975), 3.

31. Ibid., 4–5.

32. Drug Enforcement Administration, "A Study of the Illicit Opium, Morphine, and Heroin Traffic in South America 1973–1976," 14. Operation Springboard developed out of the Oscilloscope Case, which was a DEA investigation into heroin smuggling in the United States.

33. Drug Enforcement Administration, "South American Narcotics Traffic," 2. The death of Sarti and the arrest of Ricord occurred during Operation Springboard, which stemmed from information gained in the Oscilloscope Case.

34. Drug Enforcement Administration, "A Study of the Illicit Opium, Morphine, and Heroin Traffic in South America 1973–1976," 14.

35. American Embassy La Paz to Department of State, "Control of Narcotic Drugs–Narcotics Activities in Cochabamba Consular District" (1 December 1965), 1, National Archives, Records of the Drug Enforcement Administration, Subject Files of the Bureau of Narcotics and Dangerous Drugs 1916–1970, box 151; James A. Daniels to William J. Durkin, "Narcotics Intelligence Information" (12 September 1966), 1–2 National Archives, Records of the Drug Enforcement Administration, Subject Files of the Bureau of Narcotics and Dangerous Drugs 1916–1970, box 151.

36. House of Representatives Committee on Foreign Affairs, *The World Narcotics Problem*, 6, 7.

37. House of Representatives Select Committee on Narcotics Abuse and Control, *South American Study Mission August 9–23, 1977*. 14–15.

38. Daniels to Durkin, "Narcotics Intelligence Information," 2.

39. American Embassy La Paz to Department of State, "Contraband, Cocaine, and Corruption" (26 January 1969), 1, National Archives, General Records of the Department of State: Central Foreign Policy Files, Economic (1967–1969), box 885.

40. Daniels to Durkin, "Narcotics Intelligence Information," 2. Smuggling came in three forms: leaves, paste, or cocaine hydrochloride.

41. Robert A. Johnson at al, *Trends in the Incidence of Drug Use in the United States, 1919–1992* (Rockville, MD: U.S. Department of Health and Human Services Substance Abuse and Mental Health Service Administration Office of Applied Studies, March 1996), 36–42. The number of first-time heroin users reached its highest level in 1973 with 141,000 new users. After 1975 this number dropped below one hundred thousand. Conversely, the number of first-time cocaine users steadily increased, with 993,000 in 1976 and 1,098,000 in 1977.

42. William J. Durkin to Henry L. Giordano, "Memorandum: South America" (31 July 1964), 1, National Archives, Records of the Drug Enforcement Administration, Subject Files of the Bureau of Narcotics and Dangerous Drugs (1916–1970), box 153. Henry Giordano was the head of the BNDD in 1964.

43. American Embassy La Paz to Department of State, "Control of Narcotic Drugs–Narcotics Activities in Cochabamba Consular District," 1.

44. Daniels to Durkin, "Narcotics Intelligence Information," 2.

45. Durkin to Giordano, "Memorandum: South America," 2.

46. Ibid., 3; House of Representatives Committee on Foreign Affairs, *The World Narcotics Problem*, 26.

47. House of Representatives Committee on International Relations, *The Shifting Pattern of Narcotics Trafficking*, 23.

48. House of Representatives Select Committee on Narcotics Abuse and Control, *South American Study Mission August 9–23, 1977*, 10.

49. Comptroller General of the United States, "Problems in Slowing the Flow of Cocaine and Heroin From and Through South America," 1.

50. Fabio Castillo, *La Coca Nostra*, 44–62. Pablo Escobar, one of the founders of the Medellín cartel, worked as an assassin for Gómez López, the *padrino* of the North Atlantic Coast cartel. See: Darío Betancourt and Martha Luz García, *Contrabandistas, Marimberos y*

Mafiosos: Historia Social de la Mafia Colombiana, 1965–1992 (Bogotá: Tercer Mundo Editores, 1994), 43–77. The North Atlantic Coast cartel was located in the states of Magdalena and La Guajira. The Medellín cartel worked out of Antioquia and the Central Valley and the Cali cartel was situated in the Valle de Cauca. Also of note, Pablo Escobar and the Ochoas ran the Antioquia part of the Medellín cartel, and Rodríguez Gacha ran the central part of the Medellín cartel.

51. Darío Betancourt and Martha Luz García, *Contrabandistas, Marimberos y Mafiosos*, 67–68, 69. The North Atlantic Coast cartel did not become as powerful as the Medellín or Cali cartels because marijuana production was not unique to Colombia. When the Colombian government cracked down on marijuana in the early 1980s, the mafia abandoned marijuana smuggling and turned toward Mexican and U.S. domestic outlets for marijuana. For more on the Colombian antimarijuana campaign, see chapter 3.

52. Ibid.

53. House of Representatives Committee on Foreign Affairs, *The World Narcotics Problem*, 26–27.

54. House of Representatives Committee on International Relations, *The Shifting Pattern of Narcotics Trafficking*, 24.

55. House of Representatives Committee on International Relations, *The Shifting Pattern of Narcotics Trafficking*, 24.

56. House of Representatives Committee on Foreign Affairs, *The World Narcotics Problem*, 30.

57. House of Representatives Committee on International Relations, *The Shifting Pattern of Narcotics Trafficking*, 24.

58. Durkin to Giordano, "Memorandum: South America," 1–2.

59. Birch Bayh, "Report to the Senate of Birch Bayh Chairman of the Select Committee on Intelligence" (22 February 1978), 13, National Security Archive, Narcotics Collection, Panama, box 14.

60. Adolph B. Saenz to Byron Engle, "Letter: untitled" (15 July 1970), 1–4, National Archives, Nixon Presidential Materials Project, White House Special Files, Staff Member and Office Files, Egil Krogh Jr. (1969–1973), box 32. Saenz was the chief of public safety, and Engle worked for the Office of Public Safety in the Agency for International Development.

61. Bureau of Narcotics and Dangerous Drugs, "Briefing Paper on the Republic of Panama" (5 November 1971), 2, National Security Archive, Narcotics: Panama, box 14; John Dinges, *Our Man in Panama* (New York: Random House, 1990), 54.

62. Leland Riggs, "Statement of Leland Riggs Jr. for the Use of the Subcommittee on the Separation of Powers of the Committee on the Judiciary in the United States Senate" (1 December 1977). National Security Archive, Narcotics: Panama, box 14; Frederick Kempe, *Noriega: Toda la Verdad* (Buenos Aires: Grijalbo, 1990), 123.

63. John Dinges, *Our Man in Panama*, 60. Much of this information did not become public until 1978. It was withheld because the BNDD was slowly collecting information indicating that Torrijos's right-hand man, Lieutenant Colonel Manuel Noriega, had been involved in narcotics smuggling at the same time that the CIA was cultivating a close relationship with him.

64. U.S. Department of State to American Embassy Panama, "Spokesman on Expulsion of BNDD Agents" (March 1972), National Security Archive, Narcotics Collection, Panama, box 14.

65. Birch Bayh, "Report to the Senate of Birch Bayh, Chairman of the Select Committee on Intelligence," 15. At the Watergate hearings, John Dean testified that a proposal arose within the administration for Howard Hunt to undertake a plan to assassinate Torrijos. See: John Dinges, *Our Man in Panama*, 61; Frederick Kempe, *Toda la Verdad*, 125.

66. John Dinges, *Our Man in Panama*, 69–70.

67. House of Representatives Committee on Foreign Affairs, *The World Narcotics Problem*, 32.

68. Bureau of Narcotics and Dangerous Drugs, "Briefing Paper on the Republic of Panama," 5.

69. U.S. Department of State, "International Narcotics Control: Foreign Assistance Appropriations Act–Fiscal Year 1976 Budget" (1976), 18, National Security Archive, Narcotics Collection, Drug Documents: OGD, CRS, RAND, State Department INCRs, and IG Reports, box 46.

70. U.S. Department of State Press, "Report of William Rogers entitled International Narcotics Control Summary" (28 December 1971), 1, National Archives, Nixon Presidential Materials Project, Nixon Presidential Materials Staff, National Security Council Files (1969–1973), box 359. This included representatives from the State, Defense, and Treasury Deparments, as well as the AID, BNDD, CIA, and USIA.

71. Comptroller General of the United States, "If the United States Is to Develop an Effective International Narcotics Program, Much More Must be Done" (29 July 1975), Washington, DC: General Accounting Office, 72; Senate Committee on Foreign Relations, *International Narcotics Control and Foreign Assistance Certification: Requirements, Procedures, Timetables, and Guidelines*, 100th Cong., 2nd sess., March 1988, 12; Senate, *Report of the International Security Assistance and Arms Export Control Act*, 94th Cong., 2nd session, 30 January 1976, 61–62; House of Representatives Committee on International Relations, *The Shifting Pattern of Narcotics Trafficking*, 42–43. The Foreign Relations Authorization Act of 1972 and the Trade Act of 1974 amended CCINC's power to withhold aid under the Foreign Assistance Act of 1961. Withholding the sale of military equipment was adopted as a part of the 1976 amendment to the 1961 Foreign Assistance Act.

72. Senate Committee on Foreign Relations, *Protocol Amending the Single Convention on Narcotic Drugs Hearings Before the Committee on Foreign Relations*, 92nd Cong., 2nd sess., 27 June 1972, 1; U.S. Department of State Briefing Paper, "Amending Protocol to the 1961 Single Convention" (1 March 1972), 1, National Security Archive, Narcotics Collection, Drugs: Drug Documents from Presidential Libraries, box 54.

73. Senate Committee on Foreign Relations, *Protocol Amending the Single Convention on Narcotic Drugs*, 45. Statement of Charles I. Bevans, assistant legal advisor, Department of State.

74. U.S. Department of State, Office of the Historian Bureau of Public Affairs, *Chronology on International Narcotics Control 1833–1980*, 8.

75. Comptroller General of the United States, "Drug Control in South America, Having Limited Success–Some Progress but Problems are Formidable" (Washington, DC: General Accounting Office, 28 March 1978), 16.

76. Ibid., 17; U.S. Department of State, "International Narcotics Control: Foreign Assistance Appropriations Act–Fiscal Year 1978 Summary"(1978), 10–11, National Security Archive, Narcotics Collection, Drug Documents: OGD, CRS, RAND, State Department INCRs and IG Reports, box 46.

77. Sheldon B. Vance to Honorable James T. Lynn, untitled, (29 June 1976, 1, National Security Archive, Narcotics Collection, Bolivia: Joint Operations, Production Rates, Cocaine Coup, box 5. Vance was the senior advisor for narcotics control in the Department of State during 1976. See: Brent Scowcroft to President Ford, "Multiyear Budget Commitment for Narcotics Control Assistance to Bolivia(27 July 1976), 1, National Security Archive, Narcotics Collection, Bolivia: Joint Operations, Production Rates, Cocaine Coup, box 5.

78. Jim Cannon to Jim Connor, "Lynn-Scowcroft Memorandum on Commitment for Narcotics Control Assistance to Bolivia" (12 August 1976), 1, National Security Archive, Narcotics Collection, Bolivia: Joint Operations, Production Rates, Cocaine Coup, box 5. This commitment, in the years to come, would create Peruvian and Bolivian dependence on the U.S. government for assistance to maintain the War on Drugs.

79. Comptroller General of the United States, "Drug Control in South America, Having Limited Success," 17.

80. House of Representative Select Committee on Narcotics Abuse and Control, *Cocaine: A Major Drug Issue of the Seventies,* 9. For smaller purchases, campesinos received an estimated fifty dollars per one hundred kilos of coca leaves.

81. Comptroller General of the United States, "Gains Made in Controlling Illegal Drugs," 47.

82. Albert L. Brown, "Feasibility and Design of an Expanded Coca Substitution Project Being Developed by U.S. AID Mission to Bolivia," (18 August 1976), 2, National Security Archive, Narcotics, Bolivia: Joint Operations, Production Rates, Cocaine Coup, box 5.

83. Central Intelligence Agency, CIA International Narcotics Staff Notes, "Bolivia: Obstacles to Coca Crop Substitutions" (2 February 1977), 2, http://www.jeremeybigwood.net/ FOIAs/FOAI.htm (accessed 24 September 2006). Released via Freedom of Information Act request by Jeremy Bigwood. In 1976, with the collapse of the Bolivian cotton market due to a depression in international cotton prices, many inexperienced Bolivian cotton growers were forced into near bankruptcy. This caused a swelling in the production of coca and cocaine in Bolivia, as an alternative to unemployment and crop failure. See: Jaime Malamud-Goti, "Reinforcing Poverty: The Bolivian War on Cocaine," in *War on Drugs: Studies in the Failure of U.S. Narcotics Policy,* ed. Alfred W. McCoy and Alan A. Block (San Francisco: Westview Press, 1992), 70–71.

84. Albert L. Brown, "Feasibility and Design of an Expanded Coca Substitution Project Being Developed by U.S. AID Mission to Bolivia," 5.

85. Comptroller General of the United States, "Gains Made in Controlling Illegal Drugs," 47.

86. Comptroller General of the United States, "Drug Control in South America, Having Limited Success," 18.

87. Comptroller General of the United States, "Gains Made in Controlling Illegal Drugs," 47.

88. Central Intelligence Agency, CIA International Narcotics Staff Notes, "Bolivia: Obstacles to Coca Crop Substitutions" (2 February 1977), 2.

89. Drug Enforcement Administration, "Money Laundering Colombia" (August 1991), 7, National Security Archive, Narcotics Collection, Colombia: Cartels, U.S. Operations, Corruption, box 8. In the United States, money laundering was accomplished in three steps. The first and most dangerous step was the placement of proceeds into financial institutions. In step two, the money was "layered," or moved through different financial institutions to disassociate the money from its source and conceal its true ownership. The final step "integrated" the money into the legitimate economy.

90. House of Representatives Select Committee on Narcotics Abuse and Control, *Investigation of Narcotics and Money Laundering in Chicago Report of the Select Committee on Narcotics Abuse and Control,* 95th Cong., 1st sess., February 1978, 16–17.

91. Drug Enforcement Administration, "Money Laundering Colombia," 12–17.

92. Ibid., 7.

93. Ibid., 10. The individuals involved in money laundering were called "Smurfs" in the 1980s, after the cartoon characters, because they were considered little people in the money-laundering operations.

94. House of Representatives Select Committee on Narcotics Abuse and Control, *Cocaine: A Major Drug Issue of the Seventies,* 38.

95. Jack Egan, "Other N.Y. Banks Studied for Laundering Operations, *Washington Post,* 25 February 1977, sec. C, p. 9. Chemical Bank was the fifth largest bank in New York City.

96. Office of the Assistant Secretary of Enforcement and Operations, Department of the Treasury, "Currency Flows in the U.S. in 1978" (August 1979), 9. National Security Archive, Narcotics Collection, U.S. Policy/ Military: Especially DEA Reports, 10; Robert Stankey to Arthur Sinai, "Briefing Paper on Need for Florida Task Force" (25 May 1979), 2, National Security Archive, Narcotics Collection, U.S. Policy/ Military: Especially DEA Reports, box 23. The DEA believed that the large volumes of currency flowed into Florida mostly from other states and nations.

97. James Rubin, "Abstract: Washington Dateline," *Associated Press*, 6 June 1980.

98. Robert Stankey to William W. Wickerson, "Florida Currency Flow Project" (6 August 1979), 1, National Security Archive, Narcotics Collection, U.S. Policy/ Military: Especially DEA Reports, (Treasury: Operation Greenback), box 23. Wickerson was the deputy assistant secretary for enforcement within the DEA.

99. Drug Enforcement Administration, *DEA History Book 1975–1979*, http://www.usdoj.gov/ dea/pubs/history/deahistory_02.htm (accessed 10 September 2004).

100. Wayne Roberts Customs Group Supervisor, U.S. Customs Service, "Operation Greenback in Review," (1988), 2, National Security Archive, Narcotics Collection, U.S. Policy/ Military: Especially DEA Reports, (Treasury: Operation Greenback), box 23.

101. U.S. Commissioner of Customs William von Raab, U.S. Customs Service, "Who Is Doing the Wash in Florida?" (8 May 1982), 5, National Security Archive, Narcotics Collection U.S. Policy/ Military: Especially DEA Reports, (Treasury: Operation Greenback), box 23. Statement made to Bank Leadership Committee of the Florida Bankers Association.

102. Robert E. Powis, "Statement of Robert E. Powis Before the Subcommittee on General Oversight and Renegotiation for the House Committee on Banking and Urban Affairs," *Treasury News* (13 July 1982), 7, National Security Archive, Narcotics Collection, U.S. Policy/ Military: Especially DEA Reports, (Treasury: Operation Greenback), box 23.

103. House of Representatives Committee on Foreign Affairs, *Latin America in the World Economy: Hearings Before the Subcommittees on International Economic Policy and Trade and on Western Hemisphere Affairs*, 98th Cong., 1st sess., 15, 21, 23, June 1983, 21 July 1983, 58–59. Statement of Dr. Raul Prebisch; Peter H. Smith, *Talons of the Eagle: Dynamics of U.S. Latin American Relations*, 2nd ed. (Oxford: Oxford University Press, 2000), 150–151.

104. Senate Committee on Governmental Affairs, *Crime and Secrecy: The Use of Offshore Banks and Companies Hearing Before the Permanent Subcommittee on Investigations*, 98th Cong., 1st sess., 15–16 March 1983, 24 May 1983, 58–75, 300–303. Statement of Colombian currency exchange broker, Bento Ghitis-Miller.

105. Ibid. The official rate in Colombia during 1979 was forty-five pesos to the dollar.

106. Richard B. Craig, "Colombian Narcotics and United States-Colombian Relations," *Journal of Interamerican Studies and World Affairs* 23, no. 3 (August 1981): 266.

107. Comptroller General of the United States, "Drug Control in South America, Having Limited Success," 14.

108. Alfonso Chardy, "An AP News Special, Dateline: Bogotá, Colombia," *Associated Press*, 10 March 1978.

109. Senate Committee on Governmental Affairs, *Crime and Secrecy: The Use of Offshore Banks and Companies Staff Study the Permanent Subcommittee on Investigations*, 98th Cong., 1st sess., February 1983, 82.

110. Ibid., 79.

111. Ibid., 78. The national rate for Panama was only 3.6 percent annually.

112. Latin America Economic Report, "Bolivia Banks on an Economic Miracle," *Latin American Economic Report* 4 (25 June 1976): 98; Scott B. MacDonald, *Dancing on a Volcano: The Latin American Drug Trade* (New York: Praeger Books, 1988), 54–55.

113. Mario Franco and Ricardo Godoy, "The Economic Consequences of Cocaine Production in Bolivia: Historical Local and Macroeconomic Perspectives," *Journal of Latin American Studies* 24, no. 2 (May 1992): 384–385; World Bank, *2004 World Development Indicators CD-Rom* (Washington, DC: International Bank for Reconstruction and Development/World Bank, 2004). The terms of trade effect equals the capacity to import minus exports of goods and services in constant prices. Data are in constant local currency.

114. Ray Henkel, "The Bolivian Cocaine Industry," in *Drugs in Latin America: Studies in Third World Societies*, ed. Vinson H. Sutlive, et al (Williamsburg, VA: College of William and Mary, 1986), 53–80, 64, 66.

115. House of Representatives Select Committee on Narcotics Abuse and Control, *Oversight Hearings on Federal Drug Strategy*, 310–11.

116. Comptroller General of the United States, "Problems in Slowing the Flow of Cocaine and Heroin From and Through South America," 52.

117. House of Representatives, Committee on Foreign Affairs, *The World Narcotics Problem*, 25.

118. Comptroller General of the United States, "Problems in Slowing the Flow of Cocaine and Heroin From and Through South America," 50. In 1977, Ecuador observed the signs of increased narcotics consumption among sectors of its population. In addition, by the late 1970s both Peru and Bolivia witnessed the emergence of a "disturbing new trend" in drug abuse–the practice of smoking coca paste or *basuca*. See: House of Representatives Select Committee on Narcotics Abuse and Control, *South American Study Mission August 9–23, 1977*, 14; Latin America Political Report, "Brickbats and Bouquets from the Drugs Board," *Intelligence Research Ltd. Latin American Report* XIII, (2 March 1979): 67. The narcotics control board reporting this summary was a United Nations body based in Geneva.

119. House of Representatives Committee on International Relations, *The Shifting Pattern of Narcotics Trafficking*, 3.

120. Leif Roderick Rosenberger, *America's Drug War Debacle* (Aldershot, UK: Avebury, 1996), 19. Marijuana at this point had become the largest cash crop in the United States.

121. *Associated Press*, "International News, Dateline: Bogotá Colombia," 25 September 1979.

122. Comptroller General of the United States, "Problems in Slowing the Flow of Cocaine and Heroin From and Through South America," 51.

123. House of Representatives Committee on Foreign Affairs, *The World Narcotics Problem*, 30.

124. Comptroller General of the United States, "Drug Control in South America, Having Limited Success," 30.

125. Alfonso Chardy, "Dateline: Riohacha Colombia," *Associated Press*, 21 March 1978.

126. U.S. Department of State, "International Narcotics Control: Foreign Assistance Appropriations Act–Fiscal Year 1978 Summary," 11, 19, 24, 29.

127. Ibid., 31; Comptroller General of the United States, "Problems in Slowing the Flow of Cocaine and Heroin From and Through South America," 53–54.

128. Richard B. Craig, "Colombian Narcotics and United States-Colombian Relations," 263.

129. Comptroller General of the United States, "Problems in Slowing the Flow of Cocaine and Heroin From and Through South America," 45–49.

130. Comptroller General of the United States, "Drug Control in South America, Having Limited Success," 21.

131. Senate Committee on Government Operations, *Federal Drug Enforcement Part 5. Hearings Before the Permanent Subcommittees on Investigations*, 94th Cong., 2nd sess., 23–26 August 1976, 1066. From: Drug Enforcement Administration, Functions and Guidelines Relating to Operations in Foreign Countries, 30 July 1976. The amendment also required authorization from the host country for agents to operate in an undercover capacity or assist in the training of local officers.

132. House of Representatives Select Committee on Narcotics Abuse and Control, *Cocaine: A Major Drug Issue of the Seventies*, 40. The DEA had difficulty in obtaining "operational-level intelligence." Of the thirty-five DEA members assigned to South America in 1978, only one was an intelligence analyst, although five positions had been designated for intelligence specialists. As a result, only low-level traffickers in South America were captured. Complications regarding the availability of intelligence resulted in the U.S. failure to identify and break up trafficking networks. Bureaucratic incompetence had given the illicit world of narcotics the opportunity to flourish. See: Comptroller General of the United States, "Problems in Slowing the Flow of Cocaine and Heroin From and Through South America," 21.

133. House of Representatives Select Committee on Narcotics Abuse and Control, *South American Study Mission August 9–23, 1977*, 20–21.

134. Ibid., 22–23.

135. House of Representatives Committee on International Relations, *The Shifting Pattern of Narcotics Trafficking*, 24. At this point, however, the corrupting forces of the narcotics industry had extended their tentacles into every aspect of Colombian society.

136. Ibid., 9.

137. Latin America Political Report, "Brickbats and Bouquets from the Drugs Board," 67.

138. House of Representatives Select Committee on Narcotics Abuse and Control, *Cocaine: A Major Drug Issue of the Seventies*, 39.

139. Ibid.

140. Richard B. Craig, "Colombian Narcotics and United States-Colombian Relations," 262; Juan Gabriel Tokatlián, "Estados Unidos y los Cultivos Ilícitos en Colombia: Los Trágicos Equvicós de una Fumigación Futil," http://socrates.berkeley.edu:7001/Events/confrences/Colombia/workingpapers/working_paper_toaktlian.doc (accessed 17 November 2004). Tokatlián is a professor at the University of San Andres in Victoria, a province of Buenos Aires, Argentina. The U.S. ambassador in Bogotá, Diego Asencio, announced publicly and privately that Colombia would receive more assistance from the United States if it opted to fumigate. Although Colombia was considering herbicidal spraying at this time, the 1978 Percy Amendment to the International Security Assistance Act of 1961 banned the use of foreign funds for any program that used paraquat to eradicate narcotics. Colombia would be forced to go it alone if it wanted to institute herbicidal eradication. By 1981, however, Congress had overturned the Percy Amendment.

141. Richard B. Craig, "Colombian Narcotics and United States-Colombian Relations," 265.

142. Juan Gabriel Tokatlián, "Estados Unidos y los Cultivos Ilícitos en Colombia: Los Trágicos Equvicós de una Fumigación Futil," http://socrates.berkeley.edu:7001/Events/conferences/Colombia/workingpapers/working_paper_tokatlian.doc (accessed 17 November 2004). Although herbicidal eradication had some major success, it forced narcotics producers deeper into the Colombian rainforest and sent Colombia spiraling toward an intensified conflict with its campesino population.

143. Jaíme Malamud Goti, *Smoke and Mirrors: The Paradox of the Drug Wars* (San Francisco: Westview Press, 1992), 1–5.

144. Ray Henkel, "The Bolivian Cocaine Industry," in *Drugs in Latin America: Studies in Third World Societies*, 65.

145. Comptroller General of the United States, "Drug Control in South America, Having Limited Success," 8. Another paradox was the use of herbicide spraying. Herbicide-based crop eradication forced narcotics production deeper inland—into guerrilla-controlled territory. In addition, the campesinos began to farm smaller plots so that no single overflight could destroy all of their work and also so that they could hide their illicit crops among their legitimate crops.

146. Fernando Cepeda Ulloa, "Introduction," in *Latin America and the Multinational Drug Trade*, 3–20.

147. House of Representatives Select Committee on Narcotics Abuse and Control, *Oversight Hearings on Federal Drug Strategy. Hearings Before the Select Committee on Narcotics Abuse and Control*, 95th Cong., 1st sess., 23 September 1977, 6 October 1977, and 15–16 November 1977, 310–311.

148. Richard B. Craig, "Illicit Drug Traffic: Implications for South American Source Countries," *Journal of Interamerican Studies and World Affairs* 29, no. 2 (Summer 1987): 7.

149. After the cotton crash of 1975, Bolivian dictator Hugo Banzer allegedly conspired with Bolivian drug baron Roberto Suárez Gómez and earned millions of dollars annually by using the country's military to export cocaine and cocaine base. Moreover, Banzer's

secretary, son-in-law, nephew, and wife had been arrested for cocaine trafficking in the United States and Canada. See: Alexander Cockburn and Jeffery St. Clair, *Whiteout: The CIA, Drugs, and the Press* (New York: Verso Books, 1998), 181–182; Shirley Christian, "Dateline La Paz," *Associated Press*, 8 July 1977; Harold Olmos, "Dateline La Paz," *Associated Press*, 6 January 1978; Michael Levine, *The Big White Lie: The CIA and the Cocaine/Crack Epidemic an Undercover Odyssey* (New York: Thunder's Mouth Press, 1993), 55–60. Levine is a former DEA agent who worked in Bolivia at the time of the cocaine coup.

150. U.S. Department of the Army, *Country Study: Bolivia* (Washington, DC: Federal Research Division of the Library of Congress, 1997), http://lcweb2.loc.gov/frd/cs/botoc.html (accessed 10 November 2004).

151. Warren Hoge, "Man in the News, Bolivian General with Iron Fist, Luis García Meza Tejada," *New York Times*, 13 August 1980, sec. A, p. 12. For a Bolivian perspective on the coup, see: Guillermo Bedregal Gutierrez and Rudy Viscarra Pando, *La Lucha Boliviana Contra la Agresión del Narcotráfico* (La Paz: Editorial los Amigos del Libro, 1989), 117–124. Gutierrez served as the Bolivian minister of foreign relations and culture, and Pando was Bolivia's director of international affairs in the Fight Against Narcotrafficking.

152. Michael Levine, *The Big White Lie*, 59. There is speculation that the CIA had given its support to the coup because the coup prevented leftist elements from taking power in Bolivia. See: Michael Levine, *The Big White Lie*, 61–76; Alexander Cockburn and Jeffery St. Clair, *Whiteout*, 177–185. In the case of Bolivia, one can only conjecture that the intelligence-sharing difficulties between the CIA and the DEA were due to the CIA's priority—preventing communists from seizing power—taking precedence over narcotics enforcement.

153. William O. Walker III, *Drug Control in the Americas* (Albuquerque, NM: University of New Mexico Press, 1981), 200. Suárez was the primary Bolivian supplier to the Colombian cartels in the early 1980s.

154. Ibid.; Scott B. MacDonald, *Dancing on a Volcano: The Latin American Drug Trade* (New York: Praeger Books, 1988), 56–57.

Chapter 2: The Economic Role of Narcotics in Latin America, 1980–1987

1. Humberto Campodónico, "La Politica del Avestruz," in *Coca, Cocaina y Narcotráfico: Laberentino en los Andes*, ed. Diego García Sayán (Lima: Comision Andina de Juristas, 1989), 255.

2. House of Representatives Subcommittees on International Economic Policy and Trade and on Western Hemisphere Affairs, *Latin America in the World Economy*, 98th Cong., 1st sess., 15, 21, 23 June 1983 and 21 July 1983, 82; Sebastian Edwards, *Crisis and Reform in Latin America* (Oxford: Oxford University Press, 1995), 18–23.

3. House of Representatives Subcommittees on International Economic Policy and Trade and on Western Hemisphere Affairs, *Latin America in the World Economy*, 82.

4. Rudiger Dornbusch, "The Case for Trade Liberalization in Developing Countries," in *Modern Political Economy in Latin America*. ed. Jeffery Frieden, Manuel Pastor, and Michael Tomz (Boulder, CO: Westview Press, 2000), 173–178.

5. Eliana Cardoso and Ann Helwege, "Import Substitution Industrialization," in *Modern Political Economy in Latin America*, ed. Jeffery Frieden, Manuel Pastor, and Michael Tomz (Boulder, CO: Westview Press, 2000), 155–165; House of Representatives Subcommittees on International Economic Policy and Trade and on Western Hemisphere Affairs, *Latin America in the World Economy*, 15, 21, 23 June 1983 and 21 July 1983, 82. Economist Joseph Grunwald noted that Latin American economies should have retrenched following the "evaporation of Alliance (for Progress) resources," "sharp declines in other official bilateral aid funds," and the "1973–1974 oil shock."

6. Organization of American States Inter-American Specialized Conference on Traffic in Narcotic Drugs, *Socio-Economic Studies for the Inter-American Specialized Conference on Drug Traffic: First Meeting of the Inter-American Specialized Conference on Traffic in Narcotic Drugs*, 12 February 1986 (Washington, DC: Organization of American States, 22 April 1986), 49, 51.

7. Office of National Drug Control Policy, *ONDCP Drug Policy Clearinghouse Fact Sheet: Drug Use Trends* (Rockville, MD: Drug Policy Information Clearing House, October 2002), 1–2. The National Institute on Drug Abuse (NIDA) conducted the NHSDA survey between 1974 and 1991. In 1992 the newly created Substance Abuse and Mental Health Services Administration (SAMHSA) became responsible for all NHSDA surveys.

8. Ibid., 2. Between 1979 and 1985, the general trend among the number of monthly marijuana users declined steadily but still remained at high levels nationally. For instance, the number of monthly marijuana users between the ages of eighteen and twenty-five declined from 35.6 percent to 21.7 percent, while the number of monthly marijuana users between the ages of twenty-six and thirty-four remained steady at 19 percent.

9. John Wall, "U.S. Agency for International Development Evaluation Summary: Upper Huallaga Area Development Project," (Lima: *USAID*, 3 June 1988), xi, National Security Archive, Narcotics Collection, Agency for International Development Projects, box 1.

10. Secretary of State to American Embassy Lima, "Subject: International Narcotics Control Survey Report (INCSR) 1985," (January 1985), 3,, National Security Archive, Narcotics Collection, Peru: Documents from FOIA, box 31. Report drafted by INM: Rhesse. Interestingly, the report added a caveat: "precise evaluation of coca production trends in Peru" was "exceedingly difficult because most cultivation" was in "remote areas" and "climatic conditions" hindered U.S. aerial survey efforts. Peruvian government agencies estimated that coca production ranged from 60,000 hectares to 130,000 hectares.

11. House of Representatives Committee on Foreign Affairs, *U.S. Response to Cuban Government Involvement in Narcotics Trafficking and Review of Worldwide Illicit Narcotics Situation*, 98th Cong., 2nd sess., 21 and 23 February 1984, 110; Organization of American States Inter-American Specialized Conference on Traffic in Narcotic Drugs, *Socio-Economic Studies for the Inter-American Specialized Conference on Drug Traffic*, 7; Marcos Wilson, "Chapare Bolivia: World Cocaine Capital," *Estado de São Paulo* (5 December 1982), 49, National Security Archive, Narcotics Collection, Bolivia, Documents from FOIA, box 33. Released by the Drug Enforcement Administration Library through FOIA. In early 1982 other sources had put the number of hectares under cultivation as high as forty-five thousand.

12. Pat A. Lansbury to Ambassador T. Enders, "Subject: Visit of INM Assistant Secretary and Deputy to Colombia and Peru" (28 October 1981), 1, National Security Archive, Narcotics Collection, Colombia: Cartels, U.S. Operations, Corruption, box 9. In 1981 the INM assistant secretary was Dominick DiCarlo and the deputy assistant secretary was Clyde Taylor, while the ambassador to Colombia was Thomas Enders.

13. House of Representatives Committee on Foreign Affairs, *U.S. Response to Cuban Government Involvement in Narcotics Trafficking*, 126. A footnote in the INM Country Report in 1984 stated that the increase in coca leaf production was stimulated by domestic Colombian demand, the maturation of "young fields," and the identification of previously undetected fields.

14. Lansbury to Enders, "Subject: Visit of INM Assistant Secretary and Deputy to Colombia and Peru," 1; House of Representatives Committee on Foreign Affairs, *U.S. Response to Cuban Government Involvement in Narcotics Trafficking*, 126.

15. Sarita Kendall, "Economies Under the Influence of Cocaine," *Financial Times*, 24 May 1985, sec. 1, p. 4; Humberto Campodónico, "La Politica del Avestruz," 225–238. Ecuador was reputedly receiving an estimated three hundred million dollars from the narcotics trade. Humberto Campodónico's estimates match those presented here.

16. Bradley Graham, "Colombia's Economy: Strong in the Face of Rising Violence; Legal Exports, Not Drugs, Said to Underlie Continued Growth," *Washington Post*, 14 February 1988, sec. K, p. 2.

17. World Bank, *2004 World Development Indicators CD-Rom*; House of Representatives Subcommittees on International Economic Policy and Trade and on Western Hemisphere Affairs, *Latin America in the World Economy*, 94; Sarita Kendall, "Coffee Price Boost for Colombian Exports," *Financial Times*, 18 December 1985, sec. 1, p. 4.

18. Peter Montagnon, "Colombia Takes New Project Loan Route," *Financial Times*, 3 May 1983, sec. 2, p. 25. This problem was known as the "contagion theory." It postulated that Colombia's inability to obtain loans was due to the debt crisis among its neighbors, which generated fear among creditors that the economic contagion affecting the region would spread to Colombia.

19. Robert Graham, "Cautious Economic Policy Pays Dividends," *Financial Times*, 13 February 1984, sec. 1, p. 12; Sarita Kendall, "Tough Year Ahead for Industry," *Financial Times*, 13 February 1984, sec. 1, p. 14; Sarita Kendall, "Coffee Price Boost for Colombian Exports," sec. 1, p. 4.

20. World Bank, *2004 World Development Indicators CD-Rom*; Mimi Whitefield, "Colombia: An Economic Paradox," *Miami Herald*, 9 May 1988, sec. A, p. 15; Robert Graham, "Colombia: Turmoil and Achievement," *Financial Times*, 28 July 1989, sec. 1, p. 15.

21. Joseph B. Treaster, "Coffee Impasse Imperils Colombia's Drug Fight," *New York Times*, 24 September 1989, sec. A, p. 20; *Business Week*, "An Assault on Drugs, Guerrillas and Recession," 27 August 1984, 49. The ICA, an outgrowth of the Alliance for Progress, provided price supports for Colombian coffee that provided nearly 55 percent of Colombia's export income during the 1970s.

22. Sarita Kendall, "Colombia Takes a Long View on Liberalization," *Financial Times*, 8 March 1990, sec. 1, p. 6.

23. Pat A. Lansbury to Ambassador T. Enders, "Subject: Visit of INM Assistant Secretary and Deputy to Colombia and Peru," 2; Maruicio Reina, "La Mano Invisible: Narcotráfico, Economía y Crisis," in *Tras las Huellas de la Crisis Política,* ed. Francisco Leal (Bogotá: Tecer Mundo Editores, 1996), 153–79. Reprint: Charles Bergquist, Ricardo Peñaranda, and Gonzalo Sánchez, *Violence in Colombia 1990–2000: Waging War and Negotiating Peace* (Wilmington, DE: Scholarly Resources Incorporated, 2001), 82–83. (This article deals mainly with the effects of La Apetura, which is discussed later.); Francisco E. Thoumi, *Illegal Drugs, Economy, and Society in the Andes* (Baltimore: Johns Hopkins University Press, 2005), 256. Reina hypothesizes that the purchase of foreign exchange from drug trafficking added to a country's international reserves, thereby increasing the amount of money in circulation, although Reina does note that the extra foreign exchange generated by drug trafficking worked against macroeconomic adjustments. Thoumi argues that the impact of narcotics on inflation mainly depended on whether the monetary base increased as a result of the bonanza from illegal drugs.

24. Richard B. Craig, *Illicit Drug Traffic: Implications for South American Source Countries: Prepared for the Conference on International Drugs*, 44; Francisco Thoumi, *Economía, Política y Narcotráfico*, 256, 195–196; Francisco Thoumi, "Some Implications of the Growth of the Underground Economy in Colombia," 40–41. Over-invoicing of exports by front companies and the phony export of services facilitated other methods of bringing illegal foreign exchange through the Central Bank.

25. Drug Enforcement Administration Office of Intelligence, "Drug Money Laundering: Colombia" (August 1991), National Security Archive, Narcotics Collection, Colombia: Cartels, U.S. Operations, Corruption, box 8.

26. Robert E. Grosse, *Drugs and Money: Laundering Latin America's Cocaine Dollars,* (Westport, CT: Praeger Books, 2001), 40.

27. Drug Enforcement Administration Office of Intelligence, "Drug Money Laundering: Colombia," 2.

28. Robert E. Grosse, *Drugs and Money*, 40.

29. Ibid; World Bank, *2004 World Development Indicators CD-Rom*. The estimate of interest rates is based upon the percentage of current revenue and interest payments on government debt–including long-term bonds, long-term loans, and other debt instruments–to both native and foreign-born residents.

30. *Economist*, "Latin America's Killing Fields," 21.

31. Sarita Kendall, "Bogotá Chafes Under Debt Burden," *Financial Times*, 19 January 1989, sec. 1, p. 6. Other estimates indicated that the income from cocaine was more than three times the $1.2 billion earned from coffee and that as many as 1.2 million people benefited from the proceeds from the sale of coca and cocaine. See: Joseph B. Treaster, "Colombians Fear for the Economy," *New York Times*, 11 September 1989, sec. A, p. 5.

32. Stephen Fidler, "Colombia on a Tide of Money," *Financial Times*, 6 December 1991, sec. 1, p. 32.

33. Victor Mosquera Chaux, "Letter to the Editor," *New York Review of Books* 36, no. 3 (2 March 1989), http://www.nybooks.com/archives/htsearch (accessed 13 November 2006). Victor Mosquera Chaux was the Colombian ambassador to the United States in Washington, DC; he cites Dr. Urrita in his letter.

34. Douglas Farah, "Money Cleaned Colombian Style," *Washington Post*, 30 August 1998, sec. A, p. 22. The large cartels often used contraband to launder their money abroad. The cartels would convert their narco-dollars into tangible products in the U.S. and then ship the products to Colombia and sell them at discount prices for Colombian pesos. In other instances, peso brokers in the United States acted as middlemen between smugglers and narcotics traffickers. The brokers collected U.S. dollars earned from the drug trade and gave the traffickers credit. The brokers then bought pesos from smugglers in Colombia. When a deal was conducted, the smugglers received U.S. dollars in the United States to buy products to smuggle into Colombia, and the traffickers in Colombia received pesos for the U.S. dollars they had credit for. Laundered pesos from accounts in Colombia financed the purchase of quantities of goods, such as whiskey, cigarettes, and electronic devices. The contraband was brought into the Panama free trade zone and smuggled from there into Colombia, where it was sold at cheaper prices than those in the United States or Panama. In addition, until 1995, Colombian dollars earned through the cocaine trade could easily be exchanged through the ventanilla into Colombian pesos. See: Senate Caucus on International Narcotics Control, *The Black Market Peso Exchange: How U.S. Companies Are Used to Launder Money*, 106th Cong., 1st sess., 21 June 1999, 5–9. From the statement of James E. Johnson, undersecretary of enforcement, Department of the Treasury. Over-invoicing exports was another way to launder drug money.

35. American Embassy Bogotá to International Narcotics Matters Department of State, "Annual Narcotics Status Report" (31 March 1981), 12, National Security Archive, Narcotics Collection, Colombia: Cartels, U.S. Operations, Corruption, box 9.

36. Sarita Kendall, "Tough Year Ahead for Industry," sec. 1, p. 14.

37. Drug Enforcement Administration Office of Intelligence, "Drug Money Laundering: Colombia," 4.

38. Victor Mosquera Chaux, "Letter to the Editor," 2. Victor Mosquera Chaux was the Colombian Ambassador to the United States in Washington, DC.

39. Drug Enforcement Administration Office of Intelligence, "Drug Money Laundering: Colombia," 4.

40. Steve Gutkin, "An Uneasy Peace with Businesslike Barons," *USA Today*, 14 February 1990, sec. A, p. 6.

41. American Embassy Bogotá to Secretary of State Washington, DC, "Intelligence Requirements: Everything You Always Wanted to Know About Colombian Narcotics" (February 1981), 4, National Security Archive, Narcotics Collection, Colombia: Cartels, U.S. Operations, Corruption, box 9.

42. American Embassy Bogotá to International Narcotics Matters Department of State, "Annual Narcotics Status Report," 12.

43. Joseph B. Treaster, "Colombians Fear for the Economy," sec. A, p. 5.

44. Richard B. Craig, "Illicit Drug Traffic: Implications for South American Source Countries," 26.

45. New Statesman and Society, "Letter from Bogotá," *New Statesman and Society* 6, no. 283 (31 December 1993), 13.

46. Mike Reed, "Third World Report: Drug Mafia Targets Peasants in Shift to Real Estate," *Guardian*, 21 October 1988, 1.

47. Merrill Collett, "Traffickers Threaten Land Reform," *Christian Science Monitor*, 24 January 1989, 3.

48. Mauricio Reina, "La Mano Invisible: Narcotráfico, Economía y Crisis," 84.

49. Merrill Collett, "Traffickers Threaten Land Reform," 3.

50. Mike Reed, "Third World Report: Drug Mafia Targets Peasants in Shift to Real Estate," 1.

51. Merrill Collett, "Traffickers Threaten Land Reform," 3.

52. World Bank, *2004 World Development Indicators CD-Rom*; House of Representatives Subcommittees on International Economic Policy and Trade and on Western Hemisphere Affairs, *Latin America in the World Economy*, 95; William Chislett, "Debt Turns Peru Recovery into a Game of Chance," *Financial Times*, 5 January 1984, sec. 1, p. 4; Kathryn Leger, "Caught in the Crossfire of a Dirty War," *Maclean's*, 25 February 1985, 42.

53. World Bank, *2004 World Development Indicators CD-Rom*; Washington Post, "Peruvian Inflation Rate Expected to Climb to 70%," *Washington Post*, Business and Finance Roundup, 11 November 1980, sec. E, p. 2; Richard Alm and Richard L. DeLouise,"For Some Real Inflation Look at the Third World," *U.S. News and World Report*, 15 July 1985, 49.

54. Economist World Business Peru, "The Royal Hunt of the Sol," *Economist*, 26 November 1983, 77. In addition, the Peruvian economy had lost nine hundred thousand jobs.

55. Kathryn Leger, "Caught in the Crossfire of a Dirty War," 42.

56. Economist World Business Peru, "Latin American Economies: The Special Case of Peru," *Economist*, 10 January 1987, 54.

57. *Financial Times*, "Peru Retreats into Populism," 30 July 1987, sec. 1, p. 20.

58. Bradley Graham, "Peru Seen Facing Crisis; Economy, Rebel War Close in on Garcia," *Washington Post*, 2 April 1988, sec. A, p. 11.

59. *Toronto Star*, "Peru Expected to Take Action on the Export Decline," 3 April 1988, sec. H, p. 8.

60. World Bank, *2004 World Development Indicators CD-Rom*.

61. Peter Andreas, "Peru's Addiction to Coca Dollars: Why Varganomics Won't Work," *The Nation*, 16 April 1990, 514, 515; Sarita Kendall, "Economies Under the Influence of Cocaine," sec. 1, p. 4.

62. Ibid. The Banco de Crédito had branches in New York, Panama, and the Cayman Islands, which further facilitated its ability to launder narco-dollars.

63. Roberto Lerner, "The Drug Trade in Peru," in *Latin America and the Multinational Drug Trade*, ed. Elizabeth Joyce and Carlos Malamud (London: University of London Institute of Latin American Studies, 1998), 121.

64. Ibid.

65. Peter Andreas, "Peru's Addiction to Coca Dollars: Why Varganomics Won't Work," 515; Sarita Kendall, "Economies Under the Influence of Cocaine," sec. 1, p. 4.

66. Organization of American States Inter-American Specialized Conference on Traffic in Narcotic Drugs, *Socio-Economic Studies for the Inter-American Specialized Conference on Drug Traffic*, 13.

67. American Embassy Lima to the Secretary of State Washington, DC, "Upper Huallaga Area Development Project–Proposed Progress Indicators" (June 1984), 1, National Security Archive, Narcotics Collection, Peru: U.S. Operations, Sendero, Fujimori, box 6.

68. Martiza Rojas Albertini, *Los Campesinos Cocaleros del Departamiento de San Martín: Opiniones, Actitudes y Valores Hacia el Cultivo de la Coca, Producción, Comercio y Consumo de Pasta Básica de Coca* (Lima: Cerdo, 1995), 75–76.

69. Richard B. Craig, *Illicit Drug Traffic: Implications for South American Source Countries: Prepared for the Conference on International Drugs*, 25.

70. Martiza Rojas Albertini, *Los Campesinos Cocaleros*, 93–98.

71. John Wall, "U.S. Agency for International Development Evaluation Summary: Upper Huallaga Area Development Project," xii–xiii. The USAID study went on to say that cocaine paste gave a return of seven hundred dollars per kilogram.

72. Ibid., xiii.

73. Martiza Rojas Albertini, *Los Campesinos Cocaleros*, 93.

74. Bastiaan Schouten and Peter Bloom, Information Memorandum for the Assistant Administrator Latin American Countries, "Review of USAID/Peru CDSS and Action Plan" (24 June 1991), *USAID*, 2, National Security Archive, Narcotics Collection, Agency for International Development Projects, box 2.

75. World Bank, *2004 World Development Indicators CD-Rom*.

76. Edmundo Morales, *Cocaine: White Gold Rush in Peru*, 103, 109–110.

77. Richard B. Craig, *Illicit Drug Traffic: Implications for South American Source Countries: Prepared for the Conference on International Drugs*, 29.

78. Edmundo Morales, "The Andean Cocaine Dilemma," in *Drug Trafficking in the Americas*, ed. Bruce M. Bagley and William O. Walker III (Miami: University of Miami Press, 1996), 100.

79. Robert E. Grosse, *Drugs and Money*, 18.

80. Edmundo Morales, "The Andean Cocaine Dilemma," 111–12, 163.

81. Roberto Lerner, "The Drug Trade in Peru," 122.

82. Richard B. Craig, *Illicit Drug Traffic: Implications for South American Source Countries: Prepared for the Conference on International Drugs*, 29.

83. *Economist*, "Latin America's Killing Fields," 8 October 1988, 21.

84. Roberto Lerner, "The Drug Trade in Peru," 122.

85. World Bank, *2004 World Development Indicators CD-Rom*; Senate Committee on Governmental Affairs, *U.S. Government Anti-Narcotics Activities in the Andean Region of South America*, 101st Cong., 1st sess., 26–29 September 1989, 201. Statistics vary a little between the two reports, but only by small amounts.

86. World Bank, *2004 World Development Indicators CD-Rom*.

87. Checchi and Company, "A Review of AID's Narcotics Control Development Assistance Program: Prepared for Development Information and Evaluation USAID" (October 1985), 33, National Security Archive, Narcotics Collection, Agency for International Development Projects, box 1.

88. Ray Henkel, "The Bolivian Cocaine Industry," in *Drugs in Latin America*, 65. Between 1980 and 1983, campesinos earned roughly $2,000 per ton of coca leaves. Between 1984 and 1985, campesinos earned an estimated $1,500 per ton. In 1986, the price of coca leaves declined to $1,000 per ton, but rose again to $1,500 per ton in 1987.

89. Checchi and Company, "A Review of AID's Narcotics Control Development Assistance Program: Prepared for Development Information and Evaluation USAID," 33.

90. Richard B. Craig, *Illicit Drug Traffic: Implications for South American Source Countries: Prepared for the Conference on International Drugs*, 13.

91. Mac Margolis, "Bolivian Economy Hooked on Cocaine," *Christian Science Monitor*, 14 May 1986, 1; Barbara Durr, "Drugs War Creates Dilemma for Bolivia," *Financial Times*, 20 August 1986, sec. 1, p. 4.

92. Jerry R. Ladman and Jose Issac Torrico, "Chapare Financial Markets: An Assessment of and Needs for the Chapare Rural Development Project, Report Prepared for USAID Bolivia, Contract Number 511-000-S-00-2005" (La Paz: USAID, 1 March 1983), 9–10, 17, National Security Archive, Narcotics Collection, Agency for International Development Projects, box 2.

93. Andy Atkins, "The Economic and Political Impact of the Drug Trade and Drug Control Policies in Bolivia," in *Latin America and the Multinational Drug Trade*, ed. Elizabeth Joyce and Carlos Malamud (London: University of London Institute of Latin American Studies, 1998), 102.

94. Melvin Burke, "Bolivia: The Politics of Cocaine," 66. No questions were asked about where the money came from when these deposits were made.

95. U.S. Department of the Army, *Country Study: Bolivia*, http://lcweb2.loc.gov/frd/cs/botoc. html (accessed 10 November 2004); Senate Committee on Governmental Affairs, *U.S. Government Anti-Narcotics Activities*, 201; World Bank, *2004 World Development Indicators CD-Rom*. Inflation fell from 276 percent in 1986 to 15 percent in 1987. The World Bank estimates inflation at 230 percent in 1986.

96. World Bank, *2004 World Development Indicators CD-Rom*. The overvaluation of the currency through increased deposits in many respects dispels the argument that cocaine was not the primary cause for the increase in imports.

97. Roberto Laserna, *Las Drogas y el Ajuste en Bolivia: Economía Clandestina y Políticas Públicas* (La Paz: CEDLA, 1993), 44. On page 32, Laserna states that the program of adjustment rests partially on the clandestine economy, which had become a structural part of the Bolivian economy.

98. Andy Atkins, "The Economic and Political Impact of the Drug Trade and Drug Control Policies in Bolivia," 102. Many Bolivian industries struggled to compete in the domestic market as imports began to surpass exports. See: La Comisión Especial del Congreso Nacional, "Informe Parlamentario del Caso Huanchaca" (5 November 1986), in *La Guerra de la Coca: Una Sombra Sobre los Andes*, ed. Roger Cortéz Hurtado (La Paz: Centro de Información para el Desarrollo, 1992), 40. According to the commission's report, the Bolivian state's dependency on coca had encouraged a structural stabilization from narcotics trafficking, which served as an axis of capital accumulation for Bolivia.

99. Organization of American States Inter-American Specialized Conference on Traffic in Narcotic Drugs, *Socio-Economic Studies for the Inter-American Specialized Conference on Drug Traffic*, 9; Mario Franco and Ricardo Godoy, "The Economic Consequences of Cocaine," 381. The Yungas region had been Bolivia's traditional coca-growing region. According to Mario Franco and Ricardo Godoy, the Chapare was more attractive than the Yungas region because farmers could plant coca four times a year, as compared to three in the Yungas. In addition, farmers did not have to build costly terraces in the Chapare to grow coca, as they did in the Yungas.

100. U.S. Department of the Army, *Country Study: Bolivia*, http://lcweb2.loc.gov/frd/cs/botoc. html (accessed 10 November 2004).

101. Don Bostwick PhD, Joseph Dorsey PhD, and James Jones PhD, "USAID Evaluation of the Chapare Regional Development Project: Prepared for USAID Bolivia" (Washington, DC: USAID, November 1990), National Security Archive, Narcotics Collection, Agency for International Development Projects, box 2.

102. Richard B. Craig, *Illicit Drug Traffic: Implications for South American Source Countries: Prepared for the Conference on International Drugs*, 13; La Comisión Especial del Congreso Nacional, "Informe Parlamentario del Caso Huanchaca," 38. The Bolivian report claimed that 60 percent of the population benefited in one form or another from the coca trade.

103. Patricia Ellis and David Lomax, "Bolivia: The Cocaine Trade" (30 December 1982), Educational Broadcasting and GWETA: The MacNeil/Lehrer Report, Transcript #1894, 17, National Security Archive, Narcotics Collection, Bolivia, Documents from FOIA, box 33.

104. Organization of American States Inter-American Specialized Conference on Traffic in Narcotic Drugs, *Socio-Economic Studies for the Inter-American Specialized Conference on Drug Traffic*, 14; and Richard B. Craig, *Illicit Drug Traffic: Implications for South American Source Countries: Prepared for the Conference on International Drugs*, 13.

105. Melvin Burke, "Bolivia the Politics of Cocaine," *Current History* 90, no. 553 (February 1991): 67.

106. Organization of American States Inter-American Specialized Conference on Traffic in Narcotic Drugs, *Socio-Economic Studies for the Inter-American Specialized Conference on Drug Traffic*, 22; Andy Atkins, "The Economic and Political Impact of the Drug Trade and Drug Control Policies in Bolivia," 99. Mario Franco and Ricardo Godoy argue that, unlike in Peru, although coca took away laborers from agriculture, it also increased incomes. The growth in income boosted demand, which in turn caused many campesinos to become mixed-croppers to meet the demand. See: Mario Franco and Ricardo Godoy, "The Economic Consequences of Cocaine," 392–397. Franco and Godoy's argument counters that of Allison Speeding Pallet regarding the campesino economy. See: endnote 6, chapter 7.

107. Richard B. Craig, *Illicit Drug Traffic: Implications for South American Source Countries: Prepared for the Conference on International Drugs*, 14.

108. Roberto Laserna, *Las Drogas y el Ajuste en Bolivia*, 70–73.

109. Ibid., 70–73. Laserna states that the campesinos invested to acquire the means for work and production so that they could take their families out of agriculture. Consequently, they bought land to expand their enterprises, invested in education for their children, or purchased items like automobiles that they could use as taxis or to transport coca.

110. Mac Margolis, "Bolivian Economy Hooked on Cocaine," 1. Contraband items included products such as luxury goods, cars, gasoline, and items used to create coca paste from coca leaves including kerosene, toilet paper, and sulphuric acid.

111. Don Bostwick PhD, Joseph Dorsey PhD, and James Jones PhD, "USAID Evaluation of the Chapare Regional Development Project," 15.

112. Richard B. Craig, *Illicit Drug Traffic: Implications for South American Source Countries: Prepared for the Conference on International Drugs*, 14.

113. Everett G. Martin, "A Little Cattle Town in Bolivia Is Thriving as a Financial Center," *Wall Street Journal*, 17 February 1983, sec. A, p. 1.

114. Anibal Aguilar, "Exposición," in *Debate Agrario: La Economía Campesina y el Cultivo de la Coca Instituto* ed. Latinoamericano de Investigaciones Sociales (La Paz: Editorial Offset Boliviana Imprenta, 1987), 48–52.

115. Humberto Campodónico, "La Politica del Avestruz," 247, 250, 255.

116. Sarita Kendall, "Economies Under the Influence of Cocaine," sec. I, p. 4. Ecuador was receiving roughly three hundred million dollars from the narcotics trade mostly because it acted as a transshipment point. Ecuador never developed a coca-growing campesino population, as did its neighbors, Peru and Bolivia.

Chapter 3: U.S. Narcotics Control Policies in the Northern Andes, 1980–1987

1. U.S. Commissioner of Customs William von Raab, U.S. Customs Service, "Who is Doing the Wash in Florida?" 5, National Security Archive, Narcotics: Drug Documents, Treasury: Operation Greenback, box 23; United States Drug Enforcement Administration, *DEA History Book 1980–1985*, http://www.usdoj.gov/dea/pubs/history/deahistory_01.htm (accessed 9 July 2004); Lieutenant Colonel Juan L. Orama, *U.S. Military Evolution in Counternarcotics Operations in Latin America,* (Carlisle Barracks, PA: U.S. Army War College, 10 April 2001), 9; Robert E. Tomasson, "Bush Hails Coast Guard Drug Seizures," *New York Times,* 19 May 1983, sec. B, p. 12.

2. Charles Fishman, "Expanded Interdiction System, U.S. Closes Border to Illegal Drugs," *Washington Post,* 18 June 1983, sec. A, p. 7; Lieutenant Colonel Juan L. Orama, *U.S. Military Evolution in Counternarcotics Operations,* 9.

3. Ronald Reagan, "Responses to Questions Submitted by Latin American Newspapers" (30 November 1982), *The Public Papers of the Presidents of the United States* (Washington, DC: Office of the Federal Register, National Archives and Records Service, 1982), 1532.

4. American Embassy Bogotá to Department of State INM, "Annual Narcotics Status Report (ANSR 1980)" (31 March 1981), 1, National Security Archive, Narcotics Collection, Colombia, U.S. Operations, box 9.

5. Mimi Whitefield, "Ex-President of Colombia Blames U.S. for Drug Traffic," *Miami Herald,* 30 May 1981.

6. Lansbury to Enders, "Subject: Visit of INM Assistant Secretary and Deputy to Colombia and Peru, 2.

7. American Embassy Bogotá to Secretary of State Washington, DC, "Intelligence Requirements: Everything You Always Wanted to Know About Colombian Narcotics," 1.

8. Lansbury to Enders, "Subject: Visit of INM Assistant Secretary and Deputy to Colombia and Peru," 2; American Embassy Bogotá to Department of State INM, "Annual Narcotics Status Report (ANSR 1980)," 1. This cable noted that the Colombian government and the private sector "began to realize the magnitude of the drug problem." The analyst added that many Colombians realized "the negative effect" of narcotics-related corruption on Colombian institutions.

9. House of Representatives Subcommittee of Inter-American Affairs of the Committee on Foreign Affairs, *Foreign Assistance Legislation for Fiscal Year 1981, Part 6,* 96th Cong., 2nd sess., 7, 12, 26, 28 February 1980 and 6 March 1980, 115.

10. House of Representatives Subcommittee of Inter-American Affairs of the Committee on Foreign Affairs, *Foreign Assistance Legislation for Fiscal Year 1981, Part 6,* 221–222.

11. Reuters, "Antidrug Battle Outlined by Bush," *New York Times,* 17 February 1982, sec. A, p. 16.

12. *New York Times,* "U.S. Plans to Increase Patrols Near Colombia," *New York Times,* 18 November 1984, sec. A, p. 33.

13. Organization of American States, "Presentación Sobre la Coperación Marítima Entre las Bahamas, Turks y Caicos y los Estados Unidos," *Comisión Interamericana Para el Control del Abuso de Drogas,* El Trigesimo Cuarta Sesión Ordinaria, Montreal, Canada, 17–20 noviembre 2003, http://www.cicad.oas.org/es/Asambleas/CICAD34/ESP/Dia%204/pRESENTACIONBAHAMAS.htm (accessed 18 January 2007).

14. American Embassy Bogotá to Secretary of State Washington, DC, "Narcotics Assessment and Strategy Paper for Fiscal Years 1981–1985" (22 December 1981), 2, National Security Archive, Narcotics Collection, Colombia, U.S. Operations, box 9.

15. Tom Fiedler, "Diplomat: Colombia Drug Crop Cut," *Miami Herald*, 6 May 1981; American Embassy Bogotá to Secretary of State Washington, DC, "Intelligence Requirements: Everything You Always Wanted to Know About Colombian Narcotics," 3.

16. Terrence G. Grant to Mr. Joseph H. Linnemann, "The Colombian INC Program" (Washington, DC: U.S. Department of State, 1 May 1981), 3, National Security Archive, Narcotics Collection, Colombia, U.S. Operations, box 9. Linnemann was the acting assistant secretary of INM in 1981. See: American Embassy Bogotá to Department of State INM, "Annual Narcotics Status Report (ANSR 1981)," 15, National Security Archive, Narcotics Collection, Colombia, U.S. Operations, box 9; U.S. Department of State, "Fact Sheet: Narcotics Cooperation" (1981), 1, National Security Archive, Narcotics Collection, Colombia, U.S. Operations, box. 9. The SANUs received tactical support from the Colombian military.

17. American Embassy Bogotá to Secretary of State Washington, DC, "Intelligence Requirements: Everything You Always Wanted to Know About Colombian Narcotics," 1.

18. Senate Subcommittee on Terrorism, Narcotics, and International Operation of the Committee on Foreign Relations, *Drugs, Law Enforcement, and Foreign Policy*, 100th Cong., 2nd sess., December 1988, 31.

19. American Embassy Bogotá to Secretary of State, Washington, DC, "1991 Best CNP Interdiction Year Ever: Summary of 1991 Activities and Comparison to Period 1981–1991" (January 1992), 3–4, National Security Archive, Narcotics Collection, Colombia, Documents from FOIA, box 32; House of Representatives Committee on Foreign Affairs, *U.S. Response to Cuban Government Involvement in Narcotics Trafficking*, 126. Statement of Dominick DiCarlo, assistant secretary of state for Bureau of International Narcotics Matters. The statistics reported in these documents were compared with statistics presented by two International Narcotics Control Strategy Reports. See: U.S. Department of State, Bureau of International Narcotics Matters, *1989 International Narcotics Control Strategy Report* (Washington, DC: U.S. Department of State, March 1990), 75; U.S. Department of State, Bureau of International Narcotics Matters, *1985 International Narcotics Control Strategy Report to the Committee on Foreign Relations and the Committee on Foreign Affairs* (Washington, DC: U.S. Department of State, 1 February 1985), 75–76.

20. Lansbury to Enders, "Visit of INM Assistant Secretary and Deputy to Colombia and Peru," 2, 3.

21. Richard B. Craig, "Colombian Narcotics and United States-Colombian Relations," 265.

22. Juan Gabriel Tokatlián, "Estados Unidos y los Cultivos Ilícitos en Colombia: Los Trágicos Equvicós de una Fumigación Futil," http://socrates.berkeley.edu:7001/Events/confrences/Colombia/workingpapers/working_paper_toaktlian.doc (accessed 17 November 2004).

23. American Embassy Bogotá to Secretary of State Washington, DC, "International Narcotics Control-FY 1984 Budget Submission for Colombia" (7 April 1984), 2, National Security Archive, Narcotics Collection, Colombia, U.S. Operations, box 9.

24. House of Representatives Committee on Foreign Affairs, *Developments in Latin American Narcotics Control, November 1985*, 99th Cong., 1st sess., 12 November 1985, 25.

25. Robert Doherty, "Colombia Is Progressing on a Herbicide that Could Gut Coca Crop Officials Say," *Miami Herald*, 30 August 1985, sec. A, p. 1.

26. House of Representatives Staff Study Mission to Southeast Asia, South America, Central America, and the Caribbean August 1984 to January 1985, *U.S. Narcotics Control Programs Overseas*, 25.

27. Drug Enforcement Administration, "Country Profile: Colombia" (Washington, DC: Drug Enforcement Administration Office of Intelligence Strategic Section Latin American Unit, June 1988), 4, National Security Archive, Narcotics Collection, U.S. Policy/Military: Latin America General Issues, box 22.

28. American Embassy Bogotá to Secretary of State, Washington, DC, "1991 Best CNP Interdiction Year Ever," 3–4.

29. U.S. Department of State, Bureau of International Narcotics Matters, *1988 International Narcotics Control Strategy Report* (Washington, DC: U.S. Department of State, March 1989), 75; American Embassy Bogotá to Secretary of State Washington, DC, "1991 Best CNP Interdiction Year Ever," 4–5; House of Representatives Committee on Foreign Affairs, *U.S. Response to Cuban Government Involvement in Narcotics Trafficking*, 126. Statement of Dominick DiCarlo, assistant secretary of state for the Bureau of International Narcotics Matters.

30. U.S. Department of State, Bureau of International Narcotics Matters, *1989 International Narcotics Control Strategy Report*, 75; U.S. Department of State, Bureau of International Narcotics Matters, *1985 International Narcotics Control Strategy Report*, 75–76. The data for the eradication and interdiction program is a calculation of marijuana seizures and eradication in metric tons versus gross estimated marijuana production in metric tons.

31. House of Representatives Committee on Foreign Affairs, *Review of Latin American Narcotics Control Issues*, 100th Cong., 1st sess., 18 March 1987, 7. Statement of Ann Wrobleski, assistant secretary of state, Bureau of International Narcotics Matters; Drug Enforcement Administration, "Country Profile: Colombia," 4.

32. Drug Enforcement Administration, "Country Profile: Colombia," 4.

33. House of Representatives Committee on Foreign Affairs, *Developments in Latin American Narcotics Control*, 57. Five fixed-wing aircraft and one helicopter were also seized.

34. American Embassy Bogotá to Secretary of State Washington, DC, "1991 Best CNP Interdiction Year Ever," 3–4. Estimates were given in kilograms, which were converted into metric tons. See: U.S. Department of State, Bureau of International Narcotics Matters, *1988 International Narcotics Control Strategy Report*, 75.

35. American Embassy Bogotá to Secretary of State Washington, DC, "1991 Best CNP Interdiction Year Ever," 3–4. The Colombian government refused to allow the use of herbicides because technical reports described the negative effects from spraying marijuana. Notably, those reports also argued that the herbicides would not end cultivation. See: Juan Gabriel Tokatlián, "Estados Unidos y los Cultivos Ilícitos en Colombia: Los Trágicos Equvicós de una Fumigación Futil," http://socrates.berkeley.edu:7001/Events/confrences/Colombia/workingpapers/working_paper_tokatlian.doc (accessed 17 November 2004); House of Representatives Committee on Foreign Affairs, *Developments in Latin American Narcotics Control*, 46–49.

36. U.S. Department of State, Bureau of International Narcotics Matters, *1989 International Narcotics Control Strategy Report*, 75; U.S. Department of State, Bureau of International Narcotics Matters, *1985 International Narcotics Control Strategy Report*, 75–76. The data for the eradication and interdiction program is a calculation of coca seizures and eradication in metric tons versus gross estimated coca production in metric tons.

37. Drug Enforcement Administration, "Country Profile: Colombia," 4. This ranged from between fifteen thousand and seventeen thousand hectares in 1985, to between about twenty thousand and twenty-five thousand hectares in 1987.

38. Mark Whitaker, Elaine Shannon, and Ron Moreau, "Colombia's King of Coke," *Newsweek*, 25 February 1985, 19.

39. House of Representatives Committee on Foreign Affairs, *U.S. Response to Cuban Government Involvement in Narcotics Trafficking*, 19.

40. American Embassy Bogotá to Secretary of State Washington, DC, "Intelligence Requirements: Everything You Always Wanted to Know About Colombian Narcotics," 2.

41. House of Representatives Committee on Foreign Affairs, *Review of Latin American Narcotics Control Issues*, 7.

42. House of Representatives Committee on Foreign Affairs, *Developments in Latin American Narcotics Control*, 57; House of Representatives Committee on Foreign Affairs, *U.S. Response to Cuban Government Involvement in Narcotics Trafficking*, 119.

43. James H. Michel to the Deputy Secretary, "Action Memorandum: Transmission to the Senate of the Extradition Treaty Between the United States and Colombia" (Washington, DC: U.S. Department of State, 8 May 1981), 1, 2. Both nations had signed earlier treaties in 1880 and 1940.

44. House of Representatives Committee on Foreign Affairs, *U.S. Response to Cuban Government Involvement in Narcotics Trafficking*, 120.

45. Mark Whitaker, Elaine Shannon, and Ron Moreau, "Colombia's King of Coke," 19. Lehder also directed cocaine smuggling operations on Norman's Cay until 1982 from his hometown of Armenia, Colombia. See: Guy Gugliotta and Jeff Leen, *Kings of Cocaine*, 60–66, 113–116.

46. Warren Hoge, "Colombian City Is Corrupted by Cocaine," *New York Times*, 30 June 1981, sec. A, p. 6. Due to this assassination method, the Colombian government was forced to change its motorcycle laws: it became illegal for passengers to ride on motorcycles, and all motorcycle operators were required to wear vests with large identification numbers.

47. Mark Whitaker and Elaine Shannon, "Bogotá's Drug Wars," *Newsweek*, 10 December 1984, 48.

48. From a Correspondent in Bogotá, "Colombia; Coke Law," *Economist*, 29 August 1987, 35.

49. Roger Lowenstein, "Colombian Leader Battles Drug Dealers," *Wall Street Journal*, 24 December 1984, sec. A, p. 10.

50. House of Representatives Committee on Foreign Affairs, *Developments in Latin American Narcotics Control*, 30.

51. American Embassy Bogotá to Secretary of State Washington, DC, "Narcotics Guerrilla Connection in Colombia for Use in ARA Congressional Testimony" (July 1984), 1, National Security Archive, Narcotics Collection, Colombia, Cartels, box 8; Jackson Diehl, "Colombia Fights Back After Waking to Ravages of Drug Trade," *Washington Post*, 21 May 1984, sec. A, p. 1.

52. From a Correspondent in Bogotá, "Colombia; Coke Law," 35; and Mark Whitaker, Elaine Shannon, and Ron Moreau, "Colombia's King of Coke," 19.

53. Reuters, "Around the World: A Colombian Lawmaker Is Killed by Gunmen," *New York Times*, 2 August 1984, sec. A, p. 7.

54. Associated Press, "Blast at Embassy in Colombia," *New York Times*, 27 November 1984, sec. A, p. 9.

55. Jackson Diehl, "Colombia's War on Drug Trade Falters; Leading Trafficker on National Television Defends His Actions Against Anti-Imperialism," *Washington Post*, 5 March 1985, sec. A, p. 8; Guy Gugliotta and Jeff Leen, *Kings of Cocaine*, 40.

56. Reuters, "Colombian Drug Lords: The Robin Hoods of Today," *Christian Science Monitor*, 8 August 1986, 25.

57. *Newsweek*, "Drugs and a U.S. Pullout," 28 January 1985, 37.

58. Timothy Ross, "Colombia Goes After the Drug Barons," *Christian Science Monitor*, 12 January 1987, 9.

59. James Nelson Goodsell, "Drug Traffickers Retaliate Against U.S.–Colombia War on Drugs," *Christian Science Monitor*, 29 November 1984, 20.

60. Marshall Ingwerson, "U.S. Hopes Indictments Will Induce Nations to Seize Drug Smugglers," *Christian Science Monitor*, 21 November 1986, 7.

61. Timothy Ross, "Colombia Goes After the Drug Barons," 9.

62. Guy Gugliotta and Jeff Leen, *Kings of Cocaine*, 104.

63. Jacobo Arenas, *Cese el Fuego: Una Historia Política de las FARC*, (Bogotá: Editorial Oveja Negra, 1 June 2000), 10.

64. American Embassy Bogotá to Secretary of State Washington, DC, "Betancur Excoriates Drug Trafficking in National Address" (April 1984), 1, 2, National Security Archive, Narcotics Collection, Colombia: Cartels, U.S. Operations, Corruption, box 8.

65. Associated Press, "Colombian Rebels Announce Truce," *New York Times*, 27 May 1984, sec. A, p. 11. The cease-fire accord allowed the FARC to join the political fold by establishing a political party called the Union Patriotica (UP), a development of major importance. See: Ricardo Vargas Meza, "The FARC, the War, and the Crisis of State," *NACLA Report on the Americas* 31 no. 5 (March/April 1998): 3, www.nacla.org (accessed 20 February 2006).

66. American Embassy to Secretary of State Washington, DC, "Betancur Announces Cease Fire" (April 1984), 4, National Security Archive, Narcotics Collection, Colombia, Cartels, box 8; Major Luis Alberto Villamarín, *The FARC Cartel* (Bogotá: Ediciones El Faraón, 1996), 40. According to Colombia's Major Luis Alberto Villamarín, the truce with the Betancur administration was a sham set up by the FARC secretariat to boost its profits from narcotics. Villamarín adds that the FARC used the truce to extend its influence in the rural coca-growing areas in southern Colombia.

67. *Washington Post*, "The Colombian Example," 28 August 1984, sec. A, p. 14.

68. House of Representatives Committee on Foreign Affairs, *Review of Latin American Narcotics Control Issues*, 79.

69. Senate Subcommittee on Terrorism, Narcotics, and International Operation of the Committee on Foreign Relations, *Drugs, Law Enforcement, and Foreign Policy*, 31. The assassinated judges were Dr. Alfonso Reyes Echandía, Dr. Fabio Calderón Botero, Dr. Dario Velásquez Gaviria, Dr. Eduardo Gnecco Correa, Dr. Carlos Medellín Forero, Dr. Ricardo Medina Moyano, Dr. Alfonso Pati o Rosselli, Dr. Manuel Gaona Cruz, Dr. Horacio Montoya Gil, Dr. Pedro Elías Serrano Abadía, Dr. Dante Luis Fiorillo Porras. For a detailed history that gives a minute-by-minute report of events, see: Ana Carrigan, *The Palace of Justice: A Colombian Tragedy* (New York: Four Walls Eight Windows, 1993), 9–303.

70. Ibid. For a detailed account, see Ana Carrigan, *The Palace of Justice: A Colombian Tragedy* (New York: Four Walls Eight Windows, 1993).

71. United Press International, "Nicaragua Denies Charge by Reagan," sec. A, p. 3. The Colombian newspaper *El Tiempo* claimed that five Sandinistas had helped plan the raid. In addition, ten rifles belonging to the guerrillas had been supplied in 1976 to the Nicaraguan National Guard, which was overthrown by the Sandinistas in 1979. Significantly, two Belgian-made rifles were part of a lot that the Venezuelan government had supplied to the Sandinistas in 1979. The Sandinistas responded by explaining that only one-third of the Venezuelan arms shipment had ever arrived in their hands and that the remainder's whereabouts were unknown. See: Tim Coone, "Nicaragua and Colombia Defuse Row on M-19 Attack," sec. I, p. 4; *Globe and Mail*, "Around the World: Envoy Recalled by Colombia," 23 December 1985.

72. Richard B. Craig, *Illicit Drug Traffic: Implications for South American Source Countries: Prepared for the Conference on International Drugs*, 52.

73. Mark Whitaker, Elaine Shannon, and Ron Moreau, "Colombia's King of Coke," 19.

74. Bert Ruiz, *The Colombian Civil War*, 122–125. ANAPO was an independent political party that had slowly emerged in the 1960s to counter the National Front. Pinilla received ANAPO's support because he promised massive social and political reforms if elected. Colombia's press and radio stations predicted that Pinilla was going to win a landslide victory. Therefore, on the morning after the election, when Pastrana was ahead of Pinilla, many people believed that the election had been stolen. The M-19 differed from the FARC and ELN because it was mainly composed of well-educated, middle-class people who believed that change could not come through the political process.

75. Associated Press, "Colombian Rebels Announce Truce," sec. A, p. 11; Associated Press, "Obituaries: Julio Turbay; Ex-President of Colombia," *Washington Post*, 14 September 2005, sec. B, p. 6. According to William López Gutiérrez, the Sandinistas' power seizure, international recognition of the Farbundo Martí in El Salvador, official repression, and Colombia's standard-of-living crisis during the 1970s all breathed oxygen into the M-19 movement. See: William López Gutiérrez, "Las Políticas de Paz y los Procesos de Negociación en Colombia: Breve Balance y Perspectivas," *Covergencia* no. 19 (mayo-agosto 1999): 248.

76. Senate Subcommittee on Terrorism, Narcotics. and International Operation of the Committee on Foreign Relations, *Drugs, Law Enforcement, and Foreign Policy*, 31.

77. Merrill Collett, "Colombia's Drug Lords Waging War on Leftists: Traffickers Seen Allied with Extreme Right," *Washington Post*, 14 November 1987. The guerrillas demanded twelve million dollars but never received it. The Medellín cartel captured five M-19 guerrillas and held them for ransom until she was released.

78. Senate Subcommittee on Terrorism, Narcotics, and International Operation of the Committee on Foreign Relations, *Drugs, Law Enforcement, and Foreign Policy*, 31; Human Rights Watch, *Colombia's Killer Networks: The Military-Paramilitary Partnership and the United States*, (London: Human Rights Watch, 1996), 17. Law 48 made paramilitaries legal in Colombia from 1968 to 1989. The law was terminated in 1989 when Liberal presidential candidate Luis Carlos Galán was assassinated.

79. Merrill Collet, "Colombia's Drug Lords Waging War on Leftists," sec. A, p. 7.

80. Senate Subcommittee on Terrorism, Narcotics, and International Operation of the Committee on Foreign Relations, *Drugs, Law Enforcement, and Foreign Policy*, 28.

81. American Embassy Bogotá to Secretary of State Washington, DC, "Extradition: Carlos Lehder Speaks Out," (January 1984), 2, National Security Archive, Narcotics Collection, Colombia: Cartels, U.S. Operations, Corruption, box 8.

82. Associated Press, "Colombian Guerrillas Trying to Disrupt War," *New York Times*, 30 May 1982, sec. A, p. 8.

83. American Embassy Bogotá to Secretary of State Washington, DC, "M-19 Opposition to GOC Spray Campaign" (July 1984), 1, National Security Archive, Narcotics Collection, Colombia: Cartels, U.S. Operations, Corruption, box 8. Contrary to Colombian Police and U.S. embassy findings, Carlos Castaño added that Escobar corrupted Pizzaro and the M-19 and invited them to export cocaine through Panama to Havana, Cuba. See: Maruicio Aranguren Molina, *Mi Confesión*, 43.

84. American Embassy Bogotá to Secretary of State Washington, DC, "Colombian Guerrilla Calls for Drug Mafia to Kill USG Employees" (December 1984), 2, National Security Archive, Narcotics Collection, Colombia: Cartels, U.S. Operations, Corruption, box 8.

85. Sam Dillon, "Colombia Stumbling on the Path to Peace," *Miami Herald*, 11 September 1985, sec. A, p. 11.

86. *Herald* Staff and Wire Reports, "Colombia Resurrects Extradition Treaty," *Miami Herald*, 16 December 1986. An acting interim president signed the treaty in 1979.

87. Merrill Collett, "Drug Barons' Tentacles Run Deep in Colombian Society," *Christian Science Monitor*, 20 November 1987, 1.

88. *Herald* Staff and Wire Reports, "Colombia Resurrects Extradition Treaty," *Miami Herald*, 16 December 1986.

89. Rod Norland, Mark Miller, and David Gonzalez, "Snaring the King of Coke," *Newsweek*, 16 February 1987, 16.

90. Guy Gugliotta and Jeff Leen, *Kings of Cocaine*, 282–285, 303–304.

91. Alan Riding, "Colombia Effort Against Drugs Hits Dead End," *New York Times*, 16 August 1987, sec. A, p. 1; *Economist*, "Colombia: A Law in Limbo," 18 April 1987, 40.

92. Merrill Collett, "Drug Barons' Tentacles Run Deep In Colombian Society," 1; *Economist*, "Colombia: Stronger Than the State," 28 November 1987, 43.

93. Associated Press, "Extradition of Key Suspect in Drug Battle Is Blocked," *St. Petersburg Times*, 19 December 1987, sec. A, p. 2.

94. Lawrence David Aquila, "Colombia Gives U.S. Reach in Drug War, But Limits It," *Christian Science Monitor*, 1 December 1997, 2.

95. U.S. Department of the Army, *Country Study: Colombia* (Washington, DC: Federal Research Division of the Library of Congress, 1997), http://lcweb2.loc.gov/frd/cs/cotoc.html (accessed 14 December 2006).

96. William López Gutiérrez, "Las Políticas de Paz," 250. Barco promoted the Plan Nacional de Rehabilitación (PNR). The PNR was started in 1983 as a political program in the rural areas to promote campesino participation in the formulation and implementation of local investment programs funded by the government. See: Franco Armando Guerrero Albán, *Colombia y Putumayo en Medio de la Encrucijada: Narcotráfico, Fumigaciones, Economía y Soberanía* (Bogotá: Ediciones Claridad, 2005), 137.

97. María Clemencia Ramírez, *Entre el Estado y la Guerrilla*, 44–46, 70–71, 72–76. This study provides a microcosm of Colombia's civil war in Putumayo, the location of a large percentage of illegal coca farming and guerrilla/paramilitary activity. The book's main thesis postulates that the campesinos have been looking for political legitimacy, which had been denied to them in the past. As a consequence of Colombia's long-term history, their economic situation, and the War on Drugs, the campesinos have found themselves caught in the middle of Colombia's civil war as they seek political legitimacy.

98. U.S. Department of Defense, Defense Intelligence Agency, "Special Operations Policy Advisory Group" (15 January 1992), 11, National Security Archive, Narcotics Collection, Drugs: FOIA: DOD, box 39.

99. U.S. Department of Defense, Defense Intelligence Agency, "Colombian Security Force: Challenges and U.S. Assistance" (1988), 4, National Security Archive, Narcotics Collection, Colombia: Cartels, U.S. Operations, Corruption, box 8.

100. American Embassy Bogotá to Secretary of State Washington, DC, "Extradition: Carlos Lehder Speaks Out," 2; Merrill Collett, "Colombia's Drug Lords Waging War on Leftists." Although the Medellín cartel promised to disband the MAS after it reached its peace agreement with the M-19, the MAS became less of a protective force for the cartel and more of a political force. According to Alejandro Reyes, the paramilitaries achieved two objectives for the narco-traffickers: they eliminated leaders under guerrilla influence and created their own base of social support by forming the paramilitaries. See: Alejandro Reyes, "Drug Trafficking and the Guerrilla Movement in Colombia,"122.

101. Merrill Collett, "Colombia's Drug Lords Waging War on Leftists"; Rensselaer Lee, "Dimensions of the South American Cocaine Industry," *Journal of Interamerican Affairs and World Studies* 30, no. 2 (Summer/Fall 1988): 97–98; Human Rights Watch, *Colombia's Killer Networks*, 18–24; Central Intelligence Agency Office of Asian Pacific and Latin American Analysis, "Colombia: Paramilitaries Gaining Strength" (Washington, DC: Central Intelligence Agency, 13 June 1997), 4, National Security Archive, The Colombia Documentation Project, "War In Colombia Vol. III," http://www.gwu.edu/~nsarchiv/NSAEBB/NSAEBB69/part3b.html (accessed 10 April 2006). Members of the Colombian military joined the paramilitaries out of frustration with the military's inability to win against the guerrillas.

102. Fabio Castillo, *La Coca Nostra*, 213; Rensselaer Lee and Patrick Clawson, *The Andean Cocaine Industry*, 184–189.

103. Jacobo Arenas, *Cese el Fuego*, 144–145.

104. Ricardo Vargas Meza, "The FARC, the War, and the Crisis of State," www.nacla.org (accessed 20 February 2006); Ana Carrigan, "A Chronicle of Violence Foretold: State Sponsored Violence in Colombia," *NACLA Report on the Americas*, 28 no. 5 (March/April

1995): 5, http://www.hartford-hwp.com/archives/42/001.html (accessed 14 February 2006); Jonathan Steele, "Third World Review: Uphill Struggle–Colombia," *Guardian*, 4 July 1987. Between June 1986 and June 1994, more than twenty-five thousand civilians died in social and political violence.

105. Merrill Collett, "Colombian Leftwing Reels Under Dirty War Tactics," *Guardian*, 29 September 1987; Mike Reid, "Leftwing Leader Dies in Ambush," *Guardian*, 13 October 1987. Gonzalo Rodríguez Gacha was the cartel member indicted in the killing. According to AUC paramilitary leader Carlos Castaño, cocaine was the reason for Leal's assassination. Gacha accused the FARC of stealing cocaine from him at his facility in Carurú. Moreover, Castaño added that Gacha had trained four hundred men to launch attacks against the FARC in the province of La Uribe in order to break the peace. These men were trained by Israeli and British mercenaries who were retired members of each nation's armed forces. See: Mauricío Aranguren Molina, *Mi Confesión*, 97–100.

106. Mike Reid, "Leftwing Leader Dies in Ambush," *Guardian*, 13 October 1987. Rodrigo Uprimny Yepes and Alfredo Vargas Castaño explain that in spite of the insertion of a new violent faction into the power structure, elements of the state apparatus supported the dirty war. The conflict helped defend existing power against new interests and provided an opportunity to compensate for state power lost to the guerrillas. See: Rodrigo Uprimny Yepes and Alfredo Vargas Castaño, "La Palabra y la Sangre: Violencia, Legalidad y Guerra Sucia," in *La Irrupción del Paraestado*, ed. Germán Palacio (Bogotá: Fondo Editorial CEREC, 1990), 164.

107. House of Representatives Subcommittee on Inter-American Affairs of the Committee of Foreign Affairs, *Foreign Assistance Legislation for Fiscal Year 1981*, 113.

108. Cynthia Gorney, "U.S. Proposes Ambitious Plan to Limit Coca Production in Peru," *Washington Post*, 19 June 1981, sec. A, p. 30.

109. U.S. Agency for International Development (USAID), "Peru Project Paper: Upper Huallaga Valley Area Development (Amendment #2) 527–0277" (Washington, DC: USAID, 10 September 1986), 3, National Security Archive, Narcotics Collection, Agency for International Development Projects, box 1.

110. Caryn C. Hollis, "The Cocaine Industry in Peru's Upper Huallaga Valley" (January 1989), Defense Intelligence Agency, Prepared by the West Europe/Latin America Division, DDB–2200–578–89, 17, National Security Archive, Narcotics Collection, Peru: U.S. Operations, Sendero, Fujimori, (DIA Studies 1989–1991), box 7.

111. USAID, "Peru Project Paper: Upper Huallaga Valley Area Development (Amendment #2) 527–0277," 3.

112. U.S. Department of State, Bureau of International Narcotics Matters, *1985 International Narcotics Control Strategy Report*, 9.

113. John Wall, "U.S. Agency for International Development Evaluation Summary: Upper Huallaga Area Development Project," xv.

114. American Embassy Lima to Secretary of State Washington, DC, "Upper Huallaga Area Development Project" (June 1984), 1, National Security Archive, Narcotics Collection, Peru, U.S. Operations, box 6; Jackson Diehl, "Model Antidrug Drive Fails in Peru," *Washington Post*, 29 December 1984, sec. A, p. 1.

115. Edmundo Morales, "The Political Economy of Cocaine Production," 96.

116. Checchi and Company, "A Review of AID's Narcotics Control Development Assistance Program: Prepared for Development Information and Evaluation USAID," 66.

117. American Embassy Lima to Secretary of State Washington, DC, "Upper Huallaga Area Development Project," 1; House of Representatives Committee on Foreign Affairs, *U.S. Response to Cuban Government Involvement in Narcotics Trafficking*, 145.

118. Checchi and Company, "A Review of AID's Narcotics Control Development Assistance Program: Prepared for Development Information and Evaluation USAID," 70.

119. John Wall, "U.S. Agency for International Development Evaluation Summary: Upper Huallaga Area Development Project," xv.

120. Drug Enforcement Administration, "An Analysis of the Terrorist Insurgent Groups and Their Relationship to Cocaine Trafficking Organizations in the Upper Huallaga Valley of Peru" (Lima: Drug Enforcement Administration, 1 May 1989), 14, National Security Archive, Narcotics Collection, Peru: Drugs, box 36.

121. John Wall, "U.S. Agency for International Development Evaluation Summary: Upper Huallaga Area Development Project," xv.

122. American Embassy Lima to Secretary of State Washington, DC, "International Narcotics Control Strategy" (January 1989), 3–4, National Security Archive, Narcotics Collection, Peru: Documents from FOIA, box 31.

123. Central Intelligence Agency, Directorate of Intelligence, "Latin America Review: Peru" (13 September 1982), 1, National Security Archive, Narcotics Collection, Peru: U.S. Operations, Sendero, Fujimori, (CIA Reports on Sendero 1981–1988), box 7. The Sendero Luminoso was an offshoot of the Bandera Roja, which had broken away from the Movimiento Izquierda Revolucionario/Ejército de Liberación Nacional MIR/ELN alliance in 1965. The Sendero broke away from the Bandera Roja because it felt that the Bandera focused too much on the "urban areas to the detriment of the countryside" and that it was "overly de-emphasizing armed struggle." For more detail on the initial stages of the Sendero's armed struggle in Ayacucho, see: Gustavo Gorriti Ellenbogen, *Sendero: Historia de la Guerra Milenaria en el Peru*, (Lima: Editorial Apoyo, 1990) 11–380.

124. Tammy Arbuckle and Bernard Fitzsimmons, "Peru's Drug War: Vietnam-Era Methods Won't Net Narco-Guerrillas," *International Defense Review* (April 1990): 374; Abimael Guzmán Reynoso, *Guerra Popular en el Perú: Pensamiento Gonzalo*, (Lima: El Diario, 1989), 61–87.

125. Melanie S. Tammen, "Policy Analysis: The Drug War vs. Land Reform in Peru" (Washington, DC: *Cato Institute*, 10 July 1991), 4, National Security Archive, Narcotics Collection, CLIPS: Bolivia and the Andes in General, box 26.

126. Eloy Villacrez R., *Nuestra Guerra Civil: Ayacucho 80–*, (Lima: Graphos 100 Editores, 1985), 16–30. The military dictatorship exiled Villacrez who later fought in the Nicaraguan Revolution. He returned to Peru under a general amnesty in 1980 and wrote intimately about Sendero strategy and the rebellion in Ayacucho. Carlos Tapia argues that the Sendero misjudged the political situation in Peru. The Sendero did not realize that many campesinos had benefited from the military government's reforms during the 1970s, which partially broke the semi-feudal system under which they had lived. Tapia believes this misinterpretation lead to the appearance of rondas (see chapter 7) and the Sendero's eventual downfall. See: Carlos Tapia, *Autodefensa Armada del Campesinado*, (Lima: Centro de Estudios para el Desarrollo y la Participación, 1995), 13–21; Abimael Guzmán Reynoso, *Guerra Popular en el Perú*, 181–204.

127. Drug Enforcement Administration, "An Analysis of the Terrorist Insurgent Groups and Their Relationship to Cocaine Trafficking Organizations," 20. For more detail on Sendero ideology and the initial stages of their armed struggle in Ayacucho between 1979–1980, see: Gustavo Gorriti Ellenbogen, *Sendero: Historia de la Guerra Milenaria en el Peru*, 11–380; Abimael Guzmán Reynoso, *Guerra Popular en el Perú*, 342–361.

128. Martiza Rojas Albertini, *Los Campesinos Cocaleros*, 267–271. For a more detailed analysis of Sendero involvement in the narcotics trade, see chapter 5.

129. Drug Enforcement Administration, "An Analysis of the Terrorist Insurgent Groups and Their Relationship to Cocaine Trafficking Organizations," 24; Central Intelligence Agency, Directorate of Intelligence, "Latin American Review: Peru: Keeping Terrorism in Check" (3 July 1981), 15–17, National Security Archive, Narcotics Collection, Peru, CIA Reports on Sendero 1981–1988, box 7; Carlos Tapia, *Las Fuerzas Armadas y Sendero Luminoso: Dos Estrategias y un Final* (Lima: Instituto de Estudios Peruanos, 1997), 36–39.

130. Martiza Rojas Albertini, *Los Campesinos Cocaleros*, 271.

131. Drug Enforcement Administration, "An Analysis of the Terrorist Insurgent Groups and Their Relationship to Cocaine Trafficking Organizations," 24; Central Intelligence Agency Directorate of Intelligence, "Latin American Review: Peru: Keeping Terrorism in Check," 15–17.

132. Senate Committee on Foreign Relations and the Committee on the Judiciary, *International Terrorism, Insurgency, and Drug Trafficking: Present Trends in Terrorist Activity*, 99th Cong., 1st sess., 13–15 May 1985, 133, 146. Also see John Wall, "U.S. Agency for International Development Evaluation Summary: Upper Huallaga Area Development Project," xv.

133. Senate Committee on Foreign Relations and the Committee on the Judiciary, *International Terrorism, Insurgency, and Drug Trafficking*, 133.

134. Drug Enforcement Administration, "An Analysis of the Terrorist Insurgent Groups and Their Relationship to Cocaine Trafficking Organizations," 25; Senate Committee on Foreign Relations and the Committee on the Judiciary, *International Terrorism, Insurgency, and Drug Trafficking*, 133. Also see Central Intelligence Agency, Directorate of Intelligence, "Peru" (20 October 1989), 4, National Security Archive, Narcotics Collection, Peru: U.S. Operations, Sendero, Fujimori, (Max Holland Documents), box 6.

135. Checchi and Company, "A Review of AID's Narcotics Control Development Assistance Program: Prepared for Development Information and Evaluation USAID," 70.

136. Marlise Simons, "Peruvian Rebels Halt U.S. Drive Against Cocaine," *New York Times*, 13 August 1984, sec. A, p. 1.

137. House of Representatives, Staff Study Mission to Southeast Asia, South America, Central America, and the Caribbean August 1984 to January 1985, *U.S. Narcotics Control Programs Overseas: An Assessment*, 99th Cong., 1st sess., 22 February 1985, 20–21.

138. House of Representatives, Staff Study Mission to Southeast Asia, South America, Central America, and the Caribbean August 1984 to January 1985, *U.S. Narcotics Control Programs Overseas*, 20–21; U.S. Department of State, Bureau of International Narcotics Matters, *1985 International Narcotics Control Strategy Report*, 117–118.

139. American Embassy Lima to Secretary of State Washington, DC, "Ambassador Meets with Head of Joint Chiefs of Staff Zevallos; Minister of War Julia; and Foreign Minister Percovich on November 22" (November 1984), 1–2, National Security Archive, Narcotics Collection, Peru: Documents from FOIA, box 31.

140. American Embassy Lima to Secretary of State Washington, DC, "1985 INCSR Mid-Year Update" (July 1985), 2, National Security Archive, Narcotics Collection, Peru: Documents from FOIA, box 31.

141. American Embassy Lima to Secretary of State Washington, DC, "GOP Renews Regional State of Emergency in Coca-Growing Area" (December 1984), 1, National Security Archive, Narcotics Collection, Peru, Documents from FOIA, box 31; Marlise Simons, "Peruvian Rebels Halt U.S. Drive Against Cocaine," sec. A, p. 1. The U.S. expected the Peruvians to eradicate eight thousand hectares.

142. José E. Gonzales Manrique, "Guerrillas and Coca in the Upper Huallaga Valley," 107–108.

143. House of Representatives Staff Study Mission to Southeast Asia, South America, Central America, and the Caribbean August 1984 to January 1985, *U.S. Narcotics Control Programs Overseas*, 20–21; U.S. Department of State, Bureau of International Narcotics Matters, *1985 International Narcotics Control Strategy Report*, 117–118.

144. House of Representatives Staff Study Mission to Southeast Asia, South America, Central America, and the Caribbean August 1984 to January 1985, *U.S. Narcotics Control Programs Overseas*, 20–21.

145. José E. Gonzales Manrique, "Guerrillas and Coca in the Upper Huallaga Valley," 108.

146. Carlos Tapia, *Las Fuerzas Armadas y Sendero Luminoso*, 39–43.

147. Melanie S. Tammen, "Policy Analysis: The Drug War vs. Land Reform in Peru," 14; U.S. Department of State, Bureau of International Narcotics Matters, *1989 International Narcotics Control Strategy Report*, 89–90; U.S. Department of State, Bureau of International Narcotics Matters, *1985 International Narcotics Control Strategy Report*, 117–118.

148. USAID, "Peru Project Paper: Upper Huallaga Valley Area Development (Amendment #3) 527–0244" (Washington, DC: *USAID*, 30 September 1988), 6, National Security Archive, Narcotics Collection, Agency for International Development Projects, box 1. Moreover, between 1983 and 1986, a total of only 1,291 metric tons of coca leaf had been seized.

149. Richard B. Craig, "Illicit Drug Traffic: Implications for South American Source Countries," 14.

150. USAID, "Peru Project Paper: Upper Huallaga Valley Area Development (Amendment #3) 527–0244," 6.

151. Melanie S. Tammen, "Policy Analysis: The Drug War vs. Land Reform in Peru," 14.

152. American Embassy Lima to Secretary of State Washington, DC, "UNCLAS Section 11 of 12, E.1 Resource Estimates" (January 1988), 7, 15, National Security Archive, Narcotics Collection, Drug Documents, Peru: Counternarcotics, box 51.

153. American Embassy Lima to Secretary of State Washington, DC, "1986 INCSR Mid-Year Update" (July 1986), 2, National Security Archive, Narcotics Collection, Drug Documents, Peru: Counternarcotics, box 51.

154. Mike Reid, "Army Takes Over Peru Provinces," *Guardian*, 12 November 1987, 1; American Embassy Lima to Secretary of State Washington, DC, "UNCLAS Section 11 of 12, B.2 Factors Affecting Production" (January 1988), 7, National Security Archive, Narcotics Collection, Drug Documents, Peru: Counternarcotics, box 51.

155. The Institute for Counter-Terrorism, "Terrorist Organizations: Movimiento Revolucionario Tupac Amaru," http://www.ict.org.il/inter_ter/orgdet.cfm?orgid=42 (accessed 14 February 2006); Drug Enforcement Administration, "An Analysis of the Terrorist Insurgent Groups and Their Relationship to Cocaine Trafficking Organizations," 32. For more on the MRTA's origins during the 1960s, see: Sara Beatriz Guardia, *Proceso: A Campesinos de la Guerrilla Túpac Amaru*, (Lima: Compañía Impresiones y Publicidad, 1972).

156. Peru has a large Japanese immigrant population. Late in the nineteenth century, Peru offered many opportunities to Japanese farmers who were unable to find employment in Japan.

157. Barbara Durr, "Robin Hood Guerrillas on the Warpath," sec. I, p. 5.

158. American Embassy Lima (Jordan) to Secretary of State Washington, DC, "President Garcia Speaks Out Against Pucayacu Killings" (April 1986), 1, National Security Archive, Narcotics Collection, Peru: Documents from FOIA, box 31.

159. House of Representatives Committee on Foreign Affairs, *Narcotics Review in South America*, 100th Cong., 2nd sess., 17 and 22 March 1988, 4. Statement of Robert S. Gelbard, deputy assistant secretary of state for South America (1985–88). Gelbard later became the ambassador to Bolivia (1988–91) and principal deputy assistant secretary of state for inter-American Affairs (1991–93).

160. USAID, "Abbreviated PID for Upper Huallaga Area Development Project no. 527–0244" (1988), National Security Archive, Narcotics Collection, Peru-Colombia-Andes Documents Part I, PEAH, box 49.

161. American Embassy Lima to Secretary of State Washington, DC, "FY 1987 Financial Planning" (November 1986), 2, National Security Archive, Narcotics Collection, Peru: Documents from FOIA, box 31. The embassy added, "[T]he timing may never be better to push for a greater infusion of resources given the current heightened drug interest and awareness and favorable climates for drug enforcement and control."

162. John Wall, "U.S. Agency for International Development Evaluation Summary: Upper Huallaga Area Development Project," xvii.

163. Edward Schumacher, "Bolivian Leaders Tied to Lucrative Cocaine Trade," *New York Times*, 31 August 1981, sec. A, p. 1.

164. Walter Pincus, "Aid to Bolivia Ties to Progress in Cocaine War," *Washington Post*, 8 November 1982, sec. A. p. 1.

165. House of Representatives Committee on Foreign Affairs, *U.S. Response to Cuban Government Involvement in Narcotics Trafficking*, 105.

166. House of Representatives Staff Study Mission to Southeast Asia, South America, Central America, and the Caribbean August 1984 to January 1985, *U.S. Narcotics Control Programs Overseas*, 17–18; *New York Times*, "Caged Leopards of the Drug War," 12 September 1984, sec. A, p. 16.

167. Don Bostwick PhD, Joseph Dorsey PhD, and James Jones PhD, "USAID Evaluation of the Chapare Regional Development Project," 15, 16.

168. USAID, "Audit of USAID/Bolivia Chapare Regional Development Project no. 511–0543, Audit Report no 1–511–91–013" (29 August 1991), i, National Security Archive, Narcotics Collection, Agency for International Development Projects, box 1.

169. Don Bostwick PhD, Joseph Dorsey PhD, and James Jones PhD, "USAID Evaluation of the Chapare Regional Development Project," 16.

170. House of Representatives Committee on Foreign Affairs, *U.S. Response to Cuban Government Involvement in Narcotics Trafficking*, 108.

171. Jackson Diehl, "U.S. Drug Crackdown Stalls in Bolivia," *Washington Post*, 23 January 1984, sec. A, p. 1; U.S. Department of State, Bureau of International Narcotics Matters, *1989 International Narcotics Control Strategy Report*, 63–64; U.S. Department of State, Bureau of International Narcotics Matters, *1985 International Narcotics Control Strategy Report*, 52–53.

172. Jackson Diehl, "U.S. Drug Crackdown Stalls in Bolivia," sec. A, p. 1.

173. Associated Press, "Bolivian President Is Kidnapped, Then Freed in Aborted Coup," *New York Times*, 1 July 1984, sec. A, p. 1.

174. Marlise Simons, "U.S. Envoy Linked to Foiling of Bolivia Coup," *New York Times*, 6 July 1984, sec. A, p. 5.

175. *New York Times*, "Caged Leopards of the Drug War," sec. A, p. 16.

176. *Guardian*, "President Fasting: President Siles Zuazo of Bolivia on Hunger Strike in Protest at Censure of Anti-Narcotics Campaign,"*Guardian*, 27 October 1984, 1.

177. Hugh O'Shaughnessy, "Bolivian President Removes Army Chief," *Financial Times*, 31 December 1984, sec. I, p. 8.

178. Mary Helen Spooner, "Bolivians Sniff at U.S. Cocaine Plan," *Financial Times*, 11 May 1983, sec. I, p. 2.

179. American Embassy La Paz to Secretary of State Washington, DC, "Campesinos and the Battle for Coca Control in the Chapare," (August 1984), 1–2, 5, National Security Archive, Narcotics Collection, Bolivia, Documents from FOIA, box 33. Coca growers of the Yungas and Chapare formed the single organization called CONCOCA.

180. *New York Times*, "Caged Leopards of the Drug War," sec. A, p. 16.

181. U.S. Embassy La Paz to Secretary of State Washington, DC, "Campesinos and the Battle for Coca Control in the Chapare," 6.

182. Joel Brinkley, "Bolivia in Turmoil at Drug Crackdown," *New York Times*, 12 September 1984, sec. A, p. 1.

183. *Washington Post*, "Drug Projects Net Threats, Little Gain," *Washington Post*, 29 December 1984, sec. A, p. 12.

184. Mimi Whitefield, "Long Live Coca Andeans Cry," *Miami Herald*, 9 December 1985, sec. A, p. 1.

185. Bradley Graham, "Bolivian Runs Risk in Drug Drive," *Washington Post*, 17 July 1986, sec. A, p. 1.

186. Gobierno de Bolivia, "Plan Trienal de la Lucha Contra el Narcotráfico" (Noviembre 1986), in *Coca-Cronología: 100 Documentos Sobre la Problemática de la Coca y la Lucha Contra las Drogas: Bolivia, 1986–1992,* ed. Centro de Documentación y Información (Cochabamba Bolivia: Talleres Gráficos Kipus, 1992), 15–18.

187. American Embassy La Paz to Secretary of State Washington, DC, "Narcotics: Cochabamba City Again in Hands of Coca Farmers; UMOPAR Threatened" (June 1985), 1–2, National Security Archive, Narcotics Collection, Bolivia, Documents from FOIA, box 33.

188. Bradley Graham, "Bolivian Runs Risk in Drug Drive," sec. A, p. 1.

189. Douglas J. Pool et al, "Evaluation of Chapare Regional Development Project Prepared for USAID Bolivia Project no. 511–T–067" (Gainesville, FL: *Tropical Research and Development*, September 1986), 19.

190. See endnote 189 and also Richard B. Craig, *Illicit Drug Traffic: Implications for South American Source Countries: Prepared for the Conference on International Drugs*, 18; Russell Crandall, *Driven By Drugs*, 31. Russell Crandall indicates that Blast Furnace was the precedent-setting operation that "increasingly militarized" U.S. policy in the northern Andes.

191. Howard Gehring to Lieutenant General R. Dean Tice, untitled (Washington, DC: Office of the Vice President, 13 June 1986), 1, National Security Archive, Narcotics Collection, Bolivia, Documents from FOIA, box 33.

192. *Christian Science Monitor*, "U.S. Sends Troops, Helicopters to Help Bolivia Fight Drugs," 17 July 1986, 4.

193. USCINCSO Quarry Heights to Secretary of Defense Washington, DC, "Proposed Public Affairs Guidance: Blast Furnace Transition Operation" (November 1986), 1, National Security Archive, Narcotics Collection, Bolivia, Documents from FOIA, box 33; USCINSCO Quarry Heights to Aif 7084, "Situation Overview Operations, ID/SITREP/USCINCSO/060/OCT" (October 1986), 1, National Security Archive, Narcotics Collection, Bolivia, Documents from FOIA, box 33.

194. Barbara Durr, "Drugs War Creates Dilemma for Bolivia," sec. I, p. 4. For more on the NEP, see chapter 2.

195. Bradley Graham, "Drug Raids Raise Doubts in Bolivia; Role of U.S. Troops Triggers Concerns," *Washington Post*, 21 July 1986, sec. A, p. 1.

196. USCINCSO Quarry Heights to AIG 7084, "Situation Overview, ID/SITREP/USCINCSO/032/AUG" (August 1986), 1, National Security Archive, Narcotics Collection, Bolivia, Documents from FOIA, box 33.

197. *New York Times*, "Bolivian Coca Growers Are Said to Ease Siege," 12 January 1986, sec. A, p. 6; Mac Margolis, "Bolivian Economy Hooked on Cocaine," p. 1.

198. Bradley Graham, "U.S. Troops Phasing Out Bolivian Anti-Drug Drive," sec. A, p. 13.

199. Gobierno de Bolivia, "Plan Trienal de la Lucha Contra el Narcotráfico," 22.

200. U.S. Department of State, "U.S.-Bolivia Narcotics Control Agreement, Program Agreement" (24 February 1987), 4–8, National Security Archive, Narcotics Collection, Bolivia: Joint Operations, Production Rates, Cocaine Coup, box 5.

201. Mike Reid, "Cash Crisis for Bolivian Drug Battle," *Guardian*, 7 April 1987, 1.

202. U.S. Department of State, "U.S.-Bolivia Narcotics Control Agreement, Program Agreement," 7; Richard B. Craig, *Illicit Drug Traffic: Implications for South American Source Countries: Prepared for the Conference on International Drugs*, 19.

203. Mike Reid, "Cash Crisis for Bolivian Drug Battle," 1.

204. U.S. Department of State, "U.S.-Bolivia Narcotics Control Agreement, Program Agreement," 9–10.

205. Gobierno de Bolivia, "Plan Trienal de la Lucha Contra el Narcotráfico," 22.

206. Secretary of State to American Embassy La Paz, "Letter from Bolivian President Estenssoro to President Reagan" (February 1987), 1, National Security Archive, Narcotics Collection, Bolivia, Documents from FOIA, box 33; USAID, "Audit of USIAD/Bolivia's Chapare Regional Development Project Activities Managed by the Bolivian Institute of Agriculture and Cattle Technology/Chapare for the Year Ended December 31, 1989, Audit Report no. 1–511–91–17–N" (22 January 1991), 2, National Security Archive, Narcotics Collection, Agency for International Development Projects, box 2.

207. José Antonio Quiroga, "Campesino, Coca y Agricultura," in *Debate Agrario: La Economía Campesina y el Cultivo de la Coca Instituto* (December 1987), ed. Latinoamericano de Investigaciones Sociales (La Paz: Editorial Offset Boliviana Imprenta, 1987), 22. In another meeting, Quiroga stated that the Bolivian government was going back on its word because it had offered $7,800 to the campesinos for each hectare destroyed. See: José Antonio Quiroga, "Comentario," in *Debate Agrario: La Economía Campesina y el Cultivo de la Coca Instituto* (Marzo 1988), ed. Latinoamericano de Investigaciones Sociales (La Paz: Editorial Offset Boliviana Imprenta, 1988), 24.

208. Bradley Graham, "Bolivian Barometer: Coca Price Falls," *Washington Post*, 27 July 1986, sec. A, p. 1; Bradley Graham, "Drug Raids Raise Doubts in Bolivia; Role of U.S. Troops Triggers Concerns," sec. A, p. 1.

209. USCINCSO Quarry Heights to Joint Chiefs of Staff Washington, DC, "Situation Overview, ID/SITREP/USCINCSO/018/JUL" (July 1986), 1, National Security Archive, Narcotics Collection, Bolivia, Documents from FOIA, box 33; Bradley Graham, "Bolivian Barometer: Coca Price Falls," sec. A, p. 1.

210. House of Representatives Committee on Foreign Affairs, *Narcotics Review in South America*, 135.

211. Bradley Graham, "U.S. Troops Phasing Out Bolivian Antidrug Drive," sec. A, p. 13. Estimates state that prices rose from twenty dollars to sixty dollars per one hundred pounds of coca leaf. The estimate above is calculated in price per pound for clarification and consistency of argument.

212. Jay Mathews, "Bolivia Coca Output Restored, Officials Say: Impact of U.S. Aided Raids Found Fleeting," *Washington Post*, 6 February 1987, sec. A, p. 14.

213. USAID, "Bolivia: Project Paper Economic Stabilization Program project number 511–K–605" (Washington, DC: USAID,1990), 41, National Security Archive, Narcotics Collection, Agency for International Development Projects, box 2; U.S. Department of State, Bureau of International Narcotics Matters, *1989 International Narcotics Control Strategy Report*, 63–64; U.S. Department of State, Bureau of International Narcotics Matters, *1985 International Narcotics Control Strategy Report*, 52–53. Until 1987, there were no recorded statistics for Bolivian coca leaf seizures.

214. Bradley Graham, "Drug Raids Raise Doubts in Bolivia; Role of U.S. Troops Triggers Concerns," sec. A, p. 1.

215. Roger Cortéz Hurtado, "Mensaje al Congress of the Asociación Nacional de Productores de Coca," in *La Guerra de la Coca: Una Sombra Sobre los Andes*, ed. Roger Cortéz Hurtado, (La Paz: Centro de Información para el Desarrollo, 1992), 73.

216. Los Tiempos, "Campesinos Declaran Estado de Emergencia" (3 Noviembre 1987), in *Coca-Cronología: 100 Documentos Sobre la Problemática de la Coca y la Lucha Contra las Drogas: Bolivia, 1986–1992*, ed. Centro de Documentación y Información (Cochabamba: Talleres Gráficos Kipus, 1992), 68.

217. Sarita Kendall, "Economies Under the Influence of Cocaine," sec. I, p. 4. Ecuador was receiving roughly three hundred million dollars from the narcotics trade mostly because it acted as a transshipment point. Ecuador never developed a coca-growing campesino population, as did its neighbors, Peru and Bolivia.

Chapter 4: Reagan, the Drug War, and the Narco-Terrorist Nexus

1. Soviet and Cuban military aid to the Sandinista government expanded dramatically after the revolution in 1979. Within a week of their victory, the Sandinistas brought in two hundred Cuban military advisors, and the Soviet Union sent five generals to advise the Sandinista Army. Nicaragua also received Soviet-made tanks in early 1981, giving it an unprecedented advantage over its neighbors. Starting in 1981, Nicaragua sent pilots to Bulgaria and Czechoslovakia to learn how to fly Soviet MiG-17 and MiG-21 jet fighters. In 1982, Soviet military support became much more overt, as the Soviets supplied helicopters and military vehicles. See: Timothy Ashby, *The Bear in the Back Yard: Moscow's Caribbean Strategy* (Lexington, MA: Lexington Books, 1987), 109–24.

2. Scott Armstrong, "More-Potent Drugs Invade the U.S.," *Christian Science Monitor*, 27 May 1986, 1.

3. Nancy Dunne, "U.S. Fails to Stem the Rising Drug Tide," *Financial Times*, 25 July 1986, sec. 1, p. 4.

4. Brian Duffy et al, "War on Drugs: More than a Short-Term High?" *U.S. News and World Report*, 29 September 1986, 28.

5. House of Representatives Committee on Narcotics Abuse and Control and the Committee on Children, Youth, and Families, *The Crack Cocaine Crisis*, 99th Cong., 2nd sess., 15 July 1986, 2.

6. Office of National Drug Control Policy, *ONDCP Drug Policy Clearinghouse Fact Sheet*, 6. The source cited for these figures was the Drug Abuse Warning Network (DAWN).

7. Office of National Drug Control Policy, *Appendix: National Drug Control Strategy 1997, FY 1998 Budget* (Rockville, MD: Drug Policy Information Clearing House, 1997), www.ncjrs.gov/htm/data.htm (accessed 5 March 2006). The report cites ABT Associates Incorporated as the source. Data for this estimate comes from System to Retrieve Information from Drug Evidence (STRIDE), Drug Enforcement Administration, 1981–1996.

8. House of Representatives Committee on Narcotics Abuse and Control, *Cocaine Babies*, 100th Cong., 1st sess., 16 October 1987, 79. Statement of Charles Rangel.

9. Andrea Stone, "Drug Epidemic's Tiny Victims; Crack Babies Born to a Life of Suffering," *USA Today*, 8 June 1989, sec. A, p. 3; Pediatrics for Parents Inc., "Crack Babies" (Gale Group of Thomson Corporation Company, 1990); Cheryl Sullivan, "U.S. Health Care Crisis in the Making," *Christian Science Monitor*, 15 February 1989, 1. Based on the assumption that four million women were pregnant and 10 percent of them used cocaine during their pregnancy, the estimate of 375,000 is not far off. During 1992, survey data from a national sample of 2,613 women who delivered babies in fifty-two urban and rural hospitals estimated that 221,000 women who gave birth in 1992 used illicit drugs. Marijuana and cocaine were the most frequently used illicit drugs. An estimated 2.9 percent, or 119,000 women, used marijuana; another 1.1 percent, or 45,000 women, used cocaine during their pregnancy. See: Robert Mathias, "NIDA Notes: Women and Drug Use," *National Institute for Drug Awareness* 10, no. 1 (January–February 1995).

10. T. R. Reid, "New Assault Planned Against Formidable Foe; Victories Are Elusive in U.S. War Against Drugs," *Washington Post*, 10 August 1986, sec. A, p. 1.

11. Ronald Reagan, "Address to the Nation on the Campaign Against Drug Abuse" (14 September 1986), *The Public Papers of the Presidents of the United States* (Washington, DC: Office of the Federal Register, National Archives and Records Service, 1988), 1181.

12. Ronald Reagan, "Remarks on Signing the Just Say No to Drugs Week Proclamation" (20 May 1986), *The Public Papers of the Presidents of the United States* (Washington, DC: Office of the Federal Register, National Archives and Records Service, 1988) 629.

13. Michael White, "Crack at Prime Time for Ron and Nancy/U.S. President and First Lady Make Nationwide Appeal Against Drug Abuse," *Guardian*, 15 September 1986.

14. Lieutenant Colonel Juan L. Orama, *U.S. Military Evolution in Counternarcotics Operations*, 14.

15. Ronald Reagan, "Message to the Congress Transmitting Proposed Legislation to Combat Drug Abuse and Trafficking" (15 September 1986), *The Public Papers of the Presidents of the United States* (Washington, DC: Office of the Federal Register, National Archives and Records Service, 1988) 1180–1181, 1187.

16. Joel Brinkley, "Anti-Drug Law: Words, Deeds, Political Expediency," *New York Times*, 27 October 1986, sec. A, p. 18.

17. Ronald Reagan, "Remarks Announcing the Campaign Against Drug Abuse and a Question and Answer Session With Reporters" (4 August 1986), *The Public Papers of the Presidents of the United States* (Washington, DC: Office of the Federal Register, National Archives and Records Service, 1988), 1046; Joel Brinkley, "Anti Drug Law: Words, Deeds, Political Expediency," sec. A, p. 18.

18. Lieutenant Colonel Juan L. Orama, *U.S. Military Evolution in Counternarcotics Operations*, 14.

19. House of Representatives Committee on Narcotics Abuse and Control, *Implementation of the Anti-Drug Abuse Act 1986*, 100th Cong., 1st sess., 1988, 1–2, 6–7.

20. According to Ann Wrobleski, the Anti-Drug Abuse Act prevented the U.S. government from giving aircraft to foreign countries, thus the State Department had to purchase, operate, and maintain all aircraft used in Latin America. This created a greater financial burden for the INM, which was already cash poor. See: Ann Wrobleski, "Letter to the Editor," *New York Review of Books* 36, no. 3 (2 March 1989), http://www.nybooks.com/archives/htsearch (accessed 13 November 2006).

21. Joel Brinkley, "Anti Drug Law: Words, Deeds, Political Expediency," sec. A, p. 18.

22. Senate Committee on Foreign Relations, *International Narcotics Control and Foreign Assistance Certification*, 12–13.

23. House of Representatives Committee on Foreign Affairs, *U.S. International Narcotics Control Programs*, 99th Cong., 1st sess., 19 March 1985, 8–10. Emphasis added.

24. Joel Brinkley, "Drug Crops Are Up in Export Nations, State Department Says," *New York Times*, 15 February 1985, sec. A, p. 1.

25. Senate Committee on Foreign Relations, *International Narcotics Control and Foreign Assistance Certification*, 2, 4, 8.

26. K. Larry Storrs, *Drug Certification/Designation Procedures for Illicit Narcotics Producing and Transit Countries* (Washington, DC: Congressional Research Service, U.S. Library of Congress, 22 September 2003), 13. The source cites all certification between 1987 and 2001, using the "U.S. State Department's International Narcotics Control Summary." The United States did not decertify any northern Andean country until 1996, when it ruled against Colombia. However, between 1993 and 1994, Bolivia received certification only on the basis of national interest, as did Peru between 1994 and 1995.

27. U.S. Congress, "Chapter 18, Military Cooperation with Civilian Law Enforcement Officials" (1 December 1981), in *Public Law 97–86, 95th Statute*, 1114–1115, 1117, National Security Archive, Narcotics Collection, U.S. Policy/Military Action: War on Drugs (U.S. Army Information), box 17.

28. Joanne Omang, "Military Role in Drug Fight Outlined; Services Could Plan Assaults, Equip and Transport Police," *Washington Post*, 9 June 1986, sec. A, p. 4.

29. Coletta Youngers, "The War in the Andes: The Military Role in U.S. International Drug Policy, Issue Brief #2" (Washington, DC: Washington Office on Latin America, 14 December 1990, 6.

30. Joanne Omang, "Crack Down on Drugs, U.S. Is Urged; Law Makers Suggest Foreign Aid Cuts," *Washington Post*, 20 March 1985, sec. A, p. 3.

31. George C. Wilson, "The Military Urges Wider Drug War, Training Central American Teams, Blocking Transport Envisioned," *Washington Post*, 20 June 1985, sec. A, p. 22.

32. Caspar W. Weinberger to Charles B. Rangel, "Response to Letter Sent on July 18" (Washington, DC: The Pentagon, Office of the Secretary of Defense, 5 Aug 1985), National Security Archive, Narcotics Collection, U.S. Policy/Military Action: War on Drugs (U.S. Army Information), box 17. They had not conducted counternarcotics operations up to this point.

33. Caspar W. Weinberger to Thomas P. O'Neill, Jr. "Letter Regarding Public Law 99–83 Concerning Increased Assistance from the Department of Defense" (Washington, DC: The Pentagon, Office of the Secretary of Defense, 26 November 1985), National Security Archive, Narcotics Collection, U.S. Policy/Military Action: War on Drugs (U.S. Army Information), box 17.

34. George C. Wilson, "The Military Urges Wider Drug War," sec. A, p. 22.

35. There has been a great deal of debate on the issue of the narco-Communist nexus and the narco-guerrilla. Previous research into the narco-Communist nexus has divided along partisan lines. Rachel Ehrenfeld and Joseph D. Douglas have offered right-wing condemnations of Cuba and the Sandinistas, and Alexander Cockburn and Peter Dale Scott have made left-wing accusations against the CIA and the Contras. Rachel Ehrenfeld, *Narco-Terrorism* (New York: Basic Books, 1990), ix–225; Joseph D. Douglass, *Red Cocaine*, vii–179; Alexander Cockburn and Jeffrey St. Clair, *Whiteout*, vii–408; Peter Dale Scott and Jonathan Marshall, *Cocaine Politics*, vii–279.

36. Ronald Reagan, "Address to the Nation on the Situation in Nicaragua" (16 March 1986), *The Public Papers of the Presidents of the United States* (Washington, DC: Office of the Federal Register, National Archives and Records Service, 1988), 356.

37. David Hoffman, "Raid Is 1st Under Reagan Order; Bush Lobbied for Directive Over Pentagon Objections," *Washington Post*, 16 July 1986, sec. A, p. 16. This directive was first put into use during the Blast Furnace Operation in Bolivia.

38. Angus Deming and John Barry, "Reluctant Recruits," *Newsweek*, 28 July 1986, 30.

39. Ibid; David Hoffman, "Raid Is 1st Under Reagan Order," sec. A, p. 16.

40. Edward Walsh, "House Votes Anti-Drug Legislation; Measure Would Allow Use of Death Penalty, Military Intervention," *Washington Post*, 12 September 1986, sec. A, p. 1; David L. Westrate, interview by author, 10 November 2006, Buffalo, tape recording. David L. Westrate was the deputy administrator for the DEA.

41. Keith B. Richburg, "Reagan Orders Drug Trade as Security Threat, Widens Military Role," *Washington Post*, 8 June 1986, sec. A, p. 28. This language was used by Vice President Bush.

42. Ibid., 39; George Schultz, "A Forward Look at Foreign Policy" (Washington, DC: U.S. Department of State, 19 October 1984).

43. House of Representatives Committee on Foreign Affairs, *U.S. International Narcotics Control Programs*, 33.

44. Michael Satchell and Richard Z. Chesnoff, "Narcotics: Terror's New Ally," 30.

45. Reed Irvine, "Cuba's Show Trial" (Washington, DC: Accuracy in Media Incorporated, July 1989), 1; Marvin Alisky, "U.S. Mustn't Fall for Castro's Sudden Concern for Drug Smuggling," *New York City Tribune*, 7 July 1989.

46. Rachel Ehrenfeld, "Narco-Terrorism: Paper to be Presented at the USIP Meeting on Secret Warfare Activities by Transnational Groups and Non-State Entities: The Middle East and Latin America," University of Miami, 6 January 1990, 4.

47. Alfred A. McCoy, *The Politics of Heroin*, 38–41, 74–75. During the Cuban revolution, Cuban gangsters fled to the United States. This allowed the mob to set up new narcotics distribution networks through the U.S. that were unknown to U.S. police or Interpol. These connections were later exploited by Cuba and Latin America's narcotics cartels.

48. Reed Irvine, "Cuba's Show Trial," 1–2. Irvine cites a *Wall Street Journal* article printed on June 23, 1989 that cites the DEA as the source of this report.

49. George H. Gaffney to District Supervisor Casey, "Cuba-Opium and Marihuana Growth" (18 August 1965), 1–2 (Washington, DC: Records of the Drug Enforcement Administration), Bureau of Narcotics and Dangerous Drugs, Subject Files of the Bureau of Narcotics and Dangerous Drugs 1916–1970, Cuba, box 154. Gaffney was listed as the acting commissioner of narcotics.

50. Henry L. Giordano to Richard Ottineger, "Letter with Reference to Letter of October 18, 1965" (22 October 1965), 1–2 (Washington, DC: Records of the Drug Enforcement Administration), Bureau of Narcotics and Dangerous Drugs, Subject Files of the Bureau of Narcotics and Dangerous Drugs 1916–1970, Cuba, box 154. Giordano was the commissioner of narcotics.

51. Henry L Giordano to David C. Acheson, "Cuba: Your memo 3-3-66 with Attachments" (7 March 1966), 1–2 (Washington, DC: Records of the Drug Enforcement Administration), Bureau of Narcotics and Dangerous Drugs, Subject Files of the Bureau of Narcotics and Dangerous Drugs 1916–1970, Cuba, box 154. Acheson was listed as the special assistant to the secretary for enforcement.

52. David C. Acheson to Senator Henry M. Jackson, "In Connection with Mr. John N. L. White's Letter" (10 March 1966), 1 (Washington, DC: Records of the Drug Enforcement Administration), Bureau of Narcotics and Dangerous Drugs, Subject Files of the Bureau of Narcotics and Dangerous Drugs 1916-1970, Cuba, box 154.

53. Joseph D. Douglass, *Red Cocaine*, x–xi, 16–17, 68–69. Much of the information provided in this book comes from the Czechoslovakian defector General Jan Sejna. Sejna was the chief of the Communist Party at the Ministry of Defense in Czechoslovakia who defected to the United States in February 1968.

54. J. Edgar Hoover to Commissioner Bureau of Narcotics, "Letter from Independent Commandos Against Communism, Addressed August 10 1967" (28 September 1967), 1 (Washington, DC: Records of the Drug Enforcement Administration) Bureau of Narcotics and Dangerous Drugs, Subject Files of the Bureau of Narcotics and Dangerous Drugs 1916–1970, Cuba, box 154. The letter lists Castro's agents as "Garcia" (no first name), from Jackson Heights, New York; Mario Treto, from Elmhurst, New York; and Rosendo Martínez, from Tampa, Florida.

55. J. Edgar Hoover to Commissioner Bureau of Narcotics, "Alleged Hi-Jacking of Aircraft by Cuban Agents March–September 1967" (31 October 1967), 1–2 (Washington, DC:, Records of the Drug Enforcement Administration) Bureau of Narcotics and Dangerous Drugs, Subject Files of the Bureau of Narcotics and Dangerous Drugs 1916–1970, Cuba, box 154. The FBN was a precursor to the BNDD, from which the DEA was formed.

56. Egil Krogh Jr., "Heroin Politics and Policy under President Nixon," 39–42. By 1971, an estimated 15 to 20 percent of U.S. soldiers were heroin users.

57. *New York Times*, untitled, 15 January 1969, 95.

58. Rachel Ehrenfeld, "Narco-Terrorism: Paper to be Presented at the USIP Meeting on Secret Warfare Activities by Transnational Groups and Non-State Entities: The Middle East and Latin America," 4.

59. Joseph D. Douglass, *Red Cocaine,* 79.

60. Rachel Ehrenfeld, "Narco-Terrorism: Paper to be Presented at the USIP Meeting on Secret Warfare Activities by Transnational Groups and Non-State Entities: The Middle East and Latin America," 4–5.

61. House of Representatives and Senate Subcommittee on Security and Terrorism of the Committee on the Judiciary, the Subcommittee on Western Hemisphere Affairs of the Foreign Relations Committee, and the Senate Drug Enforcement Caucus, "The Cuban Government's Involvement in Facilitating International Drug Traffic," 98th Cong., 1st sess., 30 April 1983, 81.

62. Rachel Ehrenfeld, "Narco-Terrorism: Paper to be Presented at the USIP Meeting on Secret Warfare Activities," 5. Ehrenfeld cites Selwyn Rabb in the *New York Times* as the source

for this information, yet the article never mentions Ravelo-Renedo. See: Selwyn Rabb, "A Defector Tells of Drug Dealing by Cuban Agents," *New York Times*, 4 April 1983. However, testimony taken by the U.S. Congress from José Blandon, an intelligence aid to Manuel Noriega, confirms that this event did take place. See: Senate Subcommittee on Terrorism, Narcotics, and International Operations of the Committee on Foreign Relations, *Drugs, Law Enforcement, and Foreign Policy*, 65–66.

63. Michael Satchell and Richard Z. Chesnoff, "Narcotics: Terror's New Ally," 30.

64. Senate Subcommittee on Terrorism, Narcotics, and International Operations of the Committee on Foreign Relations, *Drugs, Law Enforcement, and Foreign Policy*, 46–58; Selwyn Rabb, "A Defector Tells of Drug Dealing by Cuban Agents," sec. B, p. 1.

65. Senate Subcommittee on Terrorism, Narcotics, and International Operations of the Committee on Foreign Relations, *Drugs, Law Enforcement, and Foreign Policy*, 46–58.

66. House of Representatives and Senate Subcommittee on Security and Terrorism of the Committee on the Judiciary, the Subcommittee on Western Hemisphere Affairs of the Foreign Relations Committee, and the Senate Drug Enforcement Caucus, *The Cuban Government's Involvement in Facilitating International Drug Traffic*, 45 (Testimony of Estevez Perez to the Congressional Committee, 30 April 1983), 82, 115–122.

67. Ibid., 32–33, 58. Testimony of David Lorenzo Perez to the U.S. Congress, 30 April 1983. Perez was the man who worked on the Florida side of Crump and Guillot Lara's operation.

68. Rachel Ehrenfeld, *Narco-Terrorism*, 32.

69. House of Representatives and Senate Subcommittee on Security and Terrorism of the Committee on the Judiciary, the Subcommittee on Western Hemisphere Affairs of the Foreign Relations Committee, and the Senate Drug Enforcement Caucus, *The Cuban Government's Involvement in Facilitating International Drug Traffic*, 19–20. Testimony of Crump in hearings before Congress, 30 April 1983.

70. Ibid., 83.

71. Ibid., 83–84, 686–87. This included 550 FAL rifles and ninety thousand 7.62-mm cartridges.

72. Senate Subcommittee on Terrorism, Narcotics, and International Communications, *Drugs Law Enforcement and Foreign Policy: Panama*, 100th Cong., 2nd sess., 8–11 February 1988, 106; Rachel Ehrenfeld, *Narco-Terrorism*, 44.

73. Senate Subcommittee on Terrorism, Narcotics, and International Operations of the Committee on Foreign Relations, *Drugs, Law Enforcement, and Foreign Policy*, 65.

74. Frederick Kempe, *Toda la Verdad*, 55. This occurred while George Bush was CIA director under President Ford.

75. Senate Subcommittee on Terrorism, Narcotics, and International Communications, *Drugs Law Enforcement and Foreign Policy: Panama*, 106.

76. Ibid., 146; John Dinges, *Our Man in Panama*, 131.

77. Senate Subcommittee on Terrorism, Narcotics, and International Communications, *Drugs Law Enforcement and Foreign Policy: Panama*, 100. At Noriega's trial, Carlos Lehder testified that Noriega had sent a lawyer to the cartel with a message that "if they wished to do business in Panama, the general was ready to listen." See: Dr. Ricardo Lasso Guevara, *U.S.A. vs. Noriega: Enemigos o Amigos* (Panama City: Litho Impresora Panama, 1994), 91.

78. Senate Subcommittee on Terrorism, Narcotics, and International Communications, *Drugs Law Enforcement and Foreign Policy: Panama*, 101–102.

79. John Dinges, *Our Man in Panama*, 10–13.

80. Senate Subcommittee on Terrorism, Narcotics, and International Communications, *Drugs Law Enforcement and Foreign Policy: Panama*, 101.

81. Ibid., 104; Rachel Ehrenfeld, *Narco-Terrorism*, 43.

82. Senate Subcommittee on Terrorism, Narcotics, and International Operations of the Committee on Foreign Relations, *Drugs, Law Enforcement, and Foreign Policy*, 66; Senate Subcommittee on Terrorism, Narcotics, and International Communications, *Drugs Law Enforcement and Foreign Policy: Panama*, 104.

83. Senate Subcommittee on Terrorism, Narcotics, and International Operations of the Committee on Foreign Relations, *Drugs, Law Enforcement, and Foreign Policy*, 66.

84. John Dinges, *Our Man in Panama*, 291.

85. Marvin Alisky, "U.S. Mustn't Fall for Castro's Sudden Concern for Drug Smuggling," 7 July 1989.

86. Arturo Cruz, "Anatomy of an Execution," *Commentary*, November 1989, 54.

87. Bretton G. Sciaroni, "Castro Deeply Involved in Drug Running," *Human Events*, 29 July 1989, 10.

88. Ibid.; Martin Arostegui, "Castro's Scapegoats," *National Review*, 28 December 1992, 33.

89. Julia Preston, "The Trial that Shook Cuba," *The New York Review*, 7 December 1989, 23.

90. Arturo Cruz, "Anatomy of an Execution," *Commentary*, November 1989, 55.

91. Julia Preston, "The Trial that Shook Cuba," 25.

92. Arturo Cruz, "Anatomy of an Execution," *Commentary*, November 1989, 55.

93. Julia Preston, "The Trial That Shook Cuba," 25.

94. De La Guardia's brother, Patricio, had served under Ochoa in Angola between 1987 and 1988.

95. Julia Preston, "The Trial that Shook Cuba," 30.

96. Martin Arostegui, "Castro's Scapegoats," 34, 35.

97. Bretton G. Sciaroni, "Castro Deeply Involved in Drug Running," 11.

98. House of Representatives Committee on Foreign Affairs. *Cuban Involvement in International Narcotics Trafficking*, 100th Cong., 1st sess., 25 and 27 July 1989, 5–10.

99. Julia Preston, "The Trial that Shook Cuba," 27.

100. Bretton G. Sciaroni, "Castro Deeply Involved in Drug Running," 16.

101. Ibid., 10–11.

102. U.S. Department of State, Bureau of International Narcotics Matters, *1996 International Narcotics Control Strategy Report* (Washington, DC: U.S. Department of State, March 1997), http://www.state.gov/www/global narcotics_law/1998_narc_report/carib96.html (accessed 27 July 2009); U.S. Department of State, Bureau of International Narcotics Matters, *International Control Strategy Report* (Washington, DC: U.S. Department of State, March 1999), http://www.state.gov/www/global/narcotics_law/1998_narc_report/carib98.html. (accessed 27 July 2009).

103. Senate Subcommittee on Alcoholism and Drug Abuse of the Committee on Labor and Human Resources, *Drugs and Terrorism, 1984*, 98th Cong., 2nd sess., 2 August 1984, 79, 80. Testimony of Antonio Farach.

104. Ibid., 44.

105. Ibid., 78, 83, 85.

106. Senate Subcommittee on Alcoholism and Drug Abuse of the Committee on Labor and Human Resources, *Role of Nicaragua in Drug Trafficking*, 99th Cong., 1st sess., 19 April 1985, 19. Statement of William Von Rabb, commissioner of the U.S. Customs Service. Carlton also confirmed this allegation in his testimony before Congress. See: Senate Subcommittee on Alcoholism and Drug Abuse of the Committee on Labor and Human Resources, *Nicaraguan Government Involvement in Narcotics Trafficking*, 99th Cong., 2nd sess., 11 March 1986, 44.

107. Senate Subcommittee on Terrorism, Narcotics, and International Operation of the Committee on Foreign Relations, *Drugs, Law Enforcement, and Foreign Policy*, 67. Testimony

of Floyd Carlton. See: Joel Brinkley, "U.S. Accuses Managua of Role in Cocaine Traffic," *New York Times*, 19 July 1984, sec. A, p. 6.

108. Michael Hanlon, "A Sting Avenged: Barry Seal Used to Run Drugs for Profit," *Toronto Star*, 29 March 1986, sec. M, p. 1.

109. Senate Subcommittee on Alcoholism and Drug Abuse of the Committee on Labor and Human Resources, *Role of Nicaragua in Drug Trafficking*, 99th Cong., 1st sess., 19 April 1985, 17.

110. Michael Hanlon, "A Sting Avenged: Barry Seal Used to Run Drugs for Profit," 3; Peter Dale Scott and Jonathan Marshall, *Cocaine Politics*, 99; Daniel Hopsicker, *Barry and the Boys: The CIA, the Mob and America's Secret History* (Venice, FL: Madcow Press, 2006), 268, 351. This was known as Operation Seaspray. Hopsicker adds that a close associate of Governor Bill Clinton owned the airfield where Seal operated.

111. Michael Hanlon, "A Sting Avenged: Barry Seal Used to Run Drugs for Profit," 5–6.

112. Ibid., 7; Senate Subcommittee on Alcoholism and Drug Abuse of the Committee on Labor and Human Resources, *Role of Nicaragua in Drug Trafficking*, 99th Cong., 1st sess., 19 April 1985, 17.

113. Senate Subcommittee on Alcoholism and Drug Abuse of the Committee on Labor and Human Resources, *Nicaraguan Government Involvement in Narcotics Trafficking*, 99th Cong., 2nd sess., 11 March 1986, 14, 18.

114. Peter Dale Scott and Jonathan Marshall, *Cocaine Politics*, 100.

115. Robert J. McCartney, "Accused Nicaraguan No Longer at the Ministry: Suspect Said Not to Be Government Employee," *Washington Post*, 9 August 1984, sec. A, p. 25. Allegations arose that this sting might have been a black propaganda operation to defame the Sandinista government, at a critical moment when the Reagan administration was asking for more aid for the Contras. See: Robert Parry and Peter Kornbluh, "Iran Contra's Untold Story," *Foreign Policy* no. 72 (Autumn 1988): 3–30; Alexander Cockburn and Jeffery St. Clair, *Whiteout*, 318–322; Daniel Hopsicker, *Barry and the Boys*, 17–19; Senate, Subcommittee on Terrorism, Narcotics and International Operation of the Committee on Foreign Relations, *Drugs, Law Enforcement, and Foreign Policy*, 67.

116. Senate Subcommittee on Alcoholism and Drug Abuse of the Committee on Labor and Human Resources, *Role of Nicaragua in Drug Trafficking*, 99th Cong., 1st sess., 19 April 1985, 27.

117. Joel Brinkley, "Panel Hears Details Linking Managua and Drugs," *New York Times*, 20 April 1985, sec. A, p. 3.

118. Senate Subcommittee on Alcoholism and Drug Abuse of the Committee on Labor and Human Resources, *Role of Nicaragua in Drug Trafficking*, 99th Cong., 1st sess., 19 April 1985, 25–27. Testimony of James Herring and statement of John Keeney, deputy assistant attorney general for the Criminal Division, U.S. Department of Justice.

119. Ibid., 29, 30, 35, 39–41.

120. Ibid., 31. Neither Cockburn nor Peter Dale Scott mentions Herring's testimony regarding the Vesco case.

121. Senate Subcommittee on Alcoholism and Drug Abuse of the Committee on Labor and Human Resources, *Nicaraguan Government Involvement in Narcotics Trafficking*, 99th Cong., 2nd sess., 11 March 1986, 16–17.

122. Ibid., 17.

123. Ibid., 19, 23, 24.

124. Ibid., 29.

125. Paul Boyer, ed. *Reagan as President* (Chicago: Ivan R. Dee, 1990), 242.

126. Dinesh D'Souza, *Ronald Reagan* (New York: The Free Press, 1997), 161.

127. House of Representatives Committee on Foreign Affairs, *Soviet Posture in the Western Hemisphere: Hearing Before the Subcommittee on Western Hemisphere Affairs*, 99th Cong., 1st sess., 28 February 1985, 68.

128. Ronald Reagan, "Remarks by President Reagan: The Parallel Between El Salvador and Vietnam," *Weekly Compilation of Congressional Documents* (2 March 1981): 182–83.

129. Shirley Christian, *Nicaragua: Revolution in the Family* (New York: Vintage Books: 1986), 359. The Reagan Administration insisted that the Contras were fighting to prevent the supply of arms to the Salvadorian guerrillas, while the Contras believed that they were fighting for free elections and democracy against a Communist government.

130. James M. Scott, "Interbranch Rivalry and the Reagan Doctrine in Nicaragua," *Political Science Quarterly* 112 (Summer 1997): 244; Hamilton, *Crisis in Central America*, 25. This bill became known as Boland I.

131. Dennis Volman, "Top Contras Under Scrutiny for Corruption," *Christian Science Monitor*, 11 April 1986, 1.

132. The FDN was viewed as corrupt by the press, international observers, and critics of the Somoza regime.

133. Mark Tran, "Drugs and Arrest of Contra Leader Upsets Aid Plan/ U.S. Senate to Investigate Cocaine Charges Against Nicaraguan Rebels," *Guardian*, 25 April 1986, 1.

134. Senate Subcommittee on Terrorism, Narcotics, and International Operation of the Committee on Foreign Relations, *Drugs, Law Enforcement, and Foreign Policy*, 41–42.

135. Warren Richey, "Justice Officials Find No Crime Link to Contra Leaders," *Christian Science Monitor*, 9 May 1986, 3.

136. Michael White, "Contra Heroes in Drug Deals, U.S. Acknowledges Nefarious Activities of Nicaraguan Rebels," *Guardian*, 28 August 1986, 1.

137. Warren Richey, "Justice Officials Find No Crime Link to Contra Leaders," 3. Oliver North in his diary identifies José Robelo and Sebastian Gonzalez as two FDN members suspected of smuggling. See: Oliver North, "Entry 1 April 1985," The Oliver North File: His Diaries, E-Mail, and Memos on the Kerry Report, Contras, and Drugs, National Security Archive Electronic Briefing Book No. 113, 26 February 2004, http://www.gwu.edu/~nsarchiv/NSAEBB/NSAEBB113/index.htm (accessed 13 February 2007).

138. Joanne Turnbull, "The Contras' Proxy War," *Newsweek*, 20 October 1986, 31–32. The C-123 plane that Hasenfus flew was the same plane owned by Barry Seal, who set up the operation to implicate Frederico Vaughn and the Sandinista government in narcotics trafficking. See: George Lardner Jr., "Ex-CIA Airline Tied to Cocaine; Southern Air Plane Allegedly Used in Deal for Weapons," *Washington Post*, 20 January 1987, sec. A, p. 12.

139. Lawrence E. Walsh, *Final Report of the Independent Counsel for Iran/Contra Matters* (Washington D.C: United States Court of Appeals for the District of Colombia Circuit, August 1983), xv.

140. Knut Royce (*Newsday*), "CIA Sent $10 Million from Drug Trafficking to Rebels, Witness Says," *Toronto Star*, 29 June 1987, sec. A, p. 14. Much of this money was supposedly laundered through a Costa Rican firm called Frigorificos de Puntarenas. This business held a bank account that the State Department used to transfer humanitarian aid to the Contras. See: Senate Subcommittee on Terrorism, Narcotics, and International Operation of the Committee on Foreign Relations, *Drugs, Law Enforcement, and Foreign Policy*, 45–46.

141. Michael White and Mark Tran, "Contra Links with Drugs Under Spotlight," *Guardian*, 1 July 1987, 1.

142. Senate Subcommittee on Terrorism, Narcotics, and International Operation of the Committee on Foreign Relations, *Drugs, Law Enforcement, and Foreign Policy*, 61–62. Felix Rodríguez participated in the 1961 Bay of Pigs operation and was involved in the 1967 capture of Che Guevara in Bolivia.

143. Michael O'Regan, "Bush Linked to Illegal Contra Arms Network," *The Advertiser*, 17 May 1988, 1.

144. David Hoffman, "Bush's Office Revises Rodríguez Chronology; Vice President's Staff Says Aide Met Last June With Contra Resupply Operative," *Washington Post*, 15 May 1987, sec. A, p. 16. Rodríguez worked on the resupply missions with Richard V. Secord, retired Air Force major general. Moreover, Rodríguez and Gregg had served together in Vietnam. See: Felix I. Rodríguez and John Weisman, *Shadow Warrior: The CIA Hero of a Hundred Unknown Battles* (New York: Simon and Schuster, 1989), 193–194.

145. *New York Times*, "Lies Have Wings," 12 October 1986, sec. D, p. 22; Katherine Bishop, "Contra Aid Flier Suing Company That Hired Him," *New York Times*, 25 October 1987, sec. A, p. 10.

146. *New York Times*, "Lies Have Wings," sec. D, p. 22; Martin Merzer and Jeff Leen, "Mysterious Saga of Old C-123," *Journal of Commerce*, 14 October 1986, sec. A, p. 7.

147. Alexander Cockburn and Jeffery St. Clair, *Whiteout*, 293–95.

148. *St. Petersburg Times*, "Drug Runners Allegedly Took Advantage of CIA's Network," *St. Petersburg Times*, 27 April 1987, sec. A, p. 3; Central Intelligence Agency Inspector General, "Report of Investigation: Allegations of Connections Between CIA and the Contras in Cocaine Trafficking to the United States, Lines 905–908 (Washington, DC: Central Intelligence Agency, 8 October 1998), http://ciadrugs.homestead.com/files/index-cia-ig-rpt.html (accessed 14 May 2008).

149. David Hoffman, "Bush's Office Revises Rodríguez Chronology," *Washington Post*, sec. A, p. 16; Joe Pichirallo, "How North Wove Lifeline for Contras; Secret Re-supply Network Evolved as Reaction to Congressional Ban," *Washington Post*, 4 May 1987, sec. A, p. 1.

150. David Hoffman, "Bush's Office Revises Rodríguez Chronology," *Washington Post*, sec. A, p. 16; Rod Norland, "Is There a Contra Drug Connection?," *Newsweek*, 26 January 1987, 26; *New York Times*, "Lies Have Wings," sec. D, p. 22.

151. Jonathan Kwitny, *The Crimes of Patriots: A True Tale of Dope, Dirty Money, and the CIA* (New York: W.W. Norton and Company, 1987), 60, 185; Albert A. McCoy, *The Politics of Heroin*, 38–41, 74–75. Felix Rodríguez worked for Edwin Wilson during the 1970s. Wilson was directly implicated in the Nugan-Hand Bank scandal. Rodríguez met Secord through another CIA officer named Ray Clines, who was an associate of Edwin Wilson. Wilson was eventually jailed for selling C-4 plastic explosives to Libya. See: Felix I. Rodríguez and John Weisman, *Shadow Warrior*, 207–208, 215. According to Dan Russell, after the Nugan-Hand Bank collapsed, the CIA opened a new front, known as Bishop, Baldwin, Rewald, Dillingham, and Wong to replace the bank and take over its operations throughout Asia. See: Dan Russell, *Drug War: Covert Money, Power, and Policy* (Camden, NY: Quality Books Incorporated, 1999), 358.

152. Katherine Bishop, "Contra Aid Flier Suing Company That Hired Him," sec. A, p. 10.

153. George Lardner Jr., "Ex-CIA Airline Tied to Cocaine," sec. A, p. 12.

154. Senate Subcommittee on Terrorism, Narcotics, and International Operation of the Committee on Foreign Relations, *Drugs, Law Enforcement, and Foreign Policy*, 44–45. Juan Ramón Matta Ballesteros had been arrested in 1970 for smuggling twenty kilos of cocaine into the United States. Matta was deported to Honduras where he formed SETCO in 1975, and he began to smuggle cocaine with the help of Mexican smuggler Miguel Angel Felix Gallardo. In 1978, Matta supposedly financed the overthrow of Honduran president Juan Alberto Melgar by pro-Somoza General Policarpo Paz García Castro. Matta allegedly paid off Paz García's head of intelligence, Leonides Torres Arias, for permission to run his smuggling operation. As the FDN Contras developed their base of operations in Honduras, Leonides Torres Arias put the CIA in touch with Matta to supply the Contras. See: Alexander Cockburn and Jeffery St. Clair, *Whiteout*, 280–283; Dan Russell, *Drug War*, 406–11.

155. Senate Subcommittee on Terrorism, Narcotics, and International Operation of the Committee on Foreign Relations, *Drugs, Law Enforcement, and Foreign Policy*, 44–45. Matta Ballesteros was extradited to the United States on cocaine smuggling charges in 1988.

156. Central Intelligence Agency Inspector General, "Report of Investigation: Allegations of Connections Between CIA and the Contras in Cocaine Trafficking to the United States, Line 896 (Washington, DC: Central Intelligence Agency, 8 October 1998), http://ciadrugs.homestead.com/files/index-cia-ig-rpt.html (accessed 14 May 2008).

157. Oliver North, "Entry, 9 August 1985," The Oliver North File: His Diaries, E-Mail, and Memos on the Kerry Report, Contras, and Drugs, National Security Archive Electronic Briefing Book No. 113, 26 February 2004, http://www.gwu.edu/~nsarchiv/NSAEBB/NSAEBB113/index.htm (accessed 13 February 2007).

158. Oliver North, "Entry 12 July 1985," The Oliver North File: His Diaries, E-Mail, and Memos on the Kerry Report, Contras, and Drugs, National Security Archive Electronic Briefing Book No. 113, 26 February 2004, http://www.gwu.edu/~nsarchiv/NSAEBB/NSAEBB113/index.htm (accessed 13 February 2007).

159. Rod Norland, "Is There a Contra Drug Connection?," 26.

160. Senate Subcommittee on Terrorism, Narcotics, and International Operation of the Committee on Foreign Relations, *Drugs, Law Enforcement, and Foreign Policy*, 55.

161. Mary McGrory, "The Contra-Drug Stink," *Washington Post*, 10 April 1988, sec. B, p. 1.

162. Senate Subcommittee on Terrorism, Narcotics, and International Operation of the Committee on Foreign Relations, *Drugs, Law Enforcement, and Foreign Policy*, 53–58; Rod Norland, "Is There a Contra Drug Connection?," 26.

163. Knut Royce (*Newsday*) "CIA Sent $10 Million from Drug Trafficking to Rebels, Witness Says," sec. A, p. 14.

164. Michael O'Regan, "Bush Linked to Illegal Contra Arms Network," 1.

165. Keith Schinder, "Contra Drug Inquiry Stirs Growing Interest," *New York Times*, 24 February 1987, sec. A, p. 22.

166. Michael Isikoff, "Reagan Aides Accused of Hampering Drug War; Contra Aid Had Priority Over Fighting Traffickers Hill Report Says," *Washington Post*, 14 April 1988, sec. A, p. 20.

167. Senate Subcommittee on Terrorism, Narcotics, and International Operation of the Committee on Foreign Relations, *Drugs, Law Enforcement, and Foreign Policy*, 2.

168. La Comisión Especial del Congreso Nacional, "Informe Parlamentario del Caso Huanchaca" (5 Noviembre 1986), 35–65; Rodgelio Garcia Lupo, "La CIA y la DEA Protegen el Narcotráfico en Bolivia,"*Tiempo*, 6 julio 1992, 106–107; Mabel Azuci, "Cocaína para la Contra," *El País*, 14 septiembre 1988, 6. Both articles found in Washington, DC: National Security Archive, Narcotics Collection, Clips, Bolivia and the Andes in General, box 26.

169. Gutierrez y Pando, *La Lucha Boliviana Contra la Agresion del Narcotráfico*, 170–71. Roberto Suárez Levy was killed in a shootout with Bolivian police in 1990. See: Reuters, "Bolivians Kill Trafficker's Son," *New York Times*, 24 March 1990, sec. A, p. 6. For more on the breakup of the Suárez cartel, see chapter 7.

170. Rodgelio Garcia Lupo, "La CIA y la DEA Protegen el Narcotráfico en Bolivia," *Tiempo*, 6 julio 1992, 106–107.

171. Gary Webb, "Crack Plague's Roots Are in Nicaragua War; Colombia-Bay Area Drug Pipeline Helped Finance CIA backed Contras 80s Efforts to Assist Guerrillas; Left Legacy of Drugs and Gangs in Black L.A.," *San Jose Mercury News*, 18 August 1996, sec. A, p.1.

172. Roberto Suro and Walter Pincus, "The CIA and Crack: Evidence Is Lacking of Alleged Plot; Nicaraguans Had Limited Role in Bringing Drug to U.S. Cities," *Washington Post*, 4 October 1996, sec. A. p. 1.

173. Tim Weiner, "CIA Says That It Has Found No Link Between Itself and the Crack Trade," *New York Times*, 19 December 1997, sec. A, p. 23.

174. David L. Westrate, interview by author, 10 November 2006, Buffalo, tape recording.

Chapter 5: Northern Andean Guerrillas, Drug Trafficking, and Cold War Politics

1. Senate Committee on Foreign Relations and the Committee on the Judiciary, *International Terrorism, Insurgency, and Drug Trafficking*, 300. Statement of Robert B. Oakley, director of the Office for Counter-Terrorism and Emergenc Planning, Department of State.

2. Michael Satchell and Richard Z. Chesnoff, "Narcotics: Terror's New Ally," 30.

3. Rensselaer Lee and Patrick Clawson, *The Andean Cocaine Industry*, 178; Francisco E. Thoumi, *Illegal Drugs, Economy, and Society*, 102–103.

4. American Embassy Bogotá to Secretary of State Washington, DC, "Guns for Grass: The Narc-FARC Connection," (October 1980), 1, 2–3, National Security Archive, Narcotics Collection, Colombia: Cartels, U.S. Operations, Corruption, box 8. Embassy report for INM Assistant Secretary Falco from Crigler.

5. American Embassy Bogotá to Secretary of State Washington, DC, "President Turbay Reports on the Narc-FARC Connection," (April 1981), 1, National Security Archive, Narcotics Collection, Colombia: Cartels, U.S. Operations, Corruption, box 8.

6. Ibid.

7. American Embassy Bogotá to Secretary of State Washington, DC, "Guns for Grass: The Narc-FARC Connection," 1.

8. Ibid. Ironically, the M-19 was included in the list of organizations that denounced narcotics-related corruption, but hypocritically, they had developed an alliance with the Medellín cartel.

9. American Embassy Bogotá to Secretary of State Washington, DC, "President Turbay Reports on the Narc-FARC Connection," 3.

10. James J. Brittain and R. James Sacouman, "¿Dependen las FARC-EP de la Coca?" (9 April 2006), http://www.farcep.org (accessed 19 February 2007), 1–3.

11. American Embassy Bogotá to Secretary of State Washington, DC, "FARC-M-19 Cooperation in Southern Colombia" (November 1981), 1, National Security Archive, Narcotics Collection, Colombia: Cartels, U.S. Operations, Corruption, box 8.

12. Ibid., 2.

13. American Embassy Bogotá to Secretary of State Washington, DC, "President Turbay Reports on the Narc-FARC Connection," 3.

14. María Clemencia Ramírez, *Entre el Estado y la Guerrilla*, 80–81.

15. Due to the failure of the Alliance for Progress, large landowners continued to resist agrarian land reform, and campesinos were still burdened with heavy debts. The rural areas where the campesinos lived provided a natural terrain on which to fight a guerrilla insurgency, as well as a population that was looking for a change in its status. Thus, the guerrillas maintained their *focos* (areas where guerrillas can create the conditions for revolution) in the rural areas, precisely because they knew the inhabitants were responsive to their appeals for support. See: Che Guevara, *Guerrilla Warfare*, 3rd ed. [1985] (Wilmington, DE: Scholarly Resources Incorporated, 1997), 50, 72–73; Timothy P. Wickham-Crowley, *Guerrillas and Revolution in Latin America: A Comparative Study of Insurgents and Regimes Since 1956* (Princeton: Princeton University Press, 1992), 32; Gerrit Huizer, *The Revolutionary Potential of Peasants in Latin America* (Lexington, MA: Lexington Books, 1972), 8; James F. Petras and Robert La Porte Jr., *Cultivating Revolution: The United States and Agrarian Reform in Latin America* (New York: Random House, 1971), 4.

16. American Embassy Bogotá to Secretary of State Washington, DC, "Guerrilla Involvement in Colombian Drug Trafficking" (November 1983), 2, National Security Archive, Narcotics Collection, box Colombia: Cartels, U.S. Operations, Corruption, box 8.

17. Ibid., 5.

18. Jeffrey Race, *War Comes to Long An*, 141–208 [first mention]; 3. Jeffrey Race compares a preemptive counterinsurgency strategy that uses political and economic measures to eliminate insurgencies with a reinforcement strategy that calls for military measures to defeat the insurgency.

19. American Embassy Bogotá to Secretary of State Washington, DC, "NARC/FARC Connection," (March 1984), 1, National Security Archive, Narcotics Collection, Colombia: Cartels, U.S. Operations, Corruption, box 8. Some argue that the FARC sanctioned this policy change because, around 1984, the Soviet Union reduced the amount of its aid to the Cuban Departamento de América for liberation movements in Latin America. See: Major Luis Alberto Villamarín, *The FARC Cartel*, 40.

20. Fabio Castillo, *La Coca Nostra*, 68.

21. American Embassy Bogotá to Secretary of State Washington, DC, "NARC/FARC Connection," 2, 3.

22. Ibid., 4, 5.

23. Ibid., 2. For more on the Tranquilandia raid, see chapter 3.

24. Fabio Castillo, *La Coca Nostra*, 68.

25. Secretary of State to American Embassy Bogotá, "NARC/FARC Connection," 2.

26. American Embassy Bogotá to Secretary of State Washington, DC, "Narcotics/Guerrilla Connection in Colombia" (July 1984), 2, National Security Archive, Narcotics Collection, Colombia: Cartels, U.S. Operations, Corruption, box 8. In addition, in 1983, the Colombian Army discovered ninety hectares of coca and a processing laboratory "next to an abandoned FARC camp."

27. U.S. Department of Defense, Defense Intelligence Agency, "Special Operations Policy Advisory Group," 11.

28. American Embassy Bogotá to Secretary of State Washington, DC, "Narcotics/Guerrilla Connection in Colombia," 2.

29. House of Representatives, Committee on Foreign Affairs. *Developments in Latin American Narcotics Control*, 68. Answers of Jon R. Thomas, assistant secretary, Bureau of International Narcotics Matters, Department of State. See: William López Gutiérrez, "Las Políticas de Paz," 250. Gutiérrez argues that the FARC's narcotics profits during the truce allowed the FARC to increase their number of fronts. The resulting situation made it more difficult for the Colombian army to launch counterinsurgency operations in the remote, guerrilla-controlled areas that the government had abandoned during the 1970s.

30. Secretary of State to American Embassy Bogotá, "NARC/FARC Connection," 2.

31. U.S. Department of the Army, *Country Study: Colombia*, http://lcweb2.loc.gov/frd/cs/cotoc.html (accessed 14 December 2006).

32. Richard B. Craig, "Illicit Drug Traffic: Implications for South American Source Countries," 30.

33. House of Representatives Committee on Foreign Affairs, *Developments in Latin American Narcotics Control*, 68.

34. House of Representatives Committee on Foreign Affairs, *Narcotics Review in South America*, 139. According to Ann Wrobleski, the assistant secretary of state to the Bureau of International Narcotics Matters, the "firepower imbalance between the Colombian security forces and the insurgents protecting some narcotics labs was more of an obstacle than the government-FARC truce."

35. U.S. Department of Defense, U.S. Southern Command, untitled (3 July 1996), 8, National Security Archive, Narcotics Collection, Peru-Colombia-Andes Documents Part I, Colombia FOIA, box 49. Letter of C. R. Baldwin Lieutenant Commander U.S. Navy, to Mr. Carlos M. Salinas of Amnesty International.

36. American Embassy Lima to Secretary of State Washington, DC, "Peruvian Terrorism: The Nature of the Threat" (April 1982), 8, National Security Archive, Narcotics Collection, Peru: Documents from FOIA, box 31. A petardismo was a small stick of dynamite.

37. American Embassy Lima to Secretary of State Washington, DC, "Peru: Assessment of Short Term Prospects" (September 1983), 6, National Security Archive, Narcotics Collection, Peru: Documents from FOIA, box 31.

38. American Embassy Lima to Secretary of State Washington, DC, "Peruvian Terrorism: The Nature of the Threat," 8–9.

39. American Embassy Lima to Secretary of State Washington, DC, "Peru: Assessment of Short Term Prospects," 10.

40. Central Intelligence Agency, Directorate of Intelligence, "Latin America Review: Peru," 4.

41. U.S. Congress, Senate Committee on Foreign Relations and the Committee on the Judiciary, *International Terrorism, Insurgency, and Drug Trafficking*, 146.

42. Carlos Tapia, *Las Fuerzas Armadas y Sendero Luminoso*, 39–43.

43. José E. Gonzales Manrique, "Guerrillas and Coca in the Upper Huallaga Valley," 108.

44. Carlos Tapia, *Las Fuerzas Armadas y Sendero Luminoso*, 39–43; José E. Gonzales Manrique, "Guerrillas and Coca in the Upper Huallaga Valley," 109.

45. American Embassy Lima to Secretary of State Washington, DC, "Peruvian Terrorism: The Nature of the Threat," 2.

46. Melanie S. Tammen, "Policy Analysis: The Drug War vs. Land Reform in Peru," 4.

47. RAND Corporation, "News Release: RAND Study Analyzes the Success of Terrorist Movements in Peru" (Santa Monica, CA: RAND Corporation, 1992), 9, National Security Archive, Narcotics Collection, Drugs/Research RAND Reports, box 46 (Excerpts of Scott McCormick's *Study on Sendero's Approach to the Cities*); Abimael Guzmán Reynoso, *Guerra Popular en el Perú*, 181–85.

48. Ibid, 9, 17. Bernard Fall coined the term "active sanctuaries" in his book *The Street Without Joy*. *Bases de apoyo* serves as a similar concept, although Fall referred to active sanctuaries as those located in bordering countries sympathetic to a guerrilla cause.

49. American Embassy Lima to Secretary of State Washington, DC, "Peruvian Terrorism: The Nature of the Threat," 2.

50. American Embassy Lima to DEAHQS Washington, DC, "An Analysis of the Relationship Between Peruvian Terrorist/Insurgent Groups and Cocaine Trafficking Organizations in the Upper Huallaga Valley," (August 1989), 2, National Security Archive, Narcotics Collection, Peru: Documents from FOIA, box 31.

51. Ibid.

52. Abimael Guzmán Reynoso, *Guerra Popular en el Perú*, 11–12. According to Guzmán, both Cuba and Nicaragua were revisionist because they were client states of the Soviet Union, which Guzmán considered an imperialist socialist state. Both nations denied the true revolution of the proletariat.

53. American Embassy Lima to DEAHQS Washington, DC, "An Analysis of the Relationship Between Peruvian Terrorist/Insurgent Groups and Cocaine Trafficking Organizations," 2–3.

54. Central Intelligence Agency, Directorate of Intelligence, "Peru," 4.

55. American Embassy Lima to DEAHQS Washington, DC, "An Analysis of the Relationship Between Peruvian Terrorist/Insurgent Groups and Cocaine Trafficking Organizations,"

14. According to Lee and Clawson, Peruvian traffickers were too weak to confront the Sendero because they were dependent on Colombian organizations for leadership and support. See: Rensselaer Lee and Patrick Clawson, *The Andean Cocaine Industry*, 180–82.

56. Gabriela Tarazona-Sevillano, *The Sendero Luminoso and the Threat of Narcoterrorism*, (New York: Praeger Books, 1999), 119–22. Gabriela Tarazona-Sevillano was the criminal affairs prosecutor for the Peruvian Public Ministry from 1984 to 1986. Contrary to Tarazona-Sevillano, Carlos Tapia, using captured documents from Abimael Guzmán, argues that with the exception of the UHV, the majority of the Sendero's weapons did not come from coca dollar purchases but were obtained through capture. See: Carlos Tapia, *Las Fuerzas Armadas y Sendero Luminoso*, 115–118. Edmundo Morales maintained that the cocaine underworld did not support the Sendero technically or economically because campesino coca planters and cocaine manufacturers were entrepreneurs. They could not afford to support a political crusade (like the Sendero) that was not interested in earning profits. See: Edmundo Morales, *Cocaine: White Gold Rush in Peru*, 138–40.

57. Gabriela Tarazona-Sevillano, *The Sendero Luminoso and the Threat of Narcoterrorism*, 118.

58. FBIS Asuncion to AIG, "Peru Reporters Interview Terrorists" (June 1987), 1–2, National Security Archive, Narcotics Collection, Peru: U.S. Operations, Sendero, Fujimori, box 7.

59. Martiza Rojas Albertini, *Los Campesinos Cocaleros*, 268.

60. José E. Gonzales Manrique, "Peru: Sendero Luminoso en el Valle de la Coca," 213.

61. Roger Cohen, "Cocaine Rebellion, Peru's Guerrillas Draw Support of Peasants in Coca Rich Regions," *New York Times*, 17 January 1989, sec. A, p. 1.

62. Drug Enforcement Administration, "An Analysis of the Terrorist Insurgent Groups and Their Relationship to Cocaine Trafficking Organizations," 36; American Embassy Lima to DEAHQS Washington, DC, "An Analysis of the Relationship Between Peruvian Terrorist/Insurgent Groups and Cocaine Trafficking Organizations in the Upper Huallaga Valley" (August 1989), 5.

63. Martiza Rojas Albertini, *Los Campesinos Cocaleros*, 271.

64. Gabriela Tarazona-Sevillano, *The Sendero Luminoso and the Threat of Narcoterrorism*, 116.

65. Bruce H. Kay, "Violent Opportunities: The Rise and Fall of King Coca and the Shining Path," *Journal of Interamerican Studies and World Affairs* 41, no. 3 (Autumn 1999): 106.

66. José E. Gonzales Manrique, "Peru: Sendero Luminoso en el Valle de la Coca," 216.

67. Gabriela Tarazona-Sevillano, *The Sendero Luminoso and the Threat of Narcoterrorism*, 116.

68. Ibid., 116–18.

69. Stephen G. Trujillo, "Peru's Maoist Drug Dealers," *New York Times*, 8 April 1982, sec. A, p. 25.

70. Tammy Arbuckle and Bernard Fitzsimons, "Peru's Drug War: Vietnam-Era Methods Won't Net Narco-Guerrillas," 374; Colonel Juan Muñoz Cruz, *Narcotráfico: Agresión al Peru* (Lima: El Leonciopradino, 1996), 53. Colonel Juan Muñoz Cruz estimated that during the late 1980s, the Sendero and the MRTA were responsible for nearly ten thousand flights a year.

71. Roger Cohen, "Cocaine Rebellion, Peru's Guerrillas Draw Support of Peasants," sec. A, p. 1.

72. Stephen G. Trujillo, "Peru's Maoist Drug Dealers," sec. A, p. 25.

73. Roger Cohen, "Cocaine Rebellion, Peru's Guerrillas Draw Support of Peasants," sec. A, p. 1.

74. American Embassy Lima to DEAHQS Washington, DC, "Staffdel Chambers and Ford Visit" (December 1988), 1, National Security Archive, Narcotics Collection, Peru: Documents from FOIA, box 31.

75. Secretary of State Washington, DC to American Embassy Lima, "Draft Implementation Plan for the Andean Counternarcotics Strategy-Peru" (October 1989), 2, National Security Archive, Narcotics Collection, Peru-Colombia-Andes Documents Part I, Andean Drug Summit, box 49.

76. American Embassy Lima to Secretary of State Washington, DC, "Narcotics Security: Temporary Shutdown of U.S. Support of Interdiction and Eradication" (February

1989), 1–2, National Security Archive, Narcotics Collection, Peru: Documents from FOIA, box 31. In particular, the Santa Lucia counternarcotics base located in the UHV became a target for Sendero attacks. See: American Embassy Lima to Secretary of State Washington, DC, "Security Requirements for UHV Anti-Narcotics Program" (November 1988), 1–2, National Security Archive, Narcotics Collection, Peru, Documents from FOIA, box 31; Department of the Air Force, "ACC Analytical Intelligence Report" (1992), 0011, National Security Archive, Narcotics Collection, Peru: Documents from FOIA, box 31. Report prepared by Staff Sergeant Steve Hollis.

77. American Embassy Lima to DEAHQS Washington, DC, "Staffdel Chambers and Ford Visit," 3.

78. Abimael Guzmán Reynoso, *Guerra Popular en el Perú*, 353–354. According to Guzmán's understanding of Maoist strategy, "repression is what stokes revolution." As a result, Guzmán wanted the United States and Peru to pursue a strategy that demonstrated the superiority of the proletariat over imperialism.

79. American Embassy Lima to Secretary of State Washington, DC, "New UHV Zone Commander Requests U.S. Assistance" (April 1989), 2, 5, National Security Archive, Narcotics Collection, Peru: Documents from FOIA, box 31.

80. American Embassy Lima to Secretary of State Washington, DC, "GOP/Military to De-Emphasize Eradication" (May 1989), 2–3, National Security Archive, Narcotics Collection, Peru: Documents from FOIA, box 31.

81. American Embassy Lima to Secretary of State Washington, DC, "New UHV Zone Commander Requests U.S. Assistance," 2, 4.

82. American Embassy Lima to Secretary of State Washington, DC, "GOP/Military to De-Emphasize Eradication," 5.

83. American Embassy Lima to Secretary of State Washington, DC, "New UHV Zone Commander Requests U.S. Assistance," 2–3.

84. Coletta Youngers, "The War in the Andes," 21. According to Lee and Clawson, Arciniega had become so popular in the UHV with his tactics that nearly thirty thousand people turned out in Uchiza (a former Sendero base) to support Armed Forces Day. See: Rensselaer Lee and Patrick Clawson, *The Andean Cocaine Industry*, 183.

85. Melvin Levitsky, interview by author, 31 October 2006, Buffalo, tape recording.

86. William Colby, *Lost Victory* (Chicago: Contemporary Books, 1989), 359–78.

87. David Palmer, "Peru, Drugs, and Shining Path," in *Drug Trafficking in the Americas*, eds. Bruce M Bagley and William O. Walker (Miami: University of Miami North-South Center Press, 1996), 182–83; Jose E. Gonzales Manrique, "Peru: Sendero Luminoso en el Valle de la Coca," 221; Donald J. Mabry, "The U.S. Military and the War on Drugs," 48.

88. Michael Satchell and Richard Z. Chesnoff, "Narcotics: Terror's New Ally," 30.

89. Gabreilla Tarazona-Sevillano, "Peru's Harvest of Instability and Terrorism," *Christian Science Monitor*, 16 March 1989, 19.

90. Melvin Levitsky, interview by author, 31 October 2006, Buffalo, tape recording.

Chapter 6: The Militarization of the Drug War: Bush, Panama, and the Andean Strategy

1. Bernard Weinraub, "Reagan Call for Cut in Drug Fight Ignites the Anger of Both Parties," *New York Times*, sec. A, p. 1.

2. Mary Thornton and Joanne Omang, "Commitment to Drug War Defended by Budget Chief; Lawmaker Scores Proposed Budget Cuts," *Washington Post*, 26 March 1987, sec. A, p. 4.

3. *New York Times*, "President Reagan's Drug Bust," 13 November 1987, sec. A, p. 38.

4. Victoria Churchville, "Dole: Use Military in Drug War; Candidate Links Issue to National Security," *Washington Post*, 4 March 1988, sec. A, p. 14.

5. Michael O'Regan, "U.S. Army Will Join in War on Drugs," *Courier Mail*, 20 May 1988.

6. Steven R. Belenko, *Crack and the Evolution of Anti-Drug Policy* (Westport, CT: Greenwood Press, 1993), 17.

7. Ibid., 15–17; Ronald Reagan, "Remarks on Signing the Anti-Drug Abuse Act of 1988" (18 November 1988), *The Public Papers of the Presidents of the United States* (Washington, DC: Office of the Federal Register, National Archives and Records Service, 1988), 1181.

8. George C. Wilson, "Experts Doubt Military Can Stop Flow of Drugs," *Washington Post*, 6 September 1989, sec. A, p. 19.

9. National Security Council, "NSC Strategy Options for Narcotics Control in the Andes" (Washington, DC: U.S. Department of State, 2 June 1989), 1, http://www.gwu.edu/~nsarchiv/NSAEBB/NSAEBB69/col09.pdf (accessed 30 March 2006).

10. U.S. Department of State, Office of the Inspector General, "Report of Audit: International Narcotics Control Programs in Peru and Bolivia, Memorandum 9CI–007" (Washington, DC: Department of State, March 1989), 3, National Security Archive, The Colombia Documentation Project, "War in Colombia Vol. I," http://www.gwu.edu/~nsarchiv/NSAEBB/NSAEBB69/part1.html (accessed 10 April 2006).

11. *St. Louis Post Dispatch*, "Baker Is Pessimistic About Drug War," 3 March 1989, sec. C, p. 2.

12. George C. Wilson, "Military Urged to Lead in Fight Against Drugs; Deeper Involvement Demanded at Hill Hearing," *Washington Post*, 23 February 1989, sec. A, p. 12.

13. Richard Cheney, "Memorandum for the Coordinator for Drug Enforcement Policy and Support" (Washington, DC: Office of the Secretary of Defense, 25 July 1989), National Security Archive, Narcotics Collection, Drugs: FOIA: DOD, box 39.

14. George Bush to Members of the Cabinet, "National Security Decision Directive 18" (Washington, DC: White House, 21 August 1989), 2, National Security Archive, The Colombia Documentation Project, "War In Colombia Vol. I," http://www.gwu.edu/~nsarchiv/NSAEBB/NSAEBB69/part1.html (accessed 10 April 2006).

15. National Security Council, "NSC Strategy Options for Narcotics Control," 1.

16. Lieutenant Colonel Juan L. Orama, *U.S. Military Evolution in Counternarcotics Operations*, 16.

17. Coletta Youngers, "The War in the Andes," 6.

18. Ibid., 7; Fred Kaplan, "Cheney Declares Drug War a Priority for the Pentagon," *Boston Globe*, 19 September 1989, 3; Lieutenant Colonel Juan L. Orama, *U.S. Military Evolution in Counternarcotics Operations*, 16.

19. U.S. Department of Defense, "Department of Defense Anti-Drug Policy and Action Plan (Proposed)" (Washington, DC: Department of Defense, 4 August 1989), 1, National Security Archive, Narcotics Collection, Drugs: FOIA: DOD, box 39.

20. George Bush to Members of the Cabinet, "National Security Decision Directive 18," 2.

21. Bruce M. Bagley, "The Myths of Militarization: Armed Forces in the War on Drugs" in *Drug Policy in the Americas*, ed. Peter H. Smith (Boulder: Westview Press, 1992), v–366.

22. Fred Kaplan, "Cheney Declares Drug War a Priority for the Pentagon," *Boston Globe*, 19 September 1989, 3.

23. Coletta Youngers, "The War in the Andes," 6.

24. George C. Wilson, "Experts Doubt Military Can Stop Flow of Drugs," sec. A, p. 19.

25. Bernard Adelsberger, "Cheney, Powell Set New Course in Pentagon," *Army Times*, 2 October 1989, 15.

26. George C. Wilson, "Experts Doubt Military Can Stop Flow of Drugs," sec. A, p. 19.

27. Peter Martyn, "Pentagon Seeks Salvation at Drug Summit," *Toronto Star*, 12 February 1990, sec. A, p. 13.

28. Lieutenant Colonel Juan L. Orama, *U.S. Military Evolution in Counternarcotics Operations*, 18. According to Orama, a doctrine emerged known as "military options other than war" (MOOTW), which created counternarcotics operations for conventional units in order to justify military spending.

29. Tom Hundley, "Should the Military Fight Drugs? Pentagon's New Thrust Has Sparked Controversy," *Toronto Star*, 16 February 1990, sec. A, p. 27.

30. Senate Committee on the Judiciary, *International Drug Control*. 101st Cong., 1st sess., 17 August 1989, 34–37. Statement of General Alfred Gray, commandant of the Marine Corps and member of the Joint Chiefs of Staff.

31. U.S. Department of State, Office of the Inspector General, "Report of Audit: International Narcotics Control Programs in Peru and Bolivia, Memorandum 9CI-007," 8.

32. J. Paul Scicchitano, "Vietnam Ghosts Haunt Soldiers in Drug Fight," *Army Times*, 2 October 1989, 21.

33. House of Representatives, Committee on Armed Services, *The Andean Drug Strategy and the Role of the U.S. Military*, 101st Cong., 1st sess., 9 November 1989, 23. Statement of Colonel Moynihan.

34. Senate Committee on the Judiciary, *International Drug Control*, 34–37.

35. House of Representatives Select Committee on Narcotics Abuse and Control, *Drugs and Latin America: Economic and Political Impact and U.S. Policy Options*, 101st Cong., 1st sess., 26 April 1989, 82. Statement of Bruce M. Bagley, citing: P. Reuter, G. Crawford, and J. Dave, *Sealing the Border: The Effects of Military Participation in Drug Interdiction* (Santa Monica, CA: RAND Corporation, 1988). Donald J Mabry argued that increasing the military's role in the War on Drugs exacerbated the problems faced by law enforcement agencies, because the smugglers were forced to change their smuggling techniques. It also made law enforcement more expensive because it cost more to break up smuggling networks as they became more sophisticated. Donald J. Mabry, "The U.S. Military and the War on Drugs," 45.

36. Richard Halloran, "Pentagon Says Drug War Will Cost $2 Billion," *New York Times*, 17 May 1988, sec. A, p. 17.

37. George Bush to Members of the Cabinet, "National Security Decision Directive 18," 2.

38. Melvin Levitsky, interview by author, 31 October 2006, Buffalo, tape recording.

39. House of Representatives Committee on Foreign Affairs, *Review of the President's Andean Initiative*, 101st Cong., 1st sess., 7–8 November 1989, 33.

40. Coletta Youngers, "The War in the Andes," 6.

41. House of Representatives, Committee on Foreign Affairs, *Review of the President's Andean Initiative*, 6–7.

42. U.S. Southern Command (U.S. SOUTHCOM), "Narcotics Related Assistance to the Andes" (14 September 1990), Counternarcotics Command and Management System Independent Assessment Plan, 1, National Security Archive, Narcotics Collection, CLIPS: U.S. Military War on Drugs, box 26; David C. Liner, USAID Congressional Liaison, "Summary: U.S. Economic, Military, and INM Assistance" (28 February 1992), National Security Archive, Narcotics Collection, Colombia: Cartels, U.S. Operations, Corruption, box 9.

43. House of Representatives Committee on Foreign Affairs, *Review of the President's Andean Initiative*, 52.

44. Coletta Youngers, "The War in the Andes," 5.

45. House of Representatives Committee on Foreign Affairs, *Review of the President's Andean Initiative*, 47, 60.

46. Coletta Youngers, "The War in the Andes," 13.

47. Ibid., 15; U.S. Department of Defense, U.S. Southern Command, untitled, 8. Letter of C.R. Baldwin, Lieutenant Commander U.S. Navy, to Mr. Carlos M. Salinas, Amnesty International.

48. Donald J. Mabry, "The U.S. Military and the War on Drugs," 50.

49. Senate Committee on Governmental Affairs, *U.S. Government Anti-Narcotics Activities*, 251.

50. Jim Pat Mills, "The Army's Drug War," *Army Times*, 2 October 1989, 18.

51. House of Representatives Committee on Foreign Affairs, *Review of the President's Andean Initiative*, 45.

52. Michael Isikoff and Patrick E. Tyler, "U.S. Military Given Foreign Arrest Powers," *Washington Post*, 16 December 1989, sec A, p. 1.

53. John Dinges, *Our Man in Panama*, 49; U.S. Department of Defense, Defense Intelligence Agency, "Defense Intelligence Summary: Panama" (Washington, DC: Department of Defense, 17 June 1986), 5, National Security Archive, Narcotics Collection, Panama, box 14.

54. Ramón Lamboglia, *Panama: De la Narcodictadura a Colonia Yanqui* (San José Costa Rica, 1992), 11–12, 36–37, 61. According to Ramón Lamboglia, a member of the anti-Torrijos and anti-Noriega Panamanian resistance, Torrijos's coup against Dr. Arnulfo Arias was backed by U.S. intelligence services because of Arias's anti-Yankee stance. In particular, Lamboglia argues that the U.S. Army's Military Intelligence Brigade 470 directed Torrijos's coup. The CIA's connection and influence in Panama was weak until Noriega was in power. Lamboglia argues that the CIA financed a failed counter-coup against Torrijos in December 1969 by Colonel Amado Sanjur, although Torrijos believed that Brigade 470 was behind the counter-coup.

55. U.S. Department of State, "Briefing Paper: Panama-Politics and Elections" (11 December 1983), 1, National Security Archive, Narcotics Collection, Panama, box 14; Christopher Dickey, "Fiscal, Social Woes Deter Entrants for 1984 Panamanian Election," *Washington Post*, 17 May 1983, sec. A, p. 14.

56. Ramón Lamboglia, *Panama: De la Narcodictadura a Colonia Yanqui*, 62–64. According to Lamboglia, Noriega supposedly was behind Torrijos's plane crash. Allegedly, Noriega put a bomb onboard Torrijos's plane.

57. James Nelson Goodsell, "Panama: Political Vacuum after Torrijos's Passing," *Christian Science Monitor*, 3 August 1981, 6.

58. David Gardner, "Panama's Palace Coup Postpones Power Struggle," *Financial Times*, 4 August 1982, sec. I, p. 2; Christopher Dickey, "Fiscal, Social Woes Deter Entrants," sec. A, p. 14.

59. U.S. Department of State, "Briefing Paper: Panama-Politics and Elections," 1.

60. Christopher Dickey, "Fiscal, Social Woes Deter Entrants," sec. A, p. 14.

61. U.S. Department of State, "Briefing Paper: Panama-Politics and Elections," 1.

62. Manuel Noriega and Peter Eisner, *America's Prisoner*, 59, 64–65.

63. John Dinges, *Our Man in Panama*, 149.

64. Manuel Noriega and Peter Eisner, *America's Prisoner*, 65.

65. Edward Cody, "President's Resignation Raises Doubts about Panamanian Vote," *Washington Post*, 15 February 1984, sec. A, p. 21; John Dinges, *Our Man in Panama*, 166.

66. Margot Hornblower, "Violence to be Repressed, Says Noriega; General in Panama Issues Warning," *Washington Post*, 11 May 1984, sec. A, p. 30.

67. Edward Cody, "New President Inaugurated in Panama; Military Lashes Out at Ardito Barletta," *Washington Post*, 25 September 1985, sec. A, p. 21.

68. James LeMoyne, "Elements in Ouster of Panama Chief: Beheading and a Power Duel," *New York Times*, 2 October 1985, sec. A, p. 12. Spadafora met with agents of the DEA in Costa Rica, but the DEA did not offer him protection because they considered his information fragmentary. Frederick Kempe, *Toda la Verdad*, 193.

69. American Embassy San Jose to Secretary of State Washington, DC, "Hugo Spadafora: Death Linked to Noriega" (September 1985), 1, National Security Archive, Narcotics

Collection, Panama, box 14. This same cable also mentions a Noriega-owned farm in northern Costa Rica used for drug running that was really John Hull's ranch. This definitely raises some concern regarding who knew what and who was telling the truth in the Kerry investigation.

70. James LeMoyne, "Elements in Ouster of Panama Chief," sec. A, p. 12.

71. Ramón Lamboglia, *Panama: De la Narcodictadura a Colonia Yanqui*, 68–70. Kempe states that Spadafora was a threat not only to Noriega and the Medellín cartel, but also to the CIA, because his allegations might expose their illegal efforts to arm the Contras. See: Frederick Kempe, *Toda la Verdad*, 188.

72. Manuel Noriega and Peter Eisner, *America's Prisoner*, 65.

73. James LeMoyne, "Elements in Ouster of Panama Chief," sec. A, p. 12; Manuel Noriega and Peter Eisner, *America's Prisoner*, 65. Later, it was learned that members of the PDF murdered Spadafora. They acted without orders because they were allegedly defending the PDF's honor.

74. Seymour M. Hersh, "Panama Strongman Said to Trade in Drugs, Arms, and Illicit Money," *New York Times*, 12 June 1986, sec. A, p. 1; Manuel Noriega and Peter Eisner, *America's Prisoner*, 121. In 1986, White House officials directly implicated Noriega as the originator and planner of the killing. This assertion calls into question Lamboglia's assertion that the CIA was behind the murder, but without further evidence, one can only speculate that the CIA was trying to remove Noriega from power because he was a liability. The case of Vladimiro Montesino's gunrunning operation to the FARC in chapter 8 offers another example of this kind of setup.

75. James LeMoyne, "Elements in Ouster of Panama Chief," sec. A, p. 12.

76. Seymour M. Hersh, "Panama Strongman Said to Trade in Drugs," sec. A, p. 1.

77. John Herbers, "Panama General Accused by Helms," *New York Times*, 23 June 1986, sec. A, p. 3.

78. Seymour M. Hersh, "Panama Strongman Said to Trade in Drugs," sec. A, p. 1.

79. John Herbers, "Panama General Accused by Helms," sec. A, p. 3.

80. House of Representatives Select Committee on Narcotics Abuse and Control, *Panama*, 99th Cong., 2nd sess., 19 June 1986, 2.

81. Senate Subcommittee on Terrorism, Narcotics, and International Operation of the Committee on Foreign Relations, *Drugs, Law Enforcement, and Foreign Policy*, 88.

82. Joe Pichirallo, "U.S. Probes Panama Strongman on Drug Ties; Sentiment for Ouster Grows; General Denies Role in Drug Trafficking," *Washington Post*, 11 November 1987, sec A, p. 1.

83. Birch Bayh, "Report to the Senate of Birch Bayh, Chairman of the Select Committee on Intelligence," 14.

84. House of Representatives Select Committee on Narcotics Abuse and Control, *Panama*, 40.

85. American Embassy Panama to Secretary of State Washington, DC, "The Drug Bust of a Senior PDF Officer–Many Questions but Few Answers" (July 1984), 2, National Security Archive, Narcotics Collection, Panama, box 14.

86. American Embassy Panama to Secretary of State Washington, DC, "General Staff Member Fired, Arrested for Drug Activities" (July 1984), 2–3, National Security Archive, Narcotics Collection, Panama, box 14.

87. Ibid.; Manuel Noriega and Peter Eisner, *America's Prisoner*, 200–206.

88. Seymour M. Hersh, "Panama Strongman Said to Trade in Drugs," sec. A, p. 1.

89. Senate Subcommittee on Terrorism, Narcotics, and International Operation of the Committee on Foreign Relations, *Drugs, Law Enforcement, and Foreign Policy*, 92–94.

90. John Dinges, *Our Man in Panama*, 149.

91. Frederick Kempe, *Noriega: Toda la Verdad*, 179.

92. Manuel Noriega and Peter Eisner, *America's Prisoner*, 65–66.

93. Frederick Kempe, *Noriega: Toda la Verdad*, 240, 243–247.

94. Manuel Noriega and Peter Eisner, *America's Prisoner*, 124, 65–66.

95. Ibid.; Frederick Kempe, *Noriega: Toda la Verdad*, 240.

96. Manuel Noriega and Peter Eisner, *America's Prisoner*, 66.

97. John Dinges, *Our Man in Panama*, 317.

98. Manuel Noriega and Peter Eisner, *America's Prisoner*, 124. Lawrence Eagleberger states that this meeting only touched on the subject of Nicaragua in passing. See: U.S. Department of State, Bureau of Public Affairs, *The Case Against Panama's Noriega* (by Lawrence Eagleberger), *Current Policy* no. 1222, 12 January 1990, 4.

99. U.S. Department of State, Bureau of Public Affairs, *The Case Against Panama's Noriega*, 4–6; Frederick Kempe, *Noriega: Toda la Verdad*, 243–247. Abrams was the sub-secretary of Latin American Affairs for the Department of State during the Reagan administration.

100. W. Clegg, "Panama Strongman Rejects Alleged Link with Drug Barons," *Courier-Mail*, 8 February 1988.

101. Manuel Noriega and Peter Eisner, *America's Prisoner*, 81.

102. Luis E. Murillo, *The Noriega Mess: The Drugs, the Canal, and Why America Invaded*, (Berkeley, CA: Video Books, 1995), 550–554. Murrillo's presentation of the *Pia Vesta* case is unclear and leaves information, such as the potential Sendero link or the possibility that the CIA exposed Noriega's arms shipment for its own use.

103. Ibid.; Bradley Graham, "Ship off of Peru Bore Arms, but Whose? Mystery Cargo from East Germany Creates Scandal," *Washington Post*, 29 August 1986, sec. A, p. 17.

104. Ibid.; Alan Riding, "Arms Ship Leave Wake of Mystery in Peru," *New York Times*, 31 August 1986, sec. A, p. 1.

105. Bradley Graham, "Ship off of Peru Bore Arms, but Whose?," sec. A, p. 17.

106. Ibid.; Alan Riding, "Arms Ship Leave Wake of Mystery in Peru," sec. A, p. 1.

107. Luis E. Murillo, *The Noriega Mess*, 553–554; Senate Subcommittee on Terrorism, Narcotics, and International Communications of the Committee on Foreign Relations, *Drugs, Law Enforcement, and Foreign Policy: Panama*, 165–69.

108. Luis E. Murillo, *The Noriega Mess*, 554.

109. Ibid., 553.

110. U.S. Department of Defense, Defense Intelligence Agency, "Panama: PDF Chief Under Fire" (17 June 1986), National Security Archive, Narcotics Collection, Panama, box 14.

111. Senate Subcommittee on Terrorism, Narcotics, and International Operation of the Committee on Foreign Relations, *Drugs, Law Enforcement, and Foreign Policy*, 96.

112. Oliver North to John Poindexter, "Subject: Iran" (23 August 1986), The Oliver North Diary, 1, The Oliver North File: His Diaries, E-Mail, and Memos on the Kerry Report, Contras and Drugs, National Security Archive Electronic Briefing Book No. 113 (26 February 2004), http://www.gwu.edu/~nsarchiv/NSAEBB/NSAEBB113/index. htm (accessed 4 March 2006). In the same memo by North, he indicated that Noriega had orchestrated an attack using his own agents against a Sandinista army arsenal in Managua.

113. Frederick Kempe, *Noriega: Toda la Verdad*, 259.

114. Julia Preston, "Panamanians Riot After Accusations; Colonel Details Case Against Strongman," *Washington Post*, 10 June 1987, sec. A, p. 19.

115. Jim Mulvaney, "A General with Panama in His Pocket: The Rich Pickings Behind the Struggle for Power in America's Backyard," *Guardian*, 12 June 1987. After the PDF stormed his house, Diaz Herrera was arrested and later exiled to Venezuela. See: Jim Mannion, "Panamanian Colonel to be Exiled," *Saint Petersburg Times*, 31 July 1987, sec. A, p. 2.

116. John Dinges, *Our Man in Panama*, 264.

117. Robert Graham, "Panama Leader Defended by State Department," *Financial Times*, 30 June 1987, sec. I, p. 6.

118. American Embassy Panama to Secretary of State Washington, DC, "Narcotics Money Laundering in Panama" (March 1987), 1, National Security Archive, Narcotics Collection, Panama, box 14.

119. By measuring the inflows and outflows of money to and from the United States and Panama, Fabio Castillo estimated that as much as $1,003,550,000 was laundered in Panama in 1985, in comparison with the $278,584,600 that was laundered in 1982. See: Fabio Castillo, *La Coca Nostra*, 163.

120. American Embassy Panama to Secretary of State Washington, DC, "Panamanian Reaction to DEA Money Laundering Operation (Operation Pisces)" (May 1987), 1, National Security Archive, Narcotics: Panama, box 14; Joe Pichirallo, "U.S. Probes Panama Strongman on Drug Ties; Sentiment for Ouster Grows; General Denies Role in Drug Trafficking," sec A, p. 1. The Bolivian authors Gutierrez and Pando claim that a 1989 DEA document implicates banking mogul Edmund Safra, a Brazilian who made a fortune smuggling weapons for the CIA. He allegedly used controlling banks in Panama and Brazil to wash narco-dollars earned from subsidiary banks in Bolivia and Peru. See: Gutierrez and Pando, *La Lucha Boliviana Contra la Agresion del Narcotráfico*, 402–403.

121. Senate Subcommittee on Terrorism, Narcotics, and International Operation of the Committee on Foreign Relations, *Drugs, Law Enforcement, and Foreign Policy*, 92.

122. Ibid.; Joe Pichirallo, "U.S. Probes Panama Strongman on Drug Ties," sec A, p. 1.

123. Jim Mannion, "Anti-U.S. Campaign in Panama Becomes Increasingly Bitter," *St. Petersburg Times*, 1 August 1987, sec. A, p. 1.

124. Elaine Sciolino, "U.S. Berates Panamanian Regime in Pressing for Democratic Rule," *New York Times*, 2 July 1987, sec. A, p. 1.

125. Larry Rother, "Struggle in Panama; Noriega is Adamant Despite Call for Ouster," *New York Times*, 30 July 1987, sec. A, p. 11.

126. Ibid.

127. Jim Mannion, "Anti-U.S. Campaign in Panama Becomes Increasingly Bitter," *St. Petersburg Times*, 1 August 1987, sec. A, p. 1.

128. Senate Subcommittee on Terrorism, Narcotics, and International Operation of the Committee on Foreign Relations, *Drugs, Law Enforcement, and Foreign Policy*, 84, 86.

129. Ibid. In a U.S. Department of State paper, Lawrence Eagleberger claims that Kalish made payments of one million dollars to Noriega and others in order to smuggle marijuana out of Panama. See: U.S. Department of State, Bureau of Public Affairs, *The Case Against Panama's Noriega*, 2.

130. Senate Subcommittee on Terrorism, Narcotics, and International Operation of the Committee on Foreign Relations, *Drugs, Law Enforcement, and Foreign Policy*, 84. The plane was given official status so that it could be used in a money laundering operation in which the plane would fly money out of Washington under the cover of diplomatic immunity.

131. American Embassy Washington to Secretary of State Washington, DC, "Ex Consul Blandon Continues Attacks on FDP Ranking Officers–Advocates a Blandon Plan" (February 1988), 1, National Security Archive, Narcotics Collection, Panama, box 14.

132. Senate Subcommittee on Terrorism, Narcotics, and International Operation of the Committee on Foreign Relations, *Drugs, Law Enforcement, and Foreign Policy*, 86.

133. John Maggs, "U.S. Says Noriega Sold Chemicals to Drug Lords," *Journal of Commerce*, 5 January 1990, sec. A. p. 1.

134. U.S. Department of State, Bureau of Public Affairs, *The Case Against Panama's Noriega*, 2. The Tampa grand jury also indicted Enrique Pretlet, the middleman between Kalish and Noriega.

135. W. Clegg, "Panama Strongman Rejects Alleged Link with Drug Barons."

136. Manuel Noriega and Peter Eisner, *America's Prisoner*, 202.

137. John Dinges, *Our Man in Panama*, 289–291.

138. William Branigin, "Noriega Intensifies Attacks on Domestic, Foreign Opponents," *Washington Post*, 10 February 1988, sec. A, p. 29.

139. D. Costello, "U.S. Military Told to Leave Panama," *Courier-Mail*, 10 February 1988.

140. American Embassy Panama to Secretary of State Washington, DC, "Assessment of Threat to American Community After Indictment of Noriega" (February 1988), 7, National Security Archive, Narcotics Collection, Panama, box 14. The State Department report also stated that a "normal military to military relationship" could remain at the "working level," yet this depended on Noriega.

141. Ela Navarrete Talavera, *Panama: Invasión o Revolución* (Mexico, DF: Grupo Editorial Planeta, 1990), 146.

142. Ronald H. Cole, "Joint Staff Special Historical Study, Operation Just Cause: Planning and Executions of Joint operations in Panama February 1988–January 1990 (Washington, DC: Department of Defense, Joint Chiefs of Staff, December 1990), 3, National Security Archive, Narcotics Collection, Panama, box 14. In 1988, Blandon shared evidence that Noriega signed a contract with the Soviets in 1987, who established a factory to build patrol boats. Noriega also agreed to provide services to Soviet fishing boats and the Soviet airline Aeroflot. See: Ela Navarrete Talavera, *Panama: Invasión o Revolución*, 155.

143. Ronald H. Cole, "Joint Staff Special Historical Study, Operation Just Cause," 3. The report cites the following report: "National Military Intelligence Support Team (NMIST), Panama Intelligence Task Force (ITF) to USSOUTHCOM J-2, 280150Z" (December 1989), S Pan Binder J-5/DDPMA/WHEM. Msg USCINSCO to JCS 140325Z, April 1988, TS, Pan. Fact Bk. J-3/JOD/WHEM.

144. American Embassy Panama to Secretary of State Washington, DC, "Further Reaction to Noriega Indictment" (February 1988), 1, National Security Archive, Narcotics Collection, Panama, box 14.

145. American Embassy Panama to Secretary of State Washington, DC, "Assessment of Threat to American Community After Indictment of Noriega," 7, 8.

146. Ronald H. Cole, "Joint Staff Special Historical Study, Operation Just Cause," 16.

147. Ela Navarrete Talavera, *Panama: Invasión o Revolución*, 172.

148. Ronald H. Cole, "Joint Staff Special Historical Study, Operation Just Cause," 11–12.

149. Ibid.

150. Ibid., 38–39. Ramón Lamboglia, a member of the anti-Noriega resistance, questions the necessity of the U.S. invasion of Panama. Why didn't the United States use a Stealth bomber to blow up Noriega's house, or a group of mercenaries to kill Noriega, if Noriega alone was the reason for the invasion? Lamboglia believes that the United States conducted the invasion to prevent the emergence of true democracy in Panama; the invasion protected the interests of the "Yankees" and the "Panamanian oligarchy." Lamboglia argues that the United States intended Panama to remain a North American colony, disguised as an independent republic. See: Ramón Lamboglia, *Panama: De la Narcodictadura a Colonia Yanqui*, 101.

151. *Washington Post*, "Arrest of Noriega Is Significant Milestone That Should Send a Clear Signal, Bush Says," *Washington Post*, 4 January 1990, sec. A, p. 28.

152. David Adams, "U.S. Boosts Role of Military in Drugs War," *Independent*, 16 July 1990, 11.

153. Donald J. Mabry, "The U.S. Military and the War on Drugs," 49.

154. Senate Subcommittee on Terrorism, Narcotics, and International Operations of the Committee on Foreign Relations, *Andean Drug Initiative*. 102nd Cong., 2nd sess., 20 February 1992, 42.

155. U.S. Department of State, Bureau of Public Affairs, *U.S. Economic Military and Counternarcotics Program Assistance* (18 February 1992), 1, National Security Archive, Narcotics Collection, Peru: U.S. Operations, Sendero, Fujimori, box 6.

156. House of Representatives Committee on Foreign Affairs, *Review of the International Aspects of the President's Drug Control Strategy*, 101st Cong., 1st sess., 12 September 1989, 8.

157. American Embassy La Paz to Secretary of State Washington, DC, "Preparations for the Andean Drug Summit" (November 1989), 2, National Security Archive, Narcotics Collection, Peru-Colombia-Andes Documents Part I, Andean Drug Summit, box 49.

158. American Embassy Lima to Secretary of State Washington, DC, "1989–1993 Programs Plans and Supporting Budget" (April 1987), 1, National Security Archive, Narcotics Collection, Peru: U.S. Operations, Sendero, Fujimori, (Department of State Documents 1984–1987), box 7.

159. Secretary of State Washington, DC to American Embassy Lima, "Building Support for Andean Strategy" (October 1989), 1, National Security Archive, Narcotics Collection, Peru-Colombia-Andes Documents Part I, Andean Drug Summit, box 49; Senate Committee on the Judiciary and the Caucus on International Narcotics Control, *U.S. International Drug Policy-Multinational Strike Forces-Drug Policy in the Andean Nations*, 101st Cong., 1st and 2nd sess., 6 November 1989 and 18 January 1990, 65. Senator Joseph Biden proposed a foreign debt conversion plan that designated a portion of the debt to antinarcotics efforts, but this plan was rejected. Edmundo Morales argued in 1990 that the purchase of the entire coca crop was the most effective measure to control coca. According to Morales, such a plan would prevent coca from falling into the hands of organized crime, while at the same time it would protect the campesino economy. Morales does not consider the State Department's argument that this plan only encouraged more coca production. See: Edmundo Morales, "The Political Economy of Cocaine Production," 106–107.

160. Secretary of State Washington, DC to American Embassy Lima, "Building Support for Andean Strategy," 2; House of Representatives Committee on Foreign Affairs, *Review of the International Aspects of the President's 1990 Drug Control Strategy*, 101st Cong., 2nd sess., 27 February 1990, 110. Comments from the House Foreign Affairs Committee question-and-answer session.

161. Senate Committee on the Judiciary and the Caucus on International Narcotics Control, *U.S. International Drug Policy-Multinational Strike Forces*, 73, 75.

162. Ibid., 85, 89.

163. Richard L. Millet, "The Aftermath of Invasion: Panama 1990," *Journal of Interamerican Studies and World Affairs* 32, no. 1. (Spring 1990): 13.

164. Marshall Ingwerson, "Bush Prepares for Colombia Trip," *Christian Science Monitor*, 12 February 1990, 7.

165. Secretary of State Washington, DC to American Embassy La Paz, "President Paz re. Garcia, Panama, and the Andean Summit" (December 1989), 1, National Security Archive, Narcotics Collection, Peru-Colombia-Andes Documents Part I, Andean Drug Summit, box 49.

166. *Miami Herald*, "Angry Peru Halts U.S. Sponsored Drug Fight," 23 December 1989, sec. A, p. 1.

167. Peter Riddell, "Panama Invasion Unique, U.S. Tells Latin America," *Financial Times*, 8 January 1990, sec. I, p. 3.

168. Eugene Robinson, "Latins Leery of Any U.S. Military; Opposition to Panama Invasion Could Carry Over Into Drug Issue," *Washington Post*, 9 January 1990, sec. A, p. 16. Colombian anger towards the United States became so extreme that Fulbright scholars were withdrawn from the country.

169. United Press International, "Quayle Upbeat on Latin American Peace Mission," *Christian Science Monitor*, 31 January 1990, 8.

170. Cal Thomas, "Quayle Sees Ties with Latin America Unhurt by Invasion," *St. Louis Post Dispatch*, 4 February 1990, sec. B, p. 3; *St. Louis Post Dispatch*, "Quayle Ends Tour on Sour Note," 30 January 1990, sec. A, p. 7. Quayle's trip was limited to Panama, Honduras, and Jamaica. Mexico, Venezuela, Costa Rica, Colombia, and Peru rejected him.

171. Secretary of State Washington, DC to American Embassy La Paz, "President Paz re: Garcia, Panama, and the Andean Summit," 1.

172. Marshall Ingwerson, "Bush Prepares for Colombia Trip," 7.

173. House of Representatives Committee on Foreign Affairs, *Review of the International Aspects of the President's 1990 Drug Control Strategy*, 76.

174. Ibid., 9.

175. Foreign Broadcast Information Service, "Leaders Give News Conference," *Inter-American Affairs*, FBIS–LAT–90–033, (16 February 1990): 4, National Security Archive, Narcotics Collection, Peru-Colombia-Andes Documents Part I, Andean Drug Summit, box 49. Presidents Virgilio Barco, Jaime Paz Zamora, Alan Garcia, and George Bush held a joint news conference with reporters at the presidential guest house, 15 February 1990.

176. Ibid., 3. Interview with Colombian Minister Julio Londoño Paredes, 15 February 1990.

177. Ibid., 9. Interview with President Alan Garcia, 16 February 1990.

178. John Lichfield, "Bush Claims that U.S. Firms' Laxness Is Helping Drug Barons," *Independent*, 28 April 1989, 12.

179. United Nations, United Nations Convention against Illicit Traffic in Narcotics Drugs and Psychotropic Substances, Article 12, Vienna Austria, United Nations Commission on Narcotics Drugs, 20 December 1988, 12. Chemical producers and traders must provide transaction details to their national authorities.

180. House of Representatives Committee on Foreign Affairs, *Review of the International Aspects of the President's 1990 Drug Control Strategy*, 83–84. The system for issuing import permits is a major problem for Colombia's chemical control program. The State Department's *2006 International Narcotics Control Strategy Report* states that the permits do prove reliably that the legitimate end-use for the chemicals was verified prior to issuance. Chemicals used illegally are frequently imported into the country with valid import licenses. Chemicals are also diverted or smuggled into Colombia, Peru, or Bolivia from neighboring countries, including Brazil, Ecuador, and Venezuela. Large quantities of chemicals, originating in China and shipped though Mexico, have reportedly reached Colombia. In Bolivia, traffickers have substituted inferior chemicals and recycling as a method to get around chemical control laws. See: U.S. Department of State, Bureau of International Narcotics Matters, *2006 International Narcotics Control Strategy Report Vol. I: Drug and Chemical Control* (March 2006), http://www.state.gov/p/inl/rls/nrcrpt/2006/vol1/html/62105.htm (accessed 17 January 2007). In 2005 the State Department started listing all INCSRs by the year of issuance. Thus, the 2005 report covered the year 2004, although the date of the report was given as 2005.

181. House of Representatives Committee on Foreign Affairs, *Review of the International Aspects of the President's 1990 Drug Control Strategy*, 82.

182. House of Representatives Select Committee on Narcotics Abuse and Control, *The Andean Summit Meeting, 15 February 1990,* 101st Cong, 1st sess., 7 March 1990, 33. Statement of Bernard W. Aronson, assistant secretary of state for inter-American affairs.

183. House of Representatives Committee on Foreign Affairs. *Review of the International Aspects of the President's 1990 Drug Control Strategy*, 79. Text of the Declaration of Cartagena.

184. U.S. Department of State, Bureau of Public Affairs, *U.S. Economic, Military, and Counternarcotics Program Assistance* (18 February 1992), 1.

185. House of Representatives Subcommittee on Trade of the Committee on Ways and Means, *Andean Trade Preference Act of 1991*, 102nd Cong., 1st sess., 25 July 1991, 38.

186. House of Representatives Select Committee On Narcotics Abuse and Control, *Andean Strategy*, 102nd Cong., 1st sess., 11 June 1991, 77.

187. House of Representatives Subcommittee on Trade of the Committee on Ways and Means, *Andean Trade Preference Act of 1991*, 55, 81. Statement of Bernard W. Aronson, assistant secretary of state for inter-American affairs.

188. Ibid., 169–209.

189. General Accounting Office, Report to Congressional Requesters, *Drug Policies and Agriculture: U.S. Trade Impacts of Alternative Crops to Andean Coca*, GAO/NSIAD-92-12 (Washington, DC: General Accounting Office, October 1991), 3–4.

190. House of Representatives Subcommittee on Trade of the Committee on Ways and Means, *Andean Trade Preference Act of 1991*, 169–209.

191. United States Trade Commission, *The Impact of the Andean Trade Preference Act Eleventh Report 2004 Investigation No. 332–352* (September 2005), 15.

192. House of Representatives, Subcommittee on Trade of the Committee on Ways and Means, *Andean Trade Preference Act of 1991*, 56. Statement of Bernard W. Aronson, assistant secretary of state for inter-American affairs.

193. Ibid.

194. House of Representatives Subcommittee on Trade of the Committee on Ways and Means, *Andean Trade Preference Act of 1991*, 38.

195. Montieth M. Illingworth, "U.S. Program to Andeans Faces Hurdles," sec. C, pp 1, 39.

Chapter 7: The Failure of the Andean Strategy

1. House of Representatives Select Committee on Narcotics Abuse and Control of the House Foreign Affairs Committee, *San Antonio Summit and the Andean Strategy*, 102nd Cong., 2nd sess., 26 March 1992, 3. Statement of Melvin Levitsky.

2. Simon Tisdall, "Doubts Cast on Bush Drug War," *Guardian*, 28 February 1992, 10.

3. Ricardo Soberón, "Issue Brief 6: The War on Cocaine in Peru: From Cartagena to San Antonio" (Washington, DC: Washington Office on Latin America, 7 August 1992), 9. Juan Gabriel Tokatlián, "Drug Summitry: A Colombian Perspective," 133.

4. Simon Tisdall, "Doubts Cast on Bush Drug War," 10.

5. Allison Speeding Pallet, *En Defensa de la Hoja de Coca* (La Paz: Programa de Investigación Estratégica en Bolivia, 2003), 19–27. Pallet and her investigators argue that those who develop crop-substitution programs do not understand the campesinos' way of life. Campesinos, the study contends, live as a unit that employs the whole family, whereas alternative crops are basically geared only toward men who are capable of doing the work. In addition, the campesinos' lifestyle is not driven by the desire to maximize wealth from their labor. Instead, campesinos seek a balance between acquiring the wealth to survive and maintaining a daily way of life that does not exhaust them. Coca is more cost-effective because the labor required to raise a coca crop employs the whole family and is not as labor intensive as alternative crops. Moreover, cultivation of the alternative crops requires larger parcels of land and returns a profit only once or twice a year. Coca can be picked and dried up to four times a year and uses less land to produce a profitable harvest.

6. Rensselaer Lee and Patrick Clawson, *Crop Substitution in the Andes* (Washington, DC: Office of National Drug Control Policy, December 1993), 19.

7. Ibid., 1; Allison Speeding Pallet, *En Defensa de la Hoja de Coca*, 22.

8. Lee Hamilton, "Effort to Attack Drugs at Source Falters," *Christian Science Monitor*, 17 July 1991, 19. Hamilton was a member of the House of Representatives and served on the Foreign Affairs and Joint Economic Committees.

9. Don Bostwick PhD, Joseph Dorsey PhD, and James Jones PhD, "USAID Evaluation of the Chapare Regional Development Project," 25; Rensselaer Lee and Patrick Clawson, *Crop Substitution in the Andes*, 19.

10. Don Bostwick PhD, Joseph Dorsey PhD, and James Jones PhD, "USAID Evaluation of the Chapare Regional Development Project," 25; USAID, "Audit of USAID/Bolivia Chapare Regional Development Project no. 511–0543, Audit Report no 1–511–91–013," 6–8.

11. James Painter, "Peasants Protest U.S. Role in Bolivia's Drug War," 7.

12. House of Representatives Subcommittee on Western Hemisphere Affairs of the Committee on Foreign Affairs, *The Andean Drug Strategy*, 102nd Cong., 1st sess., 26 February 1991, 45.

13. Don Bostwick PhD, Joseph Dorsey PhD, and James Jones PhD, "USAID Evaluation of the Chapare Regional Development Project," 61; Allison Speeding Pallet, *En Defensa de la Hoja de Coca*, 24–27. Pallet's study argues that labor is the only investment required for coca production, whereas investment in an alternative crop requires labor, tools, and agro-chemicals. The study contends that this added investment leads campesinos to see alternative crops as unprofitable, since the earnings from their overall investment in alternative crops are less than what they can earn from coca.

14. Rensselaer Lee and Patrick Clawson, *Crop Substitution in the Andes*, 35.

15. Don Bostwick PhD, Joseph Dorsey PhD, and James Jones PhD, "USAID Evaluation of the Chapare Regional Development Project," 61.

16. Rensselear Lee and Patrick Clawson, *Crop Substitution in the Andes*, 36.

17. Don Bostwick PhD, Joseph Dorsey PhD, and James Jones PhD, "USAID Evaluation of the Chapare Regional Development Project," 61.

18. USAID, "Abbreviated PID for Upper Huallaga Area Development Project no. 527–0244," 5, 38.

19. General Accounting Office, Report to Congressional Requesters, *Drug Policies and Agriculture*, 18–19. At seventy-five dollars per one hundred pounds, only pineapple rivaled coca, which was then overshadowed when the price of coca was at one hundred dollars per one hundred pounds.

20. USAID, "Abbreviated PID for Upper Huallaga Area Development Project no. 527–0244," 41; U.S. Department of State, Bureau of International Narcotics Matters, *1991 International Narcotics Control Strategy Report* (March 1992), 88.

21. U.S. Department of State, Bureau of International Narcotics Matters, *1991 International Narcotics Control Strategy Report*, 10.

22. House of Representatives Subcommittee on Western Hemisphere Affairs of the Committee on Foreign Affairs, *The Andean Drug Strategy*, 42.

23. U.S. Department of State, Bureau of International Narcotics Matters, *1991 International Narcotics Control Strategy Report*, 10.

24. House of Representatives Select Committee on Narcotics Abuse and Control, *Andean Strategy*, 81.

25. Office of National Drug Control Policy, *Appendix: National Drug Control Strategy 1997*, www.ncjrs.gov/htm/data.htm (accessed 5 March 2006). The report cites ABT Associates Inc. as the source. Data for this estimate comes from System to Retrieve Information from Drug Evidence, Drug Enforcement Administration, 1981–1996. The second source also comes from ABT Associates Inc. and is titled "What America's Users Spend on Illegal Drugs," 1988–93 (Spring 1995).

26. U.S. Department of State, Bureau of International Narcotics Matters, *1991 International Narcotics Control Strategy Report*, 88, 101, 122.

27. Office of National Drug Control Policy, *Appendix: National Drug Control Strategy 1997*, www. ncjrs.gov/htm/data.htm (accessed 5 March 2006). Data for this estimate comes from System to Retrieve Information from Drug Evidence, Drug Enforcement Administration, 1981–1996. This data is based on purchases of five ounces or less of cocaine.

28. Ibid.

29. House of Representatives Select Committee on Narcotics Abuse and Control, *Andean Strategy*, 30–36.

30. American Embassy La Paz to Secretary of State Washington, DC, "1991 International Narcotics Control Strategy Report" (December 1990), 20–21, National Security Archive, Narcotics Collection, Bolivia, Documents from FOIA, box 33.

31. Melanie S. Tammen, "Policy Analysis: The Drug War vs. Land Reform in Peru," 19–21.

32. Christina Lamb, "Poverty Thwarts Drugs Fight in Bolivia," *Financial Times*, 18 July 1991, sec. I, p. 3.

33. USAID, "Abbreviated PID for Upper Huallaga Area Development Project no. 527-0244," 7.

34. House of Representatives Committee on Foreign Affairs, *Review of the International Aspects of the President's Drug Control Strategy*, 8.

35. Virgilio Barco, *En Defensa de la Democracia: La Lucha Contra el Narcotráfico y el Terrorismo* (Bogotá: La Presidencia de la República, 20 julio 1990), 20–25; Rensselaer Lee and Patrick Clawson, *The Andean Cocaine Industry*, 22.

36. Eugene Robinson, "Colombian Candidate Murdered; President Sets Moves Against Drug Lords Reinstates Extradition," *Washington Post*, 20 August 1989, sec. A, p. 1. At a campaign rally filled with ten thousand people, Galán was killed by scattered automatic weapons fire. See: Associated Press, "Drug Lords Say Killings to Continue," *St. Louis Post Dispatch*, 20 August 1989, sec. A, p. 1.

37. Eugene Robinson, "Colombian Candidate Murdered," sec. A, p .1; Alan Riding, "Colombia Uses Army in Cocaine Raids," *New York Times*, 5 May 1988, sec. A, p. 3.

38. Eugene Robinson, "Colombia Seizes Aircraft, Cash in Crackdown; Arrests Continue, but Drug Kingpins Are Not Caught in Sweep," *Washington Post*, 22 August 1989, sec. A, p. 1; Virgilio Barco, *En Defensa de la Democracia: La Lucha Contra el Narcotráfico y el Terrorismo*, 55. Alejandro Reyes wrote that the war against the Medellín cartel by the Colombian police took the lives of many civilians. Consequently, neighborhood groups in Medellín began to form their own militias to control crime and defend themselves against the police. In some cases, these groups evolved into urban guerrilla cells for the FARC and the ELN in Medellín. See: Alejandro Reyes, "Drug Trafficking and the Guerrilla Movement in Colombia," 127.

39. Associated Press, "Drug Lords Say Killings to Continue," sec. A, p. 1.

40. House of Representatives Subcommittee on International Security, International Organizations and Human Rights of the Committee on Foreign Affairs, *The 1993 International Narcotics Control Strategy Report and the Future of U.S. Narcotics Policy*, 103rd Cong., 1st sess., 11 May 1993, 39.

41. INSCOM, "General Intelligence Summaries on Andes and Drug Trafficking" (1989), 0681, National Security Archive, Narcotics Collection, Colombia: Documents from FOIA, box 32. Another theory about the Avianca bombing claimed that the bombing stemmed from a war between the Cali and Medellín cartels. The war will be discussed later, but some people believed that Escobar wanted to kill Gilberto Orujela's girlfriend, who was on the plane, in retaliation for making Escobar's daughter partially deaf. A bomb set off by the Cali cartel outside Escobar's home was responsible for her deafness.

42. Stan Yarbro, "Government Steps Up Security Fearing Retaliation," Associated Press Wire, 16 December 1989.

43. *St. Louis Post Dispatch*, "Medellín Cartel Offers Peace for Pardons," 18 January 1990, sec. A, p. 1.

44. Eugene Robinson, "Barco Makes First Response to Traffickers; Colombia Said to Be in a New Situation," *Washington Post*, 20 January 1990, sec. A, p. 12.

45. House of Representatives Select Committee on Narcotics Abuse and Control, *Andean Strategy*, 59. Statement of Melvin Levitsky before the House Committee on Narcotics Abuse and Control on 11 June 1991.

46. *St. Louis Post Dispatch*, "Colombia Deserts the Drug War," 11 September 1990, sec. B, p. 2.

47. Joint Staff Washington, DC, to Info RUEADWD/OCSA Washington, DC, "Gaviria's U.S. Trip: His Own Words" (March 1991), 0420, National Security Archive, Narcotics Collection, Colombia: Documents from FOIA, box 32.

48. Douglas Farah, "Escobar Killed in Medellín," *Washington Post*, 3 December 1993, sec. A, p. 1; Douglas Farah, "Drug Lords Surrender a Victory for Colombia," *Washington Post*, 18 January 1991, sec. A, p. 14.

49. Lawrence David Aquila, "Colombia Gives Us Reach in Drug War, but Limits It," 2.

50. Al Kamen, "Colombian, Bush Vow to Win Drug War; Gaviria Visit Designed to Ease Skepticism," *Washington Post*, 27 February 1991, sec. A, p. 6.

51. Office of National Drug Control Policy, *Measuring the Deterrent Effect of Enforcement Operations on Drug Smuggling 1991–1999*, (Washington, DC: U.S. Government Printing Office, August 2001), 68. In 1993 the Cali cartel was earning an estimated thirty billion dollars a year. See: Douglas Farah, "Impact of Drugs Outlasts Escobar: Leader Seeks Deal With Colombia: Minimal Jail Time Maximum Profits," *Washington Post*, 10 December 1993, sec. A, p. 47.

52. Douglas Farah, "Cali Drug Cartel Avoids Crackdown," *Washington Post*, 5 October 1989, sec. E, p. 1.

53. Ron Chepesiuk, *Drug Lords: The Rise and Fall of the Cali Cartel* (London: Milo Books, 2005), 62–64.

54. Ron Chepesiuk, *Drug Lords*, 122–23.

55. Gustavo Veloza, *La Guerra Entre los Carteles del Narcotráfico*, (Bogotá: G.S. Editores, 1988), 82.

56. Ron Chepesiuk, *Drug Lords*, 122–23.

57. Don Podesta, "Escobar's Escape Was a Buyout," *Washington Post*, 26 July 1992, sec. A, p. 33.

58. Colin Harding, "Escobar Escape Challenges State," *Independent*, 24 July 1992, 1.

59. U.S. Southern Command (U.S. SOUTHCOM), Department of Defense, "PEPES: Perseguidos Por Pablo Escobar" (no date), 8, National Security Archive, Narcotics Collection, Peru-Colombia-Andes Documents Part I, Colombia FOIAs, box 49; American Embassy Bogotá to Secretary of State Washington, DC, "Unraveling the PEPES tangled Web" (August 1993), 2, National Security Archive, The Colombia Documentation Project, Colombian Paramilitaries and the United States, http://www.gwu.edu/~nsarchiv/NSAEBB/NSAEBB69/part3b.html (accessed 17 February 2008). According to Lee and Clawson, Medellín traffickers (supported by the Cali cartel) formed PEPES. They were traffickers who refused to pay Escobar's war taxes of two hundred thousand dollars a month to fight the Colombian government and the Cali cartel. See: Rensselaer Lee and Patrick Clawson, *The Andean Cocaine Industry*, 114.

60. Douglas Farah, "Escobar Killed in Medellín," sec. A, p. 38.

61. Ibid. According to Thoumi, the relaxation of exchange controls lessened the importance of the ventanilla siniestra. A DEA report argued that the elimination of exchange controls made it easier to bring large sums of drug money into the country disguised as foreign investment. See: Francisco E. Thoumi, *Illegal Drugs, Economy, and Society*, 189; Donald Im, "The Colombian Economic Reform: The Impact of Drug Money Laundering Within The Colombian Economy" (Washington, DC: Conference Report: Economics of the Narcotics Industry, Bureau of Intelligence and Research, U.S. Department of State and Central Intelligence Agency, 1994).

62. Stephen Fidler, "Colombia on a Tide of Money," sec I, p. 32.

63. World Bank, *2004 World Development Indicators CD-Rom*. Both statistics are percentages of annual exports and imports into Colombia.

64. Duncan Robinson, "Trading with Colombia: Tariff on Imports Slashed," *The Journal of Commerce*, 13 September 1991, sec. B, p. 4.

65. Ibid.

66. According to the FARC, unemployment, the collapse of the grain and coffee markets, and the general decline in the standard of living for campesinos as a result of liberalization turned many campesinos toward coca production. Fuerzas Armadas Revolucionarias de Colombia, *FARC: El País que Proponemos Construir* (Bogotá: Editorial La Ovjea Negra, 2001), 78.

67. Drug Enforcement Agency, "The Illicit Drug Situation in Colombia" (Washington, DC: U.S. Department of Justice, November 1993), 21.

68. U.S. Department of Defense LIC698, *Narcomercantilists: Assessing the Rise of Colombian Heroin Trafficking* (August 1992), National Security Archive, Narcotics Collection, Colombia: Documents from FOIA, box 32. The paper notes that it does not necessarily represent the opinions of the Department of Defense or the U.S. government. See: Ronald J. Ostrow, "Regional Report: Re-mapping Latin America's Drug War," *Los Angeles Times*, 7 July 1992, sec. A, p. 1.

69. U.S. Department of Defense LIC698, *Narcomercantilists*.

70. American Embassy Bogotá to Secretary of State Washington, DC, "Cultivation of Opium Poppy" (September 1991), 8, National Security Archive, Narcotics Collection, Colombia: Documents from FOIA, box 32.

71. American Embassy Bogotá to Secretary of State Washington, DC, "Colombian Government Study of Opium Poppy" (July 1992), 2, National Security Archive, Narcotics Collection, Colombia: Documents from FOIA, box 32.

72. Office of National Drug Control Policy, *Measuring the Deterrent Effect of Enforcement Operations on Drug Smuggling 1991–1999*, 68.

73. James Sutton, "U.S. Counternarcotics Strategy in Latin America: Good Intentions and Poor Results," *The Americas* 4, no. 1 (October–November 1991): 6; Nancy Nusser and Charles Holmes, "Colombian Drug Cartels Moving into Central America," *Atlanta Journal-Constitution*, 28 April 1991, sec. A, p. 10. Francisco Thoumi wrote that the profile of the Mexican cartels rose as a result of the crackdown on the Colombian cartels and U.S. interdiction efforts. The Mexicans charged a fee of up to 50 percent per shipment and often took payment in the form of cocaine. Consequently, the Mexicans started to grab a larger share of the Colombians' market on the West Coast and the western mountain region of the United States. See: Francisco E. Thoumi, *Illegal Drugs, Economy, and Society*, 101.

74. Office of National Drug Control Policy, *Measuring the Deterrent Effect of Enforcement Operations on Drug Smuggling 1991–1999*, 71.

75. Brook Larmer, "Colombians Take Over Coke Trade in Mexico," *Christian Science Monitor*, 9 January 1989, 1.

76. Frank Smyth, "The Untouchable Narco-State: Guatemalan Military Defies the DEA," *Texas Observer*, 18 November 2005, 6–20; Nancy Nusser and Charles Holmes, "Colombian Drug Cartels Moving into Central America," sec. A, p. 10; Benjamin F. Nelson, "Drug Control: U.S. Counter-Drug Activities in Central America" (Washington, DC: General Accounting Office, 2 August 1994), 1. Benajmin F. Nelson was the associate director for international affairs issues in the National Security and International Affairs Division of the GAO. Nelson notes that nearly seventy tons of cocaine annually transited through Guatemala to Mexico. Traffickers also used ships and land-and-sea air drops to transport cocaine into Central America, where it was then delivered to Mexico. Police enforcement efforts were considered lax because of low pay.

77. Juan Gabriel Tokatlián, "Estados Unidos y los Cultivos Ilícitos en Colombia: Los Trágicos Equvicós de una Fumigación Futil," http://socrates.berkeley.edu:7001/Events/confrences/

Colombia/workingpapers/working_paper_toaktlian.doc (accessed 17 November 2004); Stan Yarbro, "Colombian Anti-Drug Effort Is Challenged by Political Resistance, Cartel Shift to Heroin," *Christian Science Monitor,* 31 January 1992, 1.

78. Stan Yarbro, Colombian Anti-Drug Effort Is Challenged by Political Resistance, Cartel Shift to Heroin," 1.

79. American Embassy Bogotá to Secretary of State Washington, DC, "Media Reaction: Indians and Poppies" (May 1993), 2, National Security Archive, Narcotics Collection, Colombia: Documents from FOIA, box 32.

80. *Miami Herald,* "Colombia Halts Herbicide Spraying in Drug Crop After Peasant Protest," 22 November 1994, sec. A, p. 3; María Clemencia Ramírez, *Entre el Estado y la Guerrilla,* 185–89.

81. Drug Enforcement Agency, "The Illicit Drug Situation in Colombia" (Washington, DC: U.S. Department of Justice, November 1993), viii.

82. U.S. Department of State, Bureau of International Narcotics Matters, *1998 International Narcotics Control Strategy Report* (Washington, DC: U.S. Department of State, March 1999), 90.

83. Burt Ruiz, *The Colombian Civil War,* 178–179. Forming a coalition with the left of center, the M-19 won two seats in the Chamber of Deputies, three mayoralties, four seats in departmental assemblies, and thirty-four seats in town councils. See: Latin American Election Statistics, "Colombia: Elections and Events 1990–1994," (San Diego, CA: University of California San Diego, 16 August 2004), 9, http://sshl.ucsd.edu/collections/las/colombia/1990.html (accessed 15 April 2007).

84. Burt Ruiz, *The Colombian Civil War,* 178–79.

85. William López Gutiérrez, "Las Políticas de Paz," 256.

86. Aranguren Molina, Maruicio. *Mi Confesión,* 111–23.

87. Drug Enforcement Administration Intelligence Division, *Insurgent Involvement in the Colombian Drug Trade* (June 1994), 9, 19, National Security Archive, The Colombia Documentation Project, "War in Colombia Vol. II," http://www.gwu.edu/~nsarchiv/NSAEBB/NSAEBB69/part2b.html (accessed 10 April 2006).

88. Timothy Ross, "Colombia Tackles New Threat from Poppy Fields," *Independent,* 8 February 1992, 11.

89. American Embassy Bogotá to Secretary of State Washington, DC, "Colombian Army Second Division Commander Requests USG Assistance" (May 1991), 2, National Security Archive, Narcotics Collection, Colombia: Documents from FOIA, box 32. Francisco E. Thoumi argues that not all ELN fronts were involved in narcotics. Many of the fronts rejected using drugs to finance their revolution because it contradicted their moralistic Catholic background, inspired by one of their original founders, Camillo Torres. See: Francisco E. Thoumi, *Illegal Drugs, Economy, and Society,* 105.

90. American Embassy Bogotá to Secretary of State Washington, DC, "Media Reaction: Heroin in Colombia" (November 1991), 2, National Security Archive, Narcotics Collection, Colombia: Documents from FOIA, box 32.

91. American Embassy Bogotá to Secretary of State Washington, DC, "Colombian Government Study of Opium Poppy," 2.

92. U.S. Department of Defense, Defense Intelligence Agency to RUEKJCS/DEA Washington, DC, "Smuggling Trends in the Department of Huila" (December 1993), 3, National Security Archive, The Colombia Documentation Project, "War in Colombia Vol. II," http://www.gwu.edu/~nsarchiv/NSAEBB/NSAEBB69/part2b.html (accessed 10 April 2006).

93. Reuters, "Guerrillas New Drug Cartel, Colombian President Says," *Miami Herald,* 26 November 1992, sec. A, p. 6.

94. José Rosso Serrano Cadena, interview by author, 19 January 2007, Buffalo, Internet correspondence.

95. Drug Enforcement Administration Intelligence Division, *Insurgent Involvement in the Colombian Drug Trade*, 9, 17, http://www.gwu.edu/~nsarchiv/NSAEBB/NSAEBB69/part2b.html (accessed 10 April 2006).

96. FARC-EP, "Taller: Narcotráfico en América Latina y el Caribe" (18–19 Julio 1997), http://www.farcep.org (accessed 19 February 2007), 1–3.

97. Dick Emanuelsson, "Entrevista al Comadante Raúl Reyes: En Colombia Se Sigue Applcando el Documento Santa Fe II," in *Las Verdaderas Intenciones de las FARC*, ed. Corporación Observatorio Para la Paz (Bogotá: Intermedio Editores, 1999), 127.

98. American Embassy Bogotá to Secretary of State Washington, DC, "Violentologist's Views on Why Colombia's Insurgency Persists" (September 1992), 1–2, National Security Archive, Narcotics Collection, Colombia: Documents from FOIA, box 32.

99. American Embassy Bogotá to Secretary of State Washington, DC, "Colombian Army Second Division Commander Requests USG Assistance," 2. Francisco Thoumi questions this allegation. While Thoumi acknowledges that the guerrillas unquestionably depended on the illicit drug trade financially, he states that there is no evidence that they developed significant international marketing networks. Thus, Thoumi states that no guerrilla cartel existed, and their involvement is a matter of conjecture. See: Francisco E. Thoumi, *Illegal Drugs, Economy, and Society*, 107, 228–229. In contrast, Colombian military officer Luis Alberto Villmarín argued that the FARC was a drug cartel, which profited from coca and poppy production. See: Luis Alberto Villmarín, *El Cartel de las FARC* (Bogotá: Ediciones el Faraón, 1996).

100. Richard Sanders, "Drug Wars: Colombian Growers Fight Back When Police Spray Herbicides," *Tampa Tribune*, 26 June 1995, 4.

101. Ibid.; House of Representatives Select Committee on Narcotics Abuse and Control, *Cocaine Production in the Andes*, 101st Cong., 1st sess., 7 June 1989, 92–94. Statement by Rensselaer Lee.

102. House of Representatives Subcommittee on Western Hemisphere Affairs of the Committee on Foreign Affairs, *The Andean Drug Strategy*, 21; Drug Enforcement Agency, "The Illicit Drug Situation in Colombia," ix; American Embassy Bogotá to Secretary of State Washington, DC, "Media Reaction: Heroin and Drug Agriculture" (February 1993), 4, National Security Archive, Narcotics Collection, Colombia: Documents from FOIA, box 32. In 1992 the Colombian government created a law that forced exchange houses to report transactions that exceed seven thousand dollars a year.

103. House of Representatives Subcommittee on Western Hemisphere Affairs of the Committee on Foreign Affairs, *The Andean Drug Strategy*, 21; House of Representatives Select Committee on Narcotics Abuse and Control, *Cocaine Production in the Andes*, 92–94.

104. Central Intelligence Agency, Office of Asian Pacific and Latin American Analysis, "Colombia: Paramilitaries Gaining Strength," 7.

105. *St. Louis Post Dispatch*, "Colombian Officials Welcome U.S. Aid, Warn of Long Battle," 27 August 1989, sec. A, p. 11. According to Germán Palacio and Fernando Rojas, paramilitaries were an accepted mechanism of state repression. The relationship between the guerrillas and narco-trafficking justified political repression and prevented the incorporation of popular sectors, such as campesinos and indigenous people, into the government. Germán Palacio and Fernando Rojas, "Empresarios de la Cocaína, Parainstitucionalidad y Flexibilidad del Regimén Política Colombiano: Narcotráfico y Contrainsurgenica en Colombia," in *La Irrupción del Paraestado*, ed. Germán Palacio (Bogotá: Fondo Editorail CEREC, 1990), 86.

106. Eugene Robinson, "Bogotá Security Alleges Mercenary Aid to Cartels," *Washington Post*, 29 August 1992, sec. A, p. 1. Following the formation of the MAS, several schools funded by the Medellín cartel to train the paramilitaries, such as 01 at kilometer 9 in Puerto Boyaca-Zambito and El 50 in Santander province, were located near military garrisons. See: Fabio Castillo, *La Coca Nostra*, 221.

107. U.S. Southern Command (U.S. SOUTHCOM), Department of Defense, untitled (3 July 1996), 8. Letter of Lieutenant Commander C.R. Baldwin, U.S. Navy, to Mr. Carlos M. Salinas, Amnesty International.

108. Senate Subcommittee on Terrorism, Narcotics, and International Operations of the Committee on Foreign Relations, *Andean Drug Initiative*, 112.

109. Fabio Castillo, *La Coca Nostra*, 213–25. One campesino group in the Magdalena Medio area, known as the Movimiento Obrero Independiente y Revolucionario (MOIR), had denounced violence and Soviet imperialism and was therefore a political enemy of the FARC. The group was completely wiped out by the paramilitaries, who considered any revolutionary group to be communist sympathizers.

110. María Clemencia Ramírez, *Entre el Estado y la Guerrilla*, 105–9, 265.

111. House of Representatives Subcommittees on Human Rights and International Organizations and Western Hemisphere Affairs of the Committee on Foreign Affairs, *Human Rights in Latin America*, 102nd Cong., 1st sess., 21 February 1991, 87.

112. Randolph Ryan, "Realists in the Drug War," *Boston Globe*, 12 June 1990, sec. OpEd, p. 19.

113. Eugene Robinson, "Peruvian Victor Seeks to Shift Anti-Drug Aid; Fujimori Says U.S. Money Better Spent on Development," *Washington Post*, 12 June 1990, sec. A, p. 14.

114. Michael Isikoff, "Talks Between U.S., Peru on Military Aid Collapse," *Washington Post*, 26 September 1990, sec. A, p. 29.

115. Eugene Robinson, "U.S. Drug Effort Runs Into Latin Resistance; New Peruvian Government Turns Down $36 Million in Military Aid, Seeks Economic Help," *Washington Post*, 14 September 1990, sec. A, p. 22.

116. American Embassy Lima to Secretary of State Washington, DC, "International Narcotics Control FY 1993 Budget Estimates" (April 1991), 5, National Security Archive, Narcotics Collection, Peru: Documents from FOIA, box 31. Advisor Hernando de Soto designed the Fujimori Doctrine.

117. U.S. Embassy Lima to Secretary of State Washington, DC, "International Narcotics Control FY 1993 Budget Estimates," 5.

118. Randolph Ryan, "Realists in the Drug War," sec. OpEd, p. 19.

119. Melanie S. Tammen, "Policy Analysis: The Drug War vs. Land Reform in Peru," 22.

120. World Bank, *2004 World Development Indicators CD-Rom*.

121. General Accounting Office, *Drug Control: Long-Standing Problems Hinder U.S. Progress* (Washington, DC: General Accounting Office, February 1997), 10.

122. Pierre Kopp, *Political Economy of Illegal Drugs* (New York: Routledge, 2004), 22.

123. Malcolm Coad, "Fujimori's Shock Tactics Fail to Electrify Economy," *Guardian*, 27 November 1992, 10.

124. World Bank, *2004 World Development Indicators CD-Rom*.

125. U.S. Department of State, Bureau of International Narcotics Matters, *1989 International Narcotics Control Strategy Report*, 86; James Brooke, "Peru Builds Base to Combat Coca Production," *New York Times*, 13 June 1989, sec. A, p. 9.

126. Eugene Robinson, "U.S. Pushes for Herbicide Use on Coca; Peru Undecided on Spraying Plan," *Washington Post*, 16 June 1988, Sec. A, p. 33.

127. Michael Isikoff, "U.S. Suffering Setbacks in Latin Drug Offensive; Violence Mounting as Coca Production Soars," *Washington Post*, 27 May 1989, sec. A, p. 1; Sharon Stevenson, "Food Crops Killed by Anti-Coca Spraying in Peru," *Guardian*, 13 May 1991, 1. One Peruvian military officer reported that a U.S. official told him that if Peru did not do something about coca growing, "the defoliators would have their way."

128. James Brooke, "The Cocaine War's Biggest Success: A Fungus," *New York Times*, 22 December 1991, sec. A, p. 15; Sharon Stevenson, "Food Crops Killed by Anti-Coca Spraying in Peru," 1; Jeremy Bigwood, "The Drug War's Fungal Solution in Latin

America," paper presented as part of the symposium "Andean Seminar" at the lecture series sponsored by George Washington University and the Washington Office on Latin America, Washington, DC, 8 December 2000, 6–8; Jeremy Bigwood, "Consideraciones Sobre la Guerra Química Contra los Cultivos de Drogas: El Caso de Fusarium," in *El Uso de Armas Biológicas en la Guerra Contra Las Drogas*, ed. Elizabeth Bravo and Lucía Gallardo (Quito: Genesis Ediciones, 2001), 45–58.

129. Jeremy Bigwood, "Consideraciones Sobre la Guerra Química Contra los Cultivos de Drogas," 45–58; Eric Fichtl, "Washington's New Weapon in the War on Drugs," *Colombia Report* (30 July 2000), http://www.colombiajournal.org/colombia21.htm (accessed 20 March 2007).

130. James Brooke, "The Cocaine War's Biggest Success: A Fungus," sec. A, p. 15; Sharon Stevenson, "Food Crops Killed by Anti-Coca Spraying in Peru," 1.

131. James Brooke, "The Cocaine War's Biggest Success: A Fungus," sec. A, p. 15.

132. Jeremy Bigwood, "The Drug War's Fungal Solution in Latin America," 6–8; James Brooke, "The Cocaine War's Biggest Success: A Fungus," sec. A, p. 15; Sharon Stevenson, "Food Crops Killed by Anti-Coca Spraying in Peru," 1.

133. James Brooke, "The Cocaine War's Biggest Success: A Fungus," sec. A, p. 15.

134. U.S. Department of State, Bureau of International Narcotics Matters, *1998 International Narcotics Control Strategy Report*, 10.

135. Senate Subcommittee on Terrorism, Narcotics, and International Operations of the Committee on Foreign Relations, *Andean Drug Initiative*, 113–114.

136. James Brooke, "Peru Develops Plan to Work With U.S. to Combat Drugs," *New York Times*, 25 January 1991, sec. A, p. 2.

137. U.S. Embassy Lima to Secretary of State Washington, DC, "International Narcotics Control FY 1993 Budget Estimates," 2, 5.

138. U.S. Department of State, "An Agreement Between the United States of America and Peru on Drug Control and Alternative Development Policy" (14 May 1991), 1, National Security Archive, Narcotics Collection, Peru: U.S. Operations, Sendero, Fujimori, box 6. Fujimori then issued Decree 137–91–PCM, which ordered the armed forces and the SIN to direct the fight against terrorism and drug trafficking. See: Mariano Valerrama and Hugo Cabieses, "Questionable Alliances in the War on Drugs," 63.

139. Ricardo Soberón, "Issue Brief 6: The War on Cocaine in Peru," 4–5.

140. Eugene Robinson, "Military Joins Rule in Peru President Seizes Sweeping Powers as Troops Patrol Streets," *Washington Post*, 7 April 1992, sec A, p. 1.

141. Dan Russell, *Drug War*, 531–35. The Peruvian Congress was investigating the Barrios Altos massacre allegedly carried out by a Peruvian intelligence (SIN) death squad. Barrios Altos was a neighborhood near the Peruvian Police Intelligence headquarters and was considered a growing Sendero stronghold in Lima. One of the cars carrying the assailants was assigned to the office of Fujimori's brother.

142. Ricardo Soberón, "Issue Brief 6: The War on Cocaine in Peru," 4–5.

143. Agency for International Development, "Election Assistance to Peru" (Washington, DC: Agency for International Development Activity Data Sheet, 10 August 1992), 1. The United States even offered seven million dollars to the OAS to support the democratic process in Peru. See: *St. Louis Post Dispatch*, "Peru Leader Defends Attack on U.S. Plane," 26 April 1992, sec. A, p. 1. Almost immediately following Fujimori's ascension to power, the Peruvian Air Force fired on a U.S. C-130 cargo plane on a routine surveillance mission over the UHV and killed one crew member. Peru's Air Force claimed that the plane had no U.S. markings and was flying without an approved flight plan.

144. Joint Staff Washington, DC, to REUATAC/CDRUSAITAC Washington, DC, "USAITAC Counterintelligence Periodic Summary 91–06" (July 1991), 3, National Security Archive, Narcotics Collection, Peru, Documents Collection, http://www.gwu.edu/~nsarchiv/NSAEBB/NSAEBB96/ (accessed 12 April 2006).

145. Joint Staff Washington, DC, to REUATAC/CDRUSAITAC Washington, DC, "USAITAC Counterintelligence Periodic Summary 90–09" (October 1990), 2, National Security Archive, Narcotics Collection, Peru Documentation Project, "The Search for Truth," http://www.gwu.edu/~nsarchiv/NSAEBB/NSAEBB96/ (accessed 12 April 2006); Sam Dillon, "The Dark Past of Peru's Drug Czar," *Miami Herald*, 30 May 1992, sec. A, p. 1.

146. Arnold S. Trebach and Kevin B. Zeese, "The Wrong War in Peru," *Christian Science Monitor*, 29 May 1992, 19.

147. Amy L. Schwartz HA/PP to Norma J. Parker AID/LAC/SAM and Faye Armstrong ARA/PPC, "Follow-Up Peru" (Washington, DC: U.S. Department of State, 17 October 1991), 1, National Security Archive, Narcotics Collection, Peru: U.S. Operations, Sendero, Fujimori, box 6.

148. American Embassy Lima to Secretary of State Washington, DC, "Extra-judicial Executions in Ayacucho, Peruvian Military and Sendero Are Blamed in Separate Cases" (October 1990), 1, National Security Archive, Narcotics Collection, Peru Documentation Project, "The Search for Truth," http://www.gwu.edu/~nsarchiv/NSAEBB/NSAEBB96/ (accessed 15 April 2006).

149. Ibid., 2–3.

150. Garland Bennett, "Memorandum Human Rights Abuses on the Increase" (20 September 1988), 4, National Security Archive, Narcotics Collection, Peru Documentation Project, "The Search for Truth," http://www.gwu.edu/~nsarchiv/NSAEBB/NSAEBB96/ (accessed 15 April 2006).

151. Holly Burkhalter, "Peru Must Commit to Human Rights," *Christian Science Monitor*, 16 September 1991, 19.

152. Carlos Tapia, *Las Fuerzas Armadas y Sendero Luminoso*, 55–56.

153. Carlos Tapia, *Autodefensa Armada del Campesinado*, 19–21. Tapia adds that a war was created in the rural parts of Peru between two groups of campesinos: those who were dominated by the Sendero and those who were not. For Tapia, the Sendero did not lead a popular revolution as Mao had in China.

154. USCINCSO Quarry Heights to AIG 7084 "Rondas and Counterinsurgency in Peru" (8 September 1992), 3–4, National Security Archive, Narcotics Collection, Peru Documentation Project, "The Search for Truth," http://www.gwu.edu/~nsarchiv/NSAEBB/NSAEBB96/ (accessed 15 April 2006).

155. Carlos Basombrío Iglesias, "Sendero Luminoso and Human Rights: A Perverse Logic that Captured the Country," in *Shining and Other Paths: War and Society in Peru 1980–1995*, ed. Steven J. Stern (Durham: Duke University Press, 1998), 432–33.

156. American Embassy Lima to Secretary of State Washington, DC, "The Mind of the Beast: Sendero Luminoso Brutality," (7 August 1991), 1, National Security Archive, Narcotics Collection, Peru Documentation Project, "Peru in the Eye of the Storm," http://www.gwu.edu/~nsarchiv/NSAEBB/NSAEBB64/ (accessed 15 April 2006).

157. David L. Westrate, interview by author, 10 November 2006, Buffalo, tape recording. David L. Westrate was the deputy administrator for the DEA.

158. American Embassy Lima to Secretary of State Washington, DC, "The Mind of the Beast," 1, 3.

159. American Embassy Lima to Secretary of State Washington, DC, "Extra-judicial Executions in Ayacucho," 1.

160. Melvin Levitsky, interview by author, 31 October 2006, Buffalo, tape recording. As noted previously, Levitsky was the U.S. assistant secretary of state for narcotics matters.

161. Garland Bennett, "Memorandum Human Rights Abuses on the Increase" (20 September 1988), 2–3; Abimael Guzmán Reynoso, *Guerra Popular en el Perú*, 190–92.

162. Senate Subcommittee on Terrorism, Narcotics, and International Operations of the Committee on Foreign Relations, *Andean Drug Initiative*, 114.

163. Secretary of State Washington, DC, to American Embassy Lima, "HA A/S Schifter Meeting with Peruvian Ambassador Maclean November 27 1991" (December 1991), 1, National Security Archive, Narcotics Collection, Peru: Documents from FOIA, box 31.

164. Holly Burkhalter, "Peru Must Commit to Human Rights," 19.

165. Secretary of State Washington, DC, to American Embassy Lima, "HA A/S Schifter Meeting with Peruvian Ambassador," 1.

166. House of Representatives, Legislation and National Security Subcommittee of the Committee on Government Operations, *Oversight Investigation on the Andean Initiative*, 102nd Cong., 1st sess., 23 October 1991, 181. In addition, to restrict further proliferation of human rights abuses, Congress ordered the State Department to inform the Fujimori government that, to receive twenty million dollars in ESF funds for 1992, it needed to provide a list of military detainees and Red Cross access to military detention centers. See: Secretary of State Washington, DC, to American Embassy Lima, "Follow-Up on Peru Congressional Conditions" (November 1991), 1, National Security Archive, Narcotics Collection, Peru: Documents from FOIA, box 31.

167. House of Representatives Legislation and National Security Subcommittee of the Committee on Government Operations, *Oversight Investigation on the Andean Initiative*, 169, 181.

168. Pamela Constable, "Arrest of Peruvian Guerrilla May Shore Up Fujimori Regime," *Boston Globe*, 15 September 1992, 2.

169. Clifford Krauss, "U.S. Mindful of Setbacks in Past, Offers Guarded Praise of Capture," *New York Times*, 14 September 1992, sec. A, p. 8.

170. Linda Diebel, "Peru's Rebels Are Down But Not Out: Tupac Amaru Seen as Terrorist Lite, But a Shining Path Column Tramples On," *Toronto Star*, 9 November 1997, sec. F, p. 6; Carlos Tapia, *Las Fuerzas Armadas y Sendero Luminoso*, 152–154.

171. Central Intelligence Agency, Directorate of Intelligence, "Tupac Amaru Revolutionary Movement" (28 March, 1991), 3, 4, National Security Archive, Narcotics Collection, Peru Documentation Project, "The Search for Truth," http://www.gwu.edu/~nsarchiv/NSAEBB/NSAEBB96/ (accessed 15 April 2006).

172. Gabriela Tarazona-Sevillano, *The Sendero Luminoso and the Threat of Narcoterrorism*, 126.

173. James Brooke, "Rescue in Peru: The Rebels; for Revolutionary Group, an All Out Offensive Turns Into a Disastrous Defeat," *New York Times*, 23 April 1997, sec. A, p. 14.

174. *Herald Sun*, "Fujimori Orders Annihilation," *Herald Sun*, 1 November 1992, sec. A, p. 1. In December 1996, during Operation Breaking Silence, the MRTA seized the Japanese ambassador's residence and took 490 hostages while the ambassador was throwing a party to celebrate the Japanese emperor's birthday. The hostage crisis proved to be a strategic blunder for the MRTA. The group received a great deal of press but was strategically defeated when Fujimori ordered an assault on the ambassador's residence after four months of failed negotiations. The death of the MRTA's leader, Nestor Cerpa Cartolini, in the assault, and the incarceration of many other MRTA guerrillas demoralized the MRTA and forced the organization to terminate operations. However, surviving MRTA units threatened revenge and promised that the MRTA was "not going to die." See: Jane Diaz-Limaco, "Lima Hostage Crisis: Peruvian Rebels Break Their Silence," *Guardian*, 19 December 1996, 14; Gabriel Escobar, "Peruvian Guerrillas Hold Hundreds Hostage; Ambassadors Among Those Detained; Rebels Demand Comrades' Freedom," *Washington Post*, 19 December 1996, sec. A, p. 1.

175. Gobierno de Bolivia, "Ley del Régimen de la Coca y Sustancias Controladas: Ley 1008" (19 July 1988), in *Coca-Cronología: 100 Documentos Sobre la Problemática de la Coca y la Lucha Contra las Drogas: Bolivia, 1986–1992*, ed. Centro de Documentación y Información (Cochabamba: Talleres Gráficos Kipus, 1992), 114–55.

176. Jacqueline Williams, *Waging the War on Drugs in Bolivia* (Washington, DC: Washington Office on Latin America, 28 February 1997), 6.

177. Ibid., 5; Gobierno de Bolivia, "Ley del Régimen de la Coca y Sustancias Controladas: Ley 1008," 115; Gobierno de Bolivia, "Plan Integral de Desarrollo y Sustitución: PIDYS" (September 1988), in *Coca-Cronología: 100 Documentos Sobre la Problemática de la Coca y la Lucha Contra las Drogas: Bolivia, 1986–1992,* ed. Centro de Documentación y Información (Cochabamba: Talleres Gráficos Kipus, 1992), 176. The Bolivian government also created the Commissión por Desarrollo Alternativo (CONDAL), which was a program to give the campesinos a place to discuss their concerns regarding alternative development.

178. *Los Tiempos,* "Marcha Contra La Ley 1008" (20 septiembre 1988), in *Coca-Cronología: 100 Documentos Sobre la Problemática de la Coca y la Lucha Contra las Drogas: Bolivia, 1986–1992,* ed. Centro de Documentación y Información (Cochabamba: Talleres Gráficos Kipus, 1992), 188. The creation of coca production zones also caused a great deal of discord between the Bolivian government and campesino coca growers because the regulation was aimed mostly at coca growers in the Chapare. Those coca growers argued that Yungas growers also produced illegal coca and that the alkaloids in the Chapare's soil were solely responsible for its higher yields. See: Centro Oberera de Bolivia y Confederación de Unica de Trabajdores Campesinos, "Encuentro Nacional de Productores de Coca" (9–10 agosto 1988), in *Coca-Cronología: 100 Documentos Sobre la Problemática de la Coca y la Lucha Contra las Drogas: Bolivia, 1986–1992,* ed. Centro de Documentación y Información (Cochabamba: Talleres Gráficos Kipus, 1992), 156; José Antonio Quiroga, "Campesino, Coca y Agricultura," 12.

179. U.S. Embassy La Paz to Secretary of State Washington, DC, "Continued Bolivian Waffling on Counternarcotics" (October 1990), 5, National Security Archive, Narcotics Collection, Bolivia, Documents from FOIA, box 33.

180. Gobierno de Bolivia, "Convenio entre Bolivia y los Estados Unidos Annexo I, II, y III Del Plan Trienal Para la Lucha Contra el Narcotráfico" (9 mayo 1990), in *Coca-Cronología: 100 Documentos Sobre la Problemática de la Coca y la Lucha Contra las Drogas: Bolivia, 1986–1992,* ed. Centro de Documentación y Información (Cochabamba: Talleres Gráficos Kipus, 1992), 389–423.

181. U.S. Embassy La Paz to Secretary of State Washington, DC, "Continued Bolivian Waffling on Counternarcotics," 5.

182. U.S. Department of State, Bureau of International Narcotics Matters, *1991 International Narcotics Control Strategy Report,* 88.

183. World Bank, *2004 World Development Indicators CD-Rom*; Pierre Kopp, *Political Economy of Illegal Drugs,* 22.

184. James Painter, "Bolivia's Free-Market Plan Sputters," *Christian Science Monitor,* 15 August 1991, 3; World Bank, *2004 World Development Indicators CD-Rom.* Bolivian inflation as a percentage of GDP.

185. World Bank, *2004 World Development Indicators CD-Rom*; Pierre Kopp, *Political Economy of Illegal Drugs,* 22.

186. James Painter, "Bolivia's Free-Market Plan Sputters," 3.

187. Stephen Fidler, "Bolivia's Way to Shed State Sector: Local Version of Privatization Planned in Wake of Stabilization Success," *Financial Times,* 26 October 1994, 6; *Wall Street Journal,* "Bolivia Launches Big Sell Off," 10 June 1992, sec. A, p. 10.

188. Joint Staff Washington, DC, to Info RUEALGX/SAFE Washington, DC, "ANALIT–Implications of Bolivian Climate of Instability" (April 1992), 0623, National Security Archive, Narcotics Collection, Bolivia, Documents from FOIA, box 33.

189. Juan Pereria and Robert C Gelbard, "Correspondencia Entre el Embajador de los Estados Unidos y el Presidente de La Comisión de Politica Internacional y Culto" (17 abril 1991), in *Coca-Cronología,* 475–79.

190. Joint Staff Washington, DC, to Info RUEADWD/OCSA Washington, DC, "The Time Is Right–Our Initiative to Transfer Narcotics Enforcement to GOB and Formation of an All

Source Joint Narcotics Intelligence Fusion Center" (February 1993), 0287, 0288, National Security Archive, Narcotics Collection, Bolivia, Documents from FOIA, box 33.

191. U.S. Department of State, Bureau of International Narcotics Matters, *1993 International Narcotics Control Strategy Report* (Washington, DC: U.S. Department of State, March 1994), 92.

192. Douglas Farah, "Bolivia Seeks Aid in Drug War; President Says Funds Needed to Halt Corruption, Boost Effectiveness," *Washington Post*, 27 April 1991, sec. A, p. 12.

193. American Embassy La Paz to DEAHQS Washington, DC, "Operation Safehaven" (July 1991), 2, National Security Archive, Narcotics Collection, Bolivia, Documents from FOIA, box 33.

194. Eugene Robinson, "Cocaine Operations Shift Southward: Drugs Processed in Bolivia, Shipped from Argentina to Europe," *Washington Post*, 9 July 1991, sec. A, p. 31.

195. American Embassy La Paz to RUCOCCA/USCG IMLET Portsmouth, Virginia, "Precursor/Chemical Seizures–Methods of Concealment Encountered" (December 1992), 2, National Security Archive, Narcotics Collection, Bolivia, Documents from FOIA, box 33.

196. American Embassy La Paz to DEAHQS Washington, DC, "Operation Safehaven," 2; Drug Enforcement Administration, "La Paz Country Office Quarterly Field Management Report Fiscal Year 1996 2nd Quarter" (15 August 1996), 1, National Security Archive, Narcotics Collection, Peru: U.S. Operations, Sendero, Fujimori, box 7.

197. U.S. Southern Command (USSOUTHCOM), Operations Planning Group (OPG La Paz), "OPLAN 93–8 Operation Shutdown IV" (12 April 1993), 1, National Security Archive, Narcotics Collection, Drugs: FOIA: DOD, box 39.

198. Drug Enforcement Administration, "La Paz Country Office Quarterly Field Management Report," 4.

199. U.S. Department of State, Bureau of International Narcotics Matters, *1999 International Narcotics Control Strategy Report* (March 2000), http://www.state.gov/p/inl/rls/nrcrpt/1999/903.htm (accessed 10 April 2006); U.S. Department of State Bureau of International Narcotics Matters, *1991 International Narcotics Control Strategy Report*, 88–89.

200. Gobierno de Bolivia, "Convenio entre Bolivia y los Estados Unidos Annexo I, II, y III del Plan Trienal para la Lucha Contra el Narcotráfico," 411–423; U.S. Embassy La Paz to Secretary of State Washington, DC, "Continued Bolivian Waffling on Counternarcotics," 5. The embassy thought that Paz Zamora was "equivocating" and depended on General Hugo Banzer's support for using Bolivia's armed forces in counternarcotics operations.

201. Joint Staff Washington, DC, to Info RUEADWD/OCSA Washington, DC, "For NAS" (October 1990), 19, National Security Archive, Narcotics Collection, Colombia: Documents from FOIA, box 32.

202. U.S. Embassy La Paz to Secretary of State Washington, DC, "Continued Bolivian Waffling on Counternarcotics," 6. Much of this rivalry stemmed from Bolivia's 1952 revolution, when the police sided with the left and the Bolivian army voted to maintain the status quo. See: James Painter, "Peasants Protest U.S. Role in Bolivia's Drug War," *Christian Science Monitor*, 17 May 1991, 7.

203. U.S. Embassy La Paz to Secretary of State Washington, DC, "Continued Bolivian Waffling on Counternarcotics," 5, 6.

204. Ibid., 5.

205. *Washington Post*, "Approval Sought for Troops to Fight Bolivia's Drug War," 29 March 1991, sec. A, p. 16.

206. Joint Staff Washington, DC, to Info RUEADWD/OCSA Washington, DC, "For NAS," 20.

207. Douglas Farah, "Bolivia Seeks Aid in Drug War," sec. A, p. 12.

208. Michael Isikoff, "U.S. Protests Bolivia's Pick for Drug Unit; Aid is Suspended; Crime Ties Alleged," *Washington Post*, 5 March 1991, sec. A, p. 8.

209. Douglas Farah, "Bolivia Seeks Aid in Drug War," sec. A, p. 12.

210. Michael Isikoff, "U.S. Protests Bolivia's Pick," sec. A, p. 8.

211. Alberto Zuazo, "Dateline: La Paz Bolivia," *United Press International*, 4 April 1991, sec. I, p. 1.

212. Ibid.

213. El Comité de Coordinación de las Cinco Federaciones del Trópico de Cochabamba, Carta Abierta al Presidente Jamie Paz Zamora (27 Marzo 1991), in *Coca-Cronología: 100 Documentos Sobre la Problemática de la Coca y la Lucha Contra las Drogas: Bolivia, 1986–1992*, ed. Centro de Documentación y Información (Cochabamba: Talleres Gráficos Kipus, 1992), 448–50.

214. James Painter, "Former Minister Extradited," *Independent*, 12 December 1989, 10; House of Representatives Select Committee on Narcotics Abuse and Control, *Andean Strategy*, 84. General Arce Gomez was the interior minister for General Garcia Meza who had held the dubious title of minister of cocaine (see chapter 2). Bolivian cooperation allowed the U.S. to convict Arce Gomez on drug trafficking charges in 1991.

215. Michael Isikoff, "Bolivia Offers No-Extradition Deal to Traffickers; Offenders Must Quit Drug Trade, Name Accomplices, Give Up Assets; U.S. Cool To Policy," *Washington Post*, 19 July 1991, sec. A, p. 13.

216. James Painter, "New Extradition Treaty Heads U.S.-Bolivia Agenda," *Christian Science Monitor*, 7 May 1990, 6. Fifty U.S. Special Forces were deployed in this instance.

217. Michael Isikoff, "Bolivia Offers No-Extradition Deal to Traffickers" sec. A, p. 13. The previous extradition treaty dated back to 1900 and was used to prosecute Butch Cassidy.

218. Ricardo Zelaya, "La Extradicción Es una Nueva Arma Política," *La Razón*, August 1991, in *La Guerra de la Coca: Una Sombra Sobre los Andes*, ed. Roger Cortéz Hurtado, (La Paz: Centro de Información para el Desarrollo, 1992), 181.

219. *St. Petersburg Times*, "Bolivia Sends Suspected Cocaine Trafficker to U.S.," 11 July 1992, sec. A, p. 8; *New York Times*, "Bolivian Couple Seized on U.S. Drug Charge," 16 December 1990, sec. A, p. 34.

220. Associated Press, "Roberto Suarez Gomez, 68, King of Cocaine in Bolivia," *Plain Dealer* (Cleveland, OH), 22 July 2000, sec. B, p. 7; Malcolm Coad, "Ex-Dictator Guilty but Free in Bolivia," *Guardian*, 23 April 1993, 8. For more on the breakup of the Suarez cartel, see: Gutierrez and Pando, *La Lucha Boliviana Contra la Agresión del Narcotráfico*, 162–70.

221. Noll Scott, "Ex-President Denies Drug Role," *Guardian*, 28 March 1994, 8; *Houston Chronicle*, "Bolivian Investigation," *Houston Chronicle*, 31 March 1994, sec. A, p. 23. The allegations against Zamora came out in 1994 following his tenure as president.

222. U.S. Department of State, Bureau of International Narcotics Matters, *1993 International Narcotics Control Strategy Report*, 93–94. In 1995, Bolivia and the United States signed a bilateral extradition treaty that came into force in 1996 and mandated the extradition of nationals for the most serious offenses, including drug trafficking.

223. Michael Isikoff, "DEA in Bolivia: Guerrilla Warfare; Coca Traffic Proves Resistant," *Washington Post*, 16 January 1989, sec. A, p. 1.

224. Instituto de Estudios Internacionales Texto de la Conferencia en el foro Narcotráfico y Relaciones Internacionales, "La Guerra de las Drogras y las Nuevas Formas de Dominio" (September 1988), in *La Guerra de la Coca: Una Sombra Sobre los Andes*, ed. Roger Cortéz Hurtado (La Paz: Centro de Información para el Desarrollo, 1992), 152–55.

225. Productores de Coca, Organizaciones Sindicales, Partidos Politicos, Universidades, Organizaciones No Gubernamentales, Iglesia E Intelectuales, "Campaña de Soberania Nacional: Militarizacion No, Desarrollo Sí," (10 April 1990), in *Coca-Cronología: 100 Documentos Sobre la Problemática de la Coca y la Lucha Contra las Drogas: Bolivia, 1986–1992*, ed.

Centro de Documentación y Información (Cochabamba: Talleres Gráficos Kipus, 1992), 379.

226. James Painter, "Peasants Protest U.S. Role in Bolivia's Drug War," 7.

227. Bjorn Pettersson and Lesley Mackay, *Human Rights Violations Stemming from the War on Drugs in Bolivia* (Cochabamba: Andean Information Network, October 1993), 3.

228. *Los Tiempos*, "Masacre de Villa Tunari" (Junio 1988), in *Coca-Cronología: 100 Documentos Sobre la Problemática de la Coca y la Lucha Contra las Drogas: Bolivia, 1986–1992,* ed. Centro de Documentación y Información (Cochabamba: Talleres Gráficos Kipus, 1992), 101; Federación Especial de Trabajadores Campesinos de Trópico de Cochabama, "La Verdad Sobre el Genecidio de Villa Tunari" (Julio 1988), in *Coca-Cronología,* 102–6. The article claimed that the UMOPAR, accompanied by the DEA, fired at close range on unarmed campesinos. The campesinos also claimed that eight people were killed, ten were wounded, and seven disappeared in the Chapare River while trying to wash off the chemical gasses used against them. The newspaper *Los Tiempos* reported that five people were killed and a number of others were wounded.

229. Bjorn Pettersson and Lesley Mackay, *Human Rights Violations Stemming from the War on Drugs,* 3–4.

230. U.S. Department of Defense, Defense Intelligence Agency Washington, DC, to Info RUENAAA/CNO Washington, DC, "Coca Growers Defy Government" (March 1993), 0239, National Security Archive, Narcotics Collection, Bolivia: Joint Operations, Production Rates, Cocaine Coup, box 4. The U.S. Special Forces offered civic action projects, such as schools, clinics, and community centers, if campesino communities eradicated 30 percent of their coca. However, the campesinos rejected these projects because coca provided better returns. See: Joint Staff Washington, DC, to Info RUEADWD/OCSA Washington, DC, "Economic Alternatives and Civic Action for Chapare Campesinos Affected by Operation Ghost Zone" (April 1992), 2, National Security Archive, Narcotics Collection, Bolivia, Documents from FOIA, box 33.

231. Joint Staff Washington, DC, to Info RUEADWD/OCSA Washington, DC, "Economic Alternatives and Civic Action for Chapare Campesinos Affected by Operation Ghost Zone" (April 1992), 2, National Security Archive, Narcotics Collection, Bolivia, Documents from FOIA, box 33.

232. U.S. Department of Defense, Defense Intelligence Agency Washington, DC, to Info RUENAAA/CNO Washington, DC, "Report of INM-Funded Program Activity" (April 1994), 0014, National Security Archive, Narcotics Collection, Bolivia: Joint Operations, Production Rates, Cocaine Coup, box 4.

233. American Embassy La Paz to Secretary of State Washington, DC, "1991 International Narcotics Control Strategy Report," 2.

234. Tony Motley to Ambassador Armacost, "NSC Suggestion on Bolivia" (2 July 1984), 1, National Security Archive, Narcotics Collection, Bolivia, Documents from FOIA, box 33.

235. Motley to Armacost, "NSC Suggestion on Bolivia," 1; *Washington Post*, "Drug Projects Net Threats, Little Gain," sec. A, p. 12.

236. U.S. Department of State, "Selected Terrorism Incidents in Bolivia" (1990), 2–3, National Security Archive, Narcotics Collection, Drugs: All other Agenices and DEA, DOS and AID, box 41.

237. Memorial Institute for the Prevention of Terrorism, "Terrorism Knowledge Base: Zarate Willka," http://www.tkb.org (accessed 27 April 2006).

238. Memorial Institute for the Prevention of Terrorism, "Terrorism Knowledge Base: *Ejército Guerrillero Túpac Katari*," http://www.tkb.org (accessed 27 April 2006).

239. From FBIS Chiva Chiva to AIG 4673, "Terrorist Group Kills Two Mormon Missionaries" (May 1989), 1, National Security Archive, Narcotics Collection, Bolivia, Documents from FOIA, box 33.

240. Memorial Institute for the Prevention of Terrorism, "Terrorism Knowledge Base: *Comisión Nestor Paz Zamora*," http://www.tkb.org (accessed on 27 April 2006).

241. Joint Staff Washington, DC, to Info RUEALGX/SAFE Washington, DC, "TRANSCOM/ MAC DISUM 242," 0094, National Security Archive, Narcotics Collection, Bolivia, Documents from FOIA, box 33.

242. U.S. Embassy La Paz to USIA Washington, DC, "Media Reaction to October 10 Bombing of Marine House" (October 1990), 2–3, National Security Archive, Narcotics Collection, Bolivia, Documents from FOIA, box 33.

243. U.S. Embassy La Paz to USIA Washington, DC, "Media Reaction to Bombing of Marine House" (October 1990), 3, National Security Archive, Narcotics Collection, Bolivia, Documents from FOIA, box 33.

244. Joint Staff Washington, DC, to Info RUEADWD/OCSA Washington, DC, "GOB Claims to Have Dismantled the EGTK"(April 1992), 1963, National Security Archive, Narcotics Collection, Bolivia, Documents from FOIA, box 33.

245. Joint Staff Washington, DC, to Info RUEADWD/OCSA Washington, DC, "Emergence of New Self Proclaimed Narco-Terrorist Group Jovenes Cocaleros" (June 1992), 1361, National Security Archive, Narcotics Collection, Bolivia, Documents from FOIA, box 33.

246. U.S. Department of State, "Selected Terrorism Incidents in Bolivia" (1990), 2–3.

247. Nathaniel C. Nash, "Bolivians in Fear as Maoist Rebels Slip in from Peru," *New York Times*, 5 September 1992, sec. A, p. 1.

248. Fernando Garcia Argañarás, "The Drug War at the Supply End: The Case of Bolivia," *Latin American Perspectives* 24, no. 5 (September 1997): 71–76.

249. Central Intelligence Agency, Directorate of Intelligence, "Intelligence Memorandum: Narco-Insurgent Links in the Andes" (Washington, DC: DCI Counternarcotics Center, 29 July 1992), 6, National Security Archive, The Colombia Documentation Project, "War in Colombia Vol. II," http://www.gwu.edu/~nsarchiv/NSAEBB/NSAEBB69/part2b.html (accessed 10 April 2006).

250. Juan Gabriel Tokatlián, "National Security and Drugs: Their Impact on Colombian-U.S. Relations," *Journal of Interamerican Studies and World Affairs* 30, no. 1 (Spring 1988): 155.

Chapter 8: Clinton: From the Andean Strategy to Plan Colombia

1. Russell Crandall, *Driven By Drugs*, 36.

2. Eva Bertram et al, *Drug War Politics*, (Berkeley, CA: University of California Press, 1996), 118–19. In a dramatic shift from the Reagan and Bush administrations, the Clinton government advocated the reduction of mandatory sentencing for nonviolent narcotic possession while enacting treatment programs for drug-dependent criminals. Attorney General Janet Reno argued that the government had to seriously consider alternatives to prison sentences for drug offenders.

3. James Painter, "Foreign Focus/Drugs and the Law: South Speaks Up for Harmless Coca," *Guardian*, 21 May 1994, 12.

4. Stephen Labaton, "Reno Questions Drug Policy's Stress on Smuggling," *New York Times*, 8 May 1993, sec. A, p. 9. The Clinton administration also sought to reform the federal drug war agencies. Clinton cut the Office of National Drug Control Policy (ONDCP) staff from 146 to 25 people. The administration also supported the FBI's effort to merge the DEA into the FBI. See: House of Representatives Committee on International Relations, *Overall U.S. Counter-Narcotics Policy*, 116. This information comes from a prepared statement by Mark C. DeMier, research assistant at the National Defense Council Foundation.

5. House of Representatives Committee on International Relations, *Overall U.S. Counter-Narcotics Policy Toward Colombia: Hearing Before the Committee on International Relations*, 104th

Cong., 2nd sess., 11 September 1996, 116. This information comes from a prepared statement by Mark C. DeMier, research assistant at the National Defense Council Foundation.

6. Stephen Labaton, "Reno Questions Drug Policy's Stress on Smuggling," sec. A, p. 9.

7. Jeffrey R. Smith, "U.S. Falling Far Short in Drug War," *Washington Post*, 10 July 1995, sec. A, p. 13.

8. Jeffrey R. Smith, "Cocaine Flow Not Slowed General Says; Price Supply in U.S. Remains Unaffected," *Washington Post*, 12 January 1996, sec. A, p. 23.

9. Michael Isikoff, "White House Review Concludes Drug Interdiction Policy Is Failure," *Houston Chronicle*, 16 September 1993, sec. A, p. 17.

10. Russell Crandall, *Driven By Drugs*, 36.

11. Lieutenant Colonel Juan L. Orama, *U.S. Military Evolution in Counternarcotics Operations*, 30.

12. World Bank, *2004 World Development Indicators CD-Rom*. Estimates of Colombian debt in the billions.

13. Presidencia de la República de Colombia, *Plan Colombia: Plan Para la Paz, la Prosperidad y el Fortalecimiento del Estado* (Panamá: Editorial Portobello, 2000), 26.

14. María Clemencia Ramírez, *Entre el Estado y la Guerrilla*, 189–90. Quoted from the Colombian newspaper *El Tiempo*, 1 August 1996, sec. B, p. 4.

15. Drug Enforcement Agency, "The Illicit Drug Situation in Colombia," 10.

16. U.S. Department of State, Bureau of International Narcotics Matters, *1993 International Narcotics Control Strategy Report*, 5.

17. U.S. Department of State, Bureau of International Narcotics Matters, *1997 International Narcotics Control Strategy Report* (March 1998), http://www.state.gov/www/global/narcotics_law/1997_narc_report/policy.html (accessed 30 March 2006).

18. Drug Enforcement Agency, "The Illicit Drug Situation in Colombia," 10.

19. U.S. Department of State, Bureau of International Narcotics Matters, *1999 International Narcotics Control Strategy Report*, http://www.state.gov/p/inl/rls/nrcrpt/1999/903.htm (accessed 10 April 2006). A temporary halt in the shootdown program started in May 1994 and lasted until December 1994.

20. Juliana Velasco Iglesias, *Los Efectos de las Fumigaciones Sobre el Desarrollo Alternativo 1994–2002* (Bogotá: Ediciones Uniandes, 2003), 33–41; USAID, "USAID Alternative Development Design Document" (1999), http://bogota.usembassy.gov/wwwsad03.shtml (accessed 4 April 2007). The USAID says Plante was formed in 1996; Juliana Velasco Iglesias says 1995. In 1989 the Colombian government started to evaluate the feasibility of an alternative development program with the Programa Especial Cooperativa (PEC). Plante was a part of the Colombian government's Plan Nacional de Rehabilitación (PNR) that took over alternative development projects in 1992. The PNR was a rural political program to promote campesino participation in the formulation and implementation of local investment programs. See: Franco Armando Guerrero Albán, *Colombia y Putumayo en Medio de la Encrucijada: Narcotráfico, Fumigaciones, Economía y Soberanía* (Bogotá: Ediciones Claridad, 2005), 137.

21. Kerry Luft, "All Out War on Drugs Aimed at Appeasing U.S.," 19 February 1995, sec. C, p. 6; *Miami Herald*, "Colombia Raises Stakes in War on Drug Crops," 7 January 1995, sec. A, p. 1.

22. *Miami Herald*, "Colombia Raises Stakes in War on Drug Crops," sec. A, p. 1.

23. Richard Sanders, "Drug Wars: Colombian Growers Fight Back When Police Spray Herbicides," p. 4.

24. Juliana Velasco Iglesias, *Los Effectos de las Fumigaciones*, 33–41.

25. Ricardo Vargas Meza, *Drogas, Máscaras y Juegos: Narcotráfico y Conflicto Armado en Colombia* (Bogotá: Tercer Mundo Editores, 1999), 127–35. According to Vargas Meza, in the best

cases, herbicide spraying only acts as a temporary obstacle to illegal production. The 1994 demonstration occurred in Guaviare and Putumayo. The 1996 demonstration started in Guaviare and spread to Putumayo, Caquetá, Meta, Norte de Santander, and Bolívar. See: Juliana Velasco Iglesias, *Los Efectos de las Fumigaciones*, 33–41.

26. Juliana Velasco Iglesias, *Los Efectos de las Fumigaciones*, 38. In the book *The FARC Cartel*, Major Luis Alberto Villamarín alleges that FARC XIV and XV Front documents captured in Cauquetá prove that the FARC was the main orchestrator of the 1994 strike against aerial fumigation. See: Major Luis Alberto Villamarín, *The FARC Cartel*, 12–13, 116–18.

27. Ricardo Vargas Meza, *Fumigación y Conflicto: Políticas Antidrogas y Deslegitimación del Estado en Colombia*, (Bogotá: Tercer Mundo Editores, 1999), xxiv.

28. U.S. Department of State, Bureau of International Narcotics Matters, *1999 International Narcotics Control Strategy Report*, http://www.state.gov/p/inl/rls/nrcrpt/1999/903.htm (accessed 10 April 2006). No figures on Colombian opium cultivation or eradication exist for 1998.

29. Richard Sanders, "Colombian Growers Fight Back When Police Spray Herbicides," 4.

30. U.S. Department of State, Bureau of International Narcotics Matters, *1998 International Narcotics Control Strategy Report*, 90.

31. Drug Enforcement Administration, *The Cali Cartel: The New Kings of Cocaine*, (Washington DC: U.S. Department of Justice, Drug Enforcement Administration Intelligence Division, November 1994), 1.

32. American Embassy Bogotá to RUEHC/SECSTATE WASHDC, "Presidential Contender Samper and Ambassador Discuss Narcotics, Political, and Economic Issues" (11 February 1994), 81, National Security Archive, The Colombia Documentation Project, Colombian Paramilitaries and the United States: "Unraveling the Pepes Tangled Web," http://www.gwu.edu/~nsarchiv/NSAEBB/NSAEBB243/index.htm (accessed 17 February 2008).

33. José Rosso Serrano Cadena, *Jaque Mate*, (Bogotá: Grupo Editorial Norma, 1999), 211–16; James Risen, "U.S. Played Key Role in Arrest of Drug Lord," *Los Angeles Times*, 13 June 1995, sec. A, p. 7. U.S. policymakers also frowned on de Greiff's advocacy for legalization of narcotics.

34. American Embassy Bogotá to RUEHC/SECSTATE WASHDC, "Presidential Contender Samper and Ambassador Discuss Narcotics, Political, and Economic Issues," 82.

35. Ron Chepesiuk, *Drug Lords: The Rise and Fall of the Cali Cartel*, 196–97.

36. José Rosso Serrano Cadena, interview by author, 19 January 2007, Buffalo, Internet correspondence.

37. Ron Chepesiuk, *Drug Lords: The Rise and Fall of the Cali Cartel*, 199.

38. Laura Brooks, "Colombians Ease Ban on Extradition," *Washington Post*, 27 November 1997, sec. A, p. 44. In 1995, six of the Cali cartel's seven top leaders were arrested in a two-month period. See: Douglas Farah, "Snaring Cali Cartel Tiger, Officials Found a Pussycat," *Washington Post*, 28 August 1995, sec. A, p. 16.

39. José Rosso Serrano Cadena, interview by author, 19 January 2007, Buffalo, Internet correspondence. Francisco Thoumi argued that jailing and extraditing traffickers paradoxically cancels out narcotics control efforts, because these actions create new opportunities for other traffickers. See: Francisco E. Thoumi, *Illegal Drugs, Economy, and Society*, 368.

40. José Rosso Serrano Cadena, interview by author, 19 January 2007, Buffalo, Internet correspondence.

41. Rensselaer W. Lee III, "The Perversely Harmful Effects of Counternarcotics Policy in the Andes," in *The Political Economy of the Drug Industry: Latin America and the International System*, ed. Menno Vellinga (Miami: University Press of Florida, 2004), 188.

42. Secretary of State Washington, DC, to American Embassy Bogotá, "Delivery of Demarche to President Gaviria" (30 June 1994), 2–3, National Security Archive, The Colombia Documentation Project, Colombian Paramilitaries and the United States: "Unraveling the Pepes Tangled Web," http://www.gwu.edu/~nsarchiv/NSAEBB/ NSAEBB243/index.htm (accessed 17 February 2008).

43. Douglas Farah, "Noted Ex-Defense Minister Surrenders in Colombia's Drug Money Scandal," *Washington Post*, 16 August 1995, sec. A, p. 24; Douglas Farah, "Colombian Defends Efforts to Crimp Drug Trade," *Washington Post*, 3 June 1995, sec. A, p. 22; Douglas Farah, "U.S. Weighs Response to Clearing of Colombian Leader," *Washington Post*, 14 June 1996, sec. A, p. 17. Early estimates put the total contribution at $3.2 million, but it was later discovered that Samper had received at least six million dollars.

44. House of Representatives Committee on Government Reform and Oversight. *International Drug Control Policy: Colombia: Hearing Before the Subcommittee on National Security, International Affairs, and Criminal Justice*, 105th Cong., 1st sess., 9 July 1997, 40. This information comes from a statement by Jane E. Becker, assistant secretary for the Bureau of International Narcotics and Law Enforcement Affairs, Department of State.

45. Senate Committee on Foreign Relations, *Corruption and Drugs in Colombia Democracy at Risk: A Staff Report to the Committee on Foreign Relations*, 104th Cong., 2nd sess., February 1996, viii–2; *Washington Post*, "Bogotá to Lift Suspension of Coca Spraying: U.S. Drug Decertification Prompted Colombian Move," 8 March 1997, sec. A, p. 16; Ricardo Vargas Meza, *Fumigación y Conflicto*, 95–98. According to Vargas Meza, Colombia's desire to cooperate with the United States led the Colombian government to accept the experimental use of an herbicide called imazapyr, which is granular, not liquid like glyphosate. The use of this new herbicide is listed in the Frechette Memorandum, which advocated its use to reduce attacks on fumigation planes, since the granular herbicide could be dropped from higher altitudes. Fusarium oxysporum is also spread in pellet form.

46. Douglas Farah, "Massacres Imperil U.S. Aid to Colombia," sec. A, p. 1.

47. Human Rights Watch, "Guerra sin Cuartel: Colombia y el Derecho Internacional Humanitario" (New York: Human Rights Watch, 1998), http://www.hrw.org/spanish/ informes/1998/guerra3C.html (accessed 1 April 2007); Angel Rabasa and Peter Chalk, *Colombian Labyrinth: The Synergy of Drugs and Insurgency and Its Implications for Regional Stability* (Santa Monica, CA: RAND Corporation, 2001), 54; Organization of American States, Inter-American Commission on Human Rights, "Chapter Four, Colombia Country Report: The CONVIVIR" (1999, http://www.cidh.oas.org/countryrep/Colom99en/ chapter.4f.htm (accessed 1 April 2007). See also: Defense Intelligence Agency, "Colombian Narco-Trafficker Profiles" (September 1991), 10, National Security Archive, Narcotics Collection, Colombia Documentation Project, http://www.gwu.edu/~nsarchiv/NSAEBB/ NSAEBB131/index.htm (accessed 1 April 2007).

48. *Leahy Amendment no. 1247*, Sec 620G Prohibition on Assistance to Countries That Aid Terrorist States, U.S. Senate, 6 June 1995, S7797. The most significant charges were brought against Colombia's 12th and 24th brigades. See: U.S. Department of State, "State Department Cable: requests for further EUM (End Use Monitoring) Information Regarding COLAR (Colombian Army 12th Brigade)" (27 March 1998), 13, National Security Archive, The Colombia Documentation Project, "War in Colombia Vol. III," http://www.gwu.edu/~nsarchiv/NSAEBB/NSAEBB69/part3b.html (accessed 9 May 2006).

49. House of Representatives Committee on Government Reform, *The Narcotics Threat from Colombia*, 29. This comes from a prepared statement by Dan Burton, in an article by Burton, Dennis Hastert, and Benjamin Gilman. By holding up certain types of counternarcotics assistance to Colombia, a dispute in Congress erupted over whom to supply and what types of aid to give. The State Department held up aid in line with their interpretation of the Leahy Amendment, thus creating a rift between the State

Department and Congress. See: House of Representatives Committee on Government Reform and Oversight, *International Drug Control Policy: Colombia*, 40, 23–24.

50. House of Representatives Committee on Government Reform, *The Narcotics Threat from Colombia: Hearing before the Subcommittee on Criminal Justice, Drug Policy, and Human Resources*, 106th Cong., 1st sess., 6 August 1999, 15, 65. By the late 1990s, analysts believed that the FARC was earning over one hundred million dollars a month from processing and distributing cocaine. The FARC could pay their troops more than the government could pay the national military. Consequently, many Colombian soldiers joined the paramilitaries. This comes from a prepared statement by Congressman Dan Burton, chairperson of the Subcommittee on Drug Policy, Criminal Justice, and Human Resources (page 15) and General Barry McCaffrey, director of the Office of National Drug Control Policy (page 65). See: *Economist*, "Latin America's Other Hostages," 25 January 1997, 39. For more on the Colombian military's weak condition, see: Andrés Pastrana Arango, *La Palabra Bajo Fuego* (Bogotá: Editorial Planeta 2005), 83–92.

51. Douglas Farah, "Cocaine and the High Cost of Helicopters; White House and Congress Feud Over Extent of U.S. Anti-Drug Support for Colombia," *Washington Post*, 7 May 1998, sec. A. p. 25.

52. Human Rights Watch, "Guerra sin Cuartel: Colombia y el Derecho Internacional Humanitario" (New York: Human Rights Watch, 1998), http://www.hrw.org/spanish/informes/1998/guerra3C.html (accessed 1 April 2007); Organization of American States, Inter-American Commission on Human Rights, "Chapter Four, Colombia Country Report: The CONVIVIR" (1999), http://www.cidh.oas.org/countryrep/Colom99en/chapter.4f.htm (accessed 1 April 2007). The Colombian government announced that it would not authorize the creation of new CONVIVIR units in conflict areas. In addition, CONVIVIR units did not receive any special permit to use weapons other than personal ones.

53. Paramilitaries that joined the AUC included: Autodefensas de Córdoba y Urabá, Autodefensas de Ramón Isaza y Las de Puerto Boyacá, Autodefensas de Santander, Autodefensas de Cundinamarca, Los Traquetos de Putumayo y Caquetá and El Grupo de la Guajira. See: Maruicio Aranguren Molina, *Mi Confesión*, 199–203. Roughly 120 to 140 paramilitaries operated in Colombia in the late 1990s. The AUC's strength in the late 1990s was a reported five thousand to eight thousand soldiers. See: Marcella Gabriel and Donald Schulz, *Colombia's Three Wars*, www.colombiareport.org/colombia121.htm (accessed 8 July 2002).

54. Central Intelligence Agency, Office of Asian Pacific and Latin American Analysis, "Colombia: Paramilitaries Gaining Strength," 2.

55. Douglas Farah, "Massacres Imperil U.S. Aid to Colombia," *Washington Post*, 31 January 1999, sec. A, p. 1; Organization of American States, *Third Report on the Human Rights Situation in Colombia* (Washington, DC: General Secretariat Organization of American States, 1999), 27; Ricardo Vargas Meza, *Drogas, Máscaras y Juegos*, 142. According to Meza, Castaño and the AUC met with illegal coca syndicates in Guaviare, Caquetá, and Meta to defeat the guerrillas and turn a portion of the guerrillas' source of financing into a source for the paramilitaries.

56. Elena Alvarez, "Economic Development, Restructuring and the Illicit Drug Sector in Bolivia and Peru: Current Policies," *Journal of Interamerican Studies and World Affairs* 37 no. 3 (Autumn 1995): 137–38.

57. Barton Gellman, "Feud Hurts Bid to Stop Drug Flow, State-Defense Battle Cuts Peru, Colombia From Radar Access," *Washington Post*, 29 May 1994, sec. A, p. 1.

58. Jenni Deselm et al, "Counternarcotics in Peru–A Comprehensive Approach," *University of Michigan International Economic Development Project* (March 2007): 12. The article cites: Darren C. Huskisson, "The Air Bridge Denial Program and the Shootdown of Civil Aircraft Under International Law," *Air Force Law Review* (2005).

59. Barton Gellman, "Feud Hurts Bid to Stop Drug Flow," sec. A, p. 1.

60. R. Harris, "Forcedown Policy: Options for Colombia and Peru" (9 February 1994), 1–8, National Security Archive Peru Documentation Project, "Shootdown in Peru," http://www.gwu.edu/~nsarchiv/NSAEBB/NSAEBB44/ (accessed 30 April 2006).

61. William Jefferson Clinton to the Secretary of State, "Presidential Determination 55–59: Resumption of U.S Drug Interdiction Assistance to the Government of Peru" (8 December 1994), 1–8, National Security Archive, Peru Documentation Project, "Shootdown in Peru," http://www.gwu.edu/~nsarchiv/NSAEBB/NSAEBB44/ (accessed 30 April 2006).

62. Alexander Watson to Secretary of State, "Implementing the President's Decision on Colombia Peru Forcedown Policies" (no date), 1–8, National Security Archive, Peru Documentation Project, "Shootdown in Peru," http://www.gwu.edu/~nsarchiv/NSAEBB/NSAEBB44/ (accessed 30 April 2006). Clinton basically gave members of the U.S. military immunity from prosecution.

63. Lieutenant Colonel Juan L. Orama, *U.S. Military Evolution in Counternarcotics Operations*, 36.

64. *St. Louis Post Dispatch*, "7 Peruvian Soldiers Killed in Fighting With Ecuador," 30 January 1995, sec. A, p. 3; *New York Times*, "Peru and Ecuador to Demilitarize Border," 27 July 1995, sec. A, p. 6. Peru and Ecuador fought over the border in 1941.

65. M. Hayes, "The Shining Path of Fear," *Courier Mail*, 1 April 1995, 1.

66. Phil Davidson, "Peru Stunned by Military Aid to Drug Cartels, Army Navy and Air Force Personnel Are Helping Drug Lords," *Independent of London*, 22 July 1996, sec. I, p. 8.

67. United Nations, Office of Drugs and Crime, *Coca Cultivation in the Andean Region* (New York: United Nations, June 2005), 61. Coca cultivation dropped to ninety-four thousand hectares in 1996 and sixty-eight thousand hectares in 1997. By the end of the decade, coca cultivation in Peru would bottom out at 38,700 hectares in 1999, after which it slowly began to rise again, reaching 50,300 hectares in 2004.

68. Colonel Juan Muñoz Cruz, *Narcotráfico: Agresión al Peru*, 27–40. Colonel Juan Muñoz Cruz explains that coca growing moved to the Aguaytia Valley, Pachitea Valley, Ucayali Valley, Urubama Valley, Apurimac Valley, and Tambopata Valley. Apurimac and Urubama were the most important new valleys of production.

69. U.S. Department of State, Bureau of International Narcotics Matters, *1999 International Narcotics Control Strategy Report*, http://www.state.gov/p/inl/rls/nrcrpt/1999/903.htm (accessed 10 April 2006). According to Thoumi, one explanation for the high level of HCL production in Peru was the use of a high-level base, called queen base, which converted base into HCL in a one-to-one weight ratio. See: Francisco E. Thoumi, *Illegal Drugs, Economy, and Society*, 136.

70. Eugene Robinson, "Peru's Summit Stance Raises Questions For U.S. Anti-Drug Effort," *Washington Post*, 3 March 1992, sec. A, p. 13.

71. Owing to Clinton's reduction in funding for Andean counternarcotics programs, the State Department cut off assistance for the Santa Lucia base in the UHV. This left Peru's army solely in charge of its operations. See: General Accounting Office, "Drug Control: U.S. Antidrug Efforts in Peru's upper Huallaga Valley" (Washington, DC, General Accounting Office, December 1994), 6.

72. Martiza Rojas Albertini, *Los Campesinos Cocaleros*, 263.

73. Ibid., 261. Another campesino in Moyobamba stated that the members of the military were often "sons of the campesinos."

74. Phil Davidson, "Peru Stunned by Military Aid to Drug Cartels," sec. I, p. 8. Between 1992 and 1996, members of the Peruvian Group 8 Air Force Base (located next to the international airport in Lima) allegedly smuggled cocaine, using the pretext that their planes needed to be serviced in Russia or France. Often the planes refueled in the Canary Islands, where the Air Force members involved in the smuggling operation purportedly dropped off part of the shipment. The rest of the cargo was delivered to members of the Russian Mafia. See: Sally Bowen and Jane Holligan, *El Espía Imperfecto*, 187.

75. Francisco Reyes, "Peru's Deadly Drug Habit; Behind the Fujimori Front, Corruption, and Cocaine Trafficking Are Booming," sec. C, p. 4. Moreover, the Peruvian military almost staged a coup against the newly elected Peruvian Congress, which was investigating human rights abuses. In particular, the Congress renewed the investigation into the Barrios Altos and La Cantuta massacres by a military death squad under the direction of the SIN. See: American Embassy Lima to Secretary of State Washington, DC, "Un-named Says Army SIN Death Squad Existed" (May 1993), 1–4, National Security Archive, Narcotics Collection, Peru Project, http://www.gwu.edu/~nsarchiv/NSAEBB/NSAEBB64/ (accessed 30 April 2006).

76. Drug Enforcement Administration, "Public Allegations of Drug Trafficking Against the Head of the Peruvian Nation Intelligence Service (SIN) Vladimiro Montesinos" (27 August 1996), 1, National Security Archive, Narcotics Collection, Peru Documentation Project, "Fujimori's Rasputin," http://www.gwu.edu/~nsarchiv/NSAEBB/NSAEBB37/ (accessed 30 April 2006).

77. Sally Bowen and Jane Holligan, *El Espía Imperfecto*, 186.

78. Public Education Center, "Peru Intelligence Chief Funnels Arms to FARC; Scandals Oust Fujimori and Montesinos" (2 March 2002), http://www.publicedcenter.org/stories/peru-arms/ (accessed 4 April 2007). This Web site contains links to many international press reports on Montesinos's arms deal with the FARC.

79. Sally Bowen and Jane Holligan, *El Espía Imperfecto*, 404–06.

80. Sean Federico-OMurchu, "Peru Confirms Drugs-for-Guns Ring," *MSNBC*, 25 August 2000, http://www.msnbc.msn.com/id/3340855/ (accessed 4 April 2007).

81. Mariano Valerrama and Hugo Cabieses, "Questionable Alliances in the War on Drugs," 58–60; Clifford Krauss, "The World: Cold War Echoes; Our (and Their) Man in Peru," *New York Times*, 8 October 2000, sec. D, p. 3.

82. Kathi Austin and Jason Felch, "A Colombia Arms Deal and the Peril of Blowback," *Washington Post*, 3 March 2002, sec. B. p. 5. A French arms dealer, Charles Acelor, was first contacted by Montesinos and the Aybar brothers. Acelor, believing that this was a legitimate government deal, put them in touch with Soghanalian. See: Milagros Trujillo Zavala, "Del Jet Set Mundial . . . Al Penal de San Jorge ¿Quién rayos es Charles Acelor?" *Caretas* (27 Febrero 2003), http://www.caretas.com.pe/2003/1761/articulos/acelor.phtml (accessed 4 April 2007.

83. *La Republica* (Lima), "Peru: Lebanese Arms Dealer Details Jordanian Weapons Sale for Colombian FARC" (23 January 2004), http://www.nisat.org/blackmarket/america/latin_america_&_caribbean/South_America/peru/2004-01-23%20Lebanese%20Arms%20Deal er%20Details%20Jordanian%20Weapons%20Sale%20for%20Colombian%20FARC.html (accessed 4 April 2007).

84. Ibid. The details of the operation and Montesinos's role grew clearer as more information became public. There were two explanations for the operation's financing. In the first, the FARC agreed to pay Montesinos in cash by selling cocaine to a Brazilian trafficker, Luiz Fernando da Costa, also known as Fernandinho. With the earnings from the sale of cocaine, the FARC paid between $250 and $600 for each weapon; Montesinos had paid Jordan fifty-five dollars each for the weapons. In the second, presented by MSNBC, former Russian KGB and military members who were part of the Russian Mafia flew IL-76 cargo planes loaded with the weapons from the Ukraine to Jordan, where they refueled and received diplomatic clearance to head to Iquitos in Peru. In Iquitos, the Peruvians and Ukrainians exchanged the weapons for cocaine. The source of the cocaine is unclear, although it supposedly came from the FARC. The Peruvians then sold the weapons to the FARC for cash. See: Sally Bowen and Jane Holligan, *El Espía Imperfecto*, 404–405; Sean Federico-OMurchu, "Peru Confirms Drugs-for-Guns Ring" (25 August 2000); Public Education Center, "Peru Intelligence Chief Funnels Arms to FARC; Scandals Oust Fujimori and Montesinos" (2 March 2002). Estimates of what the FARC paid for each weapon vary, but the general idea was that the FARC sold a kilo of cocaine—which cost between $250 and $600 to make—for each weapon.

85. Sally Bowen and Jane Holligan, *El Espía Imperfecto*, 411.

86. Mariano Valerrama and Hugo Cabieses, "Questionable Alliances in the War on Drugs," 58–60; Clifford Krauss, "The World: Cold War Echoes," sec. D, p. 3. A videotape that showed Montesinos bribing an opposition legislator to switch to President Alberto Fujimori's party seriously damaged Fujimori's presidency. Secret videos that Fujimori made of himself became public following his escape to Venezuela, leading to further allegations of extortion, bribery, and gunrunning. See: La Biblioteca Anticorrupción del Congreso de la República, *En La Sala de Corrupción Videos y Audios de Valdimiro Montesinos 1998–2000* (Lima: Fondo Editorial del Congreso del Perú, 2004). A temporary president, Valentín Paniagua, took control of Peru until 2001, when Toledo beat Garcia in the national election.

87. Sally Bowen and Jane Holligan, *El Espía Imperfecto*, 398–404.

88. Jeremy McDermott, "Peru Trial Links CIA to Drug Terrorists," *Scotsman*, 15 February 2004, http://www.informationclearinghouse.info/article5666.htm (accessed 4 April 2007); Tim Golden, "CIA Links Cited on Peru Arms Deal That Backfired," *New York Times*, 6 November 2000, sec. A, p. 3.

89. Sally Bowen and Jane Holligan, *El Espía Imperfecto*, 408–409.

90. Jeremy McDermott, "Peru Trial Links CIA to Drug Terrorists," *The Scotsman*, 15 February 2004.

91. Reuters, "Escobar Brother Fingers Fujimori," *Montreal Gazette*, 21 December 2000, sec. B, p. 1.

92. Sally Bowen and Jane Holligan, *El Espía Imperfecto*, 180–81. Montesinos and the Auerllano brothers had a ship ten kilometers off the shore of Pisco that fabricated cocaine. They shipped the cocaine from either the port of Callao or the international airport in Lima and then delivered it to the Yucatán. The shipments, which used a reputable front company, were rarely inspected.

93. For further allegations against Montesinos, see: Mariano Valerrama and Hugo Cabieses, "Questionable Alliances in the War on Drugs," 58–60; Clifford Krauss, "The World: Cold War Echoes," sec. D, p. 3; Kevin G. Hall, "CIA Paid Millions to Montesinos," *Miami Herald*, 3 August 2001. Robert Gorelick was the CIA head of station in Peru and Montesinos's handler.

94. Stephen Fidler, "Bolivia's Way to Shed State Sector: Local Version of Privatization Planned in Wake of Stabilization Success," 6; World Bank, *2004 World Development Indicators CD-Rom*. Bolivian annual percentage of GDP growth.

95. World Bank, *2004 World Development Indicators CD-Rom*. Bolivia's adult population was estimated at roughly 3.8 million people at the time.

96. Presedencia de la República de Bolivia, *¡Por la Dignidad! Estrategia Boliviana de la Lucha Contra el Narcotráfico* (La Paz: Ministerio de Gobierno, 1998), 6–7. By 1998, estimates calculated that the cocaine industry employed between 6.7 percent and 13.5 percent of the economically active population. See: Francisco E. Thoumi, *Illegal Drugs, Economy, and Society*, 155.

97. Michael Isikoff, "DEA in Bolivia: Guerrilla Warfare," sec. A, p. 1.

98. Gabriel Escobar, "Change in Bolivia: Nobody Said It Would Be Popular," *Washington Post*, 17 April 1996, sec. A, p. 28.

99. Gabriel Escobar, "Latin America's Poor Not Helped by Reforms; U.N. Says Ills Remain Despite Economic Change," *Washington Post*, 13 April 1996, sec. A, p. 25.

100. Jack Epstein, "Latin American Bolivian Coca Czar Opposes U.S., Defends Crops," *Globe and Mail*, 29 October 1996, sec. A, p. 12.

101. Pablo Stefanoni and Hervé Do Alto, *La Revolución de Evo Morales*, 55.

102. Sally Bowen, "Bolivia in a Fix Over Anti-Coca Leaf Campaign," *Financial Times*, 3 August 1995, 3.

103. Freddy Condos Riveros, *La Agresión: Así Sentimos los Cocaleros* (La Paz: Ediciones Alkhamari, 1994), 15–16.

104. Freddy Condos Riveros, *La Agresión*, 67–69.

105. *San Francisco Chronicle*, "South America: U.S. Cuts Aid to Bolivia Because of Coca Crop," 24 February 1995, sec. A, p. 14.

106. Gabriel Escobar, "Keeping Coca a Cash Crop," sec. A, p. 18.

107. Associated Press, "Bolivia Needs Dollars 2Bn to Stem Cocaine Output," *Financial Times*, 11 November 1994, 4.

108. Sally Bowen, "Bolivia in a Fix Over Anti-Coca Leaf Campaign," 3.

109. Jack Epstein, "Coca Czar Protests U.S. War on Drugs," *Christian Science Monitor*, 26 September 1996, 1.

110. U.S. Department of State, Bureau of International Narcotics Matters, *1998 International Narcotics Control Strategy Report*, 85.

111. United Nations International Drug Control Program, *1997 World Drug Report* (Oxford: Oxford University Press, 1997), 142.

112. Jim Abrams, "GOP Seeks Shift in War on Drugs," *Chicago Sun-Times*, 25 December 1994, 31.

113. Office of National Drug Control Policy, *1999 National Drug Control Strategy* (Washington, DC: Office of National Drug Control Policy, 1999), 42, 46.

114. Office of National Drug Control Policy, *ONDCP Drug Policy Clearing House Fact Sheet*, 1–2.

115. House Republican Policy Committee, "Clinton Raises the White Flag: Policy Statement on How to Win the War on Drugs" (18 September 1996), http://www.fas.org/irp/news/1996/hrpc_drugs.htm (accessed 10 March 2007).

116. Substance Abuse and Mental Health Services Administration, "National Drug Survey Results Released" (Washington, DC: SAMHSA Press Office, 20 August 1996), 1.

117. Jim Abrams, "GOP Seeks Shift in War on Drugs," 31.

118. Douglas Farah, "Cocaine and the High Cost of Helicopters," sec. A, p. 25.

119. Mary Beth Sheridan, "Fujimori: U.S. War on Drugs Has Failed," *Miami Herald*, 10 December 1994, sec. A, p. 25.

120. House of Representatives Subcommittee on Western Hemisphere Affairs of the Committee on International Relations, *Anti-Drug Effort in the Americas and the Implementation of the Western Hemisphere Drug Elimination Act,* 106th Cong., 1st sess., 3 March 1999, 10–43. Statement of Rand Beers, assistant secretary of International Narcotics and Law Enforcement Affairs of the Department of State.

121. House of Representatives Subcommittee on the Western Hemisphere of the Committee on International Relations, *A Review of the Andean Initiative*, 107th Cong., 1st sess., 28 June 2001, 33–36. Statements of James F. Mack, deputy assistant secretary of state for International Narcotics and Law Enforcement Affairs of the Department of State and Michael Deal, acting assistant administrator for the Bureau for Latin America and the Caribbean of USAID.

122. United Nations Office of Drugs and Crime, *Coca Cultivation in the Andean Region*, 61. By 2005, coca production in Bolivia increased to 26,500 hectares, whereas in Peru, production declined slightly to thirty-eight thousand hectares. The State Department notes the continued presence of the Sendero in the UHV in their 2007 international narcotics control report. See: U.S. Department of State, *2007 International Narcotics Control Strategy Report* (Washington, DC: U.S. Department of State, March 2007), http://www.state.gov/p/inl/rls/nrcrpt/2007/ (accessed 17 April 2007).

123. U.S. Congress Subcommittee on Western Hemisphere Affairs of the Committee on International Relations, *Anti-Drug Effort in the Americas*, 10–43. Statement of Rand Beers, assistant secretary of International Narcotics and Law Enforcement Affairs of the Department of State.

124. Clifford Krauss, "Bolivia at Risk of Some Unrest Is Making Big Gains in Eradicating Coca," *New York Times*, 9 May 1999, sec. A. p. 6; Viceministero de Desarrollo Alternativo,

Plano Dignidad, 9, 53–55. Plan Dignidad was supposed to rid Bolivia of the "illegal drug circuit" by the year 2002. Plan Dignidad also called for more agro-industry investment and said that Bolivia's campesinos needed to move from being traditional producers to commercial producers.

125. Sacha Sergio Llorenti, *El Silencio Es Complicé: Los Derechos Humanos en el Trópico de Cochabamba y La Guerra Contra Drogas* (La Paz: Editorial Offset Boliviana, 1999), 5–180. This book documents countless incidents of violence and human rights violations resulting from Banzer's Plan Dignidad. See: Mariano Valerrama and Hugo Cabieses, "Questionable Alliances in the War on Drugs," 65.

126. Clifford Krauss, "Bolivia at Risk of Some Unrest," sec. A. p. 6; Catherine Elton, "Peru's Coca Growers Protest U.S. Anti-Drug Policies," *Christian Science Monitor*, 30 August 1999, 7.

127. Martin Jelsma, "Breve Historia de la Guerra Química y Biológica Contra las Drogas," in *El Uso de Armas Biológicas en la Guerra Contra Las Drogas*, ed. Elizabeth Bravo and Lucía Gallardo (Quito: Genesis Ediciones, 2001), 19–33; Jenni Deselm et al, "Counternarcotics in Peru–A Comprehensive Approach," *University of Michigan International Economic Development Project* (March 2007): 15.

128. United Nations Office of Drugs and Crime, *Coca Cultivation in the Andean Region*, 61. Since 2000, coca production has risen in all three countries. This fact challenges Lee and Clawson's questioning of the profitability of planting coca. Repression may have temporarily suppressed coca cultivation, but the increase in planting shows that coca remains a fundamental part of the Andean economy. See: Rensselaer Lee and Patrick Clawson, *The Andean Cocaine Industry*, 144–45.

129. Presidencia de la República de Colombia, *Plan Colombia*, 2; Andrés Pastrana Arango, *La Palabra Bajo Fuego*, 42–45.

130. Presidencia de la República de Colombia, *Plan Colombia*, 5.

131. Ibid., 8, 11–15.

132. Ibid., 19–21.

133. Karen DeYoung, "Colombia's U.S. Connection Not Winning Drug War," *Washington Post*, 6 July 1999, sec. A, p. 10; Larry Rohter, "Colombia Guerrillas Agree to Start Peace Talks," *New York Times*, 4 May 1999, sec. A, p. 5. The Zona de Distensión was located in central-western Colombia, between the states of Huila, Caquetá, Guaviare, and Meta. Other sources have called it the Zona de Despeje.

134. Andrés Pastrana Arango, *La Palabra Bajo Fuego*, 330–65.

135. Karen DeYoung, "For Rebels It's Not a Drug War: Colombian Government Agrees Conflict Has Other Causes," *Washington Post*, 10 April 2000, sec. A, p. 1; Colombian Peace Process Project, *Peace Process in Colombia 1998–2001* (Bogotá, 5 December 2001), http://www.cursos.uexternado.edu.co/colombiapaz/index.htm (accessed 6 March 2007).

136. Robert E. White, "Shadows of Vietnam: The Wrong War," *American Diplomacy* vol. 5, no. 3 (2000): 1, http://www.ciaonet.org (accessed 6 March 2007). Robert White was the former ambassador to El Salvador during their civil war. White went on this fact-finding trip with Representative William Delahunt. At one point, the State Department went so far as to hold secret meetings with the FARC in Costa Rica to keep the peace process on track. See: Douglas Farah, "U.S. Officials, Colombian Rebels Meet," *Washington Post*, 5 January 1999, sec. A, p. 8.

137. Andrés Pastrana Arango, *La Palabra Bajo Fuego*, 127–29.

138. Senate Caucus on International Narcotics Control of the Subcommittee on International Trade, *U.S. Assistance Options for the Andes*, 106th Cong., 2nd sess., 22 February 2000, 50. Testimony of Barry McCaffrey.

139. Douglas Farah, "Pact Near on Aid to Colombia," *Washington Post*, 9 October 1999, sec. A, p. 2.

140. Larry Rohter, "Like Carrot, Stick Fails With Rebels in Colombia," *New York Times*, 27 September 1999, sec. A, p. 9.

141. Larry Rohter, "Plan to Strengthen Colombia Nudges U.S. for 3.5 Billion," *New York Times*, 18 September 1999, sec. A, p. 6. The March 1999 FARC assassination of three U.S. citizens who were indigenous aid workers seriously damaged any support in the United States for Pastrana's peace negotiations. However, the murder of these missionaries led to condemnation of the State Department's negotiations with the FARC in Costa Rica. See: Andrés Pastrana Arango, *La Palabra Bajo Fuego*, 162–67.

142. Larry Rohter, "Like Carrot, Stick Fails With Rebels," sec. A, p. 9. FARC commanders feared a repeat of the "dirty war" against the Patriotic Union, which raised a problem for the negotiations. The government did not grant the ELN their own neutral zone. Fearing that they might be left out of any negotiations, the ELN began to step up their operations.

143. Alberto Garrido, *Guerrilla y Plan Colombia*, 35–37. Statement of Simón Trinidad, the official voice for the FARC at the bargaining table. The FARC said that Plan Colombia was a counterinsurgent war disguised by the War on Drugs.

144. Karen DeYoung, "For Rebels It's Not a Drug War," sec. A, p. 1.

145. Larry Rohter, "Armed Forces in Colombia Hoping to Get Fighting Fit," *New York Times*, 9 December 1999, sec. A, p. 9.

146. Tad Szulc, "The Drug War: Plan Colombia: Chillingly Familiar," *Toronto Star*, 24 August 2000, 1; Larry Rohter, "Plan to Strengthen Colombia," sec. A, p. 6.

147. U.S. Department of State, "Support for Plan Colombia" (2003), http://www.state.gov/p/wha/rt/plncol/ (accessed 3 March 2007).

148. Howard La Franchi, "Drug War Escalates, Neighbors Weary," *Christian Science Monitor*, 30 August 2000, 1. The United States would provide roughly $416 million for twenty fumigation planes and the delivery and maintenance of sixty-one Black Hawk and Huey combat helicopters by 2002. The plan limited the maximum number of U.S. personnel to five hundred troops and three hundred civilian contractors in Colombia at any given time. Human Rights Watch criticized the administration for having about one thousand military/civilian contractors with links to the United States working in Colombia. See: Robert Lawson, "DynCorp: Beyond the Rule of Law," *Information Network of the Americas* (27 August 2001), www.colombiareport.org/colombia78.htm (accessed 27 August 2001), 1.

149. U.S. Department of State, Bureau of Western Hemisphere Affairs, "United States Support for Plan Colombia" (19 July 2000), 2, http://www.state.gov/www/regions/wha/colombia/fs_000719_plancolombia.html (accessed 15 October 2002). Another $110 million was offered to Bolivia for its counternarcotics operations. See: *Wall Street Journal*, "World Watch: The Americas: U.S. to Boost Ecuador-Bolivia Outlays," 21 August 2000, sec. A, p. 12.

150. Gobierno de Colombia, "Plan Colombia," (Washington, DC: Embajada de Colombia, julio 2003), 1–2, http://www.colombiaemb.org/opencms/opencms/plancolombia/results.html (accessed 20 April 2007). In 2005, Colombia was producing 144,000 hectares of coca, up from the estimate of 136,000 hectares in 2000. See: U.S. Department of State, *2007 International Narcotics Control Strategy Report*, http://www.state.gov/p/inl/rls/nrcrpt/2007/ (accessed 17 April 2007).

151. *Wall Street Journal*, "World Watch–The Americas: Talks to Begin on Plan Colombia," October 16 2000, sec. A, p. 25; Howard La Franchi, "A Strike Against Plan Colombia," *Christian Science Monitor*, 2 November 2000, 6; David Adams and Paul de la Garza, "Rising Violence Precedes Plan Colombia," *St. Petersburg Times*, 5 November 2000, sec. A, p. 1; Carlos Lozano Guillén, *Reportajes desde el Caguan: Proceso de Paz con las FARC-EP* (Bogotá: Colección Izquierda Viva, 2001), 115–20. According to the CIA, the paramilitaries stepped up operations against the guerrillas as early as 1998, to ensure that they remained on an equal footing with them during Pastrana's peace negotiations and to bolster popular opinion in their favor since many thought the government was losing the war. See: Central Intelligence Agency, Office of Asian Pacific and Latin American Analysis, "Colombia: Paramilitaries Assuming a Higher Profile" (31 August 1998), 1–2, National Security Archive, Narcotics Collection, Colombia Documentation Project, "War

in Colombia Vol. III," http://www.gwu.edu/~nsarchiv/NSAEBB/NSAEBB69/col64.pdf (accessed 20 April 2007).

152. Larry Rohter, "Colombia Guerrillas Agree to Start Peace Talks," sec. A, p. 5; Douglas Farah, "U.S. Officials, Colombian Rebels Meet," *Washington Post*, 5 January 1999, sec. A, p. 8; Gary M. Leech, *Killing Peace*, 76–83.

153. Steven Dudley, "Colombia Sets Negotiations with a Second Rebel Group; Army Forces to Pull Out of Guerrilla Stronghold," *Washington Post*, 26 April 2000, sec. A, p. 28; Reuters, "Rebel Leader Apologizes to Catholics for Abduction," *Globe and Mail*, 8 June 1999, sec. A, p. 25. The ELN took forty-one passengers and crew members hostage from the hijacked plane. In the church kidnapping, the ELN took 143 people hostage but released eighty-four soon after the incident. As part of the peace deal, the ELN released many of the hostages.

154. Andrés Pastrana Arango, *La Palabra Bajo Fuego*, 330–65.

155. Steven Dudley, "Colombia Sets Negotiations," sec. A, p. 28.

156. Scott Wilson, "Rightist Forces Thwart Leader in Colombia; Takeover of Rebel-Held Area Puts Peace Effort at Risk," *Washington Post*, 19 April 2001, sec. A, p. 13.

157. Andrés Pastrana Arango, *La Palabra Bajo Fuego*, 306–9.

158. Robert Collier, "Drug War in the Jungle: U.S. Financed Campaign Aims to Beat Traffickers and Rebels," *San Francisco Chronicle*, 17 December 2000, sec. A, p. 1.

159. Jeremy McDermott, "Drug War Ravages Colombia," *Scotsman*, 26 March 2001, 10.

160. Jeremy McDermott, "Rebels in Deal over Prisoners," *Daily Telegraph*, 4 June 2001, sec. A, p. 14. Further complicating the peace process was the discovery that three IRA members were training the FARC in urban combat techniques inside the Zone. See: John Murray Brown and James Wilson, "Colombia Details Fresh IRA Link to Guerrillas," *Financial Times*, 18 September 2001, sec. A, p. 8.

161. Adam Isacson, *Was Failure Avoidable: Learning From Colombia's 1998–2002 Peace Process*, paper presented as part of the "Dante B. Fascell North-South Center Working Paper Series," University of Miami North-South Center, March 2003, 29.

162. Scott Wilson, "Colombian Rebels Use Refuge to Expand Their Power Base; FARC Pushes Boundaries of Government-Backed Safe Haven," *Washington Post*, 3 October 2001, sec. A, p. 25.

163. Jeremy McDermott, "New Godfathers of Colombia's Cocaine Trade," *Scotsman*, 3 June 2001, sec. A, p. 20.

164. Andrés Pastrana and James Wilson, "Colombia Seeks More U.S. Aid to Fight Rebels," *Financial Times*, 18 April 2002, sec. A, p. 36; Andrés Pastrana, "High Stakes in Colombia," *Washington Post*, 15 April 2002, sec. A, p. 21; Andrés Pastrana Arango, *La Palabra Bajo Fuego*, 414–19, 434–40.

165. U.S. Department of the Treasury, "Treasury Targets 15 Leaders of Colombian Narco-Terrorist Group" (Washington, D.C.: Department of the Treasury Press Report HP-661, 1 November 2007), http://www.ustreas.gov/press/releases/hp661.htm (accessed 25 January 2007).

166. Andrés Pastrana Arango, *La Palabra Bajo Fuego*, 441–59.

167. Diana Jean Schemo, "U.S. to Change Strategy in Narcotics Fight in Colombia," *New York Times*, 8 August 1998, sec. A. p. 2.

168. Reuters, "U.N. Official Criticizes U.S. Aid Plan for Colombia" (21 February 2000), www.colombiasupport.net/200002/unwire-criticism-0223.html, (accessed 21 October 2002). The crop substitution program targeted the relatively small states of Cauca and Putumayo, because of the difficulty in organizing a successful program. See: Karen DeYoung, "A Long Way From Coca to Coffee," *Washington Post*, 11 October 2000, sec. A, p. 18.

169. Robert E. White, "Shades of Vietnam," *Washington Post*, 8 February 2000, sec. A, p. 23. White argues that "the $1.3 billion spent on Plan Colombia for war could be used

more constructively to build farm-to-market highways that would peacefully carry the government's authority into the remote areas." See: Presidencia de la República de Colombia, *Plan Colombia*, 50.

170. Phil Stewart, "Colombia Defends Coca Program, U.S. Questions Aid," *Reuters News*, 2 April 2002, http://ca.news.yahoo.com/020403/5/lfov.html (accessed 21 October 2002).

171. Juliana Velasco Iglesias, *Los Effectos de las Fumigaciones*, 26–32.

172. *Associated Press*, "U.N. Criticizes Drug Crop Spraying in Colombia," 25 July 2001, http://www.poppies.org/news/99605986278102.shtml (accessed 2 November 2002).

173. Jeremy McDermott, "Drug War Ravages Colombia," 10.

174. *Associated Press*, "U.N. Criticizes Drug Crop Spraying in Colombia," available from http://www.poppies.org/news/99605986278102.shtml (accessed 2 November 2002).

175. Karen DeYoung, "A Long Way From Coca to Coffee," sec. A, p. 24.

176. Scott Wilson, "U.S. Doubts Effects of Coca Plan: Alternative Program Fails to Win Over Colombian Farmers," *Washington Post*, 7 April 2002, sec. A, p. 13.

177. Paul de la Garza and David Adams, "U.S. Program Failing to Halt Drug Crops, Report Charges," *St. Petersburg Times*, 27 February 2002, sec. A, p. 11.

178. T. Christian Miller, "U.S. Finds Substitution for Coca Failed in Colombia," *Los Angeles Times*, 29 March 2002, sec. A, p. 1.

179. Michael Shifter, "This Plan Isn't Working; U.S. Military Aid Alarms Colombia Neighbors," *Washington Post*, 10 December 2000, sec. B, p. 4; Central Intelligence Agency, Office of Asian-Pacific and Latin American Analysis, "Colombia-Venezuela: Continuing Friction Along the Border" (1 October 1997), 1, National Security Archive, Narcotics Collection, Colombia Documentation Project, "War in Colombia Vol. II," http://www.gwu.edu/~nsarchiv/NSAEBB/NSAEBB69/col40.pdf (accessed 20 April 2007). The document explains Venezuelan-Colombian differences concerning border skirmishes with the FARC and ELN. For more information regarding the spillover effect of the War on Drugs along the Ecuadorian border, see: Salomón Cuesta Zapata and Patricio Trujillo Montalvo, *La Frontera de Fronteras Putumayo: Violencia, Narcotráfico, y Guerrilla* (Quito: Fundación de Investigaciones Andino Amazónicas Abya Yala, 1999), 5–163. In particular, the authors discuss the guerrilla-paramilitary conflict in Putumayo and how it crossed over into Ecuador's border states of Carchi, Esmereldas, and Sucumbíos.

Conclusion: U.S. Drug Policy Comes Full Circle

1. International Crisis Group, "Coca, Drugs and Social Protests in Bolivia and Peru," *International Crisis Group Latin American Report* 12 (3 March 2005): 1.

2. U.S. Department of State "Excerpt: Bush Budget Includes $731 Million for Andean Counterdrug Initiative" (9 April 2001), http://www.usembassy.it/file2001_04/alia/a1040901.htm (accessed 25 January 2007); K. Larry Storrs and Nina M. Serafino, "Andean Regional Initiative (ARI): FY2002 Supplemental and FY2003 Assistance for Colombia and Neighbors" (Washington, DC: Library of Congress Congressional Research Service, 6 September 2002); White House Office of the Press Secretary, "Fact Sheet: The Andean Regional Initiative" (23 March 2002), http://www.state.gov/p/wha/rls/fs/8980.htm (accessed 10 January 2007).

3. K. Larry Storrs and Nina M. Serafino, "Andean Regional Initiative (ARI): FY2003 Supplemental and FY2004 Assistance for Colombia and Neighbors" (Washington, DC: Library of Congress Congressional Research Service, 27 August 2003).

4. K. Larry Storrs and Nina M. Serafino, "Andean Regional Initiative (ARI): FY2002 Supplemental and FY2003 Assistance for Colombia and Neighbors"; Center for

International Policy's Colombia Program, "Supplemental Aid for 2002," *Center for International Policy* 8 (January 2003), http://ciponline.org/colombia/02supp.htm (accessed 10 January 2008).

5. Drug Enforcement Administration, National Drug Intelligence Center, "National Drug Threat Assessment 2008" (October 2007), http://www.usdoj.gov/dea/concern/18862/cocaine.htm (accessed 22 July 2008).

6. Gary Leech, "Bush and Uribe Undermine UN Security Council," *Colombia Journal*, 16 December 2002, http://www.colombiajournal.org/colombia144.htm (accessed 20 March 2008).

7. Jan McGirk, "Colombia's New Hardline Preisdent Prepares for War on Marxist Rebels," *Independent of London*, 28 May 2002, sec. F, p. 13.

8. Human Rights Watch, "Guerra sin Cuartel: Colombia y el Derecho Internacional Humanitario" (New York: Human Rights Watch, 1998), http://www.hrw.org/spanish/informes/1998/guerra3C.html (accessed 1 April 2007); Angel Rabasa and Peter Chalk, *Colombian Labyrinth: The Synergy of Drugs and Insurgency and Its Implications for Regional Stability* (Santa Monica, CA: RAND Corporation, 2001), 54; and Organization of American States, Inter-American Commission on Human Rights, "Chapter Four, Colombia Country Report: The CONVIVIR" (1999), http://www.cidh.oas.org/countryrep/Colom99en/chapter.4f.htm (accessed 1 April 2007).

9. U.S. Department of Defense, Defense Intelligence Agency, "Colombian Narco-Trafficker Profiles" (September 1991), 10, National Security Archive, Narcotics Collection, Colombia Documentation Project, available from http://www.gwu.edu/~nsarchiv/NSAEBB/NSAEBB131/index.htm (accessed 1 April 2007).

10. *Human Rights Watch*, "Colombia: Demobilization Scheme Ensures Injustice," 18 January 2005, http://www.hrw.org/english/docs/2005/01/18/colomb10032.htm (accessed 2 February 2008); *Human Rights Watch*, "Colombia: Letting Paramilitaries Off the Hook," January 2004, http://hrw.org/backgrounder/americas/colombia0105/index.htm (accessed 2 February 2008).

11. U.S. General Accountability Office, "Plan Colombia: Drug Reduction Goals Not Fully Met, But Security Has Improved; U.S. Agencies Need More Detailed Plans for Reducing Assistance, GAO-09-71" (October 2008), 26.

12. Gary Leech, "Two Perspectives from the Colombian Left," www.colombiajournal.org (accessed 13 October 2007). See: Toby Muse, "Former Colombia Spy Chief Arrested," *Associated Press Wire*, 23 Feburary 2007; Toby Muse, "Colombia Foreign Minister Resigns," *Associated Press*, 19 February 2007; *Wall Street Journal*, "Foreign Minister Quits Amid Colombia Scandal," 20 February 2007, sec. A, p. 10. Allegations have been made that in 2002 the CIA secretly shipped weapons to arm the AUC via Israel's Mossad. In this case, Israeli arms dealers bought three thousand assault rifles from Nicaraguan security forces, claiming that they would be sold to Panamanian security forces. However, the Panamanian government denied any knowledge of the incident, and the weapons were diverted to the AUC. See: Raúl Reyes, "Una Carta de un Amigo," http://www.farc-ep.org (accessed 5 May 2002); Gary Leech, "Another Contra Scandal," http://www.colombiajournal.org/colombia121.htm (accessed 8 July 2002).

13. Juan Forero, "Cousin of Colombian President Arrested in Death Squad Probe: Mario Uribe Seized After Failed Bid for Political Asylum in Costa Rica Embassy," *Washington Post*, 23 April 2008, sec. A. p. 12; *Associated Press*, "Leading Colombian Party Chief Arrested," 25 July 2008.

14. Frank Bajak, "Colombian Preisdent Uribe Seeks Election Redo," *Associated Press Wire*, 27 June 2008.

15. Libardo Cardona, "Colombia Spy Chief Probes Alleged Wiretapping," *Associated Press Wire*, 21 February 2009.

16. Patrick Markey, "Analysis: Colombia Wiretap Scandal Mars Success," *Reuters*, 24 February 2009, http://www.alertnet.org/thenews/newsdesk/N23377680.htm (accessed

24 May 2009); *La Semana*, "El Espionaje Era Peor," 25 abril 2009, http://www.semana. com/noticias-nacion/espionaje-peor/123258.aspx (accessed 5 June 2009); *La Semana*, "Ex funcionarios del DAS niegan haber recibido órdenes de la Presidencia," 18 mayo 2009, http://www.semana.com/noticias-nacion/ex-funcionarios-del-das-niegan-haber-recibido-ordenes-presidencia/124126.aspx (accessed on 4 June 2009).

17. Tyler Bridges, "Uribe Seeks New Elections; Foes Raise Cries of Dictator," *Miami Herald*, 28 June 2008, http://www.miamiherald.com/entertainment/music/latin-world/v-print/story/586421.html (accessed 22 July 2008).

18. Frank Bajak, "Report: No Re-election for Uribe in Colombia," *Associated Press Wire*, 2 February 2009.

19. Terra Actualidad, "El 80 Por Ciento de los Colombianos Tienen una Imagen Favorable de Uribe," *El Tiempo* (Colombia), 24 enero 2008, http://eltiempo.com.co/actualidad/articulo/html/acu8216.htm (accessed 2 February 2008); Toby Muse, "Colombian Troops Kill Rebel Leader," *Buffalo News*, 2 March 2008, sec. A, p. 5.

20. *BBC News*, "Colombians in March Protest," 4 February 2008, http://news.bbc.co.uk/2/hi/americas/7225824.stm (accessed 3 March 2008).

21. *El Tiempo*, "Universitarios marcharán el jueves para protestar contra los violentos," 7 March 2008, http://www.eltiempo.com/nacion/boyaca/2008-03-04 (accessed 3 March 2008).

22. Frank Bajak, "Colombians March Against Kidnappings," *Associated Press*, 21 July 2008; Katharine West, "The March of the Forgotten," 10 March 2008, http://www.colombiajournal.org/colombia277.htm (accessed 10 May 2008).

23. Katharine West, "The March of the Forgotten," 10 March 2008.

24. Patrick Markey, "Colombia Says Police Fired on Indigenous Protesters," *Reuters*, 23 October 2008; Frank Bajak, "Colombia Fires 25 Soldiers in Civilian Deaths," *Associated Press Wire*, 29 October 2009.

25. Reuters, "Colombia Rebel Group Breaks off Peace Talks" 27 July 2007, http://www.cnn.com/2007/WORLD/americas/07/27/colombia.rebels.reut/index.html (accessed 5 February 2007).

26. Gary Leech, "Two Perspectives from the Colombian Left," www.colombiajournal.org.

27. Toby Muse, "Senior Colombian Rebel Commander Killed," *Associated Press Wire*, 1 March 2008.

28. José de Córdoba, "Rebels Flail in Colombia After Death of Leader," *Wall Street Journal*, 28 May 2008, sec. A, p. 1.

29. Ibid., Juan Forero and Steven Dudley, "Tough Intellectual Takes Rebel Reins in Colombia," *Washington Post*, 9 June 2008, sec. A, p. 1.

30. *RTT News*, "Colombia Refutes Ransom Payment to FARC For Hostage Release," http://www.nasdaq.com/aspxcontent/newsStoryPrintVer.aspx?cpath=20080707%5cACQRT T200807070106RTTRADERUSEQUITY_0034.htm&&mypage=newsheadlines&title= Colombia+Refutes+Ransom+Payment+To+FARC+For+Hostage+Release&symbol=& title=Colombia%20Refutes%20Ransom%20Payment%20To%20FARC%20For%20Host age%20Release (accessed 22 July 2008); Patrick McDonnell and Chris Kraul, "Colombia Leaders Call Ransom Story Absolutely False," *Los Angeles Times*, 7 July 2008, http://www.latimes.com/news/nationworld/world/la-fg-colombia7-2008jul07,0,7390815.story?track=rss (accessed 22 July 2008). The source on the ransom information came from Jean Pierre Gontard, a Swiss intermediary with the FARC.

31. Gary Leech, "Colombia Hostage Rescue Endangers Lives of Journalists and Aid Workers," *Colombia Journal*, 7 July 2008, http://www.colombiajournal.org/colombia285.htm (accessed 22 July 2008).

32. U.S. Department of State, Bureau of International Narcotics Matters, *2008 International Control Strategy Report Vol. I*, (March 2008), http://www.state.gov/p/inl/rls/nrcrpt/2008/

vol1/html/100776.htm (accessed 10 May 2008). Ironically, the report states that, while 157,000 hectares of coca were cultivated in 2006, the U.S. and Colombian government eradicated 171,613 hectares of coca aerially and 42,110 hectares manually. It is hard to understand how it is possible to eradicate more hectares than were cultivated and still have 610 metric tons of HCL produced in 2006. The INCSR provides no explanation for this discrepancy.

33. National Drug Intelligence Center, "National Drug Threat Assessment 2008."

34. Toby Muse, "Coca Cultivation Surges in Colombia," *Associated Press Wire,* 16 March 2008.

35. U.S. General Accountability Office, "Plan Colombia: Drug Reduction Goals Not Fully Met," 1–5, 46–50.

36. Juan Forero, "Colombia's Low-Tech Coca Assault: Uprooting Bushes by Hand Preferred Over U.S. Funded Aerial Spraying," *Washington Post,* 7 July 2007, sec. A, p. 1; Associated Press, "U.S. Reducing Aid to Coca-growing Area of Colombia," *Arizona Daily Star,* 12 October 2006, http://www.azstarnet.com/sn/printDS/150692 (accessed 25 February 2008).

37. National Drug Intelligence Center, "National Drug Threat Assessment 2008."

38. Sibylla Brodzinsky, "Can Chávez Free FARC Hostages?," *Christian Science Monitor,* 6 September 2007.

39. Alan Clendenning, "Iran Strengthens South America Ties," *Associated Press Wire,* 27 September 2007; FARC-EP, "Entrevista a Manuel Marulanda Velez Comandante en Jefe de las FARC-EP," 4 March 2002, http://www.farcep.org/?node=2,761,1&highlight=Movmiento%20Bolivariano (accessed 18 October 2007).

40. Frank Bajak and John Leicester, "Interpol: Colombia Has Real Rebel Data," *Associated Press Wire,* 16 May 2008.

41. Kelly Hearn: FARC's Uranium Likely a Scam, *Washington Times,* 19 March 2008, http://www.washingtontimes.com/apps/pbcs.dll/article?AID=/20080319/FOREIGN/51731 (accessed 19 March 2008).

42. Ben Freeman, "Move to Renew Colombia Ecuador Ties Collapses," *Associated Press Wire,* 24 June 2008.

43. Gonzalo Solano, "Ecuador Says U.S. Must Leave Manta Air Base," *Associated Press Wire,* 29 July 2008; Frank Bajak, "Ecuador's Challenge: Dislodging Colombian Rebels," *Associated Press Wire,* 30 August 2008.

44. Christopher Toothaker, "Chávez: Colombia Incursion Would Be War," *Associated Press Wire,* 2 March 2008.

45. José de Córdoba, "Venezuela's Chávez Urges End to Colombia's Insurgency," *Wall Street Journal,* 9 June 2008, sec. A, p. 6.

46. José de Cordoba, "Chavez Lets Colombia Rebels Wield Power Inside Venezuela," *Wall Street Journal,* 25 November 2008, sec. A, p. 1.

47. Ibid.; Mary Anastasia O'Grady, "Dancing with the Wolves," *Wall Street Journal,* 15 October 2007, sec. A, p. 22; John Carlin, "El Narcosanctuario de la FARC," *El Pais* (Madrid), 16 December 2007, http://www.elpais.com/articulo/portada/conexion/venezolana/elpepusocdmg/20071216elpdmgrep_1/Tes.

48. Ian James and Frank Bajak, "Venezuela Becomes Cocaine Conduit," *Associated Press Wire,* 1 July 2007.

49. *Associated Press,* "Venezuela, U.S. May Renew Drug Cooperation," 17 July 2008.

50. *Associated Press,* "Chavez Rejects U.S. Report on Drug Trafficking," 28 February 2009.

51. Christopher Toothaker, "Chávez Kalashnikov Factory Plan Stirs Fear," *Washington Post,* 18 June 2006, http://www.washingtonpost.com/wp-dyn/content/article/2006/06/18/AR2006061800565_pf.html (accessed 30 June 2008).

52. Luke Harding, "Russia-Venezuela: Chávez in Moscow to Sign $2 Billion Arms Deal," *Guardian,* 23 July 2008, p. 21; *Associated Press,* "Chávez: Russian Jets Can Repel Attack on

Venezuela," 3 August 2008; *Associated Press,* "Venezuela Denies Report of Russian Base," 23 July 2008.

53. Christopher Toothaker, "Russian Warships Hold Exercises With Chavez's Navy," *Associated Press Wire,* 2 December 2008; China Economic Net, "Russia Seeks Military Presence in Cuba," *China Economic Net,* 8 August 2008, http://en.ce.cn/World/Europe/200808/08/t20080808_16427739.shtml (accessed 4 June 2008).

54. Mary Anastasia O'Grady, "Dancing with the Wolves," sec. A, p. 22; John Carlin, "El Narcosanctuario de la FARC," *El Pais* (Madrid), 16 December 2007, http://www.elpais.com/articulo/portada/conexion/venezolana/elpepusocdmg/20071216elpdmgrep_1/Tes; U.S. Department of State, Bureau of International Narcotics Matters, *2001 International Control Strategy Report* (March 2002), http://www.state.gov/p/inl/rls/nrcrpt/2001/rpt/8479.htm; U.S. Department of State, Bureau of International Narcotics Matters, *2006 International Control Strategy Report Vol.I.* (March 2006), http://www.state.gov/p/inl/rls/nrcrpt/2006/vol1/html/62108.htm.

55. U.S. Department of State, Bureau of International Narcotics Matters, *2001 International Control Strategy Report* (March 2002), http://www.state.gov/p/inl/rls/nrcrpt/2001/rpt/8479.htm; U.S. Department of State, Bureau of International Narcotics Matters, *2006 International Control Strategy Report Vol.I.* (March 2006), http://www.state.gov/p/inl/rls/nrcrpt/2006/vol1/html/62108.htm.

56. Casto Ocando, "Acusan a Cuba de formar guerrilleros en campamento turístico venezolano," *El Nuevo Herald,* 4 October 2008, http://www.elnuevoherald.com/noticias/america_latina/cuba/story/296933.html (accessed 4 June 2009).

57. Nerda Pickler, "Couple Accused of Spying for Cuba for 30 Years," *Buffalo News,* 6 June, 2009, sec. A, p. 5.

58. *Associated Press,* "Nicaragua Pledges Drug Cooperation," 5 February 2007.

59. U.S. Department of State*, 2007 International Narcotics Control Strategy Report Vol. I,* http://www.state.gov/p/inl/rls/nrcrpt/2007/.

60. *Associated Press,* "Nicaragua to Break off Relations with Colombia," *New York Post,* 7 March 2008, http://www.nysun.com/foreign/nicaragua-to-break-off-relations-with-colombia/72528/?print=0341586121 (accessed 10 May 2008); *United Press International,* "Nicaragua Renews Ties with Colombia," 17 March 2008, http://www.upi.com/Top_News/2008/03/12/Nicaragua_renews_ties_with_Colombia/UPI-32911205371742/ (accessed 30 June 2008).

61. José de Córdoba, "Colombia Clashes with Nicaragua Over Guerrilla Tie," *Wall Street Journal,* 28 July 2008, sec. A, p. 8.

62. *Associated Press,* "Nicaragua President Open to FARC Talks," 17 July 2008.

63. U.S. Department of State*, 2007 International Narcotics Control Strategy Report Vol. I,* http://www.state.gov/p/inl/rls/nrcrpt/2007/.

64. Sarah Grainger, "Mexican Drug Gang Menace Spreads in Guatemala," *Associated Press Wire,* 18 February 2009.

65. Devlin Barrett, "DEA Says Mexican Drug Cartels Are Creeping South," *Associated Press Wire,* 15 April 2009.

66. Hispanic Center for Latin American Research, "Kabiles: The New Lethal Force in the Mexican Drug Wars," Hispanic Center for Latin American Research, 31 January 2009, http://www.hacer.org/current/Mex158.php (accessed 5 April 2009).

67. U.S. Department of State, Bureau of International Narcotics Matters, *2009 International Control Strategy Report Vol. I* (March 2009), http://www.state.gov/p/inl/rls/nrcrpt/2009/vol1/html/62108.htm (accessed 22 May 2009).

68. U.S. Department of State*, 2007 International Narcotics Control Strategy Report Vol. I,* http://www.state.gov/p/inl/rls/nrcrpt/2007/.

69. *Associated Press,* "Bolivian Leader Defends His Drug Policy," 20 September 2006.

70. International Crisis Group, "Coca, Drugs and Social Protests in Bolivia and Peru," 17.

71. *Associated Press*, "Bolivia Opens New Front in Coca Fight," 11 April 2007.

72. Carlos Valdez, "Cocaine Flows Over Brazil-Bolivia Border," *Associated Press Wire*, 10 June 2007.

73. *Associated Press*, "Chavez: Venezuela Won't Tolerate Secession in Bolivia," 9 May 2008.

74. Paola Flores, "Bolivia, U.S. Seek to Heal Wounded Ties," *Associated Press Wire*, 4 July 2008.

75. Dan Keane, "Civil War Talk Stokes Bolivian Fears," *Associated Press Wire*, 30 September 2007; Dan Keane, "Bolivia Sets Vote on New Constitution," *Associated Press Wire*, 29 February 2008.

76. Carlos Valdez, "4th Bolivian State Moves Towards Autonomy," *Associated Press Wire*, 22 June 2008; Carlos Valdez, "Bolivian Voters Back Pro-Indigenous Constitution," *Associated Press Wire*, 26 January 2009.

77. Antonio Regalado and David Luthnow, "Bolivia Politics Roiled by Killing of Alleged Assassins," *Wall Street Journal*, 18 April 2009, sec. A, p. 5.

78. Carlos Valdez, "4th Bolivian State Moves Towards Autonomy."

79. Rick Kearns, "Diplomatic Efforts Seek to Mend Damaged U.S.-Bolivia Relationship," *Indian Country Today*, 1 August 2008, http://www.inidiancountry.com/content.cfm?id=1096 417850&print=yes (accessed 2 August 2008).

80. Dan Keane, "Morales Ups Rhetoric Against U.S. Anti-Drug Aid," *Associated Press Wire*, 5 October 2008; Carlos Valdez, "Bolivian President Suspends U.S. Anti-Drug Efforts," *Associated Press Wire*, 3 November, 2008.

81. Carlos Valdez, "Bolivian President Seeks Improved U.S. Relations," *Associated Press Wire*, 21 May 2009.

82. U.S. Department of State, Bureau of International Narcotics Matters, *2008 International Control Strategy Report Vol. I*, http://www.state.gov/p/inl/rls/nrcrpt/2008/vol1/html/100776. htm; This estimate counts only areas visibly under cultivation and in no way accounts for cultivation in remote, inaccessible areas.

83. Leslie Josephs, "Peru Economy Booms, but García Unpopular," *Associated Press Wire*, 28 July 2007; Milagros Salazar, "Peru: Government Puts Renewed Emphasis on Forced Coca Eradication," *Inter Press News Service Agency*, 2 April 2007, http://ipsnews.net/print. asp?idnews=37182 (accessed 28 February 2008).

84. Andrew Whalen, "Peru's Hot Economy Wracked by Growing Conflicts," *Associated Press Wire*, 19 November 2008.

85. Milagros Salazar, "Peru: Government Puts Renewed Emphasis on Forced Coca Eradication," http://ipsnews.net/print.asp?idnews=37182.

86. International Crisis Group, "Coca, Drugs and Social Protests in Bolivia and Peru," 17.

87. Jenni Deselm et al, "Counternarcotics in Peru—A Comprehensive Approach," 19. The article cites the *Reuters* report: "Cocaine Labs Should Be Bombed," *Reuters,* 2 April 2007.

88. Marco Aquino, "Coca Is the Only Option for Some Peruvian Farmers," *Reuters*, 17 July 2007.

89. Ibid., Milagros Salazar, "Peru: Government Puts Renewed Emphasis on Forced Coca Eradication," http://ipsnews.net/print.asp?idnews=37182.

90. International Crisis Group, "Coca, Drugs and Social Protests in Bolivia and Peru," 7, 15.

91. Groups claiming to be affiliated with the Shining Path have also openly identified with coca growers and drug traffickers and have engaged in violent ambushes of police and intimidation of alternative development teams in coca-growing areas. Eight police officers were killed in December 2005. Five police officers and two employees from Peru's state-run coca company, ENACO, were killed in December 2006. In March 2007 a Sendero ambush wounded two military officers. U.S. Department of State, *2006 International Narcotics Control Strategy Report Vol. I*, http://www.state.gov/p/inl/rls/nrcrpt/2007/; U.S.

Department of State, *2007 International Narcotics Control Strategy Report Vol. I*, http://www.state.gov/p/inl/rls/nrcrpt/2007/. Attacks increased in 2008, occurring in the coca-growing areas of the Upper Huallaga Valley and the Cochabamba Valley. In April 2009 an attack was launched in the Apurimac-Ene River Valley in southeastern Peru. See: Andrew Whalen, "Peru Says 14 Killed in Shining Path Attack," *Associated Press Wire*, 10 October 2008; *Associated Press*, "4 Peru Police Killed in Ambush by Suspected Rebels," 30 November 2008; *Associated Press*, "Peru Military Says 13 Soldiers Dead in Ambushes," 13 April 2009.

92. *Associated Press*, "Peru Military Says 13 Soldiers Dead in Ambushes," 13 April 2009.

93. Sam Logan and Ashley Morse, "The FARC's International Presence: An Overview," *Samuel Logan: Security and Democracy* (December 2006): 3–4, 6, http://www.samuellogan.com/publications/The-FARCs-International-Presence.pdf (accessed 22 July 2008). The report claims that the FARC sends roughly six men not in uniform across the border at a time.

94. Ted Galen Carpenter, *Bad Neighbor Policy: Washington's Futile War on Drugs in Latin America*, 223–33.

Index

Italicized page numbers refer to charts.
Italicized "map" after page numbers refers to maps.

356 Index